"We don't have the money, so we have to think."

Ernest Rutherford (1871–1937)

Speculation

Dane Mitchell

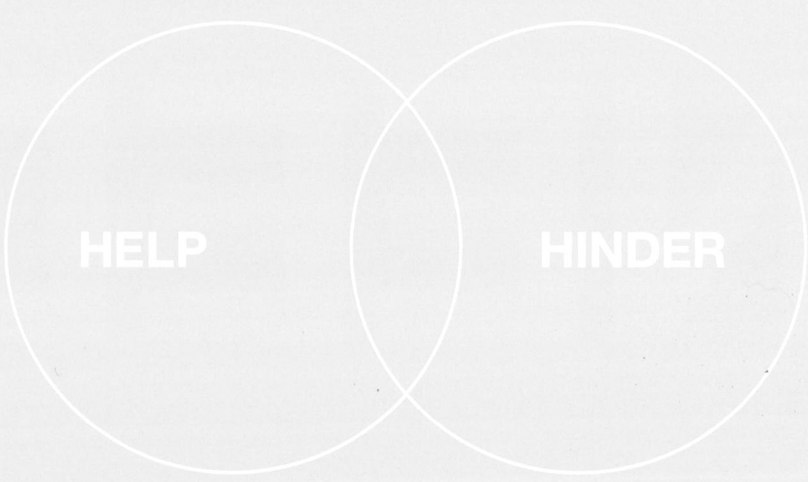

HELP
HINDER

NEED

CALL

+39 347

HELP?

NOW
5900902

THIS PUBLICATION

HAS BEEN CURSED

Yvonne Todd

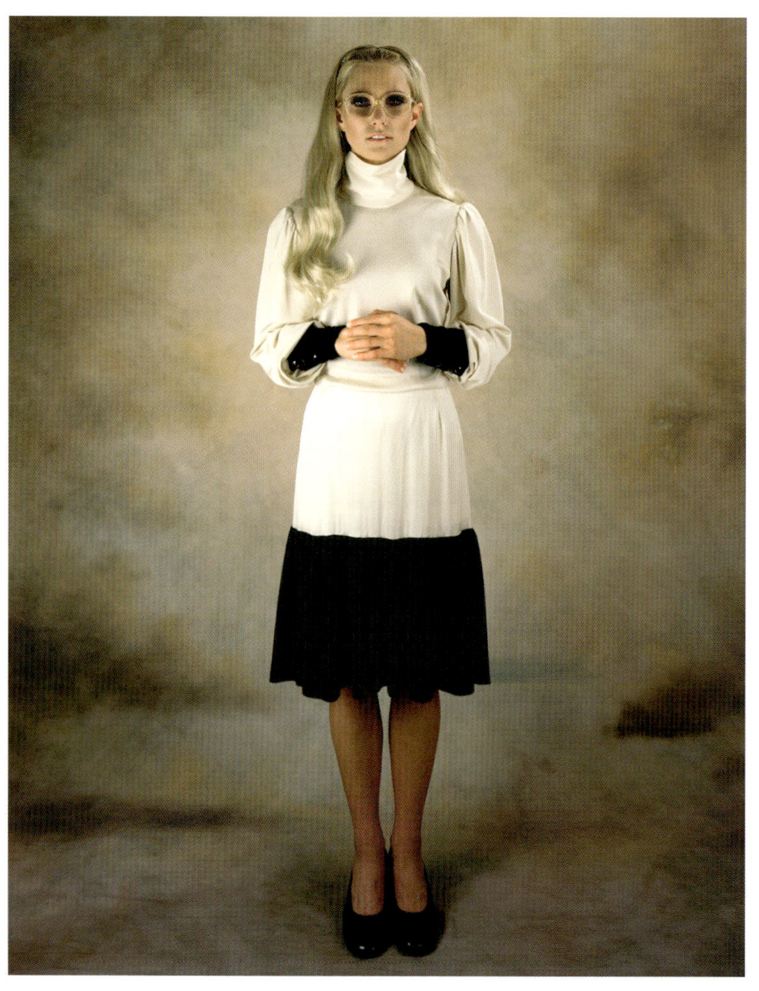

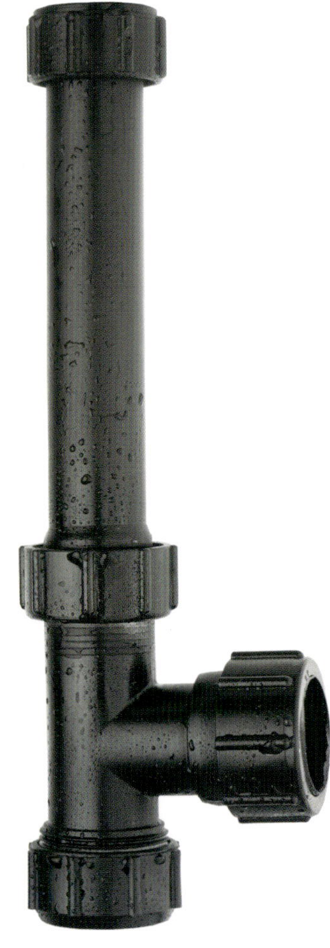

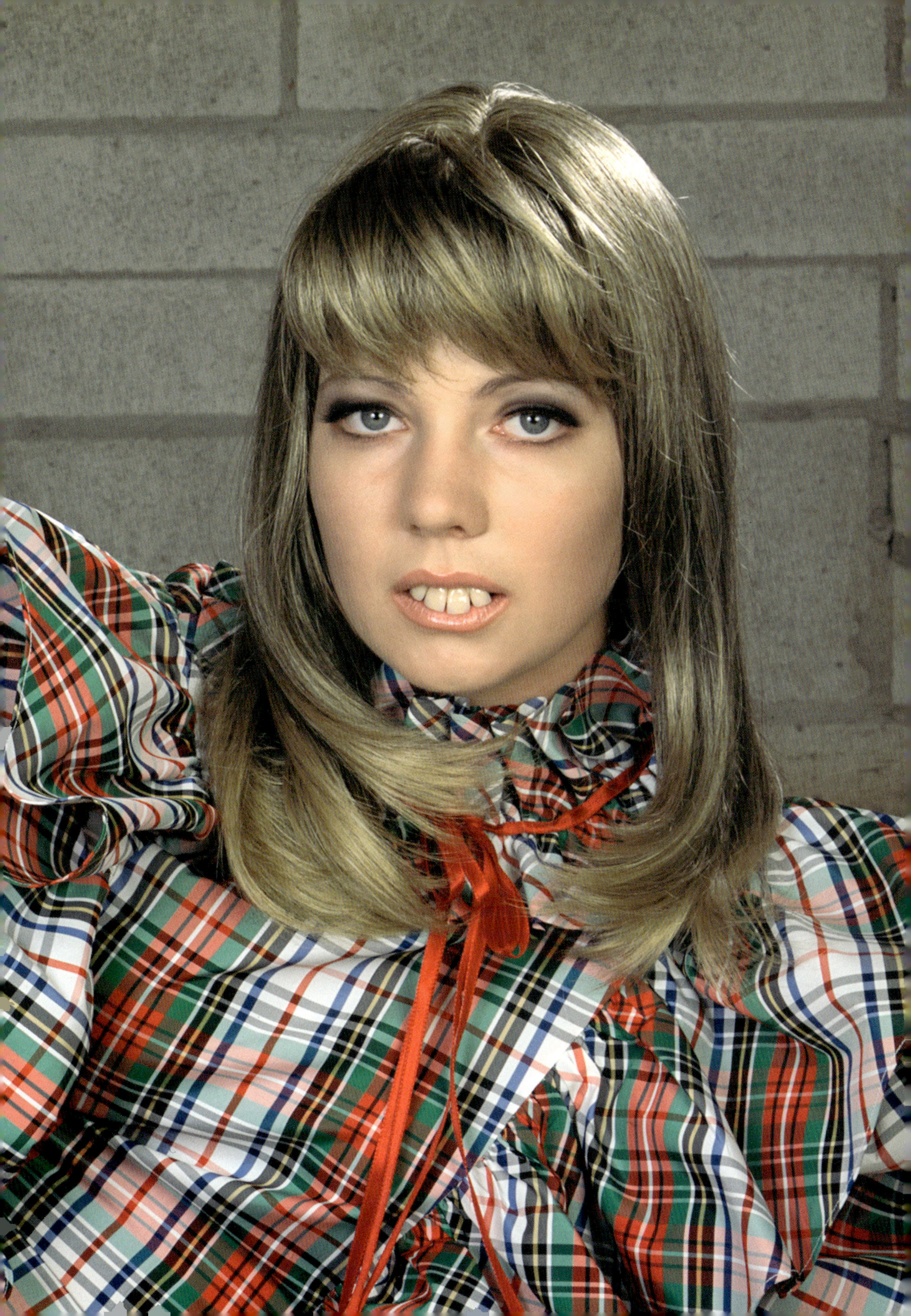

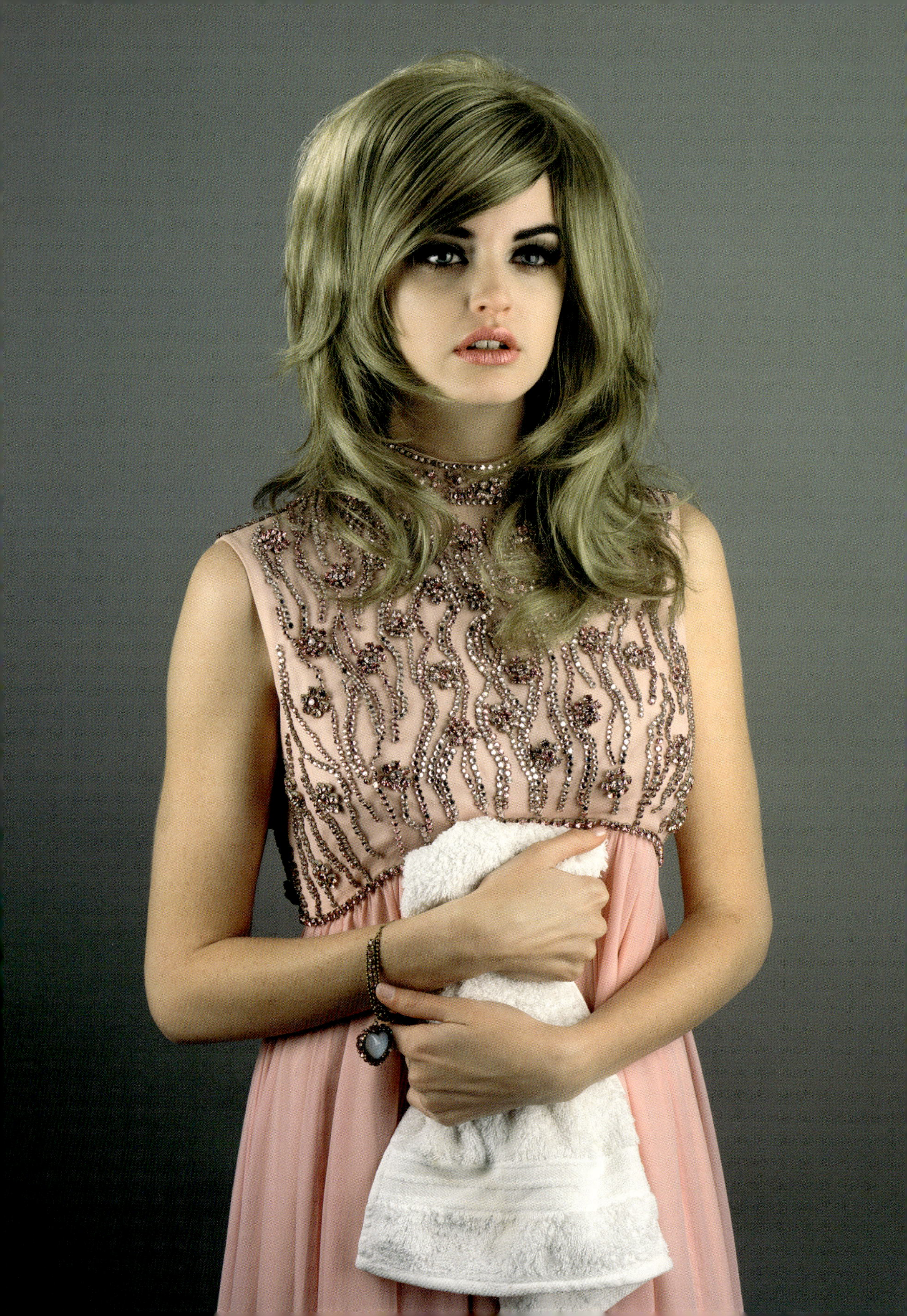

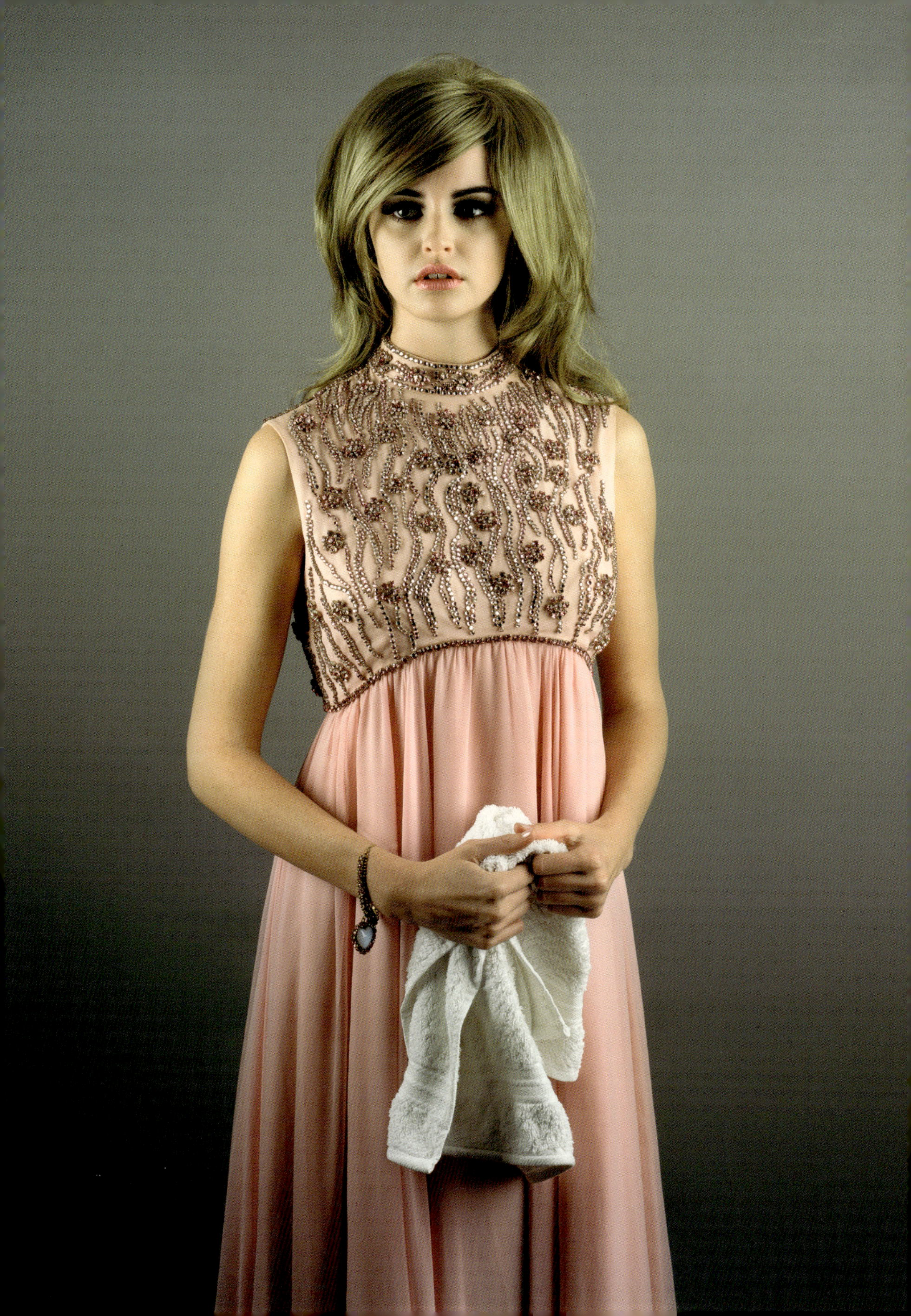

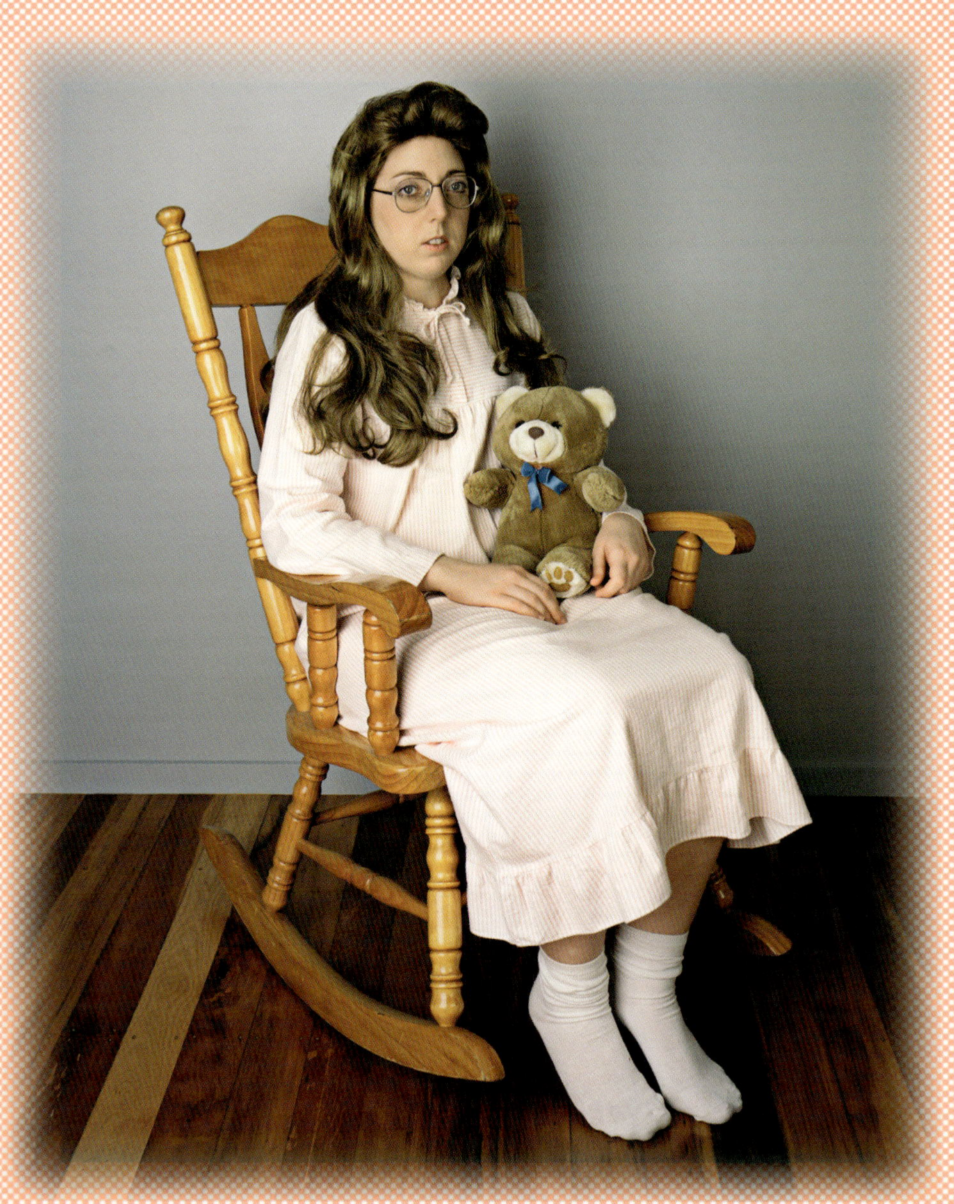

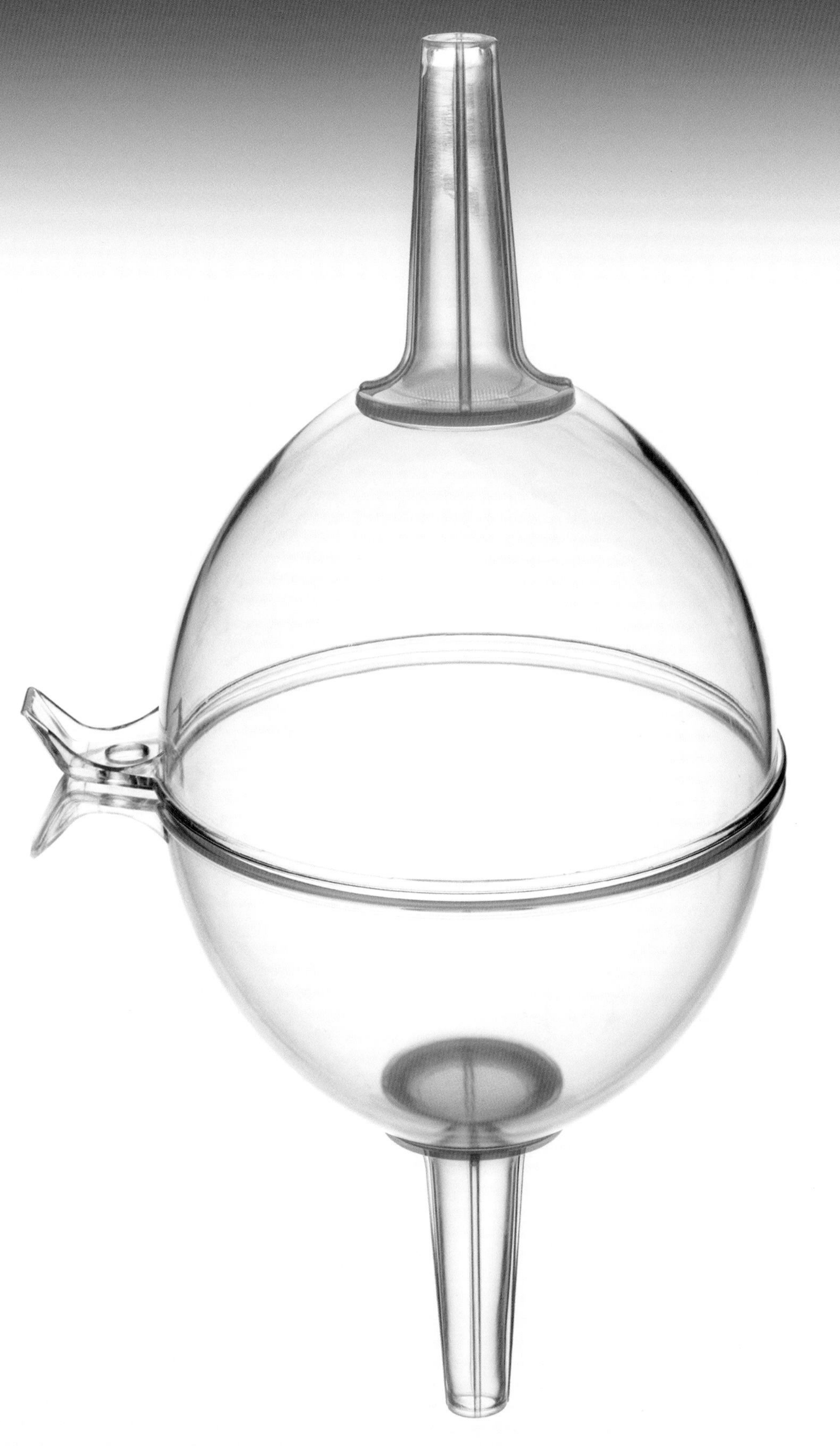

Andrew Barber

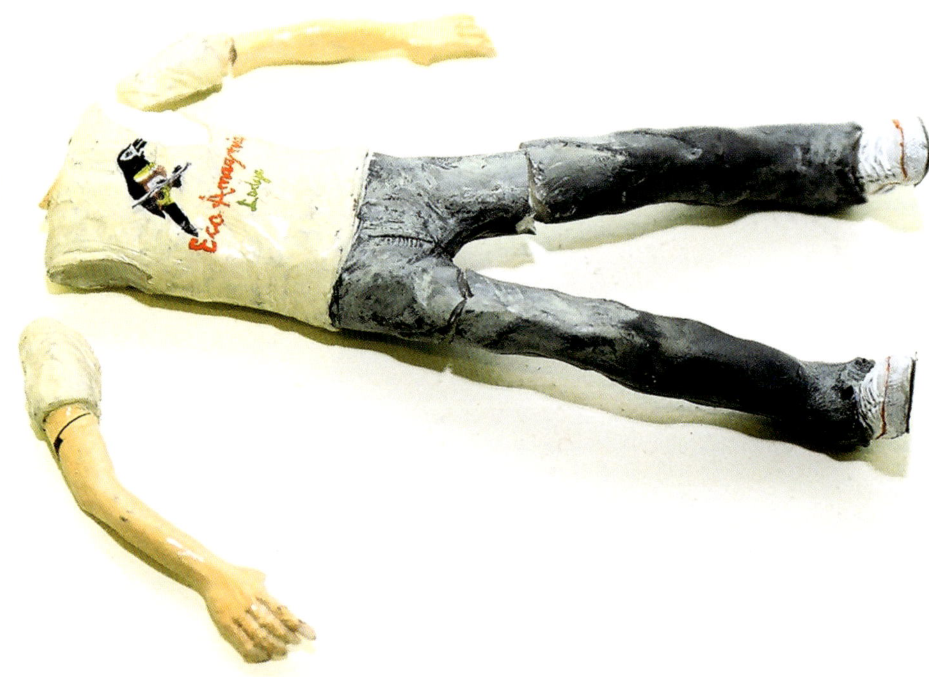

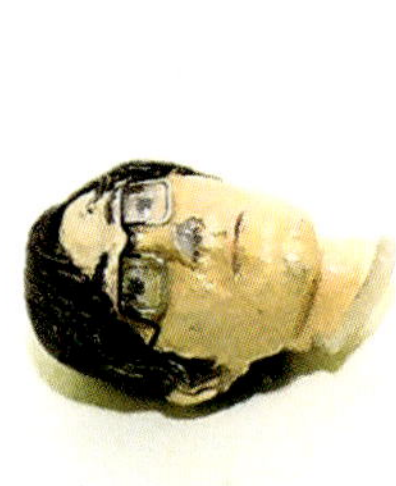

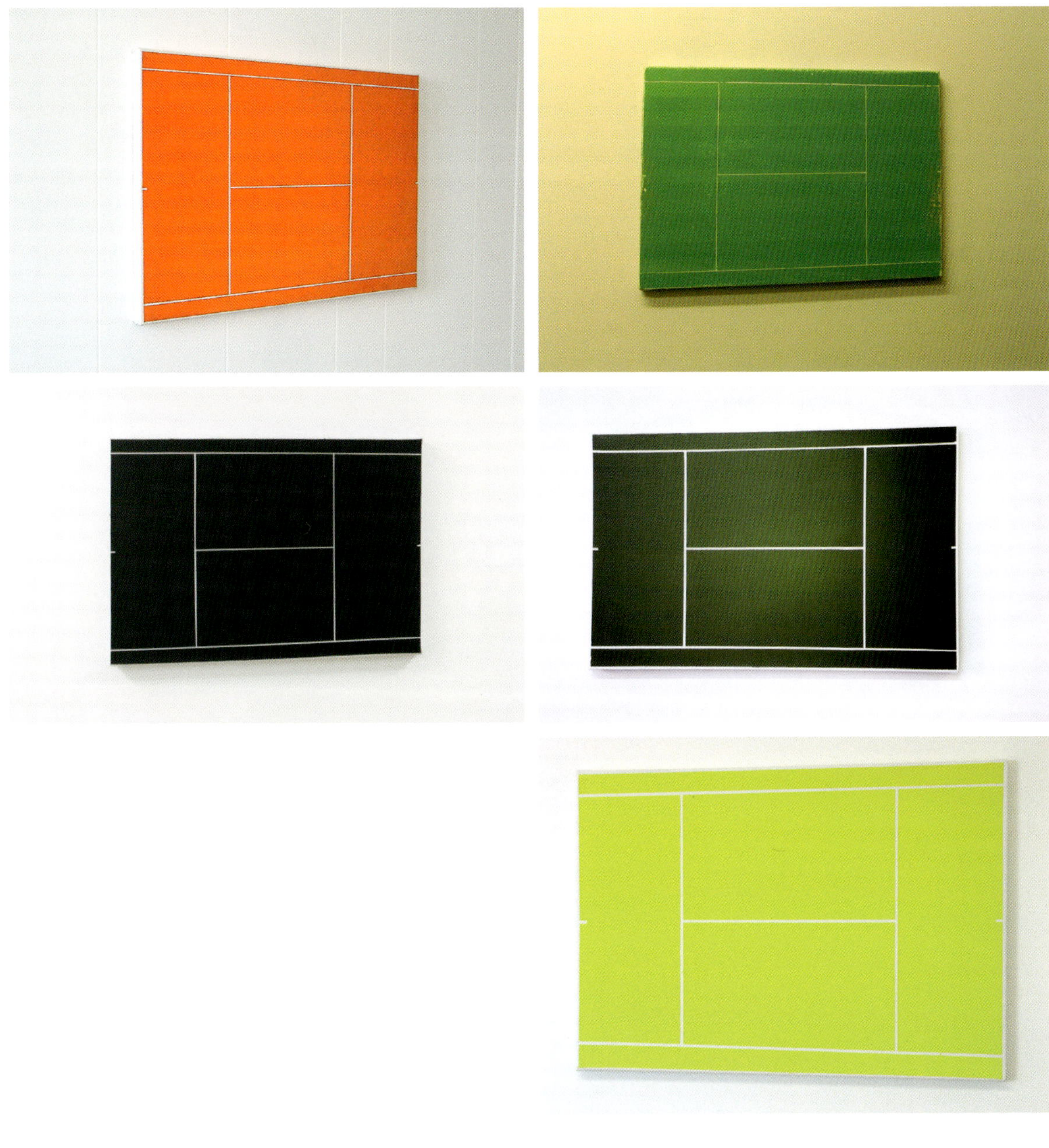

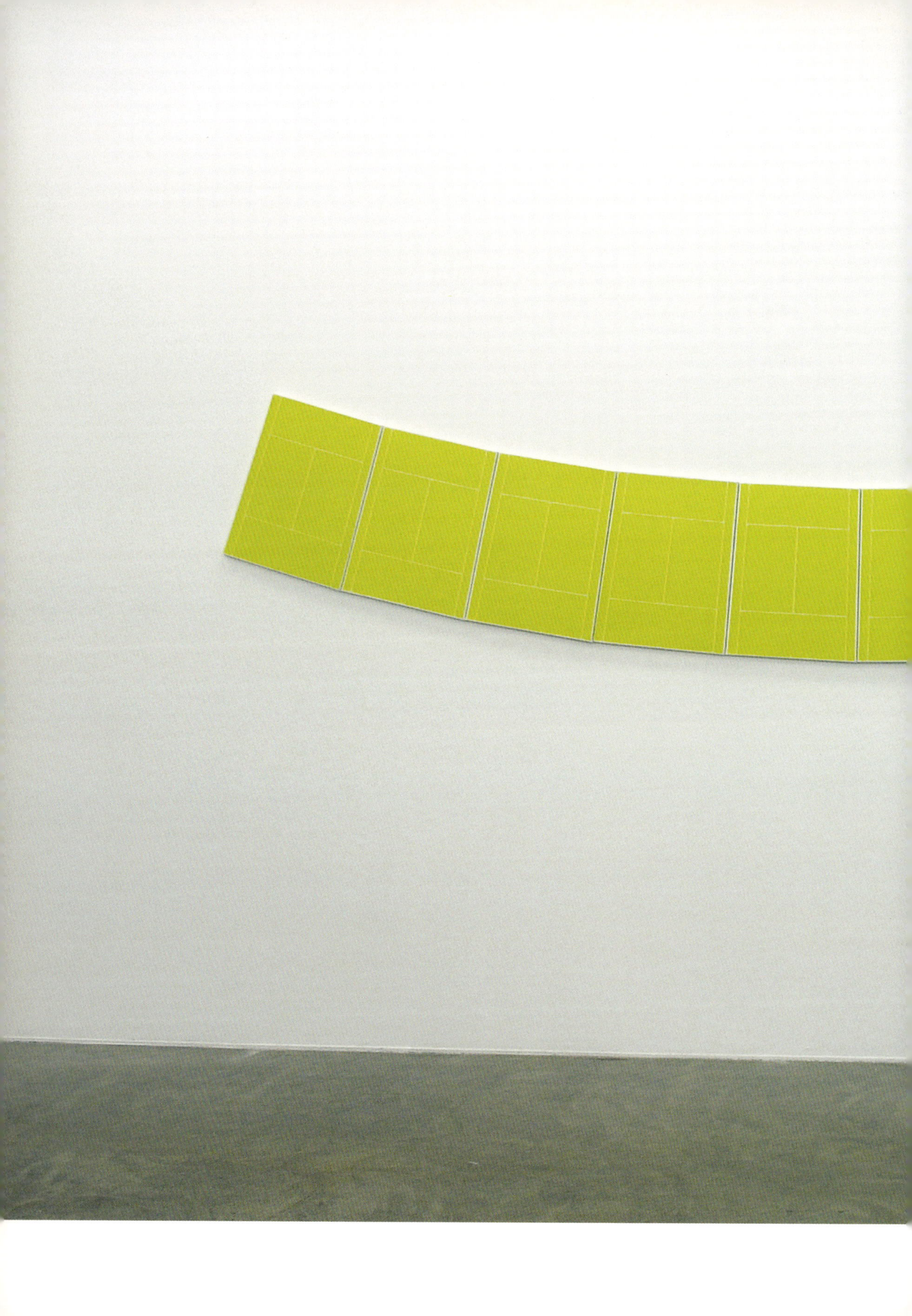

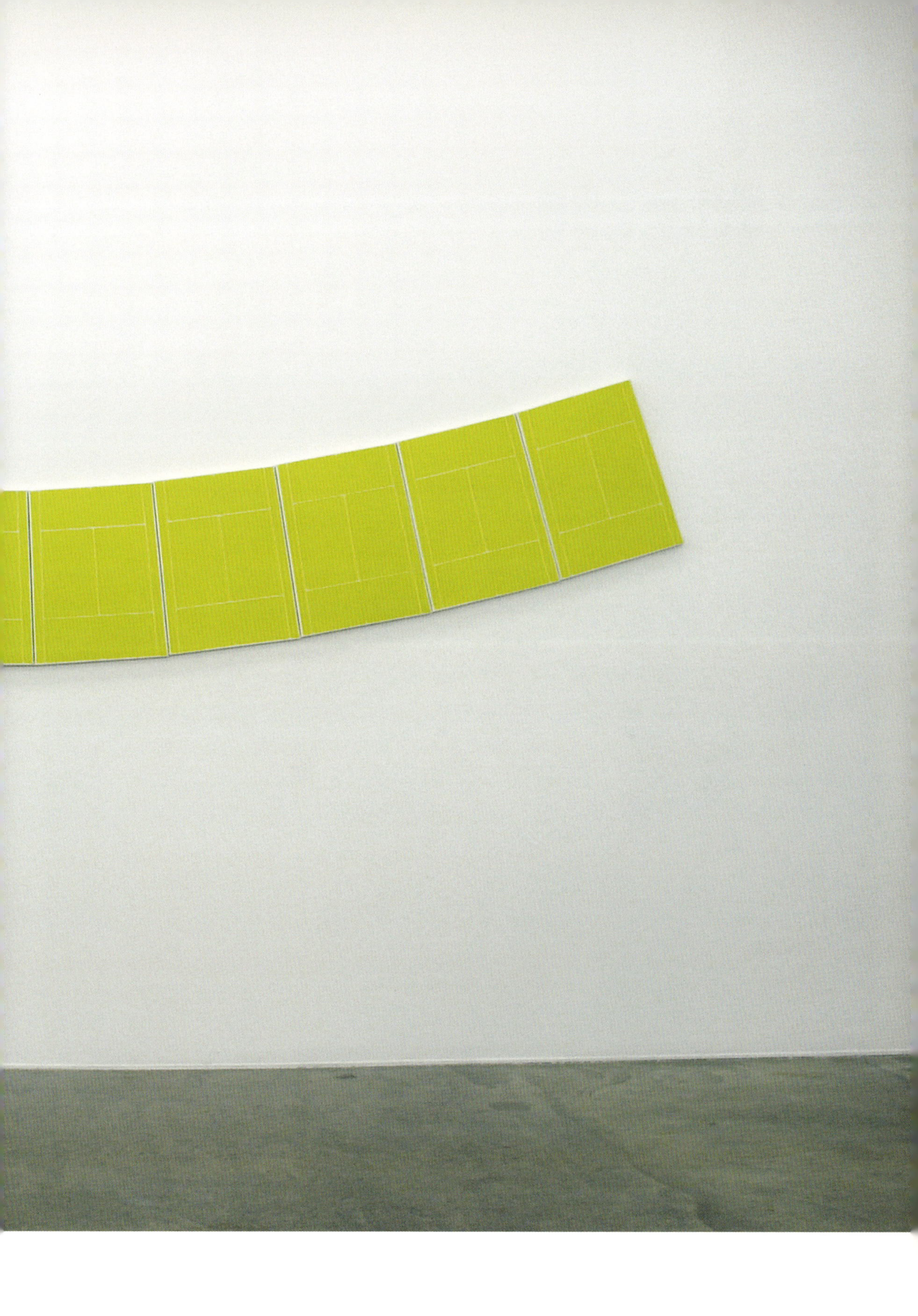

Ani O'Neill

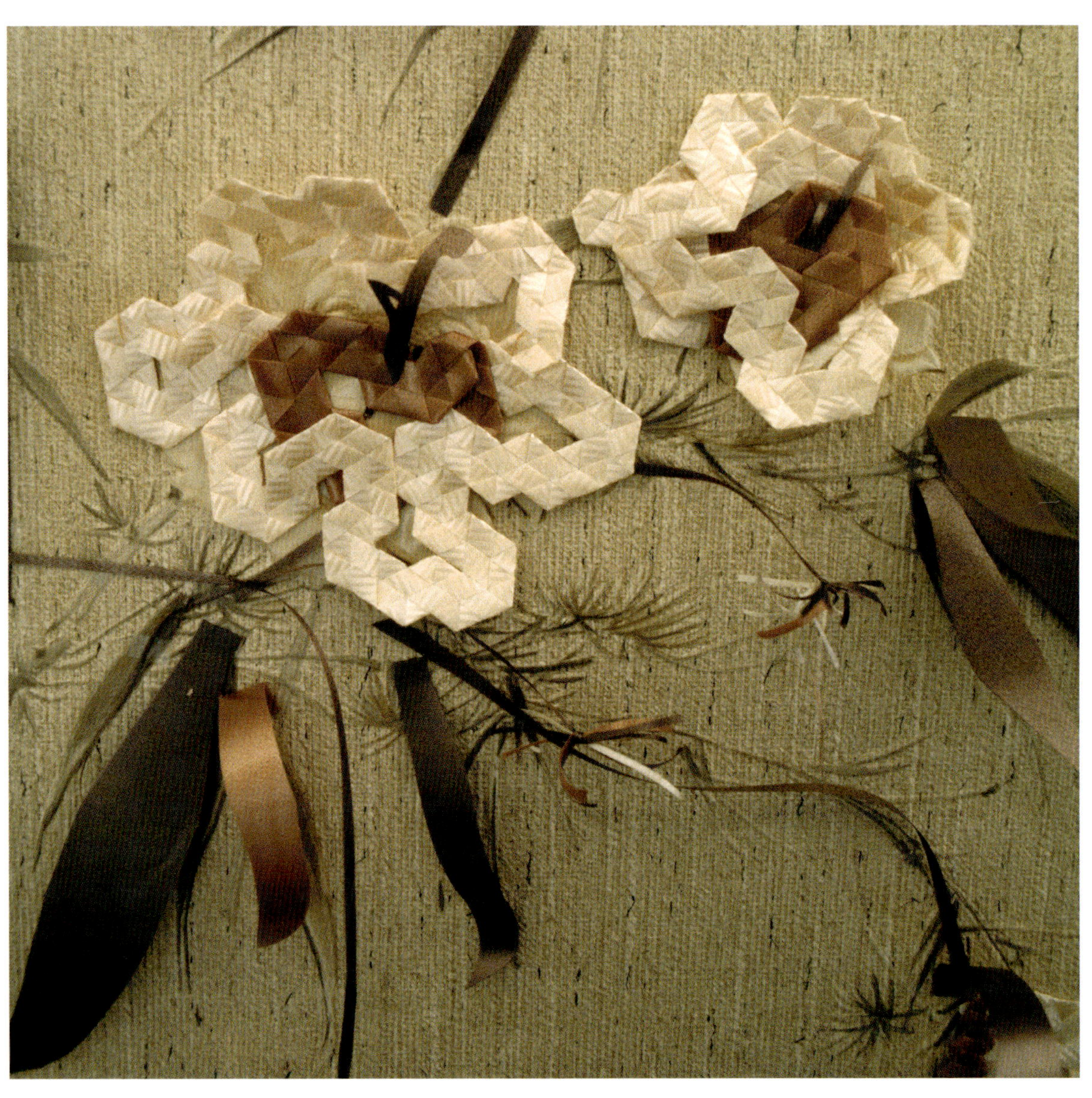

Pretty subtle wallpaper, 1993 (detail), old telephone exchange building, Auckland

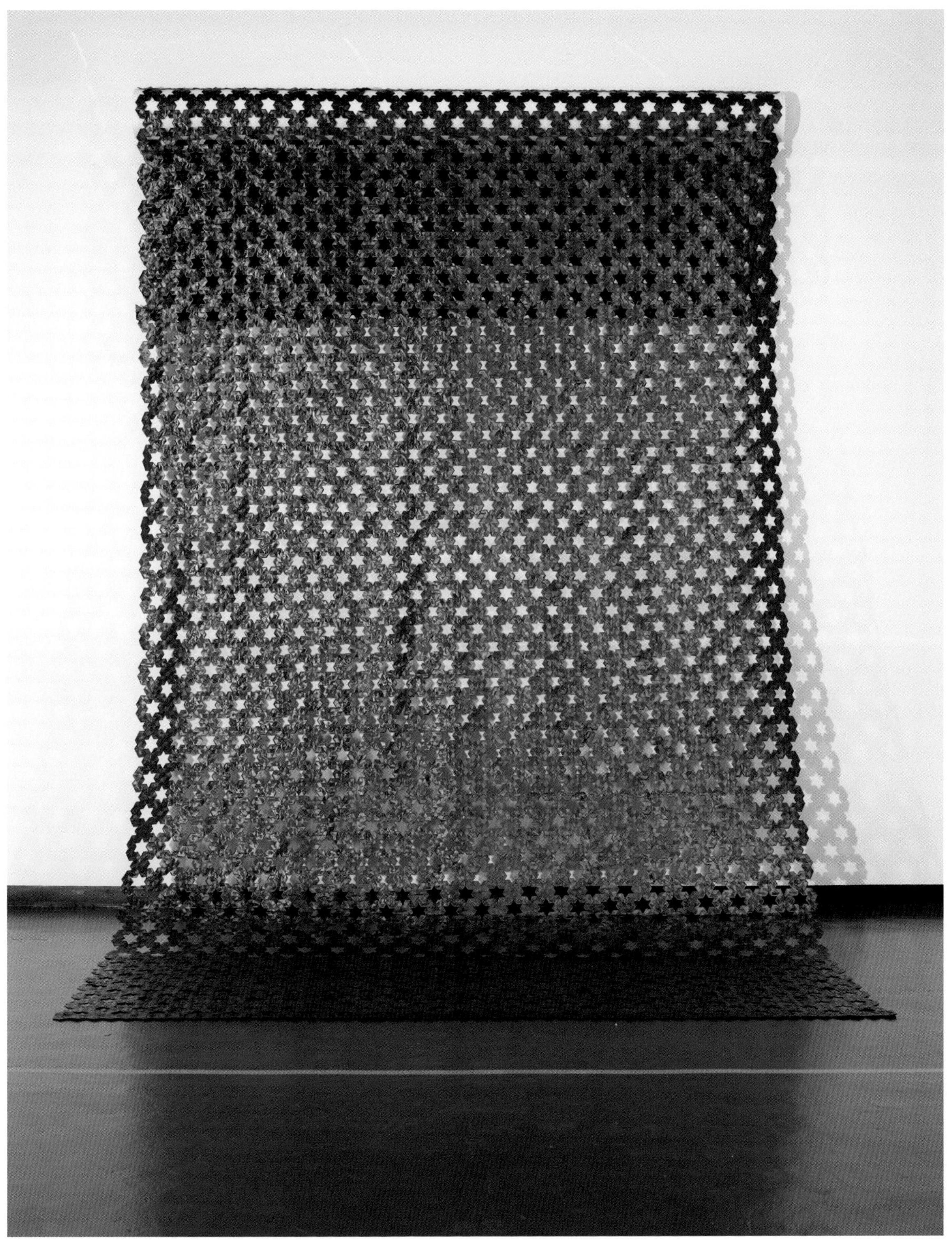

Star By Night, 1993. Collection of Te Papa Tongarewa Museum of New Zealand, Wellington

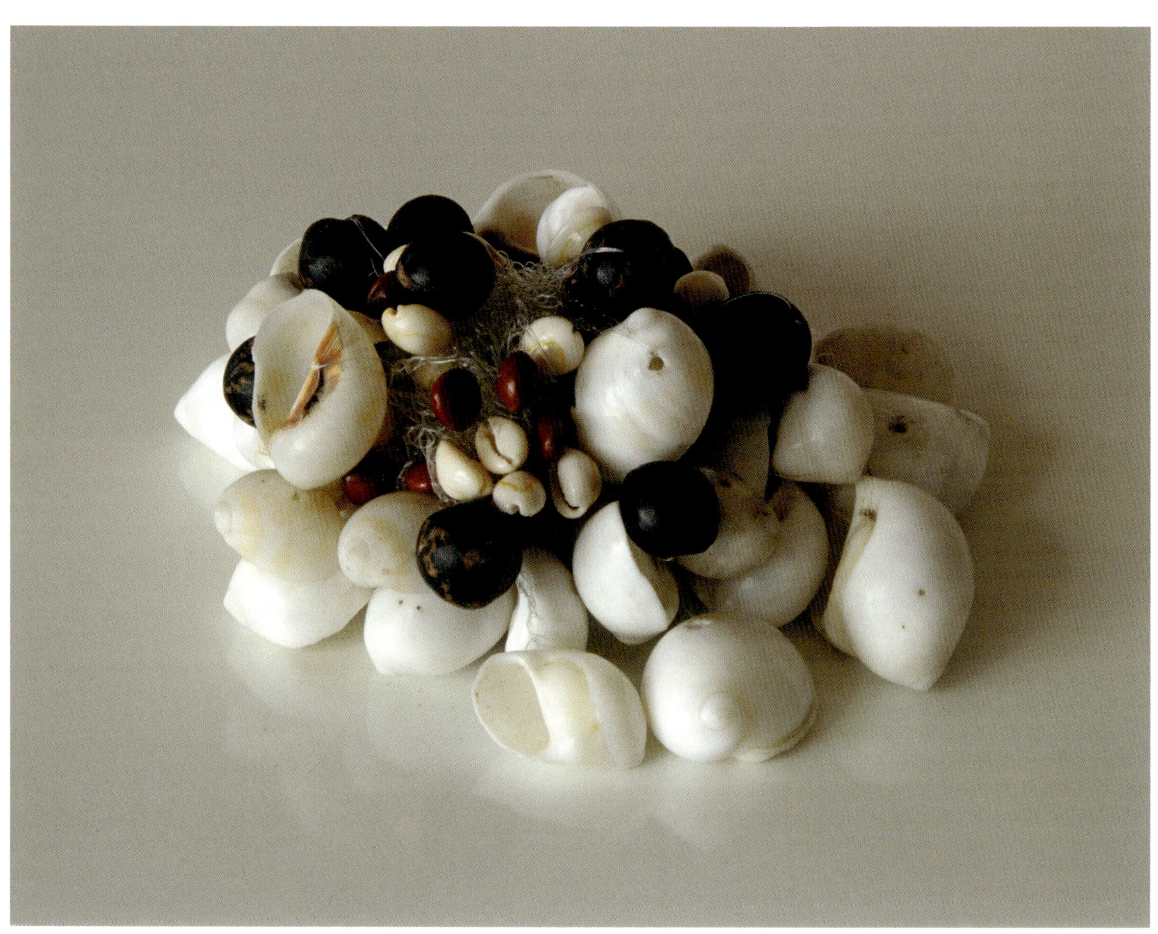

Ei scrumble no. 4, 2002. Sue Crockford Gallery, Auckland

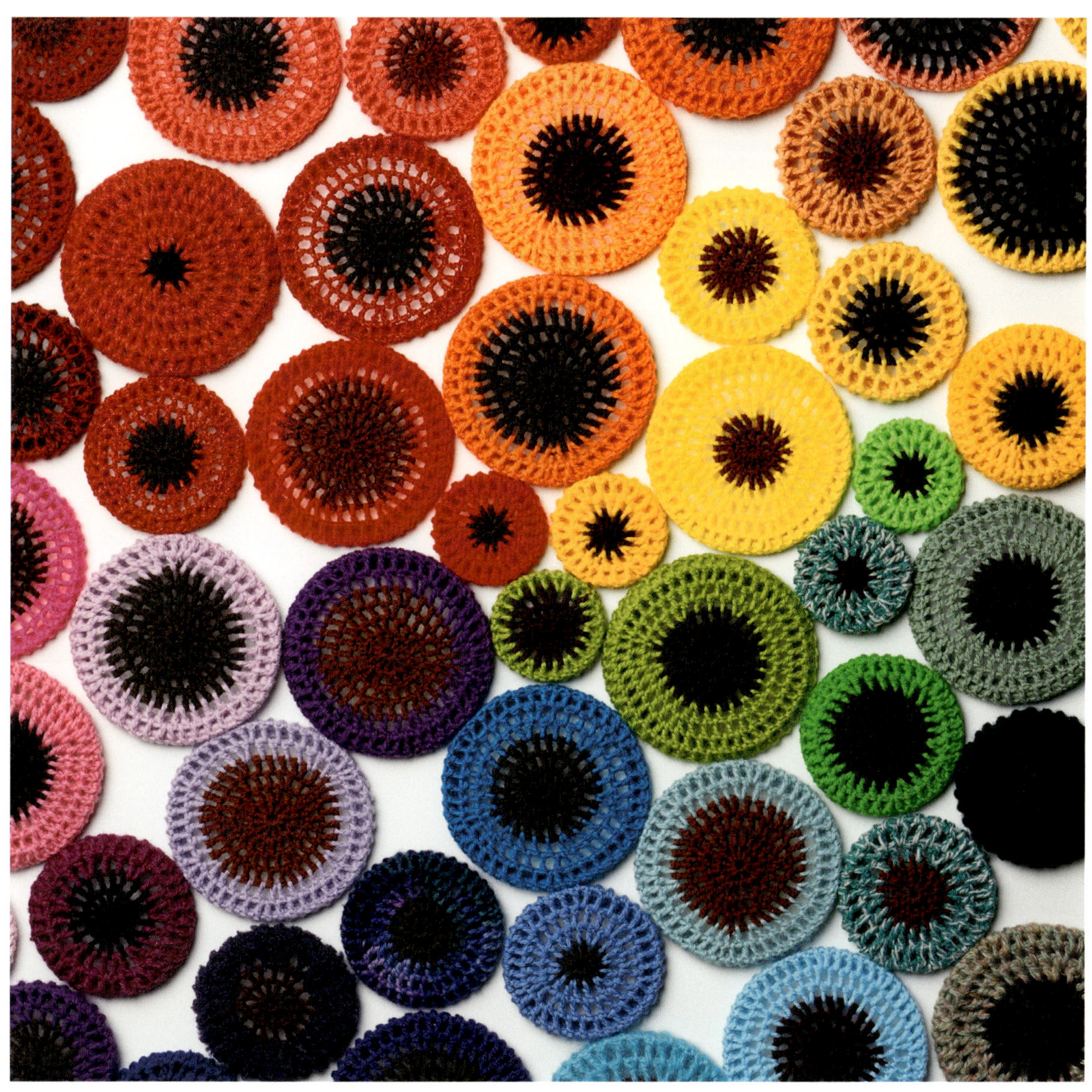

Rainbow Country, 2000 (detail). Collection of Te Papa Tongarewa Museum of New Zealand, Wellington

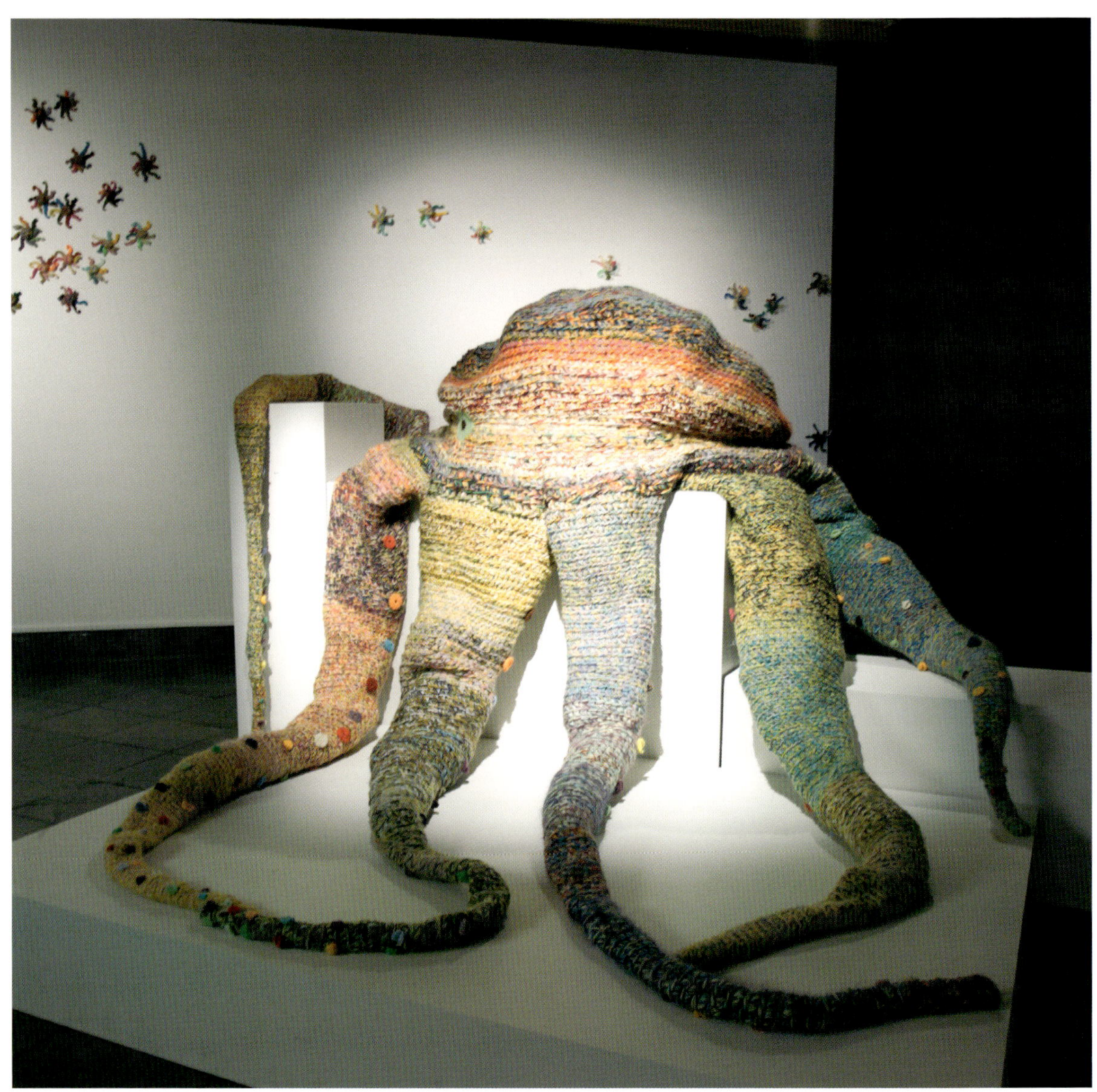

Fresh Eke, 2002. Waikato Museum of Art and History (2005), Hamilton

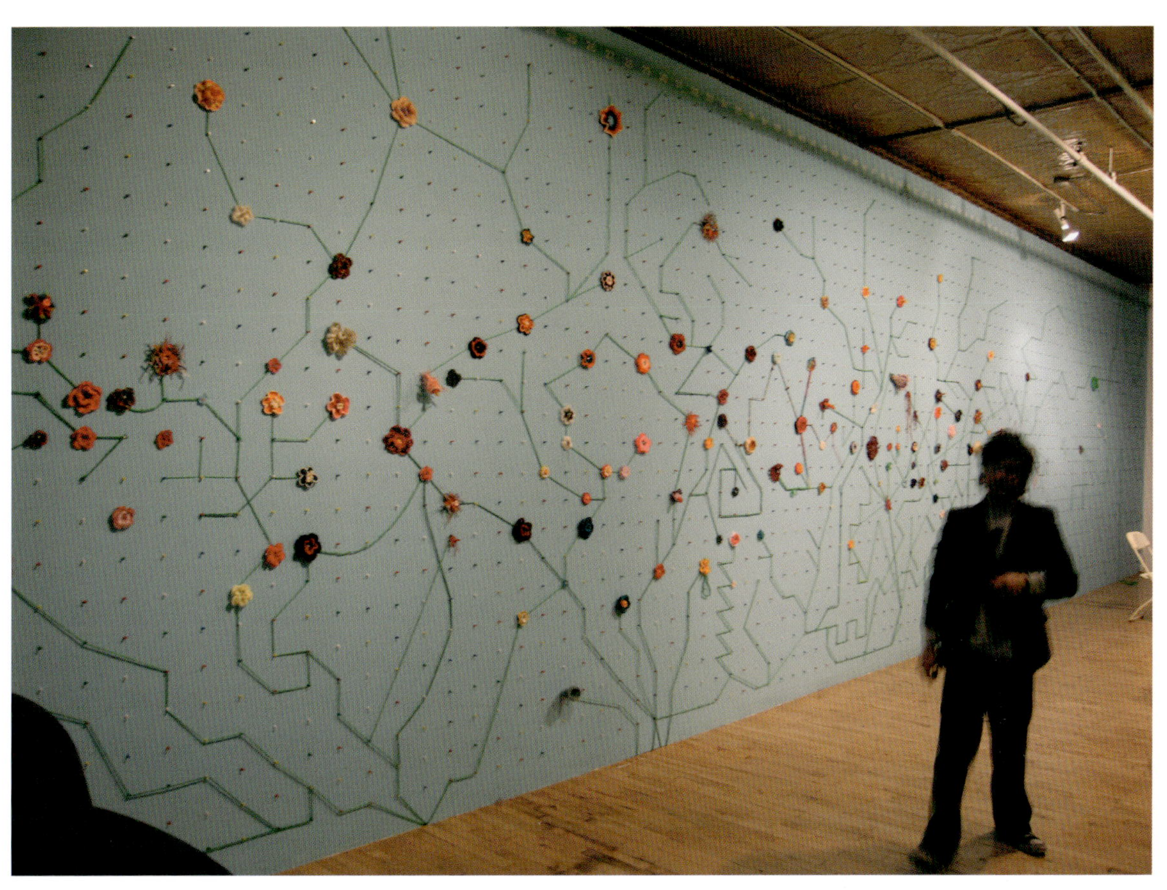

The Buddy System, 2001–. Art In General (2004), New York

Daniel Malone

32

Exhibition posters
May–December 2006

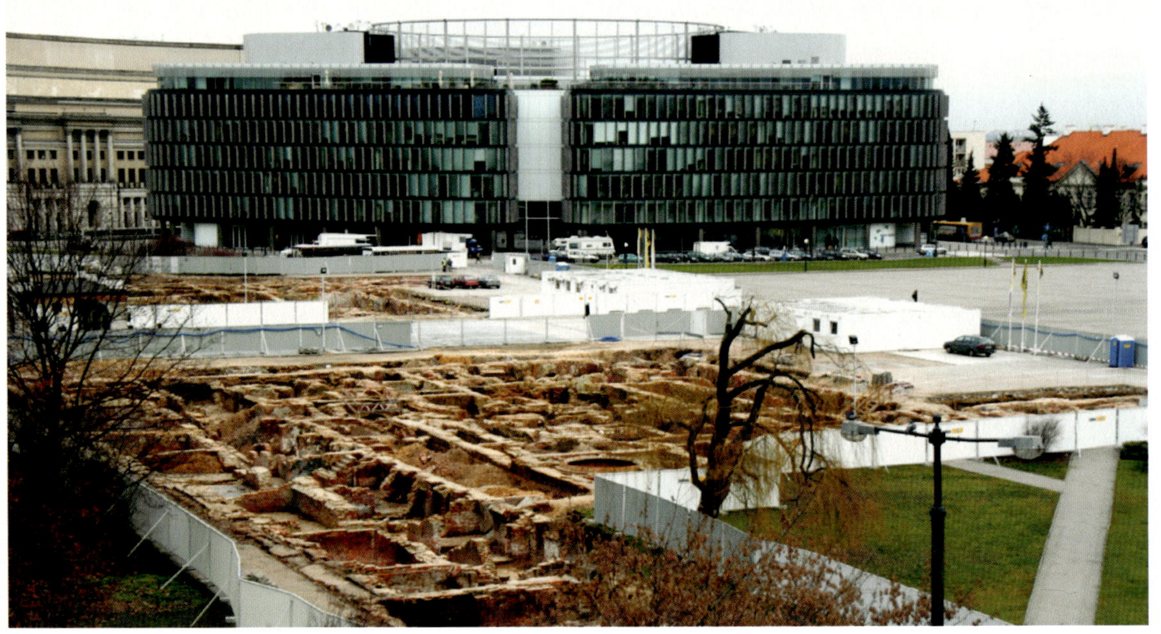

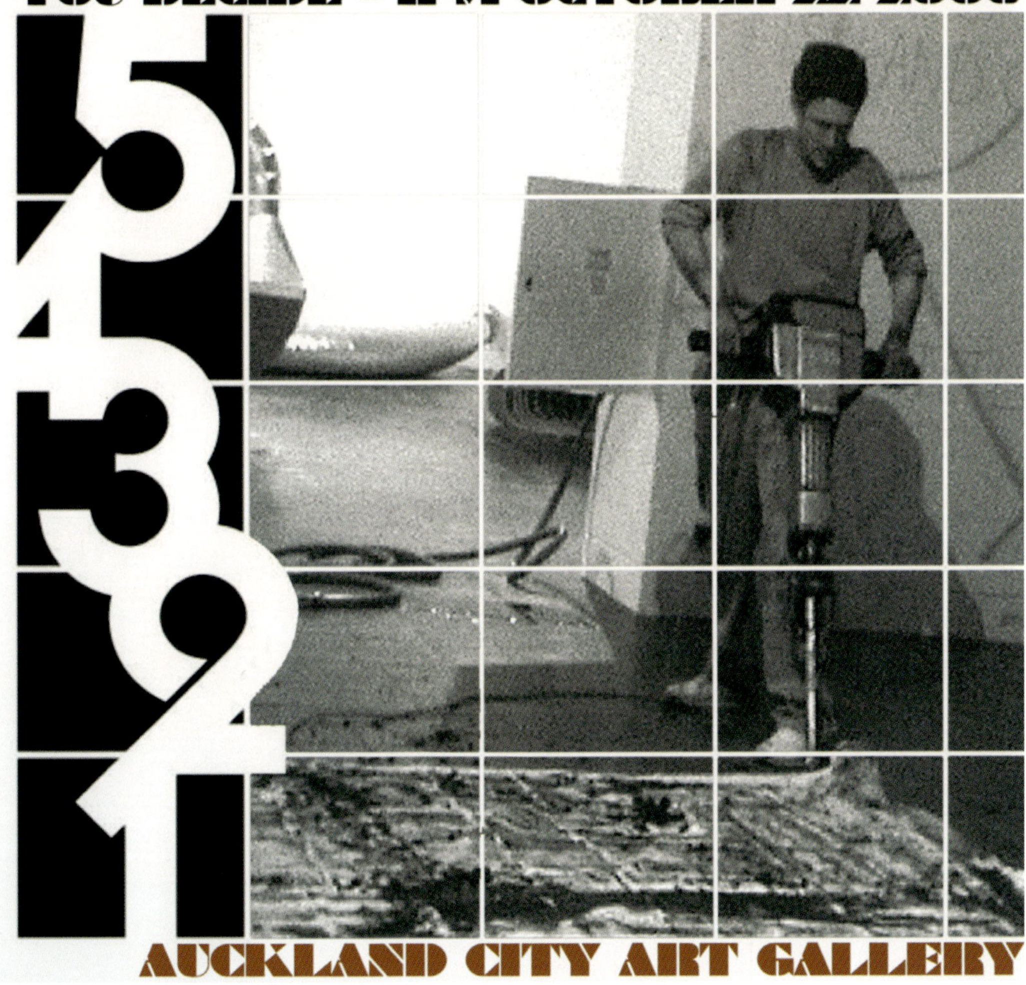

FLOOR PIECE?
70'S STYLE
PROJECT OR PROTEST
YOU DECIDE – 11PM OCTOBER 22 2006
5
4
3
2
1
AUCKLAND CITY ART GALLERY

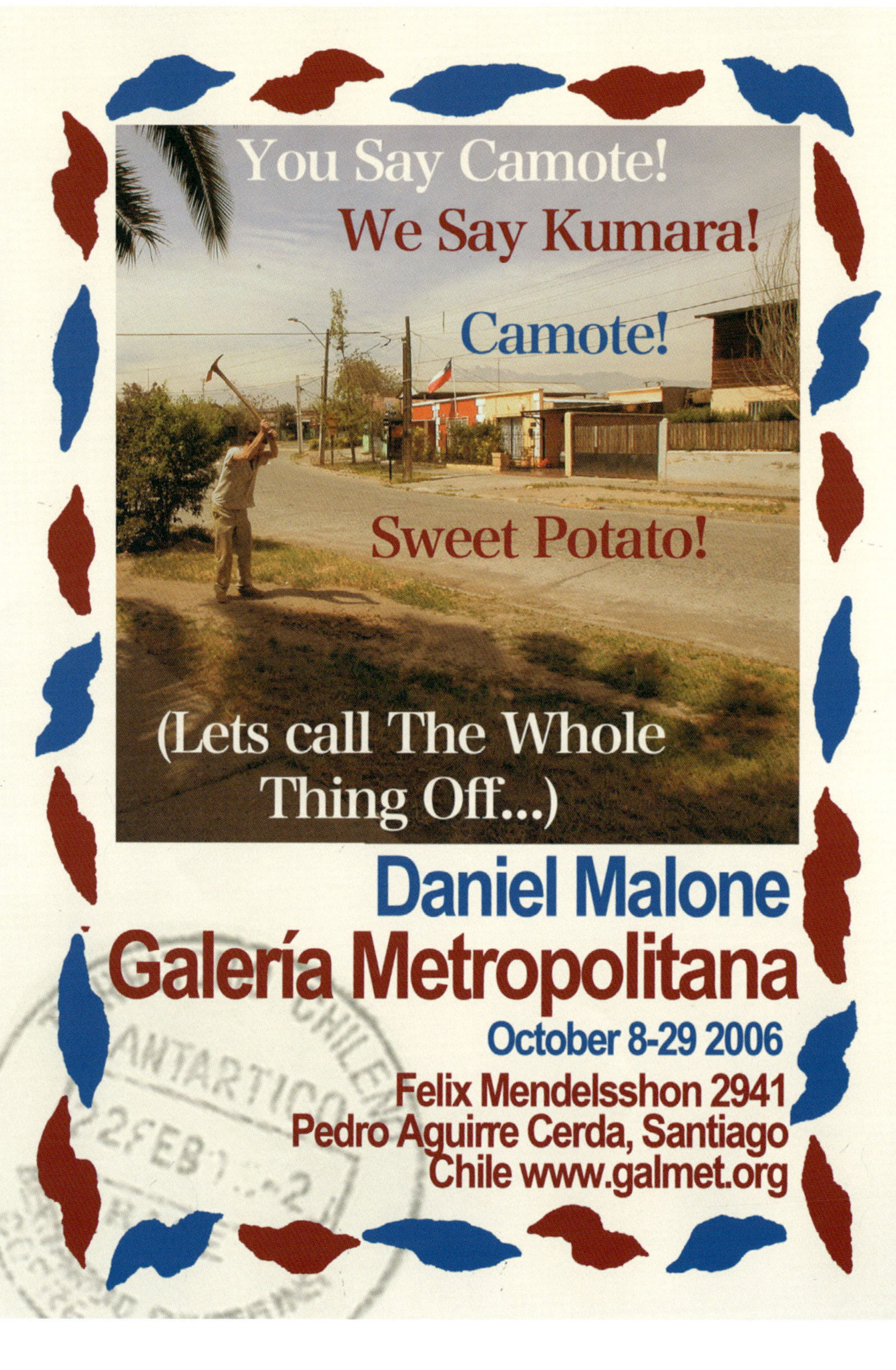

You Say Camote!
We Say Kumara!
Camote!
Sweet Potato!
(Lets call The Whole Thing Off...)
Daniel Malone
Galería Metropolitana
October 8-29 2006
Felix Mendelsshon 2941
Pedro Aguirre Cerda, Santiago
Chile www.galmet.org

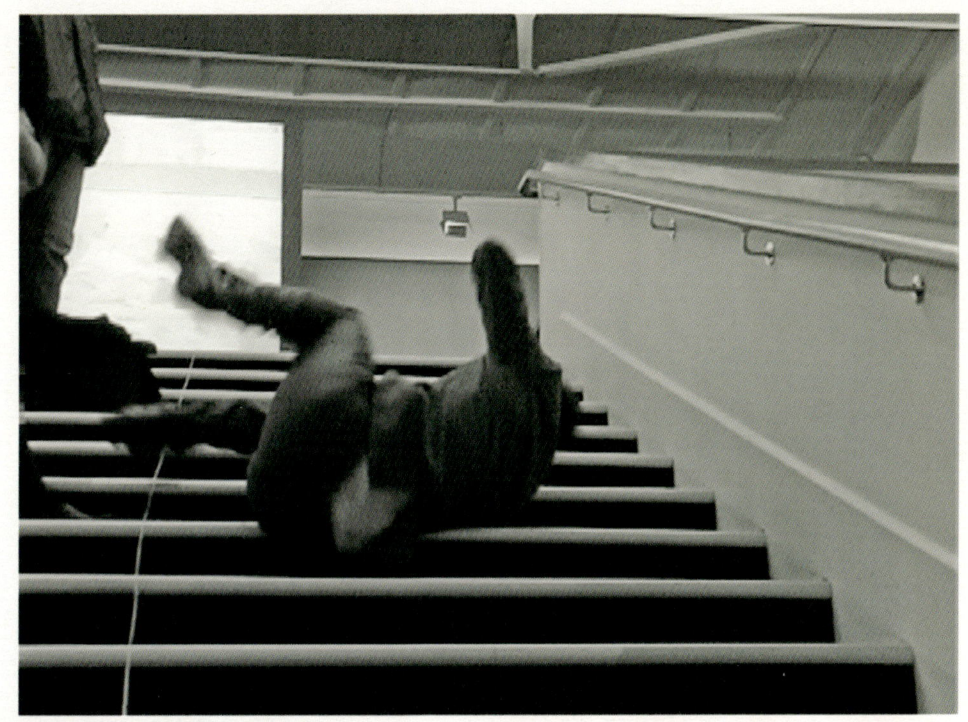

THE FALL

The Taken as an Art-Political Statement

Daniel Malone

**Govett-Brewster Art Gallery
New Plymouth, New Zealand
2 pm, 9 September, 2006**

STEAL THIS SMILE!

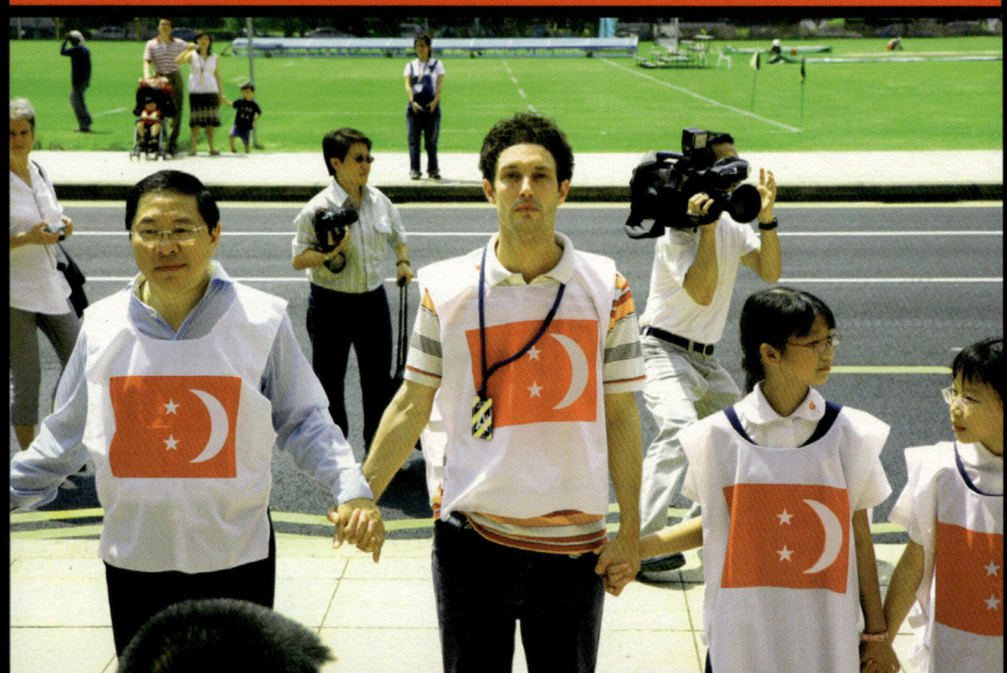

INVITATION TO PARTICIPATE

Seeking 500 volunteers to join hands around City Hall in a re-enactment of Abbie Hoffman's 1967 attempt to levitate the Pentagon at the opening of the inaugural Singapore Biennale, a contemporary art event held as part of Singapore Global City 2006 which also includes annual meetings of the IMF and World Bank in the same building. The theme of this biennale is Belief. All participants given flag-artwork to take away aftewards.

All welcome, assemble Pandang fields, 10am, September 2nd

Six shots recorded from a Glock .21 handgun purchased illegally & fired at the site of the 1965 New York World's Fair Flushing, Queens, September 3 1998

DER VERSCHOLLENE ‹AMERIKA›

Three lathe-cut acetate 7" records

Each unmarked side containing three minutes of silence & a single gunshot, each in a different place

May 16th– June 24th 2006 GROUND ZERO MALONE

ceramics
records
silk dyed tissue

At Artists Space

38 Greene St, SOHO, Manhattan, NY, NY,

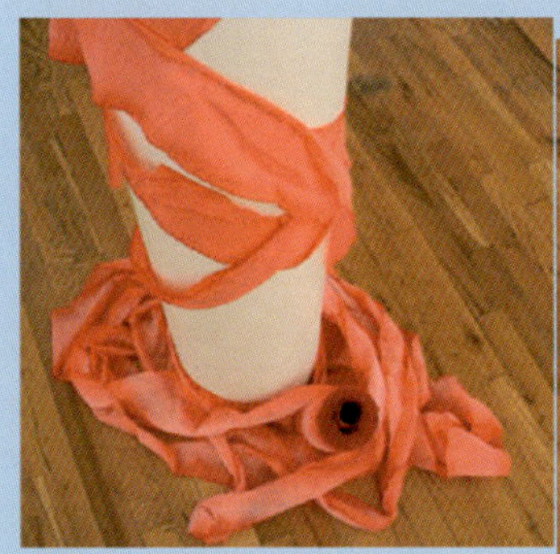
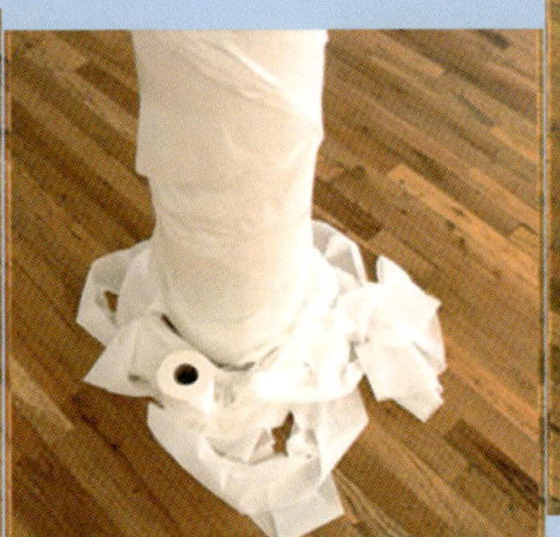
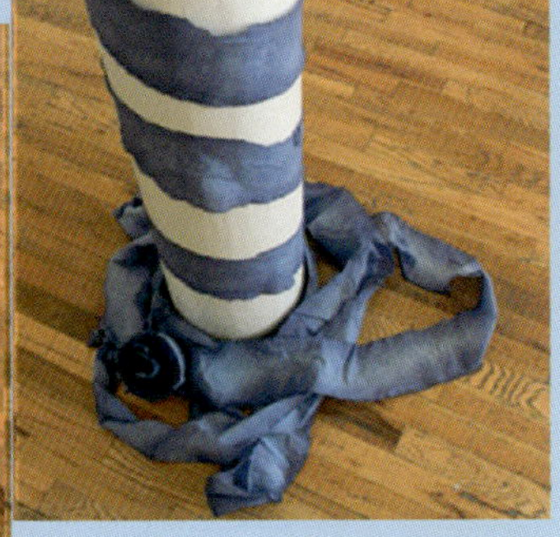

Bill Hammond

38

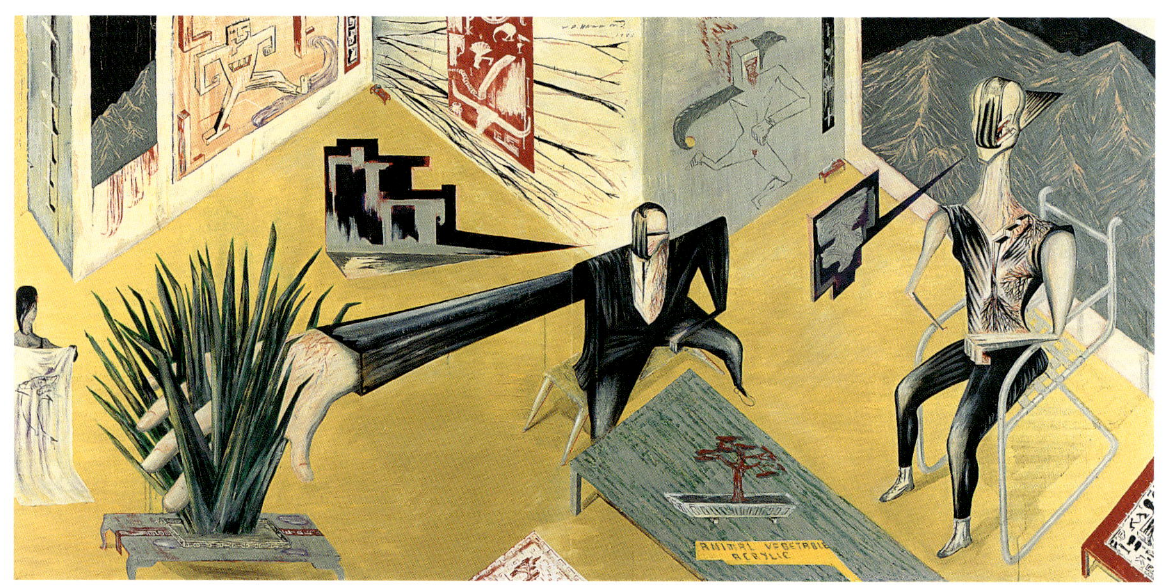

Animal Vegetable Acrylic, 1988
acrylic on canvas
1605 x 3130mm
Collection: M Webster

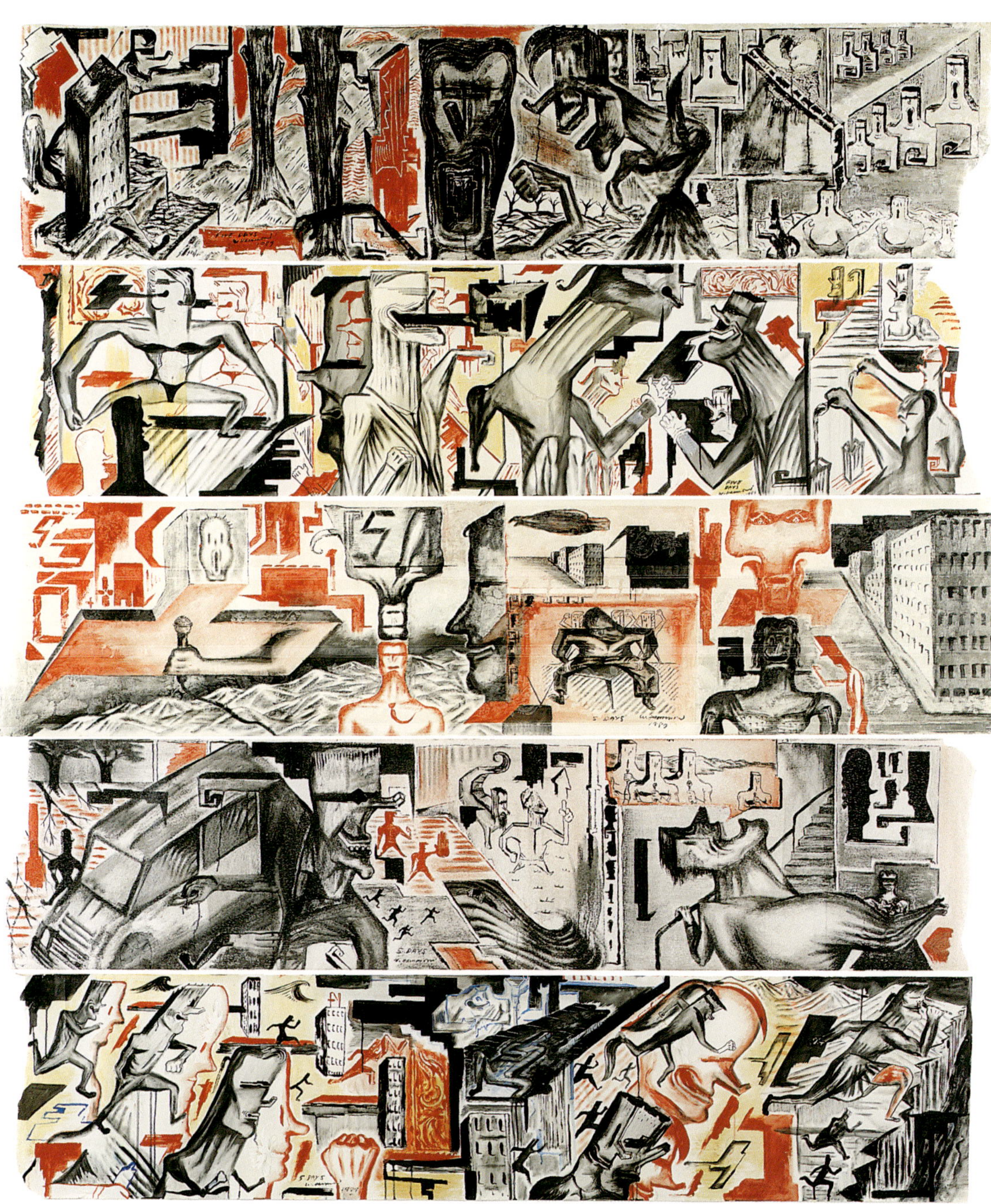

Five Days, 1989
acrylic on wallpaper
installed dimensions: 2665 x 2270mm
Collection: Dunedin Public Art Gallery

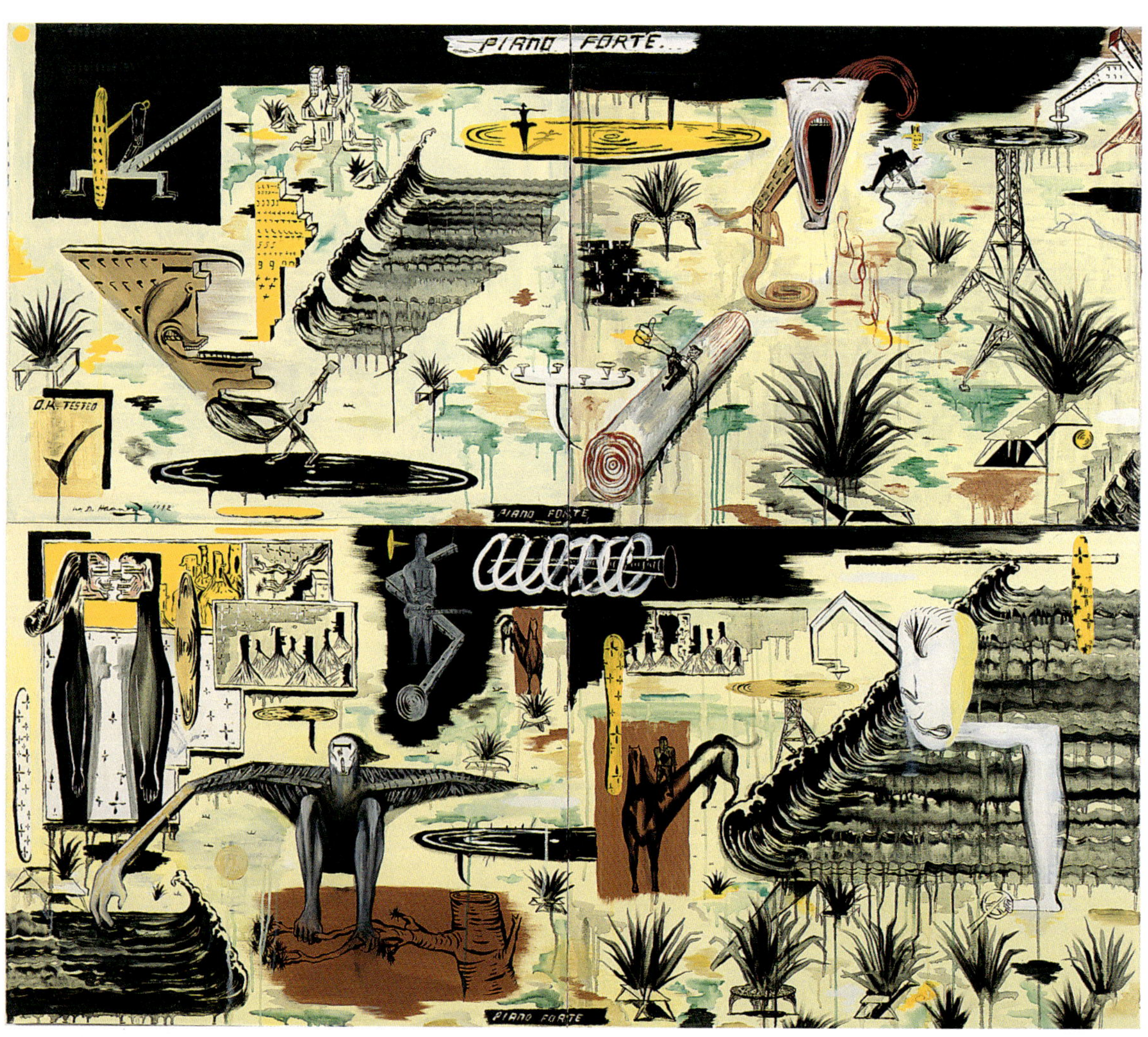

Piano Forte, 1992
acrylic on canvas
1605 x 1805mm
Collection: M Webster

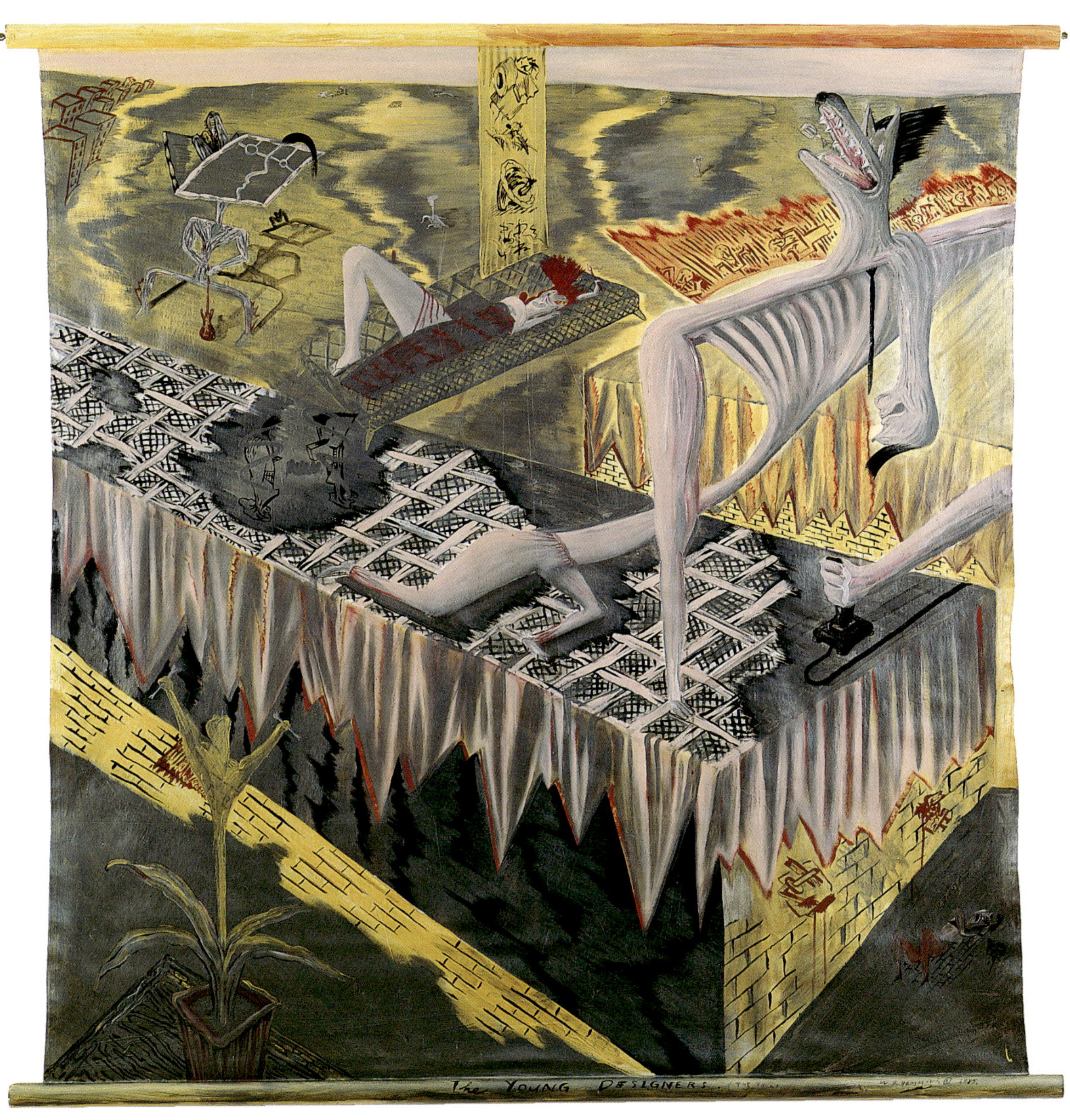

The Young Designers, 1985
acrylic on canvas
1970 x 1925mm
Collection: Auckland Art Gallery Toi o Tamaki

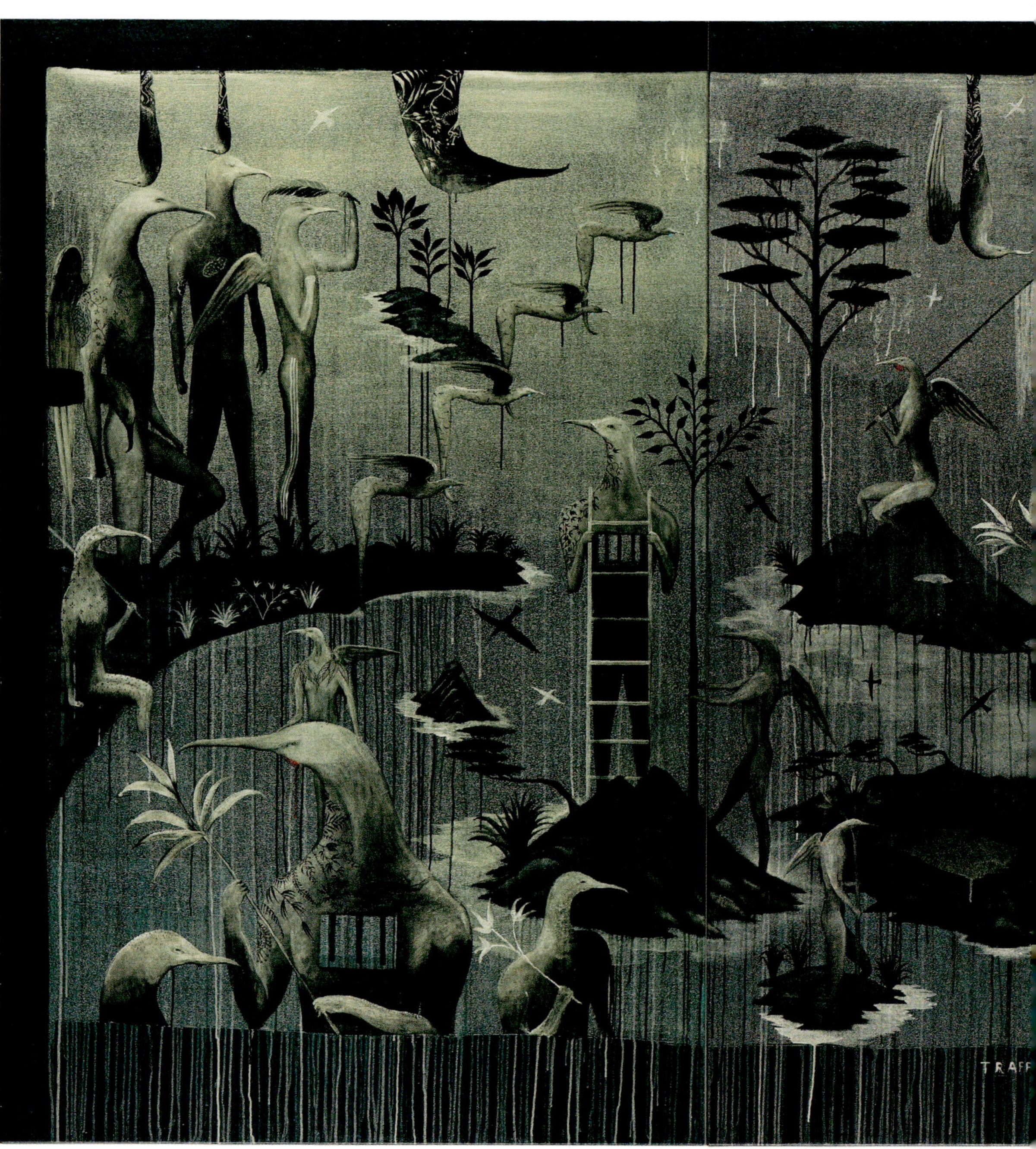

Traffic Cop Bay, 2003
acrylic on canvas
2000 x 3750mm
Collection: Museum of New Zealand Te Papa Tongarewa

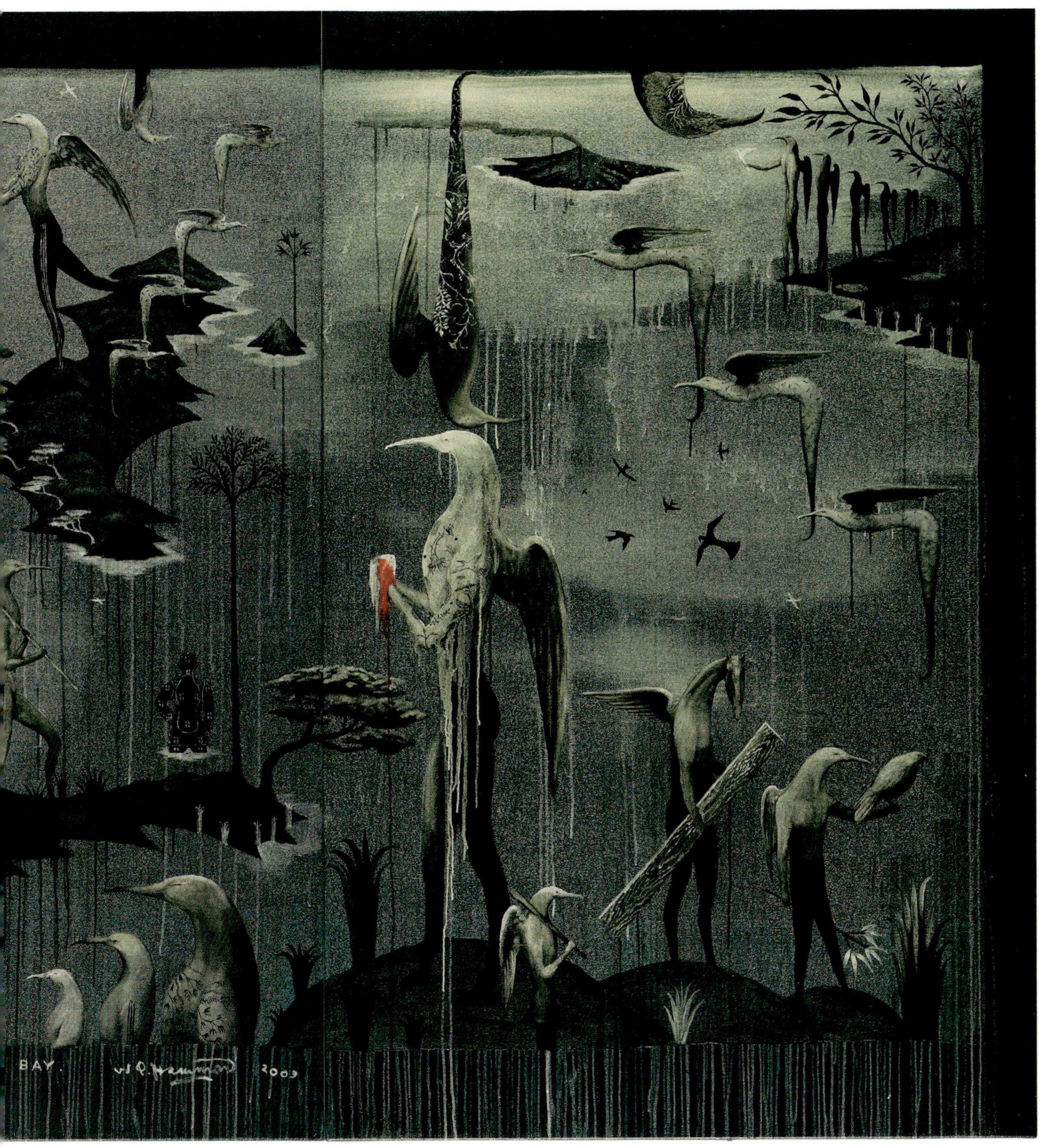

BAY.
2009

Julian Dashper

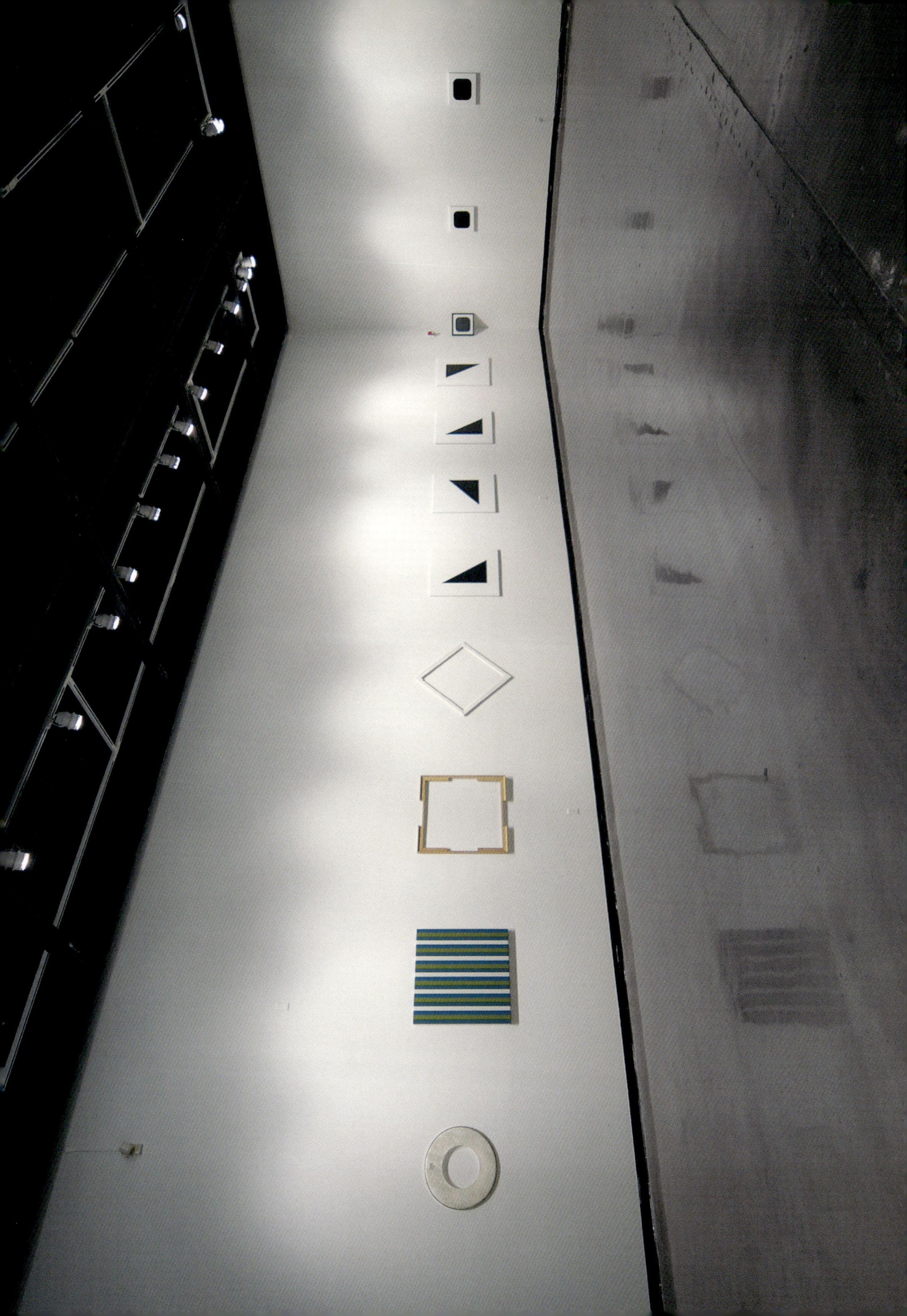

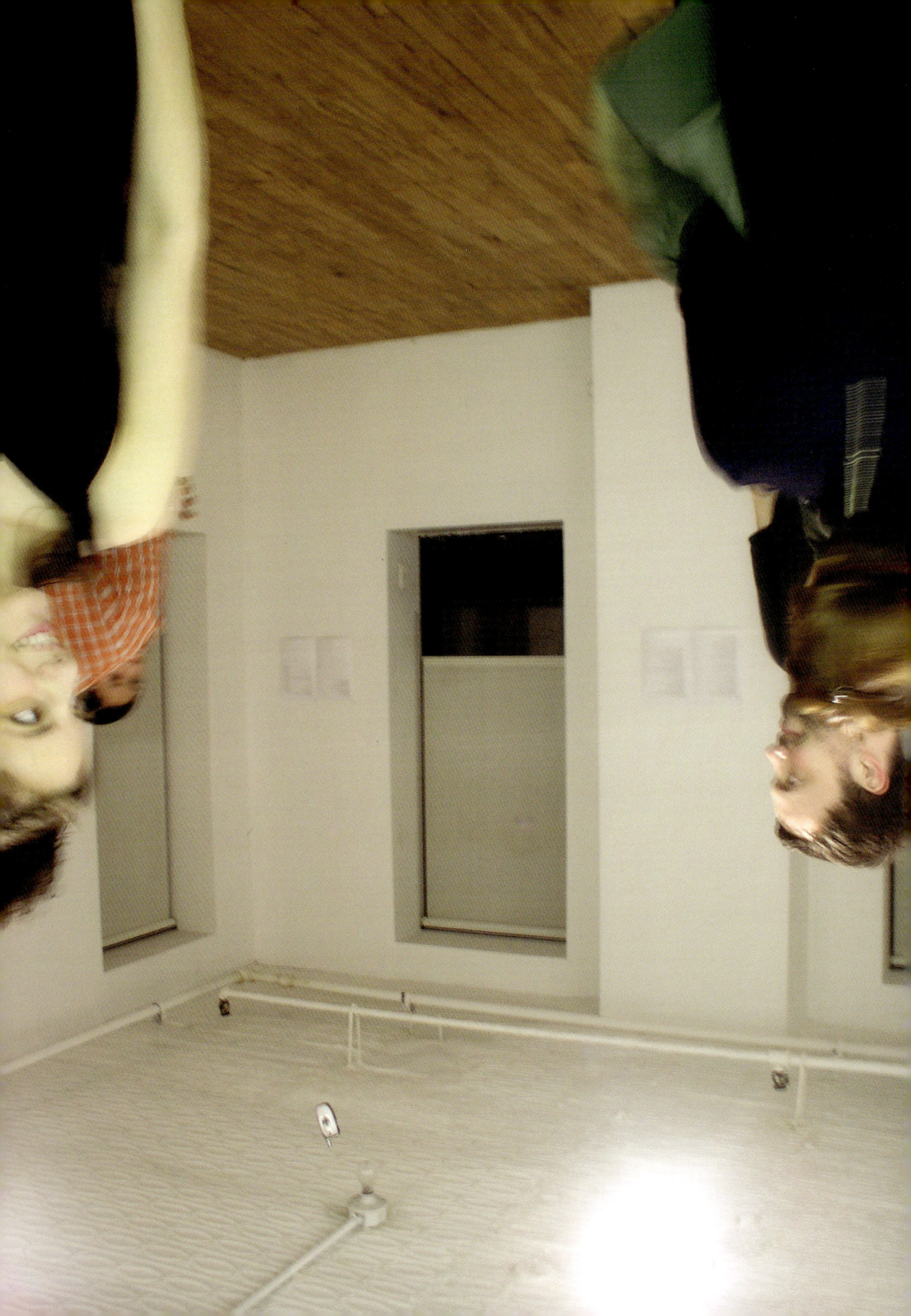

Julian Dashper
SOLO EXHIBITIONS continued

2000   **Stuff**, London, *Julian Dashper, New Zealand*
        Room 211, Hotel Winston, Amsterdam, *Kamer 211*
        Galerie Stadt München, Amsterdam, *Julian Dashper*
        PS, Amsterdam, *I love Amsterdam and Amsterdam loves me*
        Sue Crockford Gallery, Auckland, *For immediate release*
        Sarah Cottier Gallery, Sydney
        Hamish McKay Gallery, Wellington
        Blue Oyster Gallery, Dunedin, *The last solo exhibition in the world*

2001   **The Chinati Foundation**, Marfa, Texas, *Locker Plant Locker Plant* (publ)
        Sue Crockford Gallery, Auckland, *Selected Masterpieces*
        BBQ Project, Berlin, *Julian Dashper is not coming to Berlin*
        Showcase NL, Amsterdam, *Julian Dashper*
        Showcase, Wellington, *Julian Dashper*

2002   **PS**, Amsterdam, *Introducing Donald Dashper* (publ)
        Sue Crockford Gallery, Auckland, *Unique Pictures* (publ)
        rm 401, Auckland, *The JD Show*
        Sarah Cottier Gallery, Sydney
        Campbelltown City Bicentennial Art Gallery, Campbelltown, Sydney *Blue Circles* (publ)

2003   **te tuhi - the mark**, Manukau City, Auckland *Blue Circles* (publ)
        Artspace, Sydney, *Julien Dashper* (publ)
        City Gallery, Wellington, *Blue Circles* (publ)
        Texas Gallery, Houston, *Unique Records* (publ)
        Michael Lett, Auckland, *Unleash Fury*

2004   **Sue Crockford Gallery**, Auckland, *The early Dutch works*
        Canary, Auckland, *Untitled (portrait of Ben Curnow)*
        Mop Projects, Sydney
        Hamish McKay Gallery, Wellington, *The secret*

2005   **CCNOA**, Brussels, *Julian Dashper*
        Showcase NL, Amsterdam, *Julian Dashper*
        PS, Amsterdam, *One new painting and one new record by Julian Dashper*
        Sioux City Art Center, Sioux City, Iowa,
        Midwestern Unlike *You and Me: New Zealand's Julian Dashper* (publ)
        Kaliman Gallery, Sydney, *15 minutes in Australia*

2006   **Sheldon Memorial Art Gallery**, Lincoln, Nebraska,
        Midwestern Unlike *You and Me: New Zealand's Julian Dashper* (publ)
        Esso Gallery, New York, *Julian Dashper : Future Call 1994-2006, Untitled (C.V.) 1979-2006*
        Aratoi Wairarapa Museum of Art and History, Masterton, *Dashper again and again* (publ)
        Whangarei Art Museum Te Wharetaonga o Whangarei, Whangarei,
        Painting problems: the work of Julian Dashper 1990-2006 (publ)
        Ulrich Museum of Art, Wichita, Kansas,
        Midwestern Unlike *You and Me: New Zealand's Julian Dashper* (publ)
        Hamish McKay Gallery, Wellington, *Both sides now*
        Sue Crockford Gallery, Auckland, *It is what it isn't*

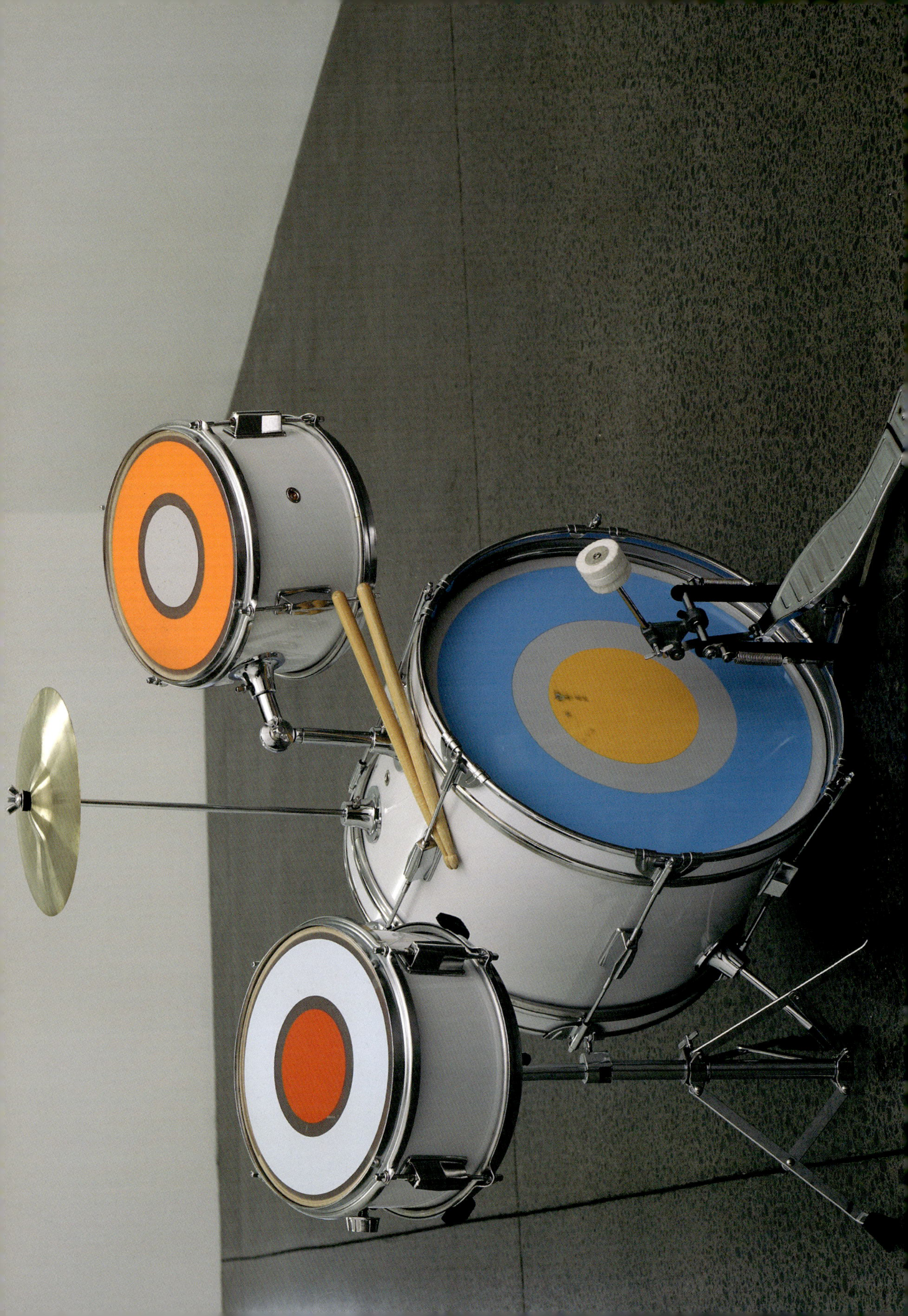

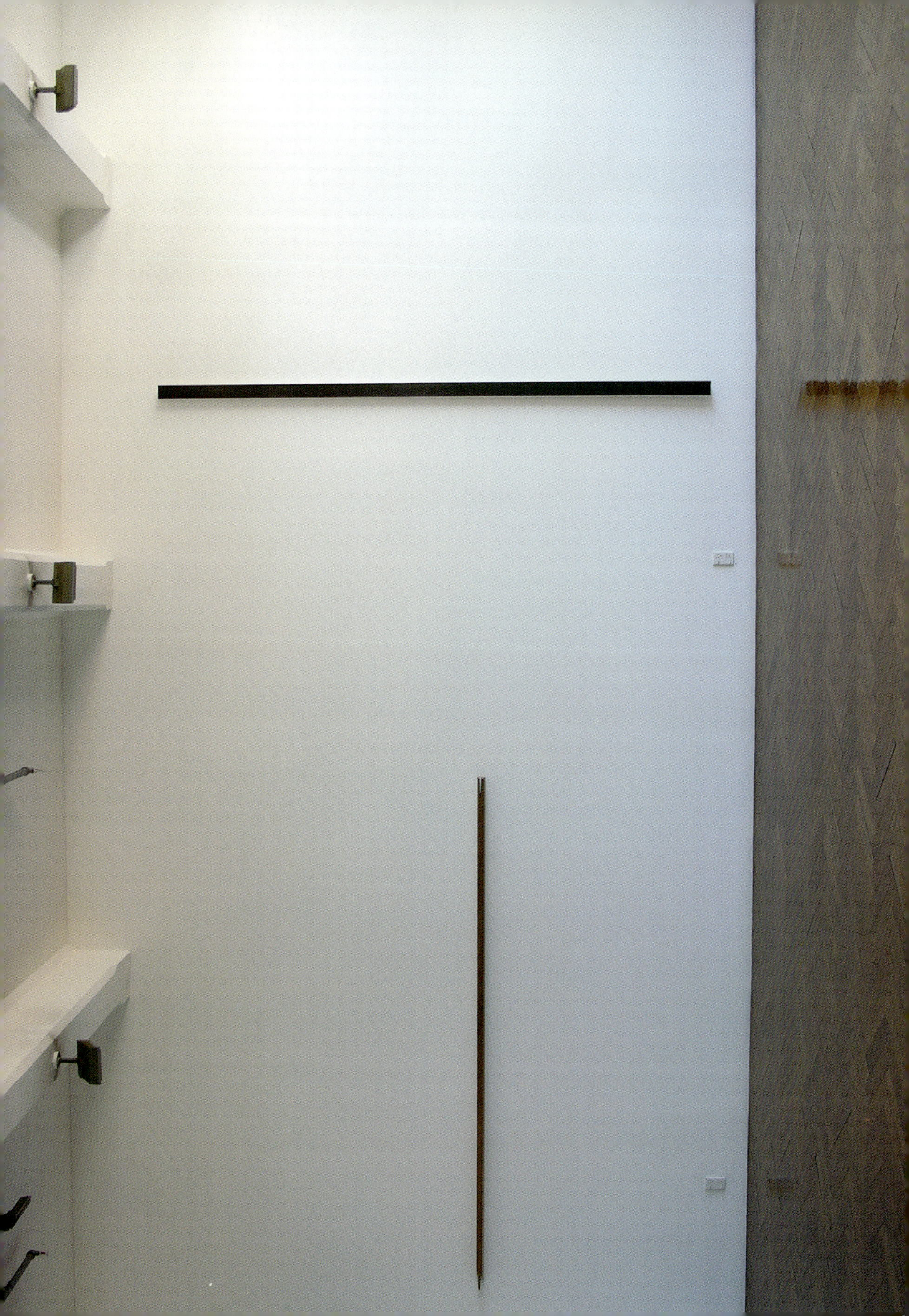

Ronnie van Hout

EUROPA 2007

Two Biennale's coincide..... Today, he is going to sell all of his eighties art..... Damien's exhibition closes in February...... Late one evening, the old painter was re-reading his old reviews.

Question: Does Damien's show close in February?

DOCUMENTA 12

An unknown artist backing up
to look at a painting knocks over
a sculpture and damages it.
Rushing from the gallery he
accidentally drops his sunglasses
on the ground. The dealer, who is
unaware of the damaged sculpture
calls out. "Hey, you! Stop!"
The artist turns around, sees
the dealer and confesses the
damage to the sculpture....

Question: Why did he do this?

BASEL 07

A semi-famous artist has just stolen some catalogues from your stand at Liste. An important director of a well known Art institution, who swings by, sees the artist as he is running away. The director thinks he is running to catch the start of a video screening nearby. You can talk quickly to the director before the artist enters the screening room.

Question: What do you say?

Münster 07

An artist is about to grafitti a dealer gallery. Drunkenly he sneaks around avoiding the motion detectors and alarms. If he is caught, the gallery will never represent him. As he is about to tag the side of of the gallery he steps on something soft. He hears a screech, then something soft and furry runs past him toward the front of the gallery. Immediately the alarm sounds.

Question: Why did the alarm go off?

VENICE 2007

You went to the Venice Biennale for the vernissage. In the morning the sky is blue and the sun is shining. However, walking around the Giardini later, the sky becomes gray and it starts to rain.
You forgot to bring your umbrella.

Question: What do you think?

Sriwhana Spong

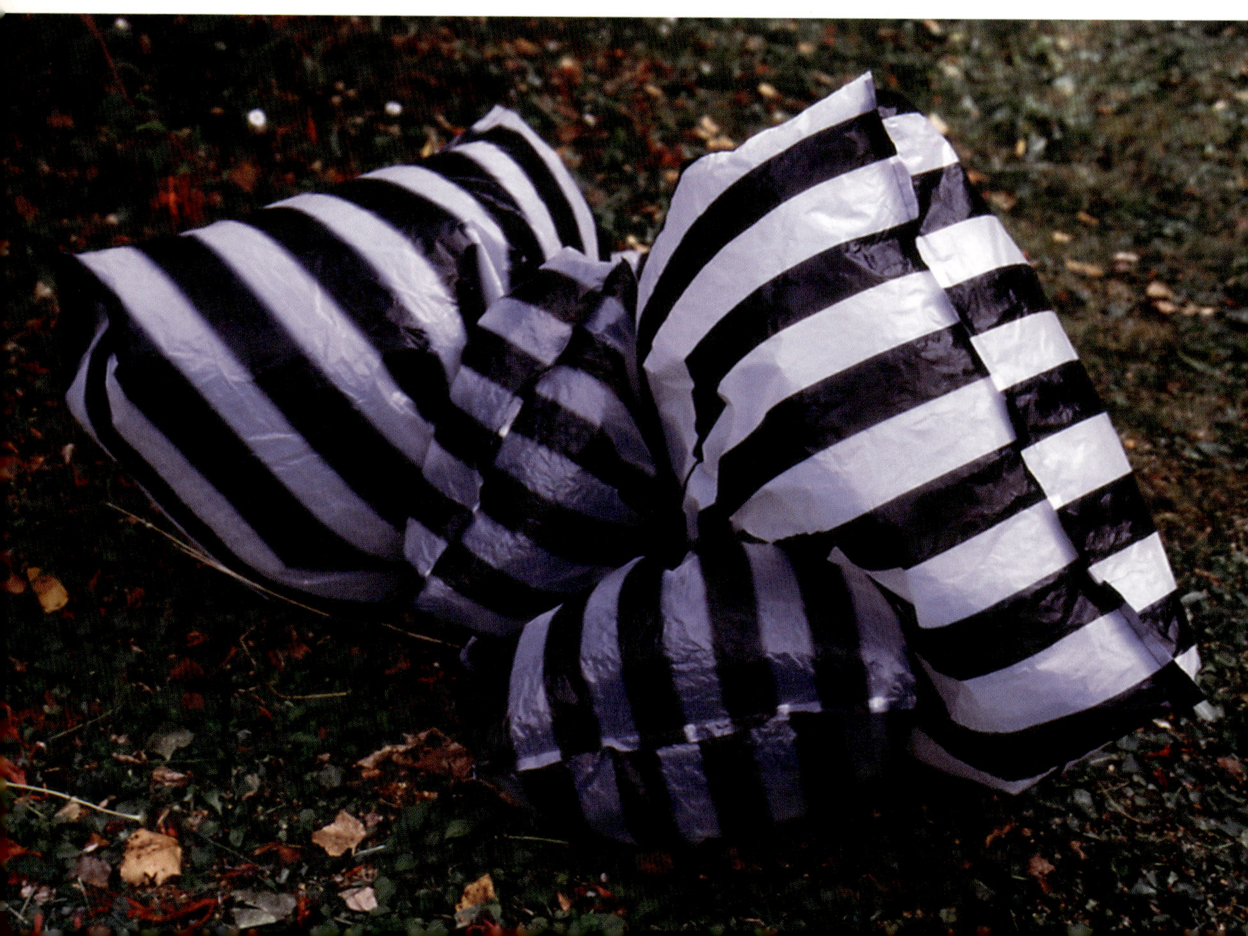

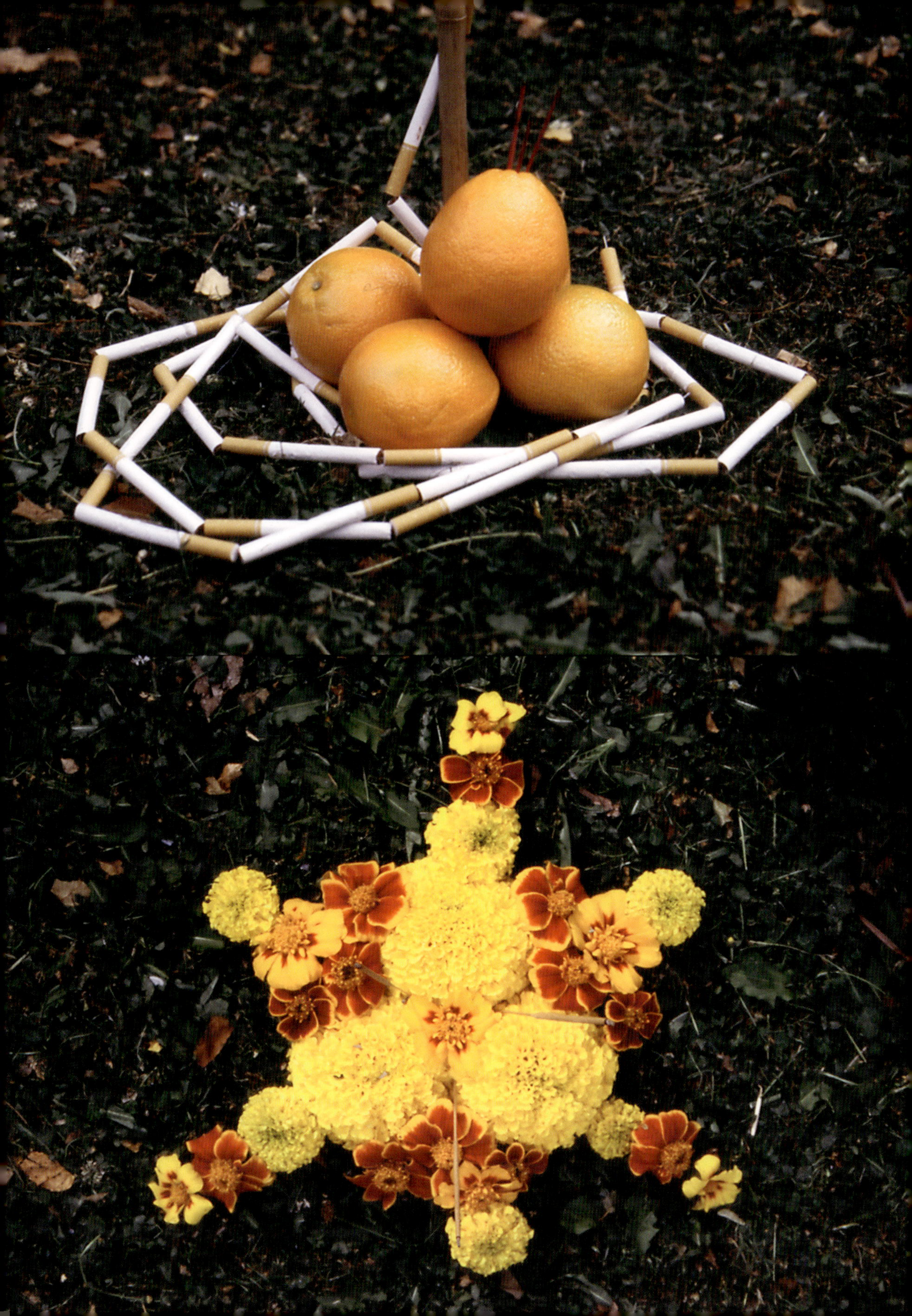

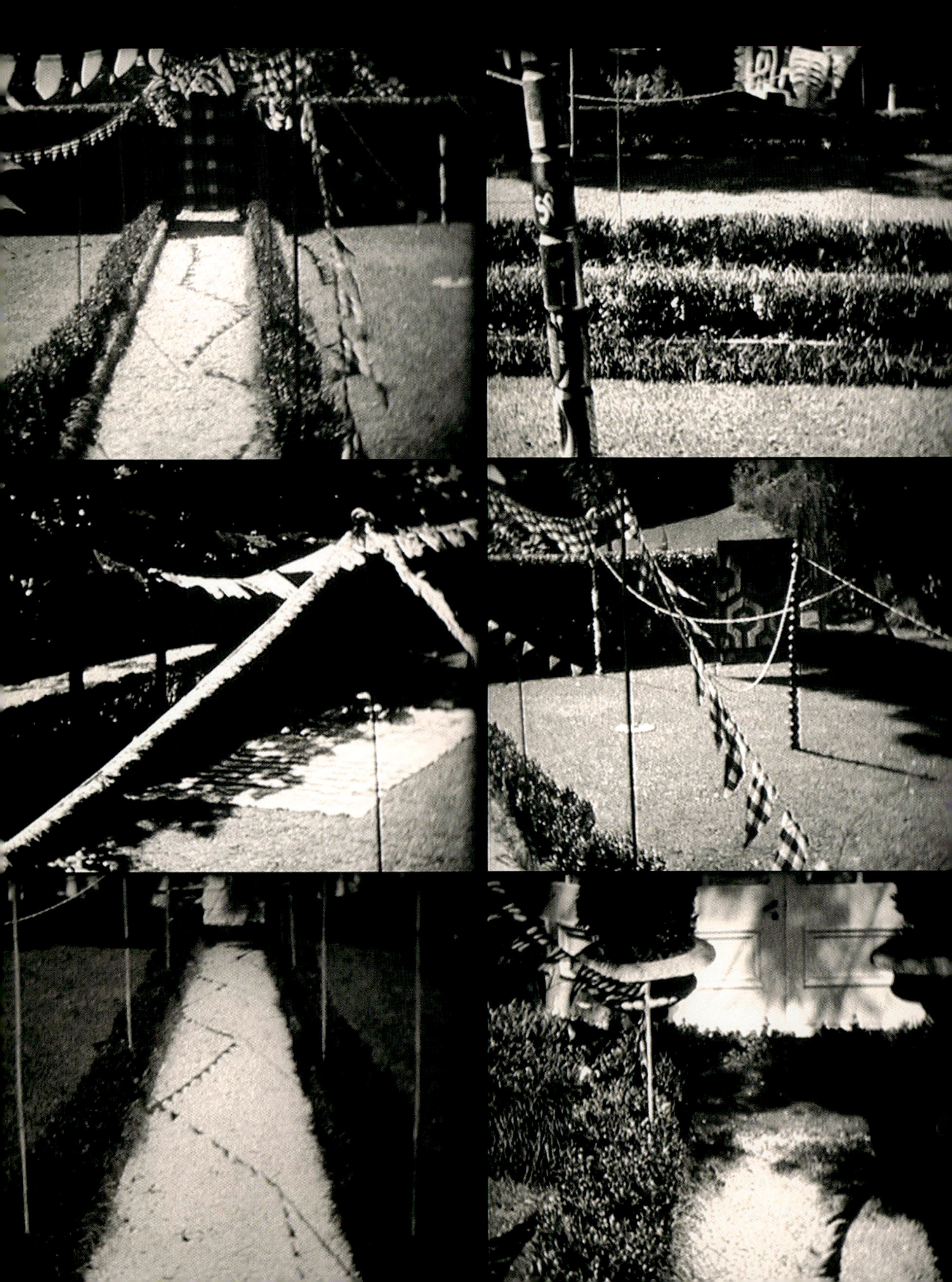

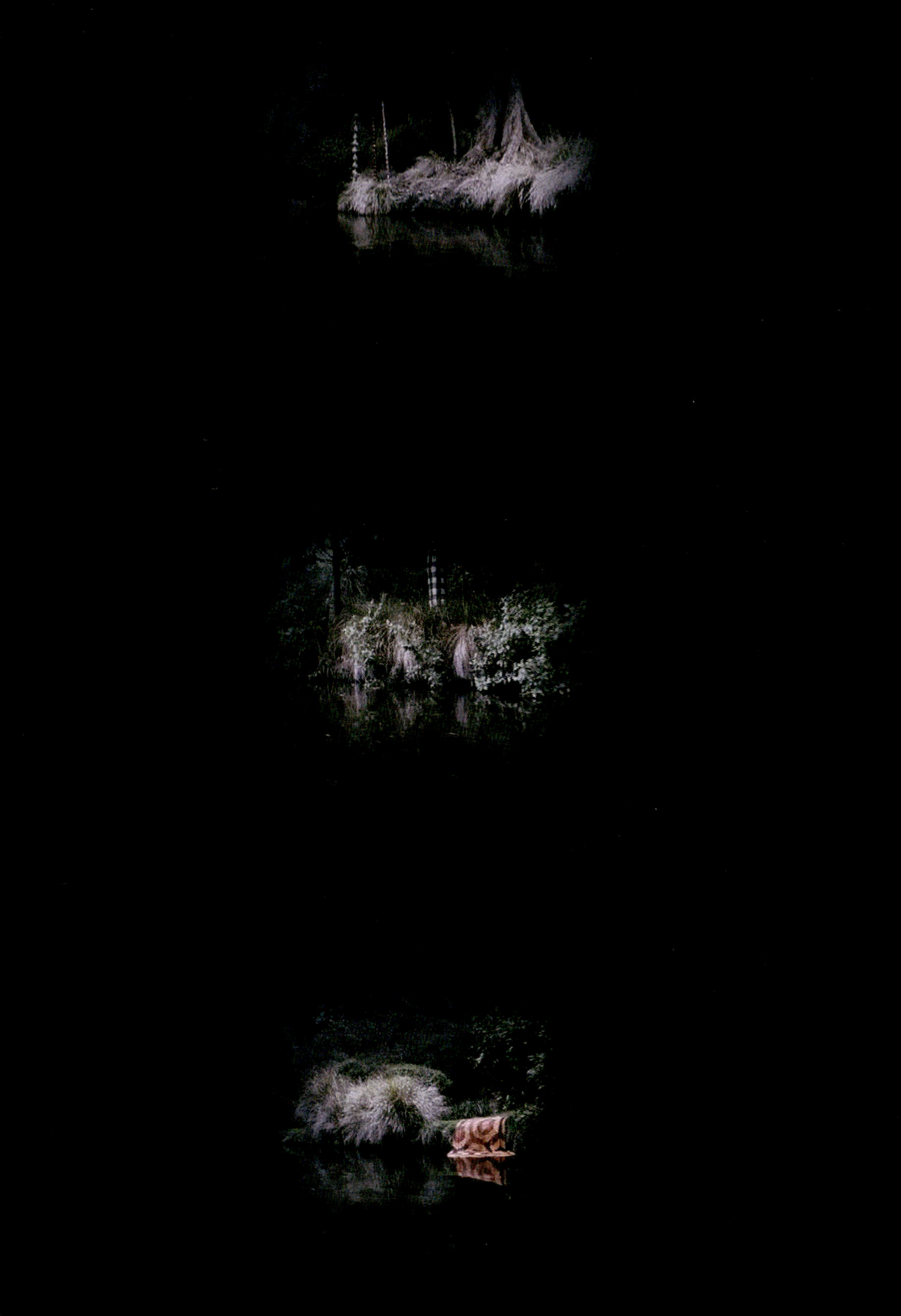

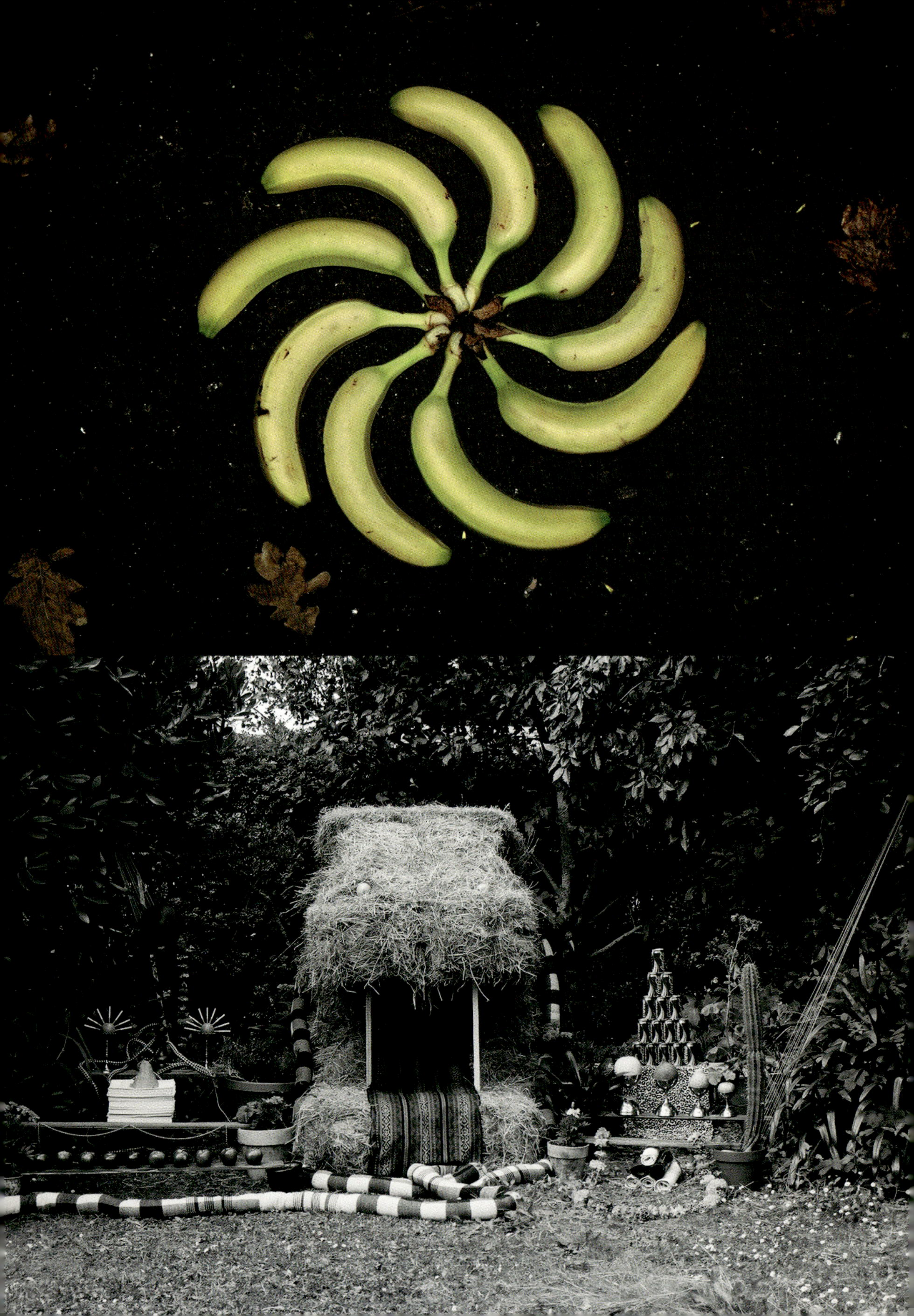

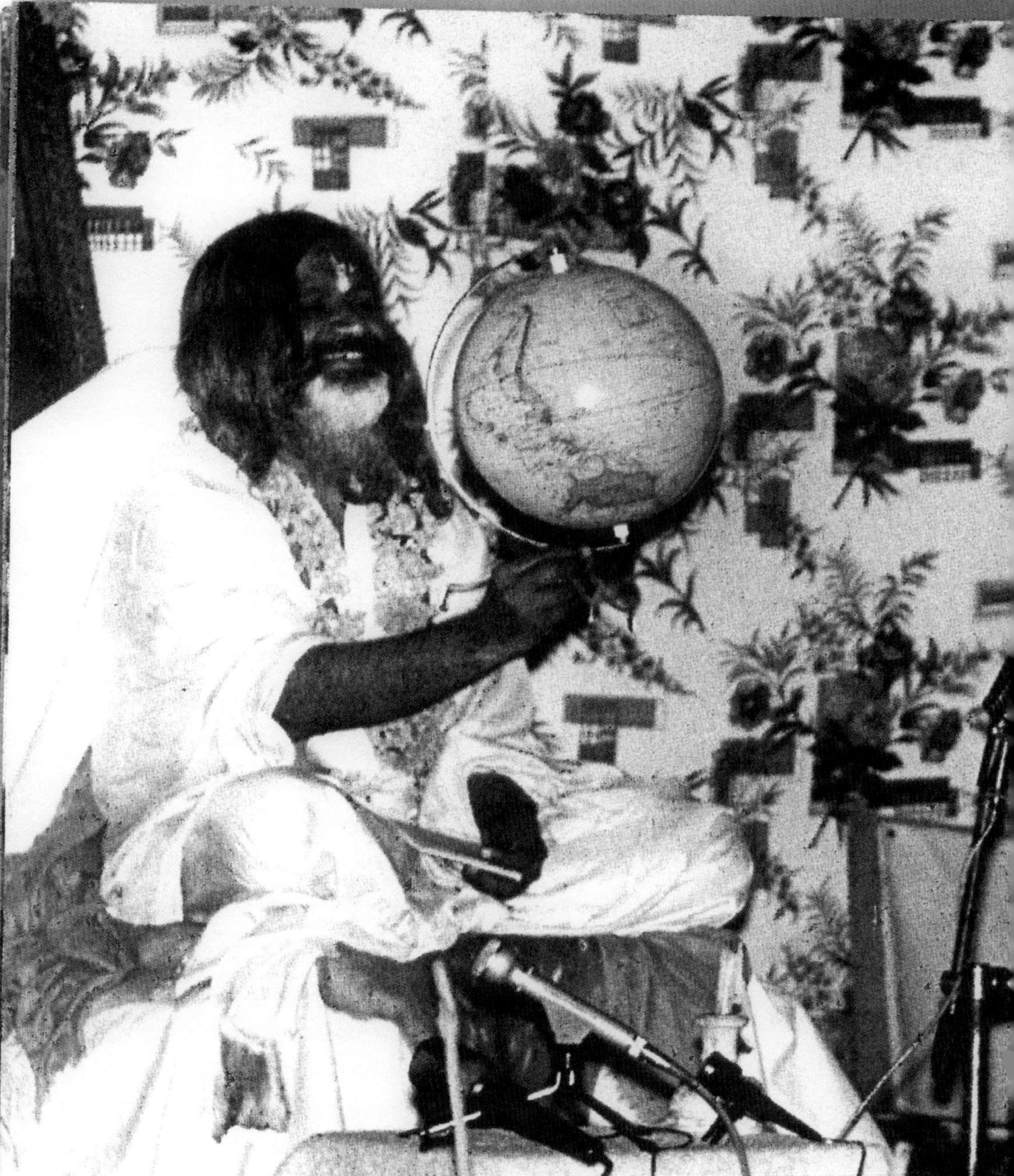

ABOVE: "The Maharishi presented George Harrison with a cake and a plastic globe turned upside-down. 'This is the world,' he said. 'It needs to be corrected.' We sang 'Happy Birthday' to George, and then when the laughter and applause subsided, the Hindu porters laughed and danced and threw firecrackers at one another in the doorway of the lecture hall."

Judy Millar

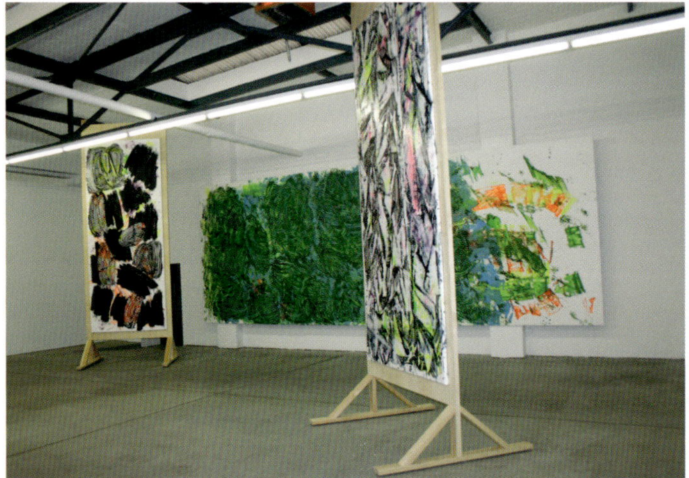

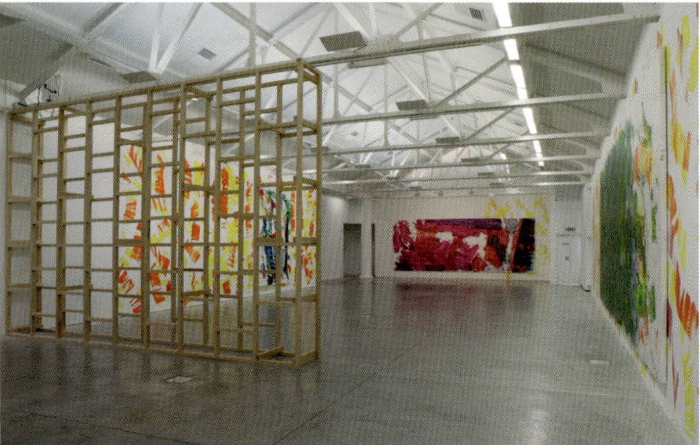

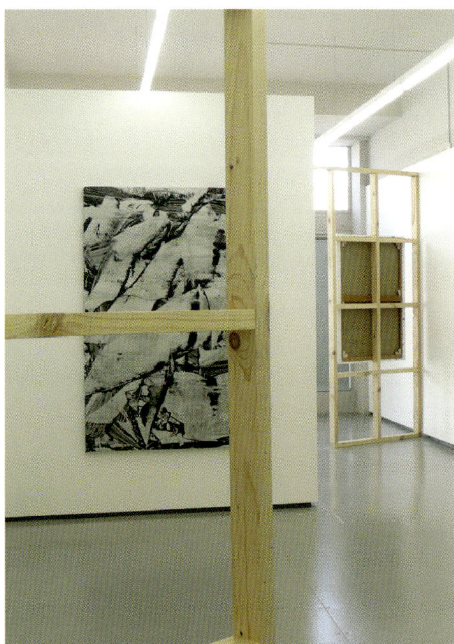

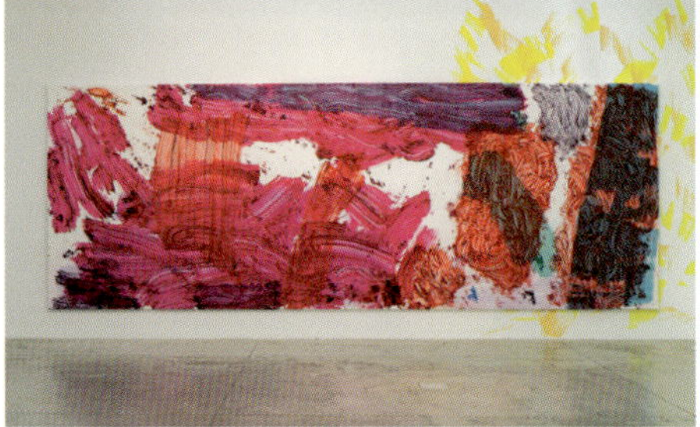

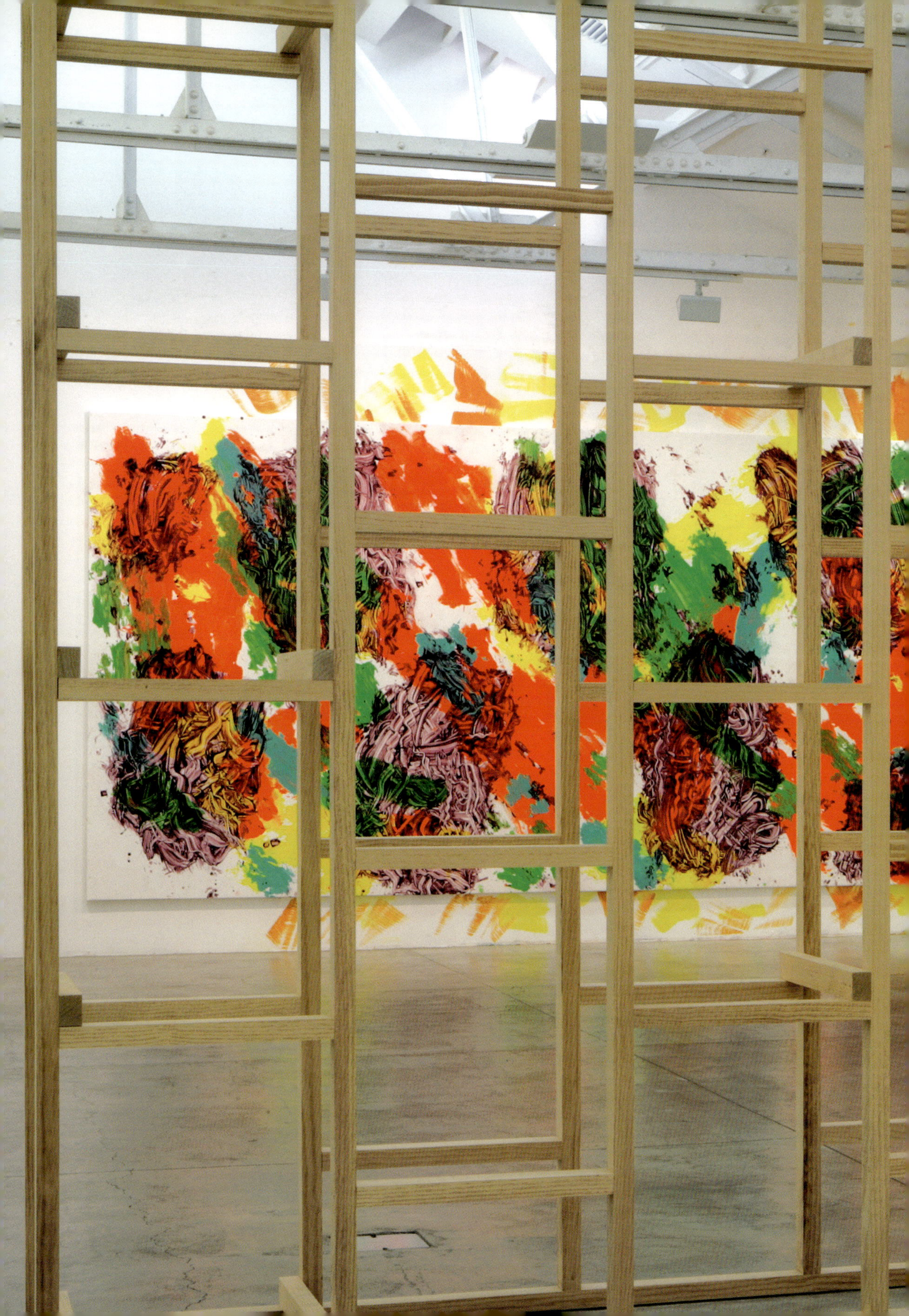

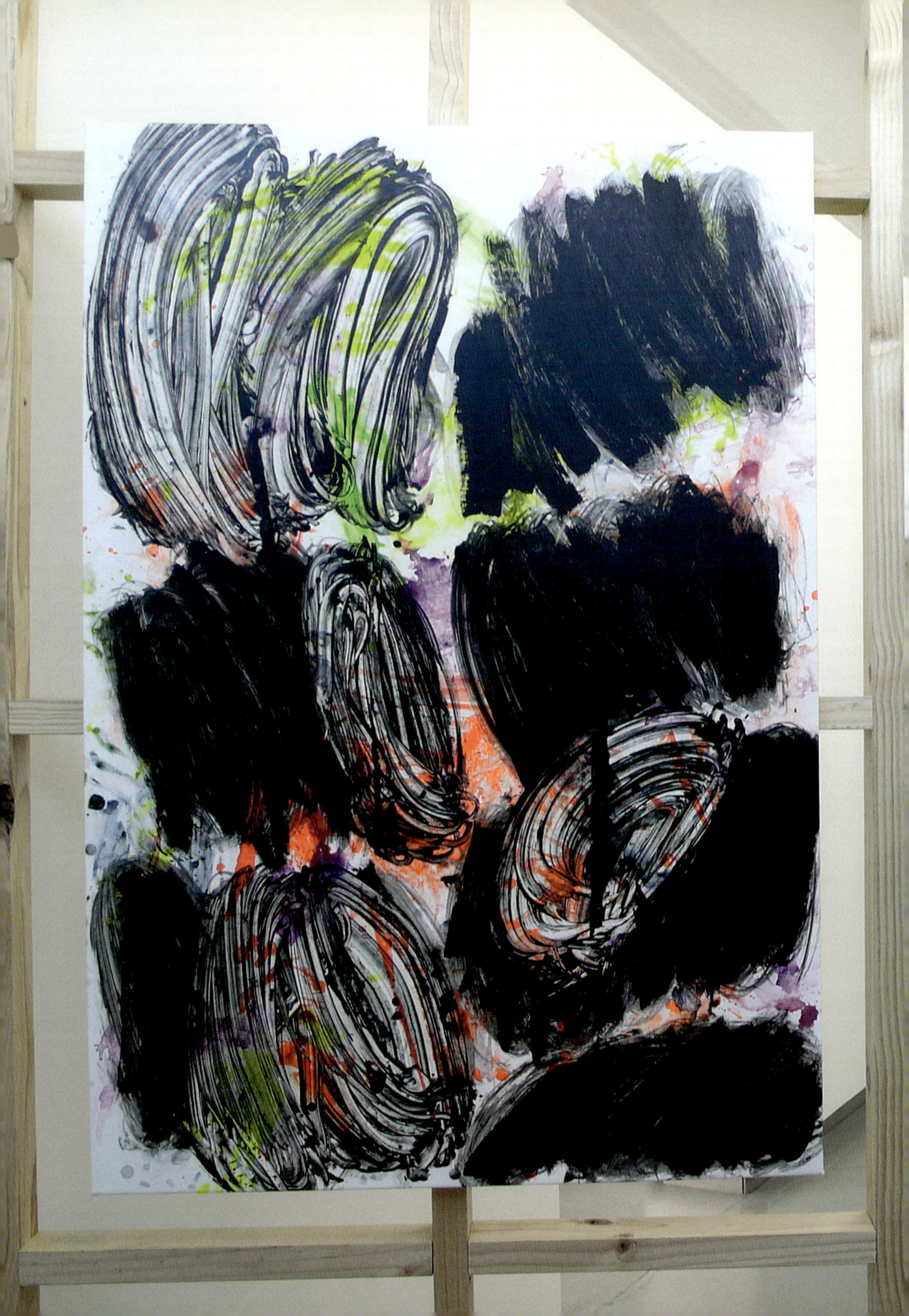

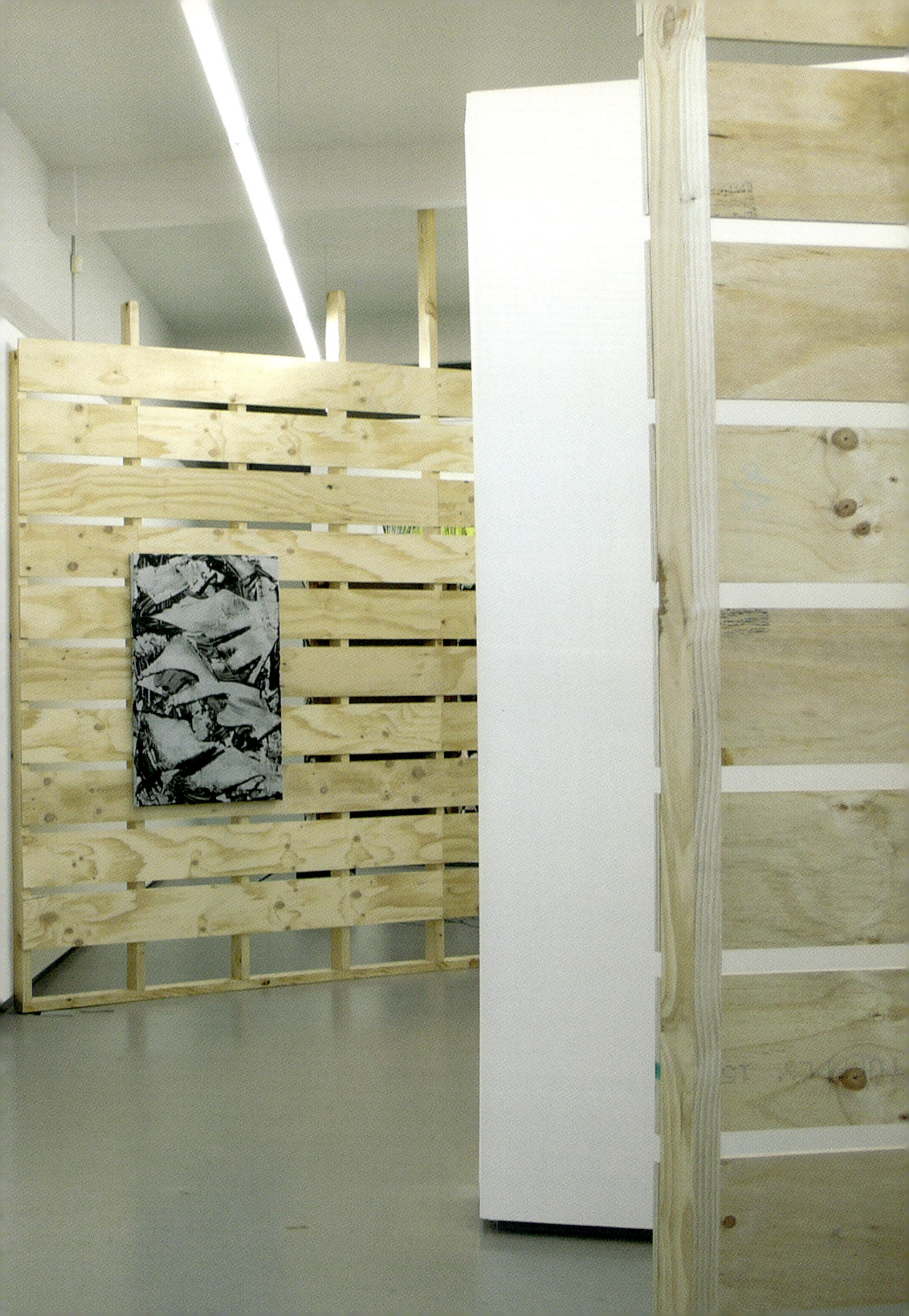

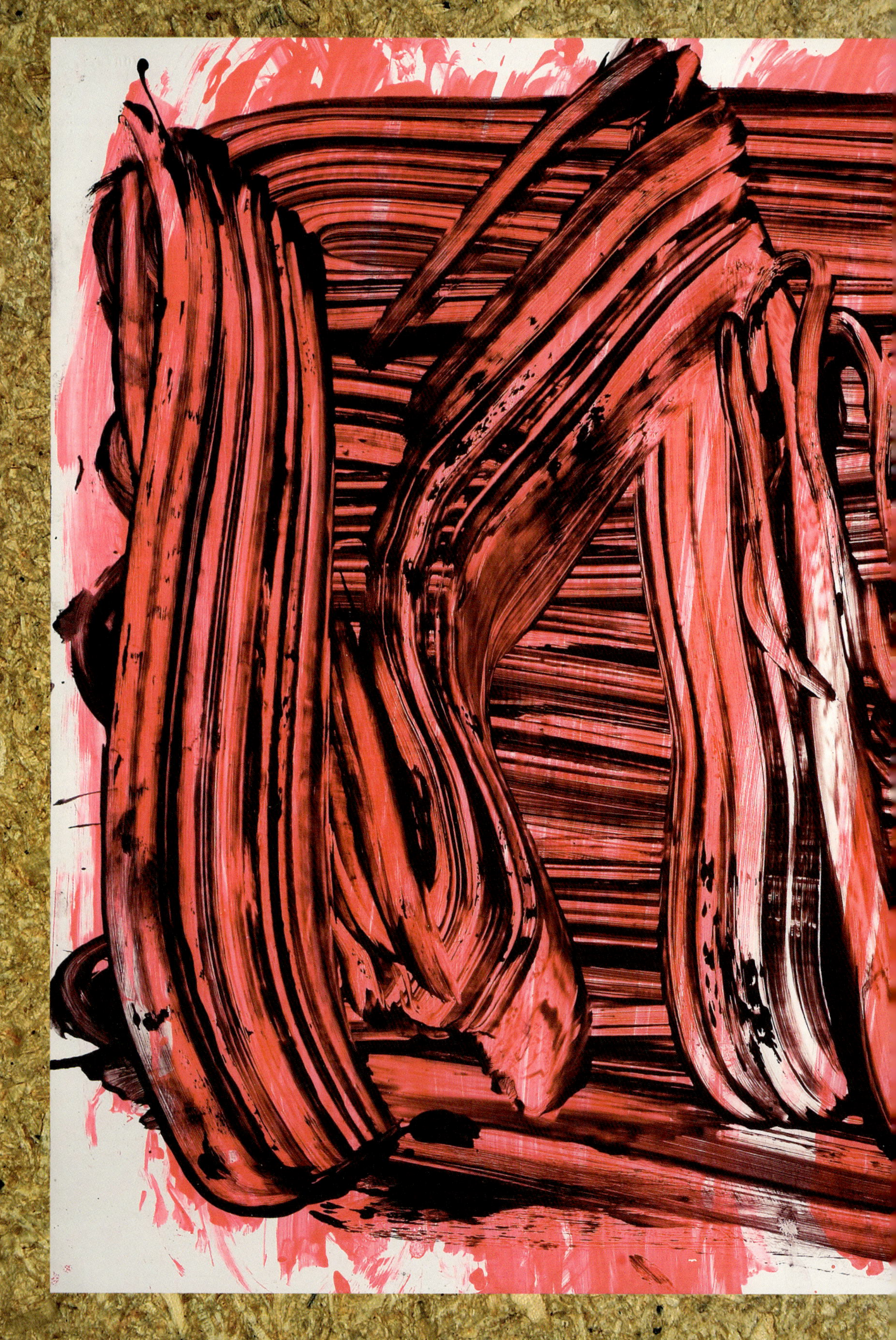

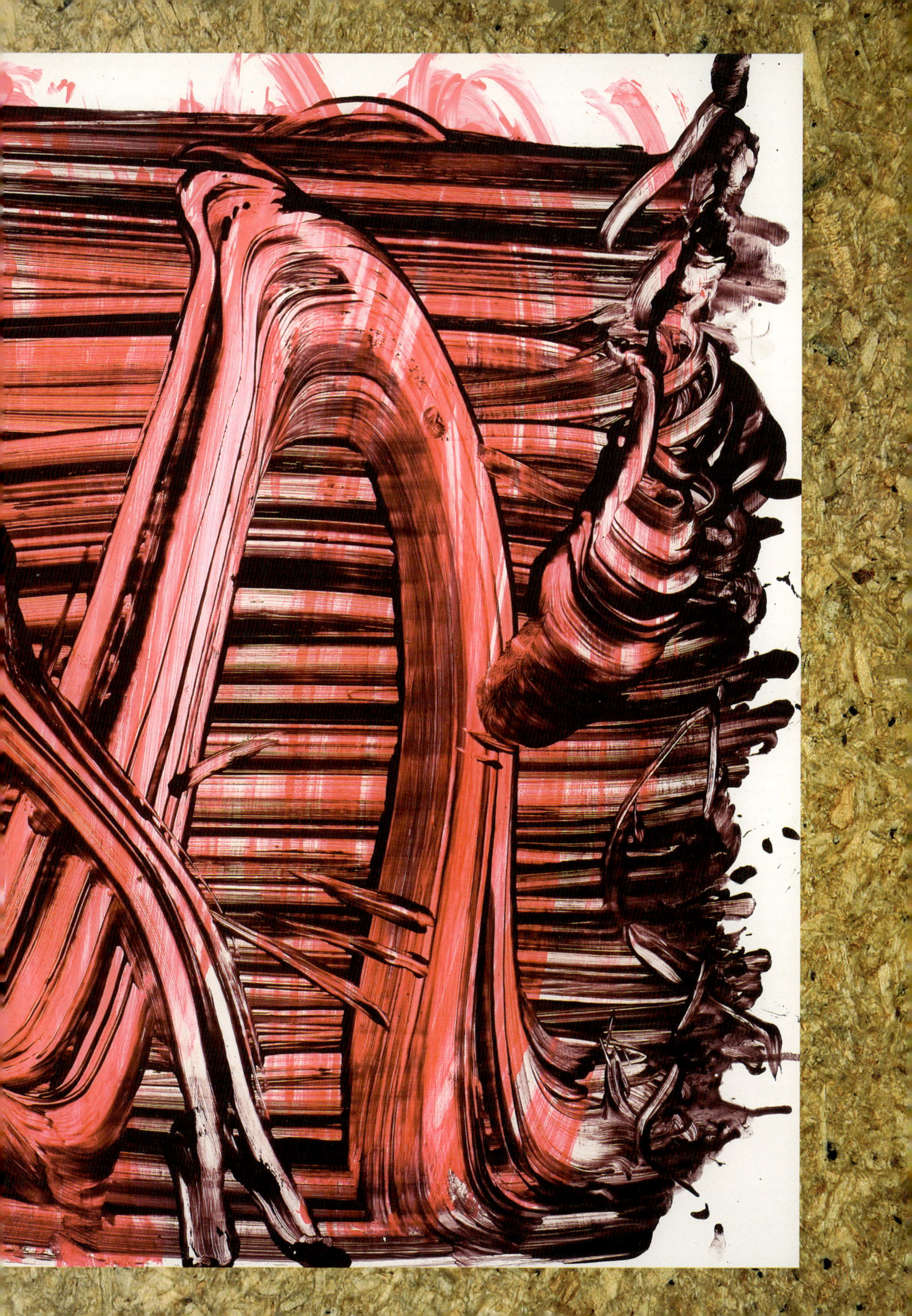

Bill Culbert

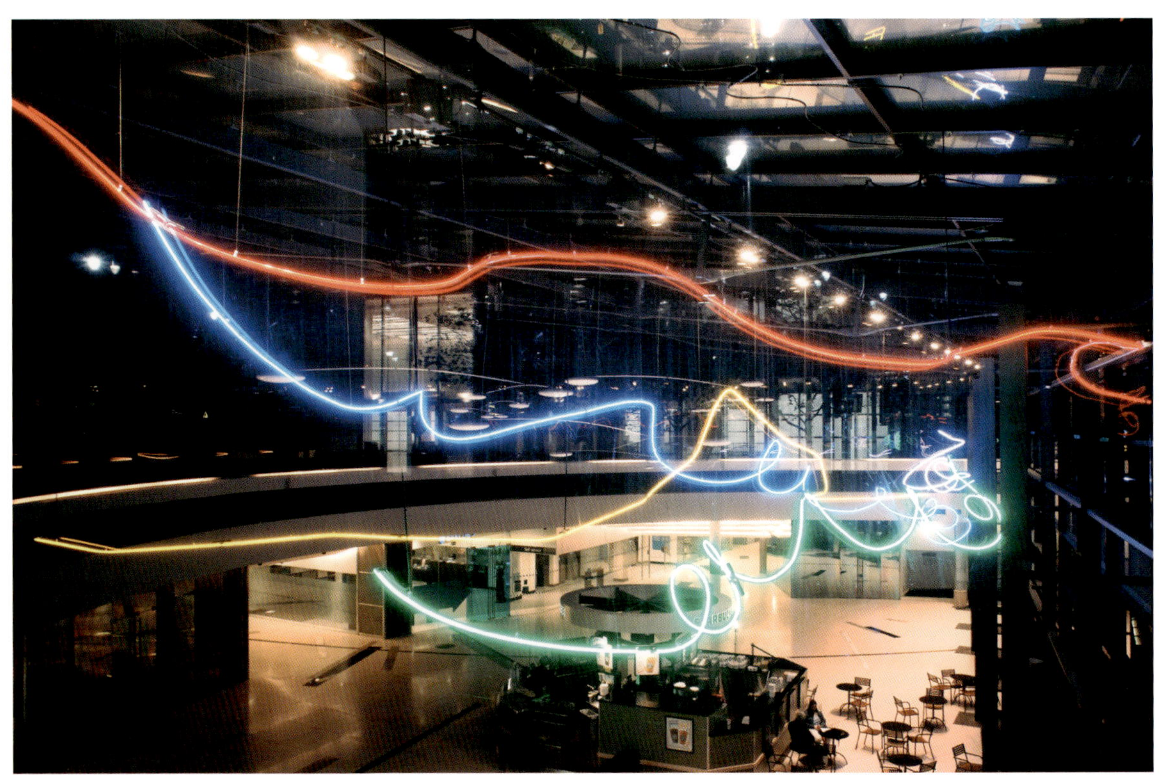

Coup de Foudre
Canary Wharf, London
2006
Photo: Philip Vile

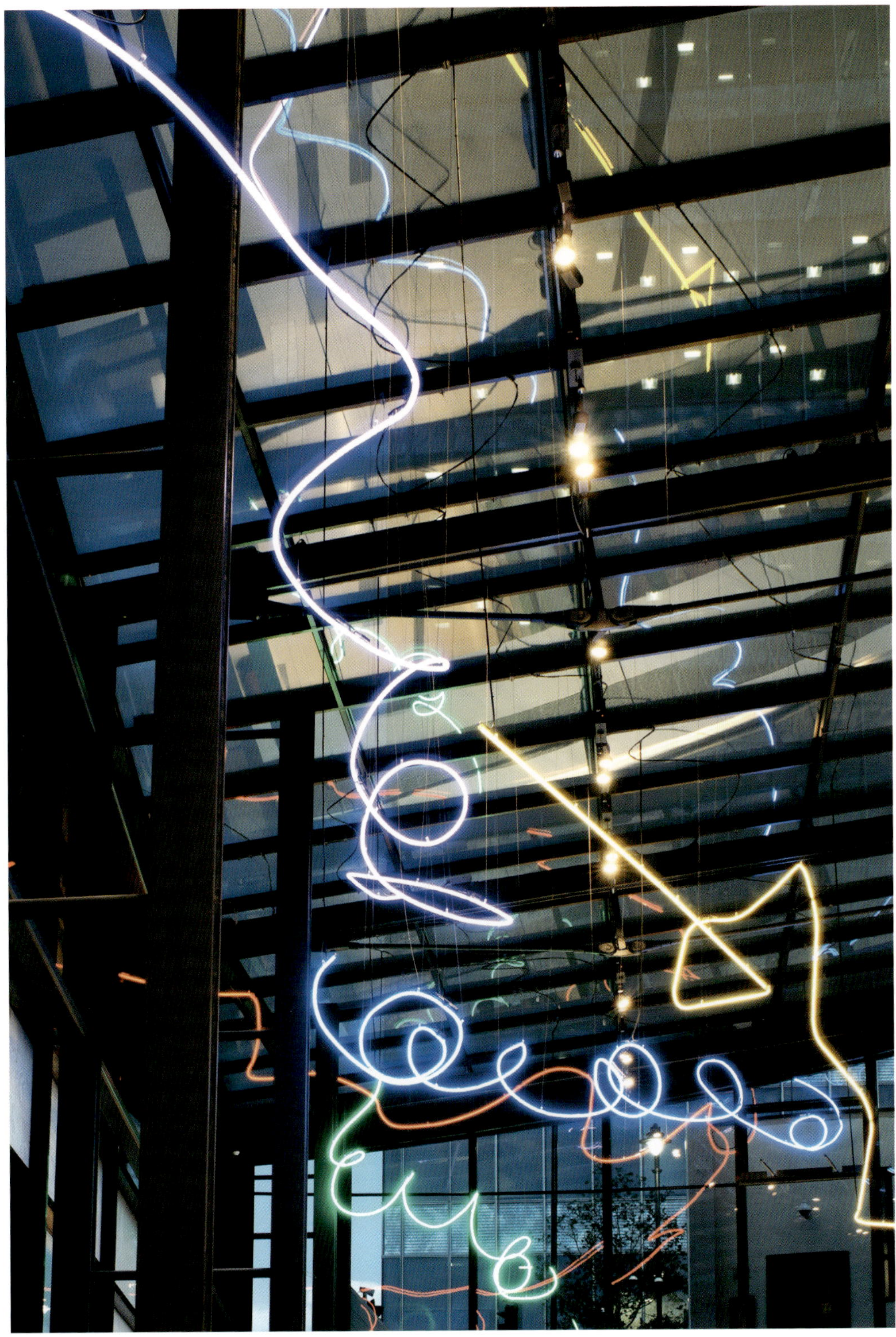

Coup de Foudre
Canary Wharf, London
2006
Photo: Philip Vile

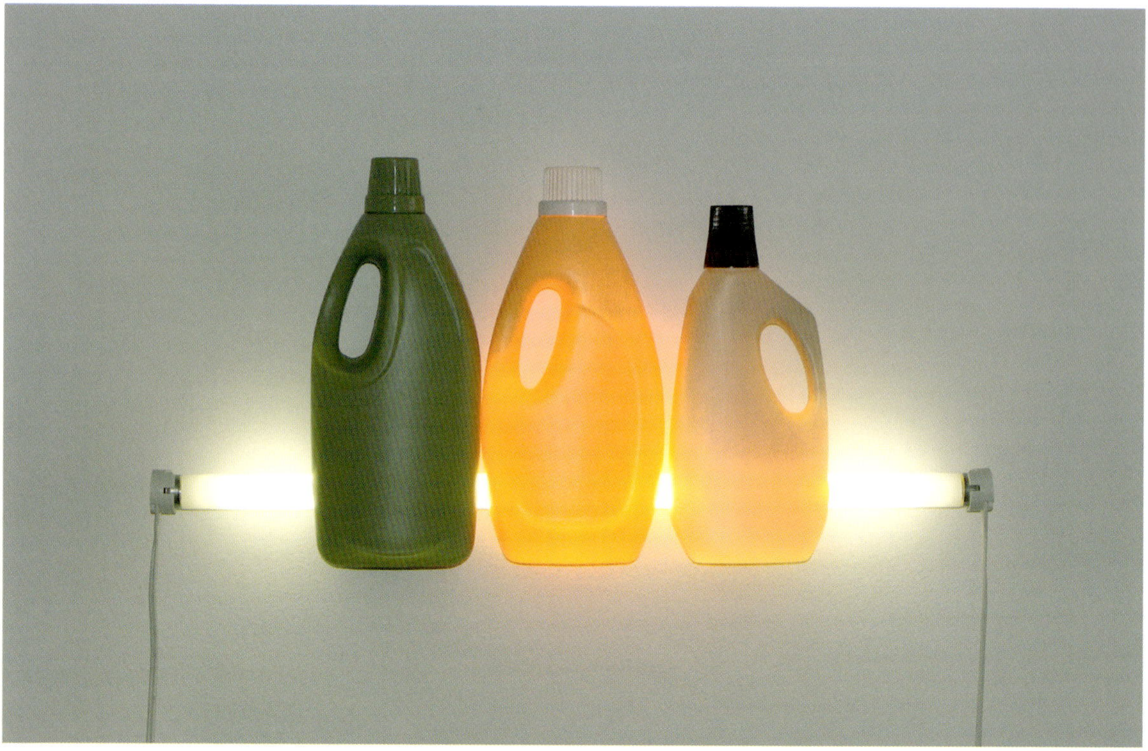

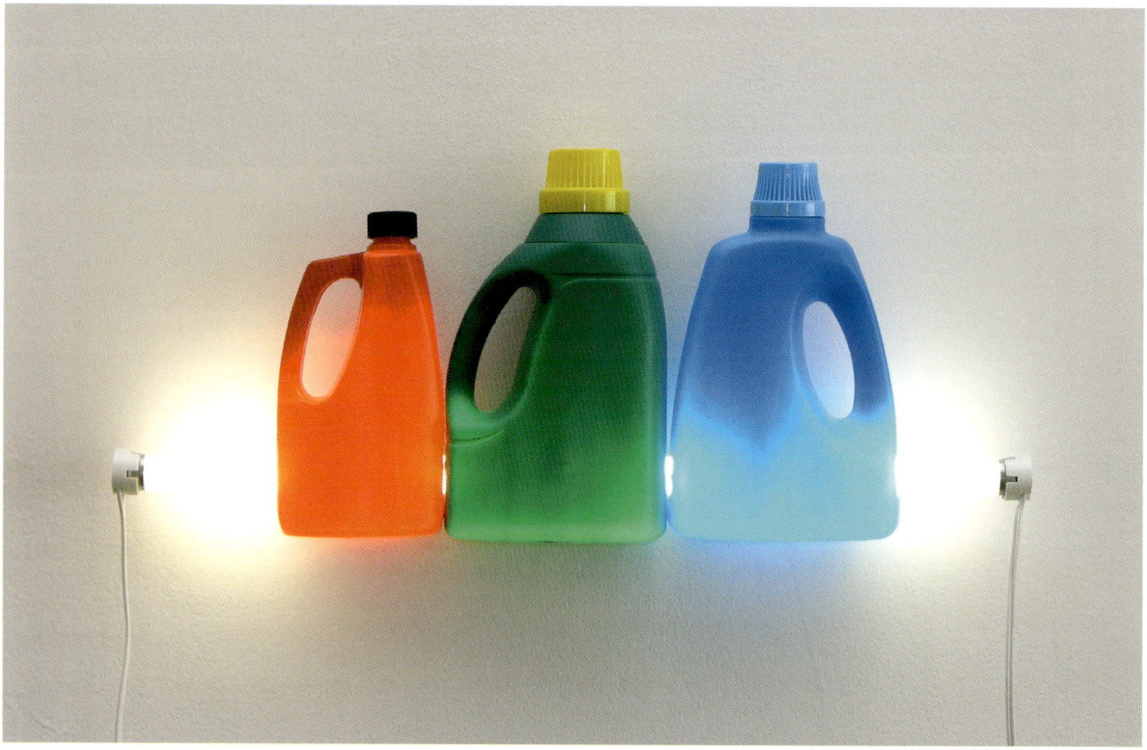

Orakei Suite I
2006
plastic bottles, fluorescent tube
30 x 60cm
Courtesy of the artist and Sue Crockford Gallery, Auckland

Orakei Suite II
2006
plastic bottles, fluorescent tube
30 x 60cm
Courtesy of the artist and Sue Crockford Gallery, Auckland

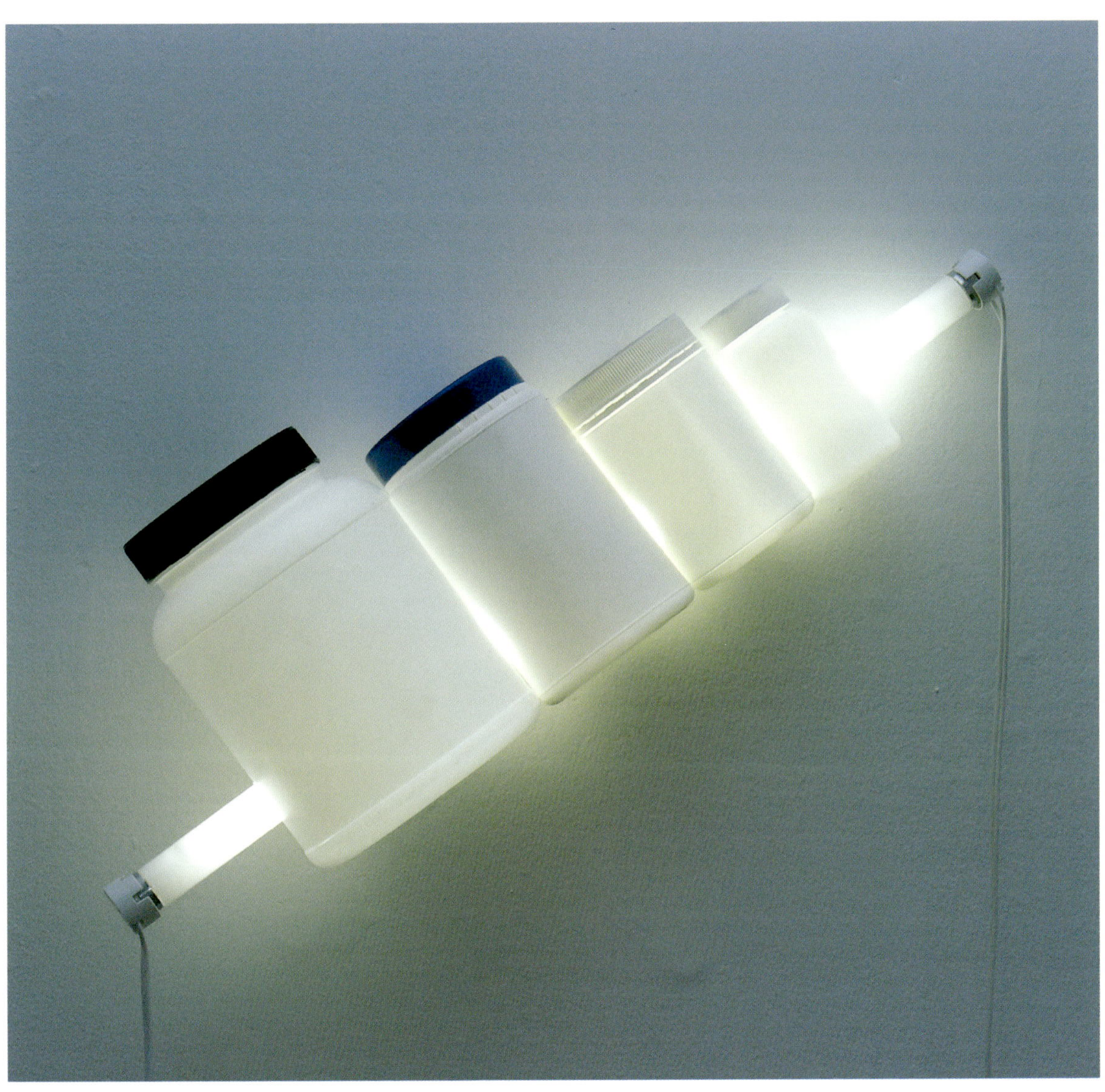

Just Jars
2006
plastic bottles, fluorescent tube
30 x 60cm
Courtesy of the artist and Sue Crockford Gallery, Auckland

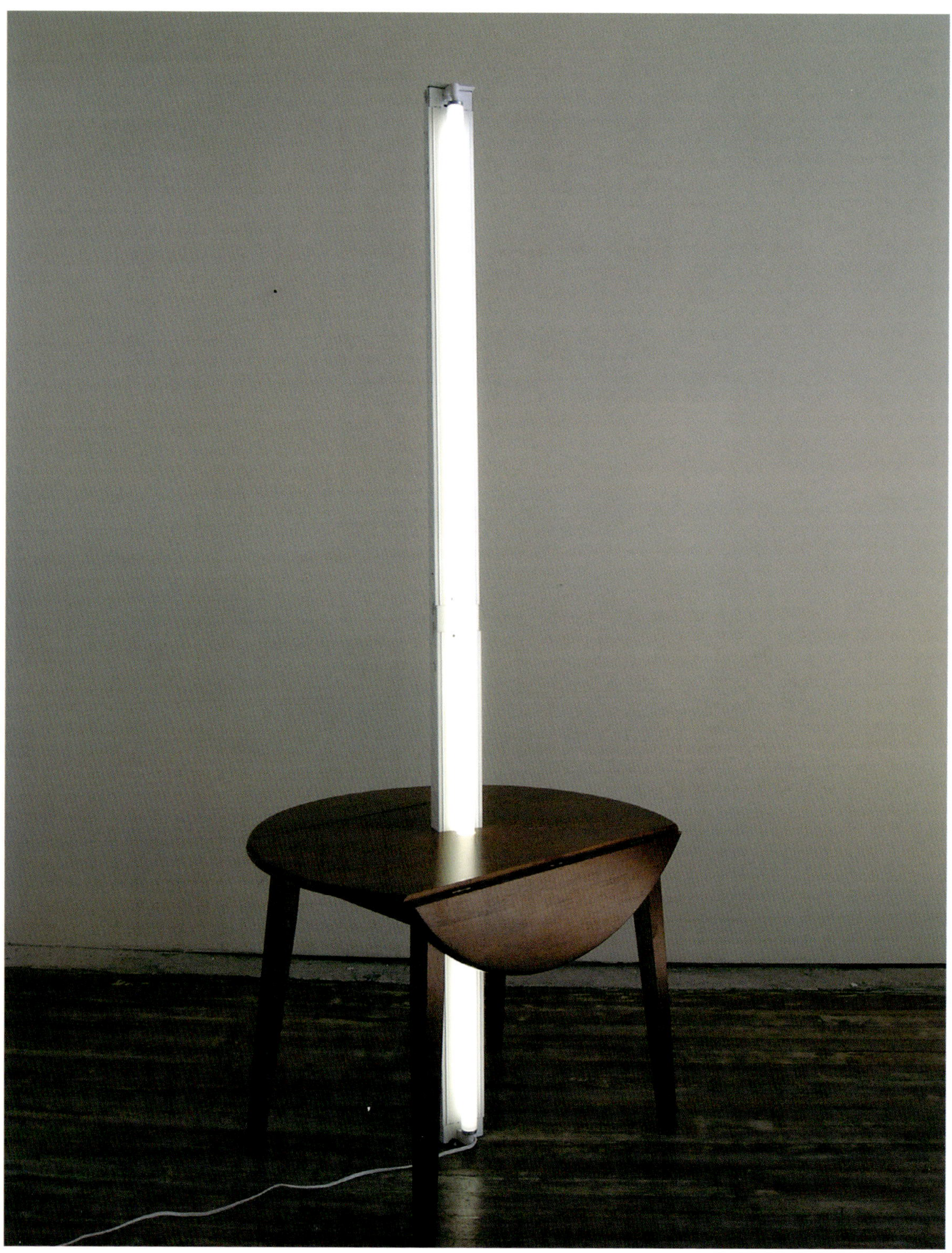

Table Lamp #3
2007
wooden table with fluorescent tube
Courtesy of LINCART, San Francisco

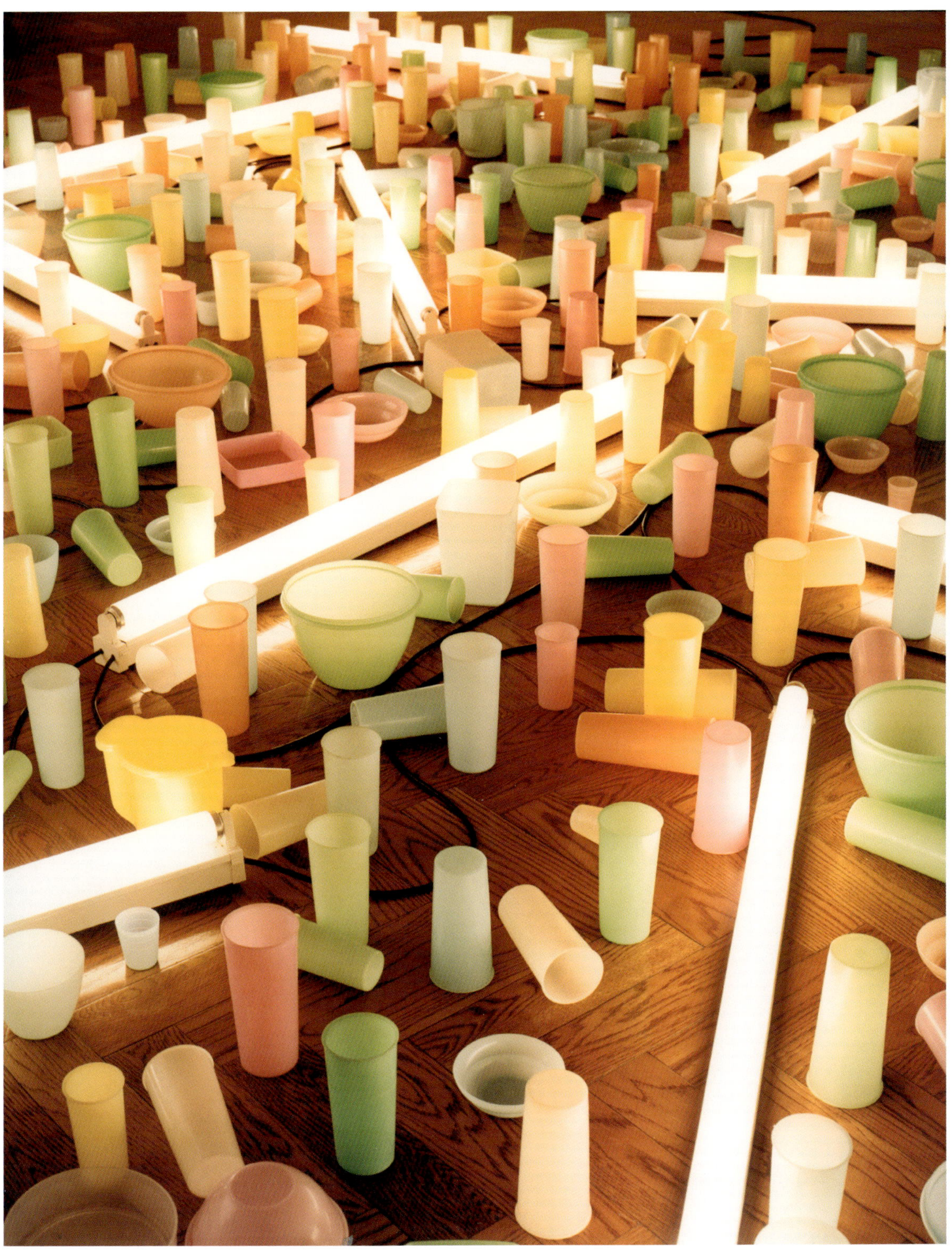

Spacific Plastic
2001
tupperware, fluorescent tubes
3 x 7m
Courtesy of the artist and Sue Crockford Gallery, Auckland

Maddie Leach

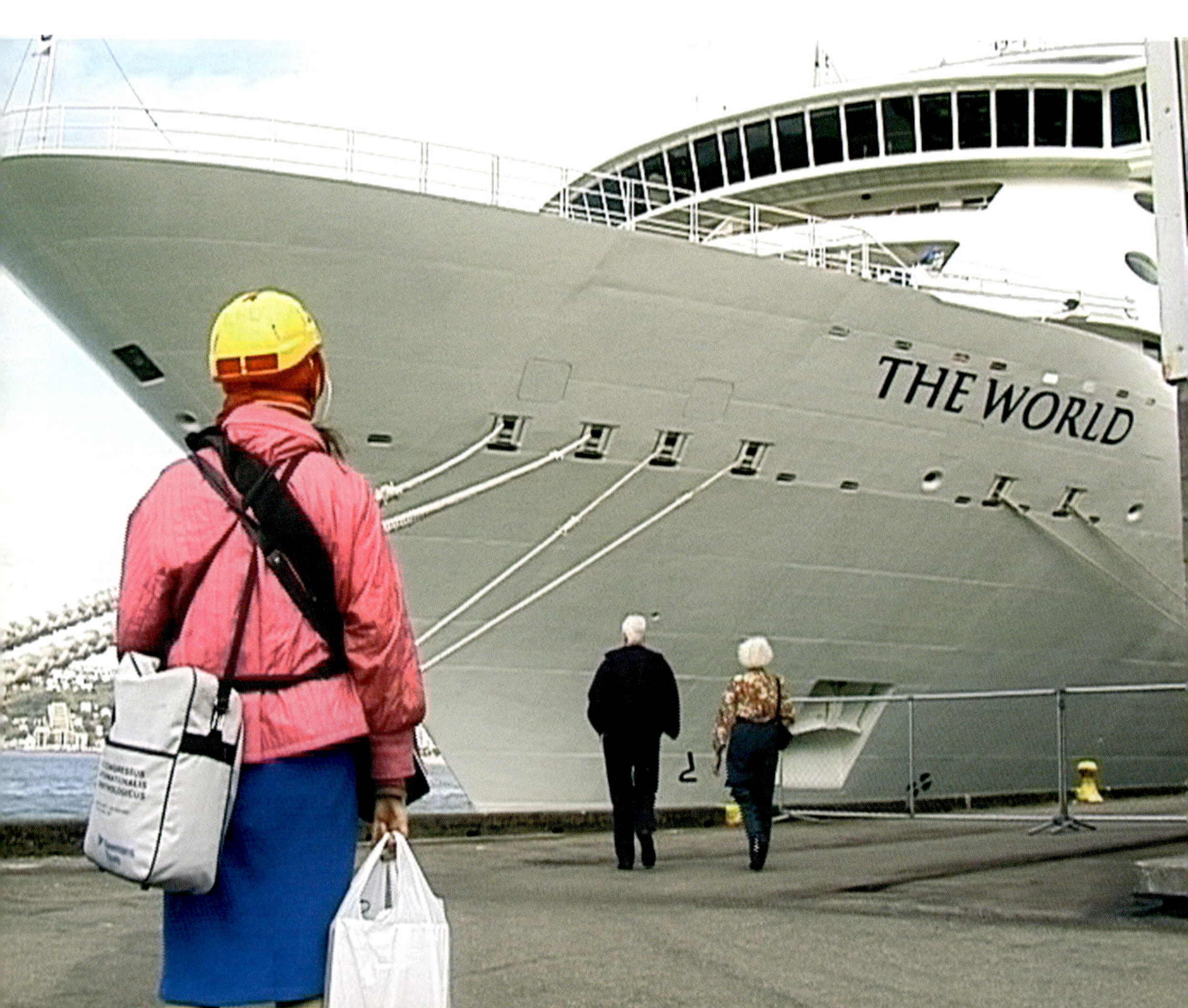

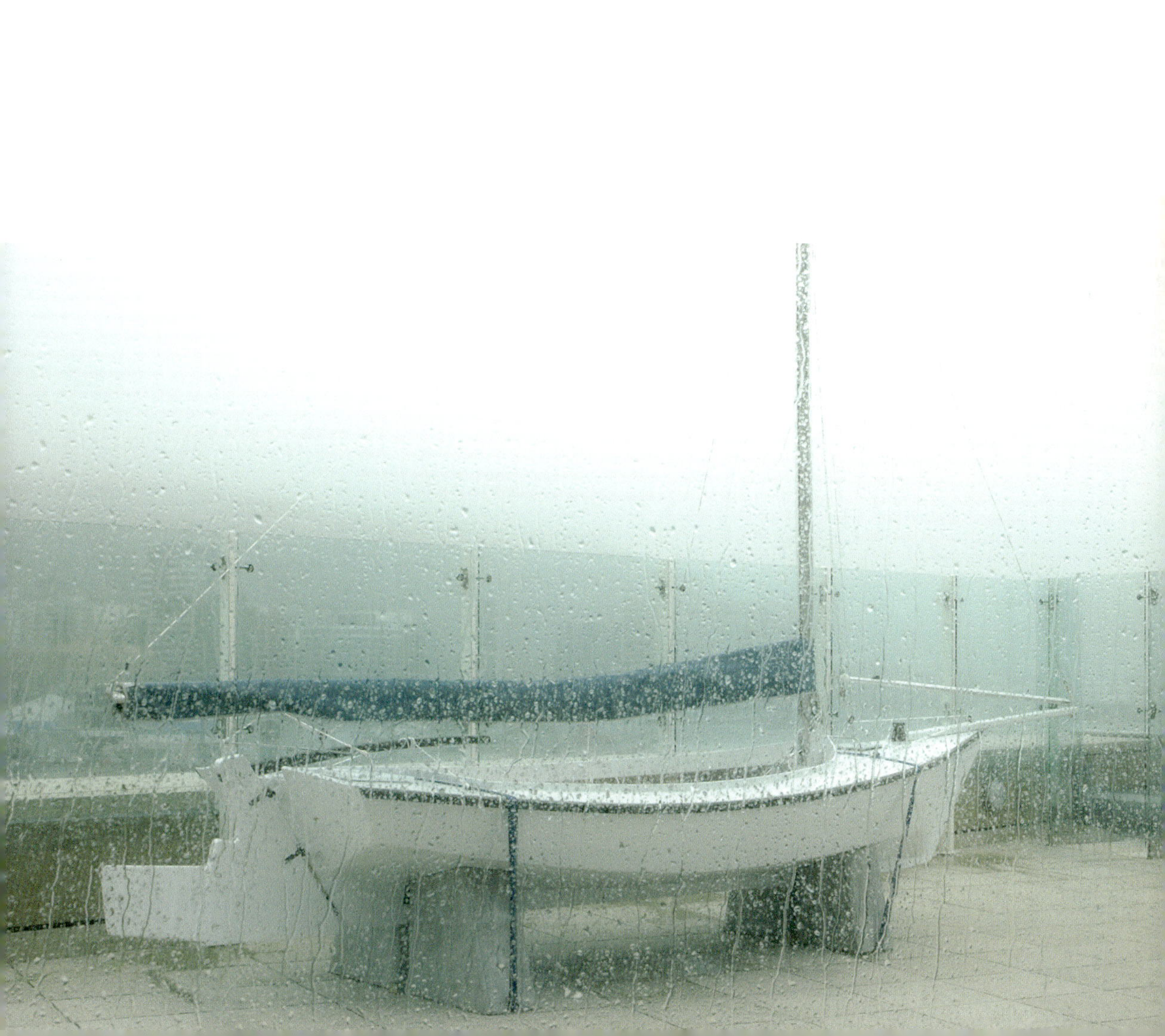

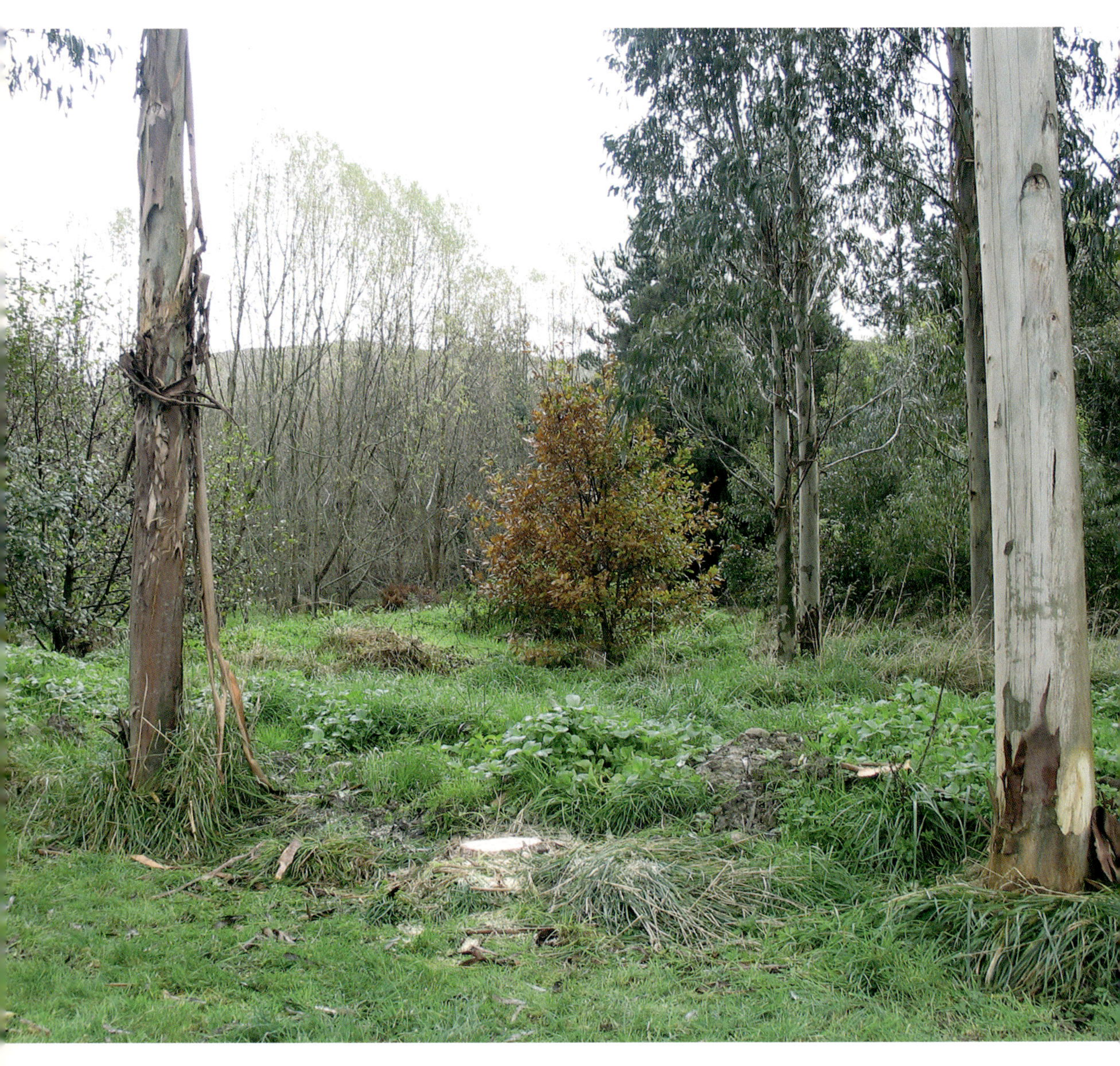

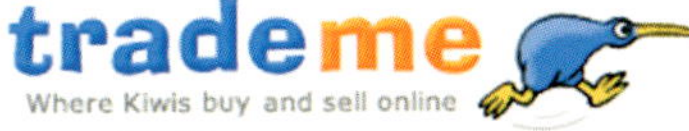

Logout   ❓ **Help**

Home | **Browse** | **Sell** | **My Trade Me** | **Community**

Items I'm selling Watchlist My account My favourites My feedback   8:57 pm

Hi Maddie, You have been automatically logged in on this computer. Click here if you don't want this to happen.

🔨 Lawson Cypress

Current bid: $167.00   Closes: Mon, 6 Mar

Seller's options - only you can see this section	hide ⌃

Current bid:	$167.00 **vinccenzo** (7 ★)	Edit pricing
Start price:	$100.00	Sell similar item
Reserve:	$225.00	Promote
		Withdraw

📈 Bids: **13**   Bidders/Watchers: **23**   Views: **692**

Rough-sawn, approx 1 cube 6x2 (150x50) No 1 grade Lawson. Quality timber from the Taranaki district. Has been carefully stacked and air-dried for the last two and half months in the Govett-Brewster Art Gallery in New Plymouth.

There are 40 planks at approx 3m lengths each. Straight and strong. Minor warping on very top layer.

A durable, sweet-smelling timber excellent for interior and exterior applications.

Buyer to collect or arrange transport from New Plymouth.

Add a comment to your auction

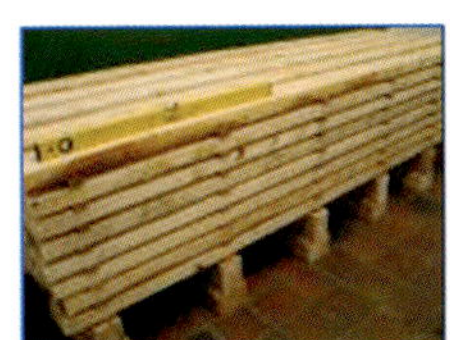

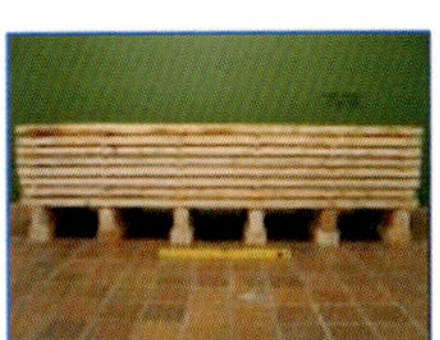

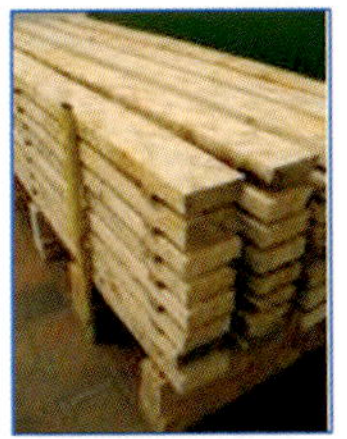

Click to enlarge

👀 Add to watchlist   ✉ Email to a friend   🖨 Printer friendly page

Closes **9:54 am, Mon 6 Mar.** This auction may auto-extend. ❓
Auction Number: 48887967

About the seller	**Payment / shipping**
prairiedusk (1 ★)	**Location:** Wellington City, Wellington [local]
100% positive feedback	**Shipping:** Buyer to collect
Member since April 2005	**Payment:** cash, bank deposit
AV Address Verified Nov 2005	**SafeTrader:** Doesn't support SafeTrader learn more
Seller's other listings	
Read seller's feedback	Read our Safe Buying Advice

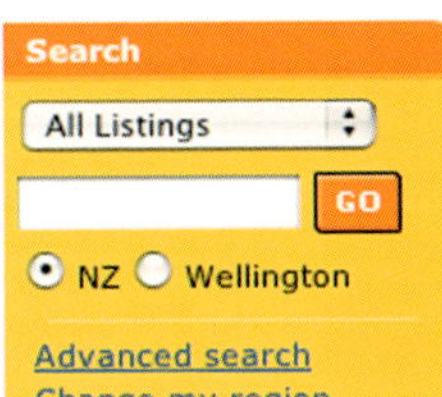

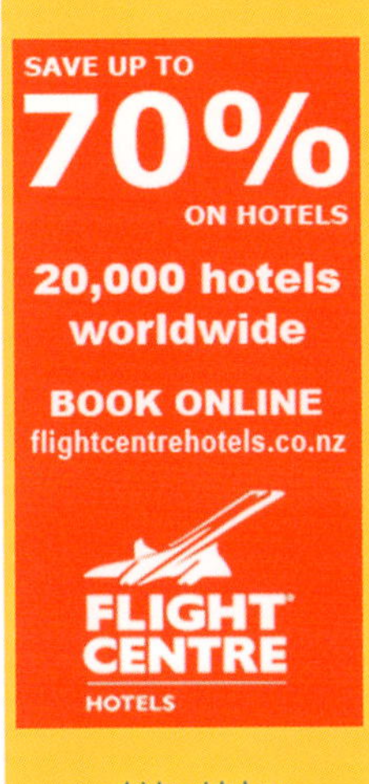

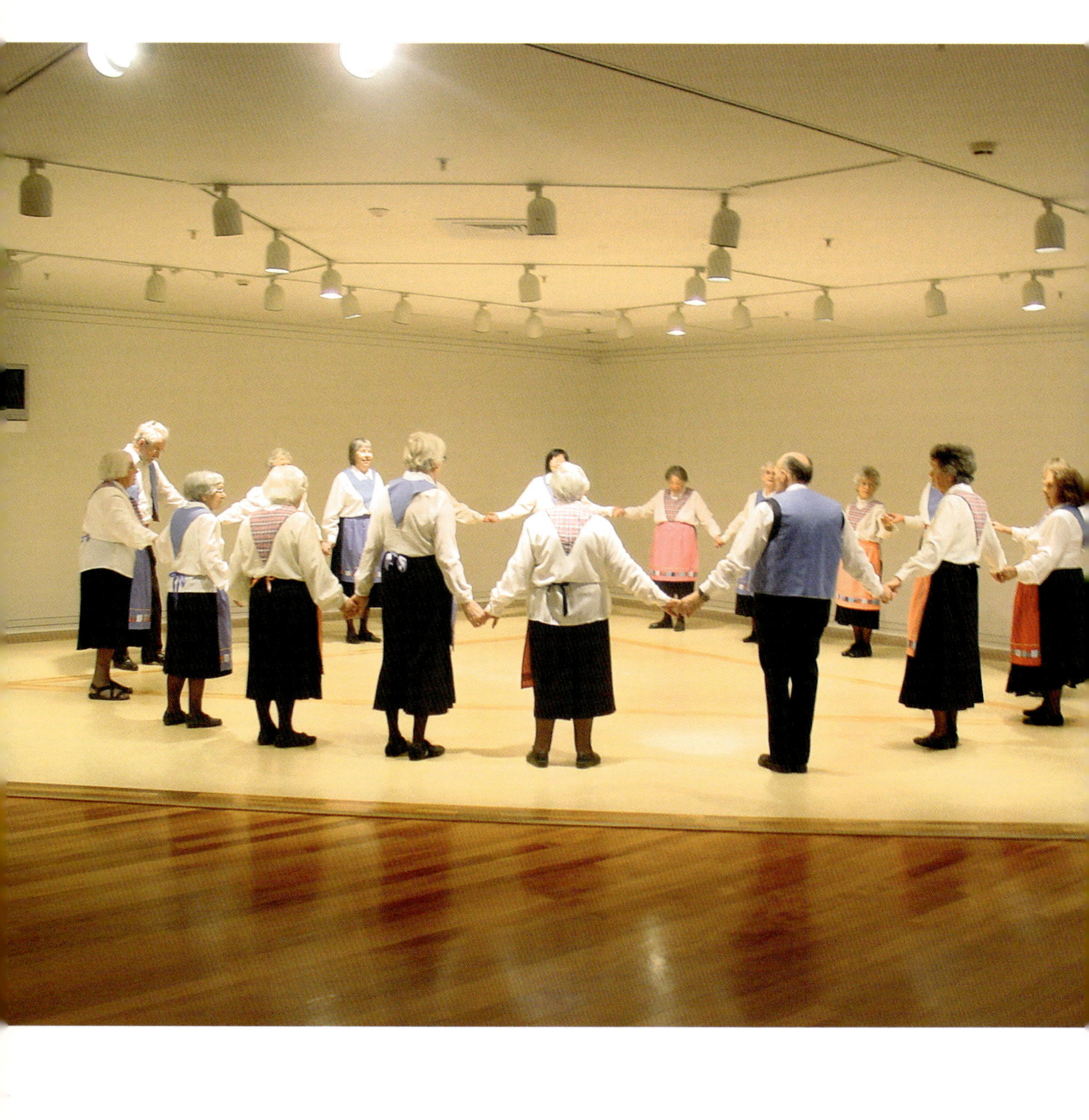

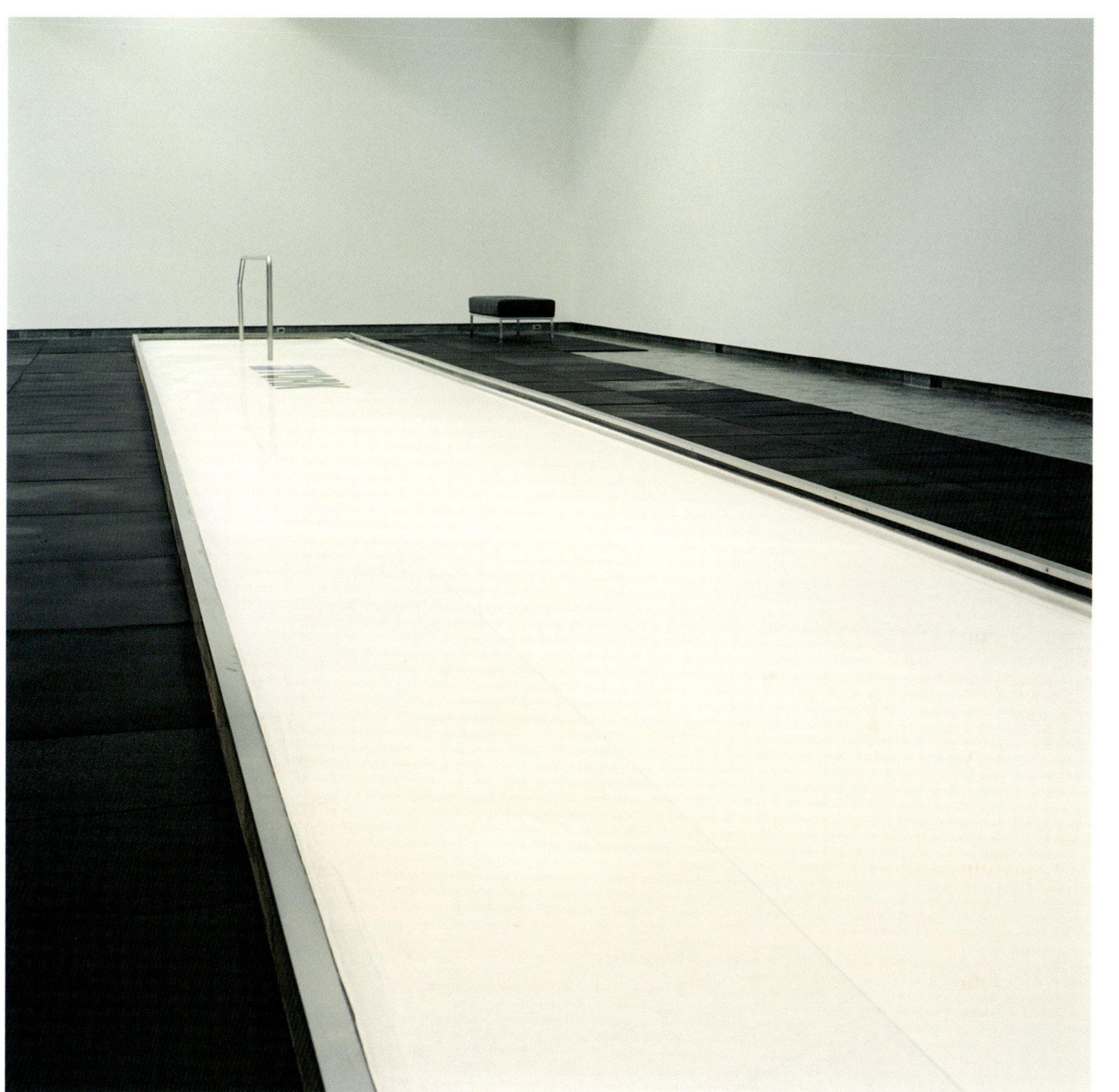

Jim Speers

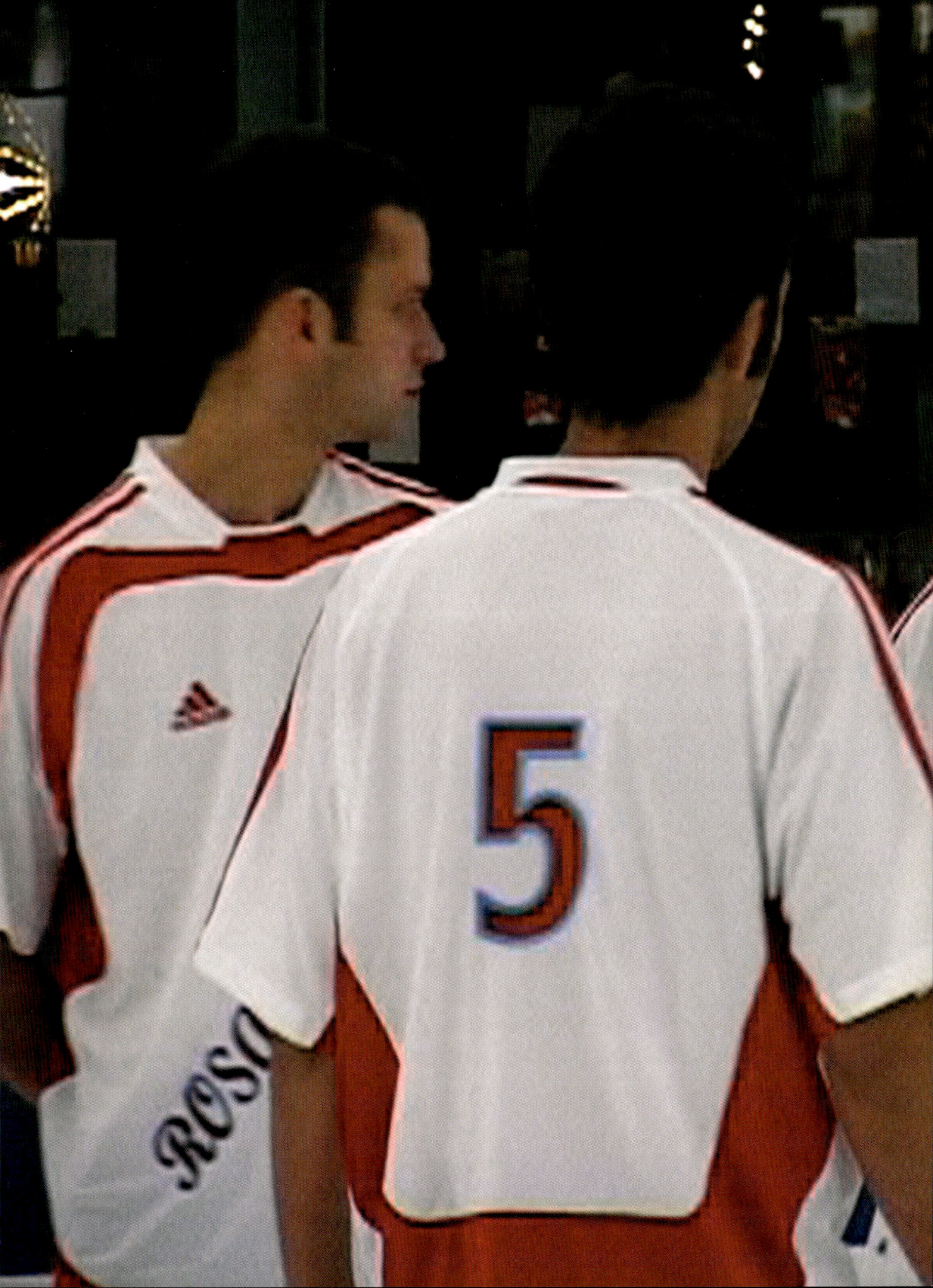

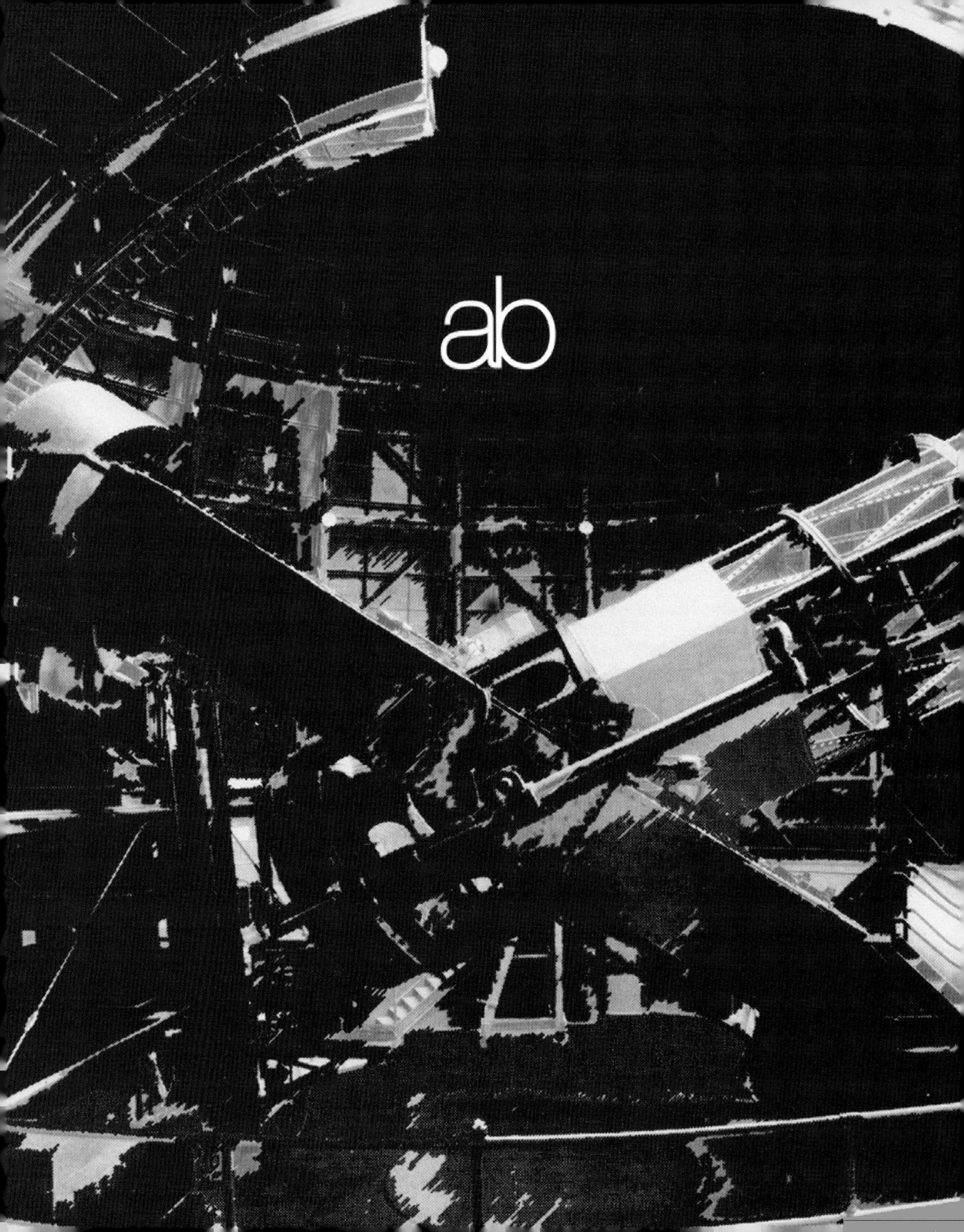

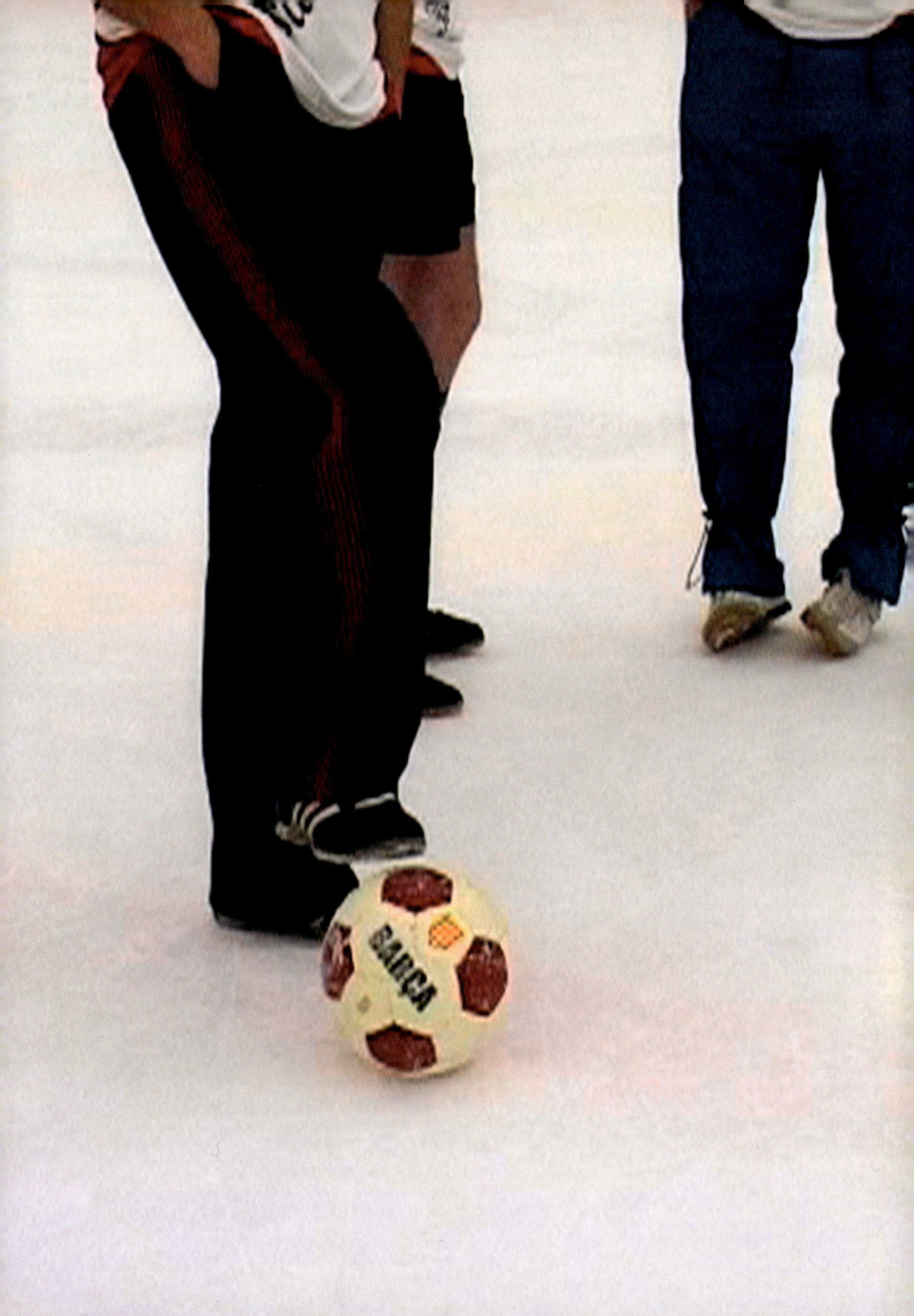
BARÇA

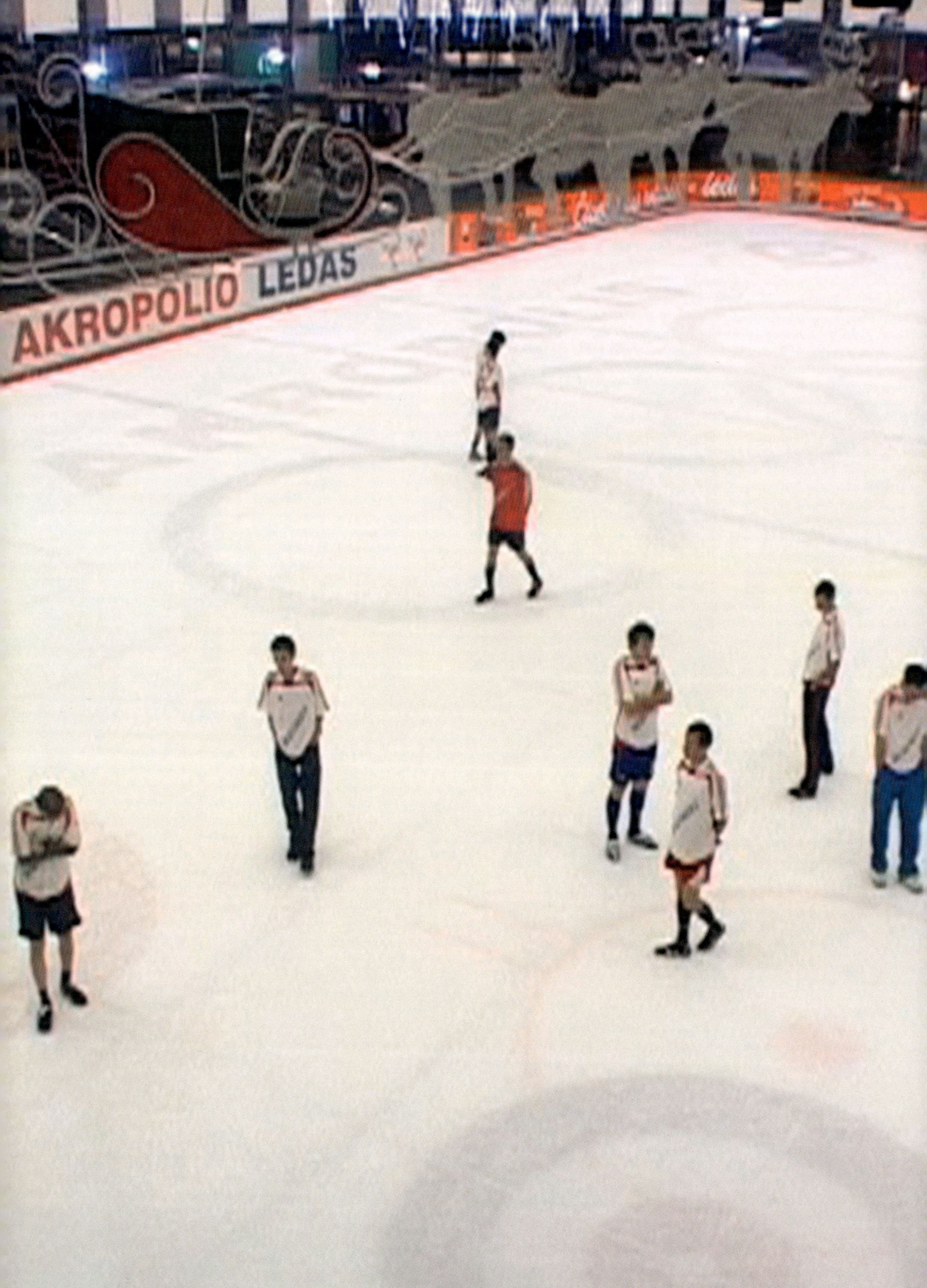
AKROPOLIO LEDAS

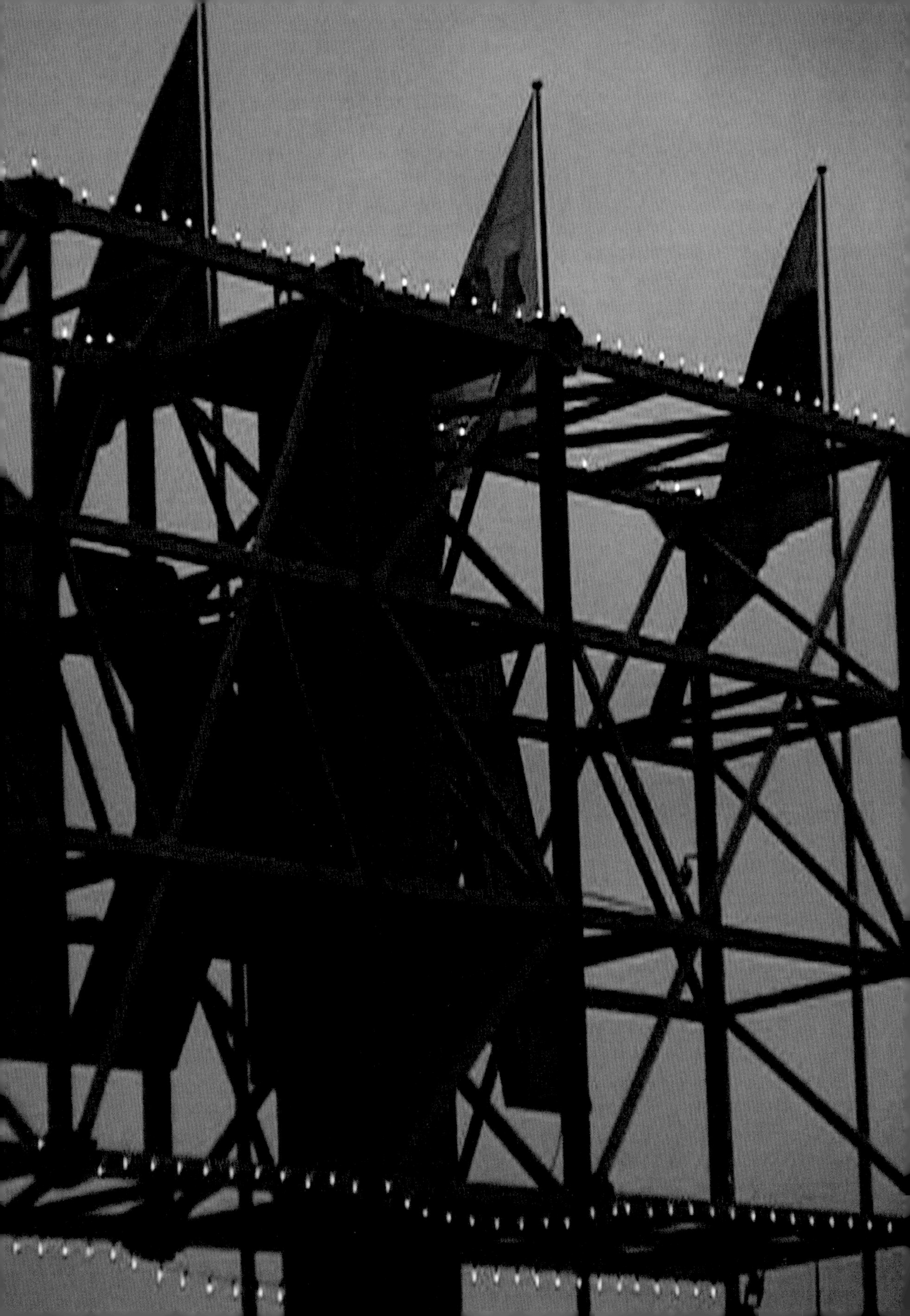

Mladen Bizumic

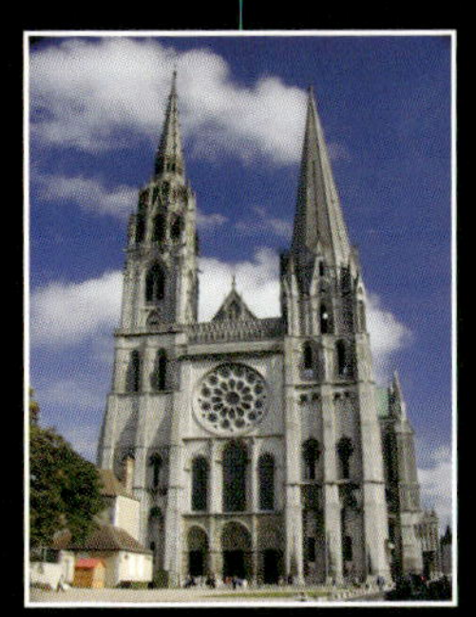

A LABYRINTH AT PABLO ELEMENTARY SCHOOL
POJOAQUE VALLEY SCHOOLS, NEW MEXICO

DURING THE WINTER OF 2003, VIOLA ESPINOZA'S
2ND GRADE CLASS AND GAIL HERRERA'S
GRADE 3/4 (MULTI-AGE) CLASS RESEARCHED,
PLANNED AND BUILT A LABYRINTH
MODELLED ON A DESIGN FROM
CHARTRES CATHEDRAL IN FRANCE.

RULES FOR WALKING THE LABYRINTH
SUGGESTED BY STUDENTS

- WAIT ON THE 'PAUSING STONE'
- THINK ABOUT WHAT YOU WANT TO DO
  ON THE LABYRINTH
- COUNT SLOWLY TO 20 AFTER SOMEONE
  HAS ENTERED BEFORE YOU ENTER
- TAKE TIME TO RELAX
- BRING A GOOD THOUGHT - MAYBE
  SOMETHING YOU ARE THANKFUL FOR
  OR SOMETHING YOU WOULD LIKE TO
  CHANGE IN YOUR LIFE
- WALK SLOWLY
- STEP ASIDE IF OTHERS WANT TO PASS
- BE SILENT
- STAY IN YOUR OWN 'BUBBLE'
- RESPECT EACH OTHER'S SPACE
- NO PUSHING, KICKING, TRIPPING
- TAKE CARE OF THE LABYRINTH
- REPLACE STONES THAT GET MOVED
- PICK UP THE TRASH

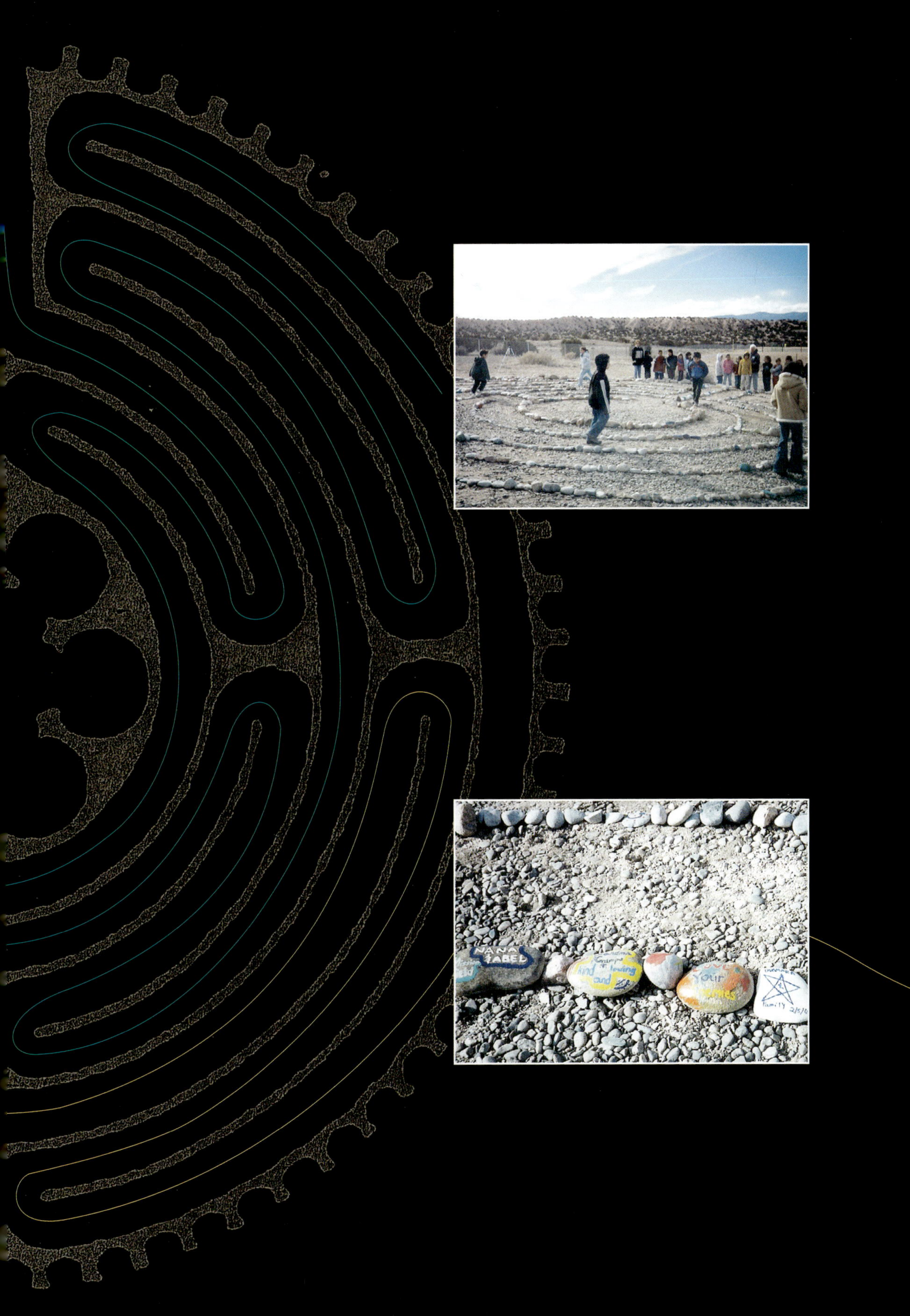

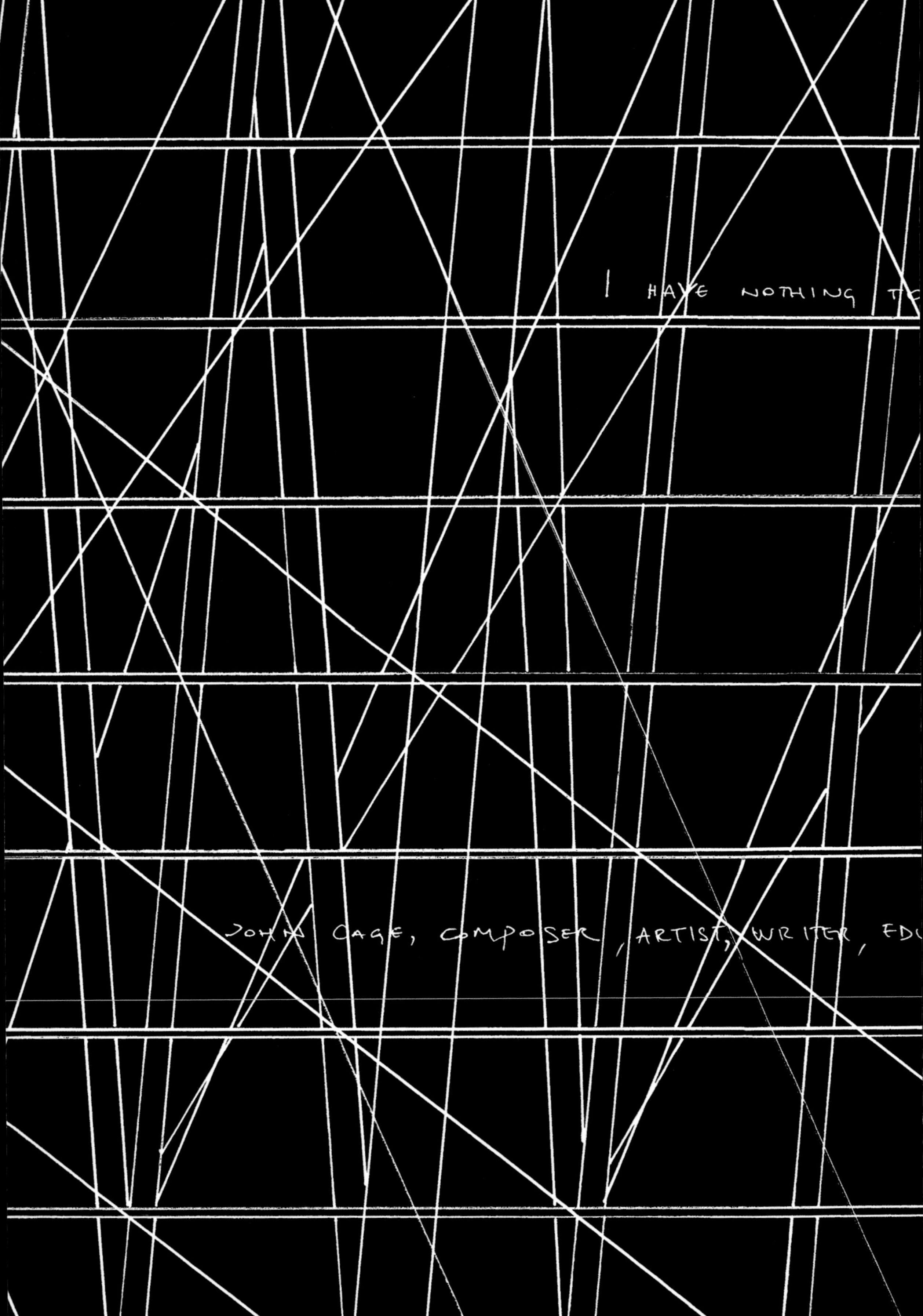

I HAVE NOTHING T
JOHN CAGE, COMPOSER, ARTIST, WRITER, EDU

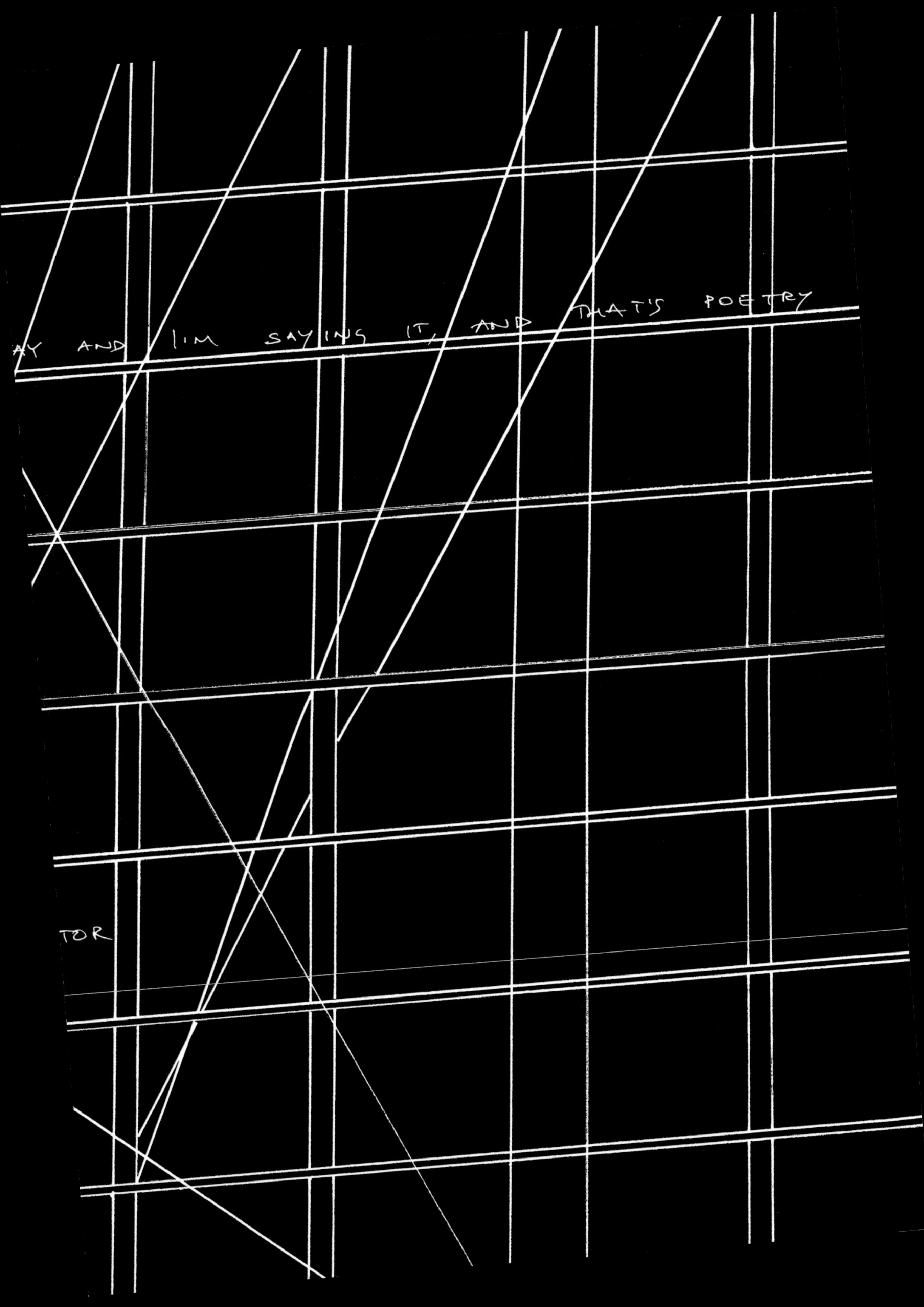
AY AND I'M SAYING IT, AND THAT'S POETRY
TOR

Stella Brennan

Stills and narration from *Theme for Great Cities*
2003
mono DVD, 3 minutes

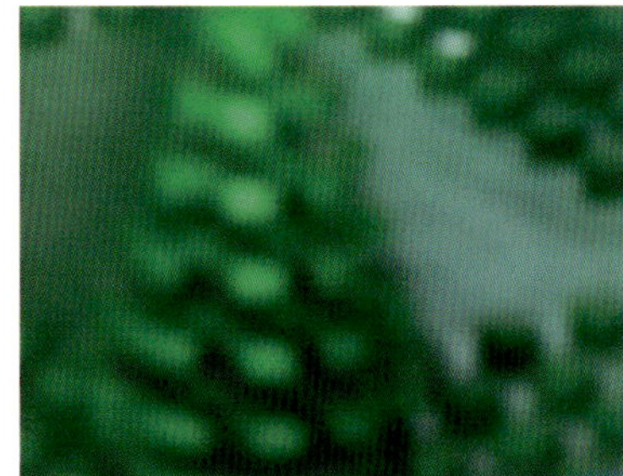
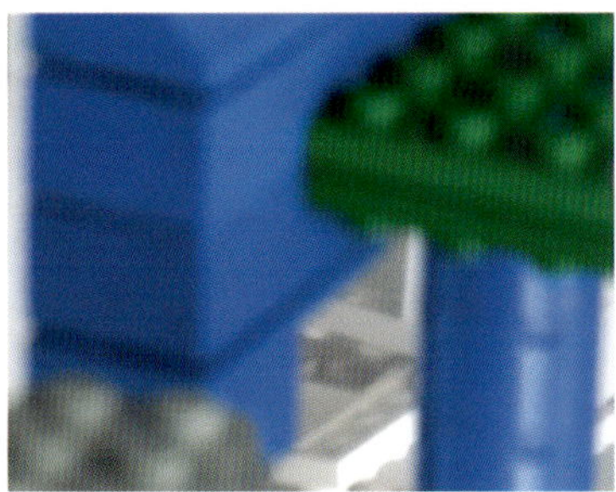
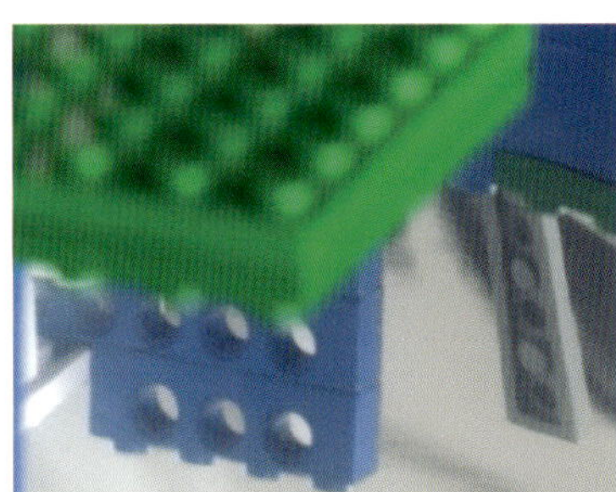
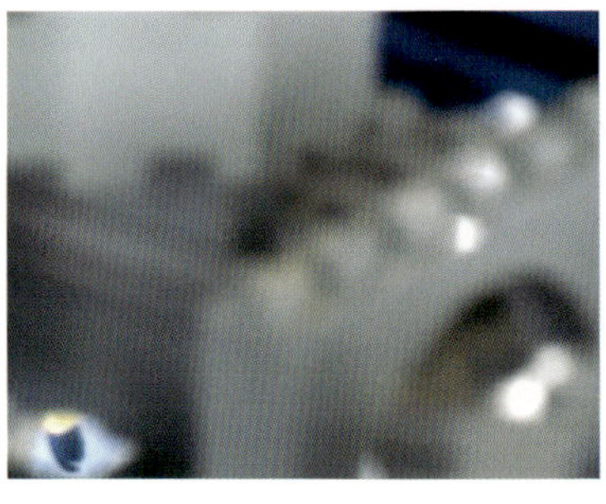

STELLA BRENNAN
THEME FOR GREAT CITIES
2003

TEXT FROM
COMMENTS AGAINST URBANISM
RAOUL VANEIGEM
1961

URBANISM IS THE MOST CONCRETE AND PERFECT
FULFILMENT OF A NIGHTMARE.

THE IDEAL URBANISM IS THE PROJECTION IN SPACE OF A
SOCIAL HIERARCHY WITHOUT CONFLICT. ROADS, LAWNS,
NATURAL FLOWERS AND ARTIFICIAL FORESTS LUBRICATE
THE MACHINERY OF SUBJECTION AND MAKE IT ENJOYABLE.
AS IT COMBINES MACHIAVELLIANISM WITH REINFORCED
CONCRETE, URBANISM'S CONCIENCE IS CLEAR.

WE ARE ENTERING UPON THE REIGN OF POLICED
REFINEMENT. THE ART OF REASSURANCE – URBANISM KNOWS
HOW TO EXERCISE IT IN ITS PUREST FORM: THE ULTIMATE
CIVILITY OF A POWER ON THE VERGE OF ASSERTING TOTAL
MIND CONTROL.

WHAT SIGNS SHOULD WE RECOGNISE AS OUR OWN? A FEW
GRAFFITI, WORDS OF REJECTION OR FORBIDDEN GESTURES,
HASTILY SCRAWLED, IN WHICH CULTURED PEOPLE ONLY
TAKE AN INTEREST WHEN THEY APPEAR ON THE WALLS OF
SOME FOSSIL CITY LIKE POMPEII. BUT OUR OWN CITIES
ARE EVEN MORE FOSSILISED.

WE WOULD LIKE TO LIVE IN LANDS OF KNOWLEDGE, AMID
LIVING SIGNS LIKE FAMILIAR FRIENDS. THE REVOLUTION
WILL ALSO BE THE PERPETUAL CREATION OF SIGNS THAT
BELONG TO EVERYONE.

WHEREEVER BUREAUCRATIC CIVILISATION HAS SPREAD, THE
ANARCHY OF INDIVIDUAL CONSTRUCTION HAS BEEN
OFFICIALLY SANCTIONED, AND TAKEN OVER BY THE
AUTHORISED ORGANISMS OF POWER, WITH THE RESULT THAT
THE BUILDING INSTINCT HAS BEEN EXTIRPATED LIKE A
VICE AND ONLY BARELY SURVIVES IN CHILDREN AND
PRIMITIVES AND AMONG THOSE WHO, UNABLE TO CHANGE
THEIR LIVES, SPEND THEM DEMOLISHING AND REBUILDING
THEIR SHACKS.

PROJECT FOR A REALISTIC URBANISM: REPLACE
PIRANESI'S STAIRCASES WITH ELEVATORS, TRANSFORM
TOMBS INTO OFFICE BUILDINGS, LINE THE SEWERS WITH
TREES, PUT TRASH CANS IN LIVING ROOMS, STACK UP THE
HOVELS, AND BUILD ALL CITIES IN THE FORM OF
MUSEUMS. MAKE A PROFIT OUT OF EVERYTHING, EVEN OUT
OF NOTHING.

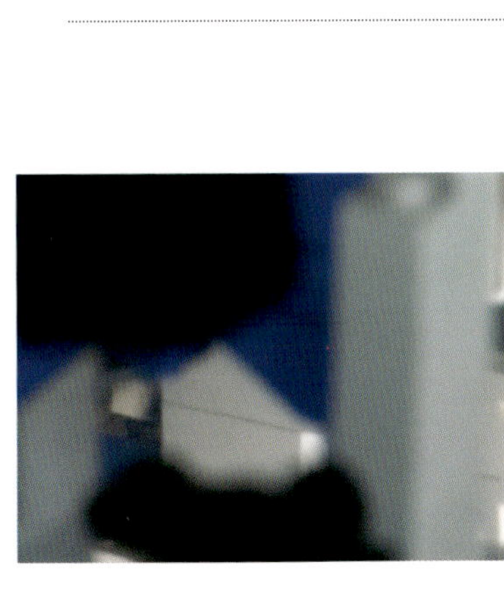

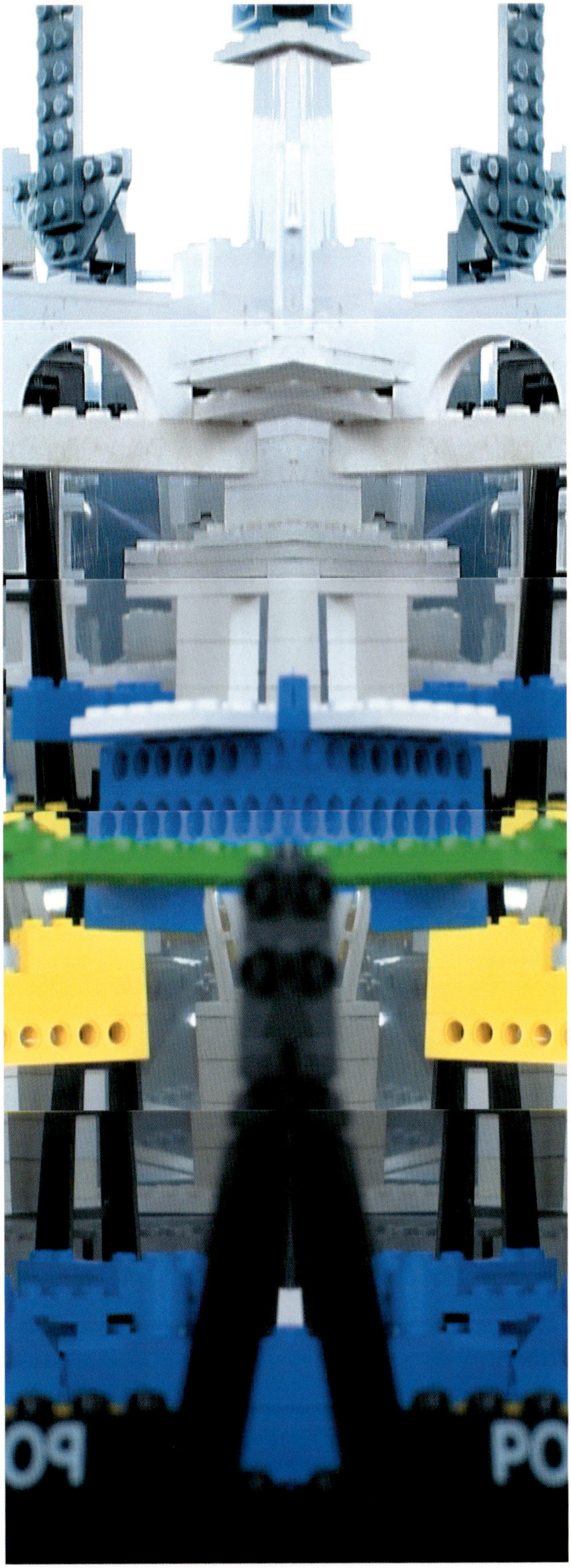

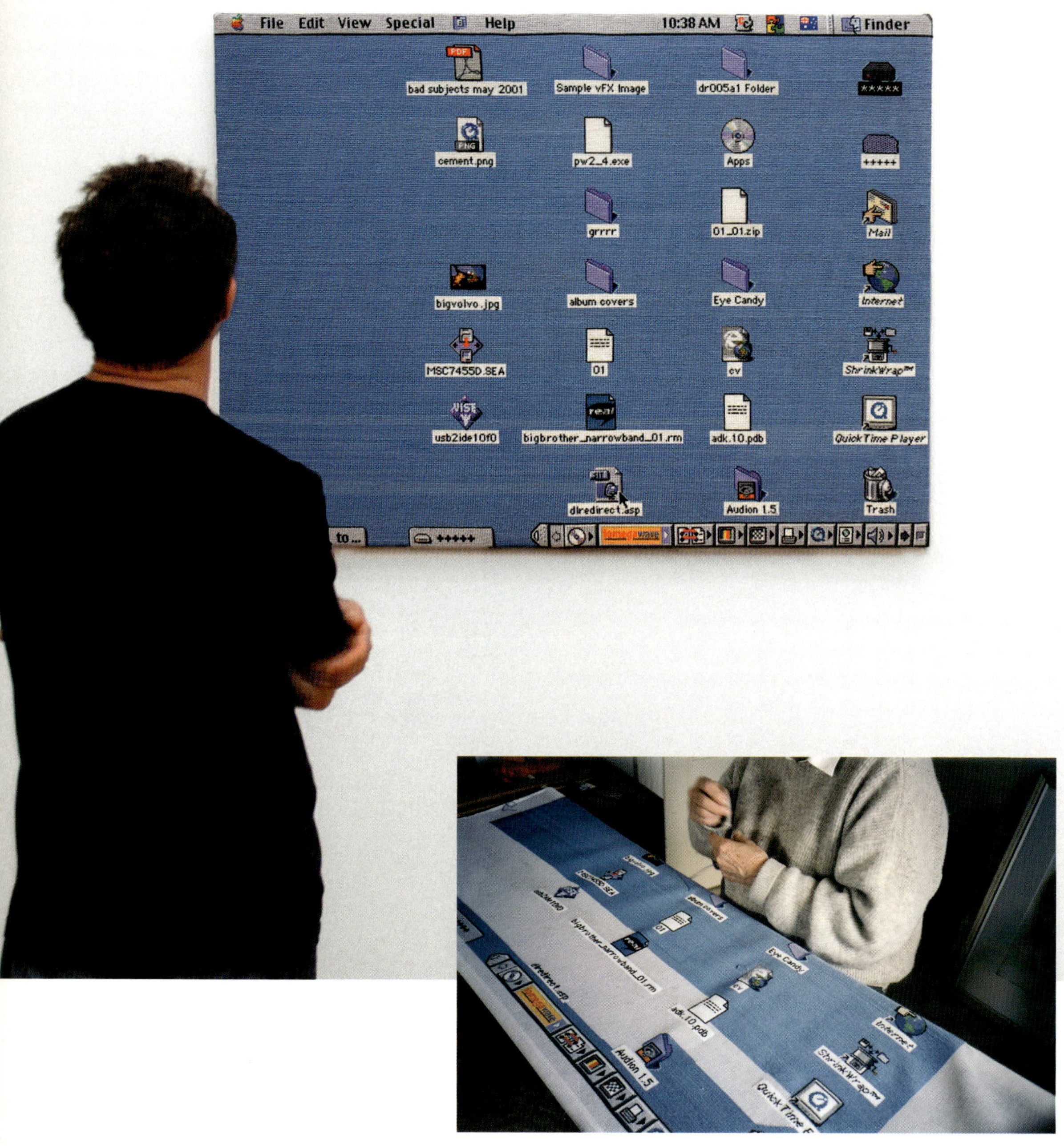

Tuesday, 3 July 2001, 10:38am
2001–2002
needlepoint embroidery, cotton on canvas
860 x 1150mm

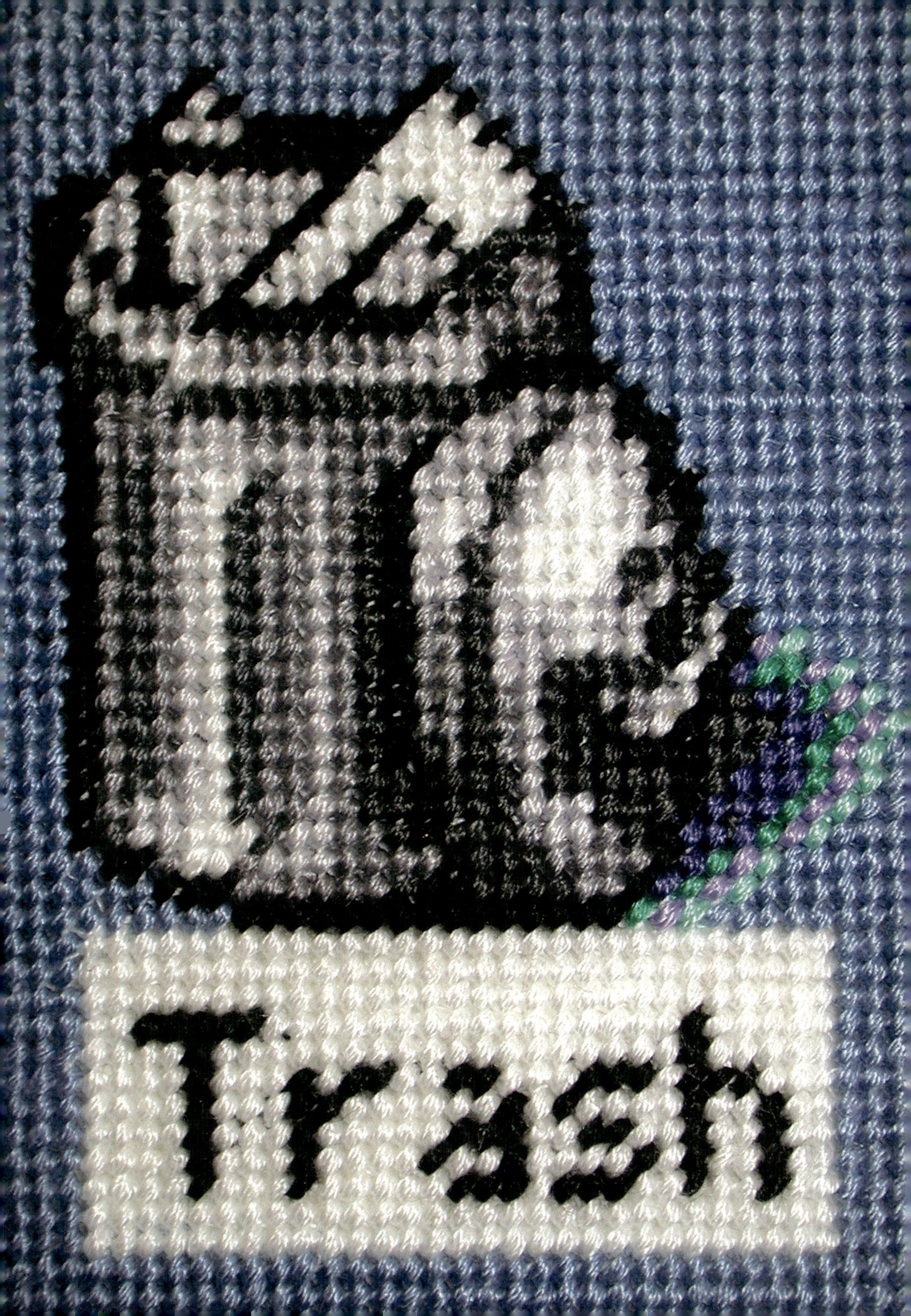

Trash

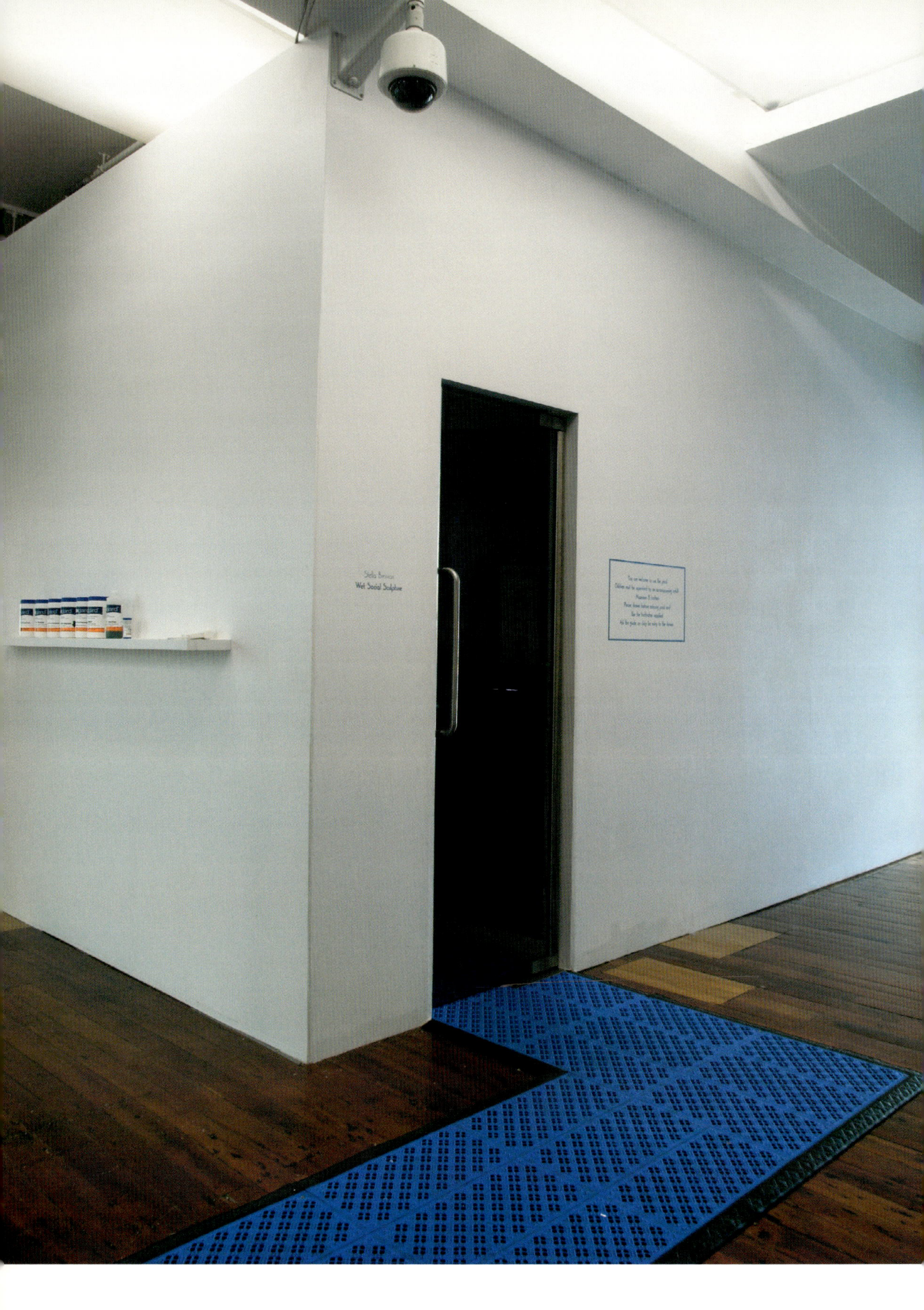

Stella Brennan
Wet Social Sculpture

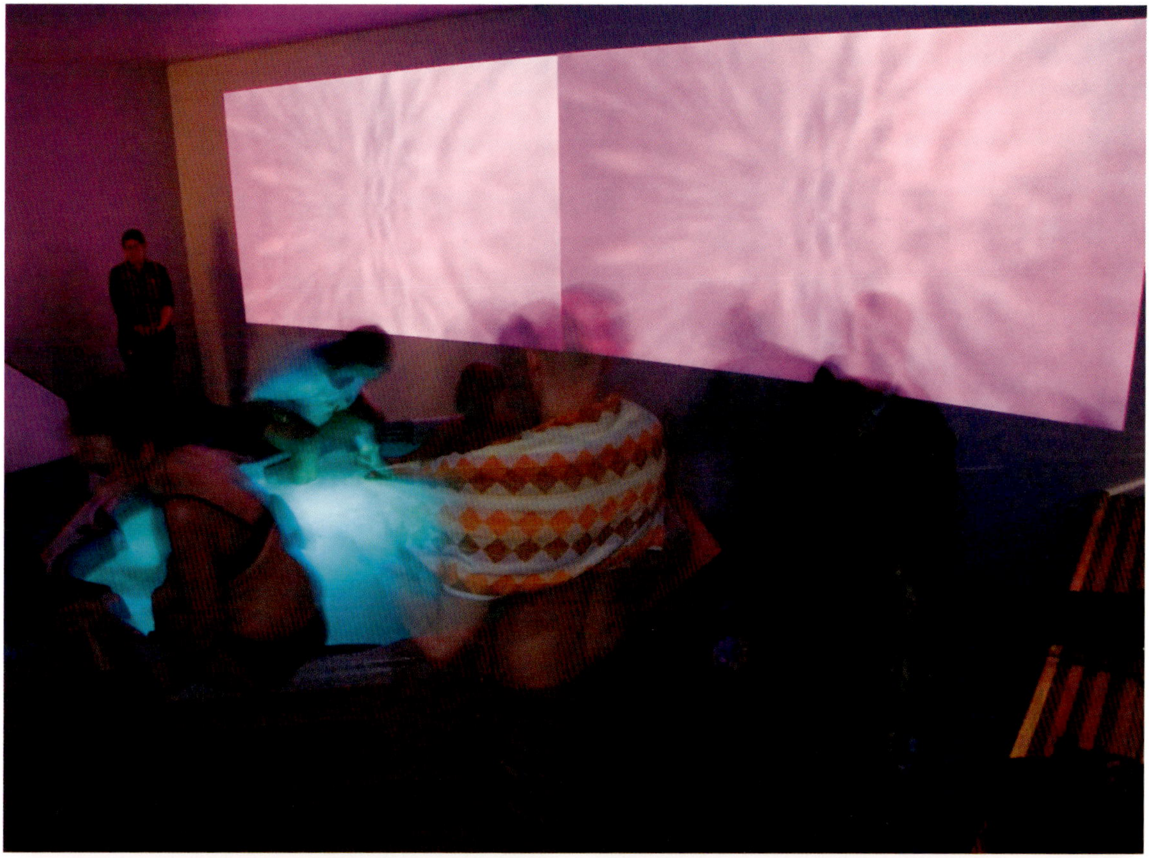

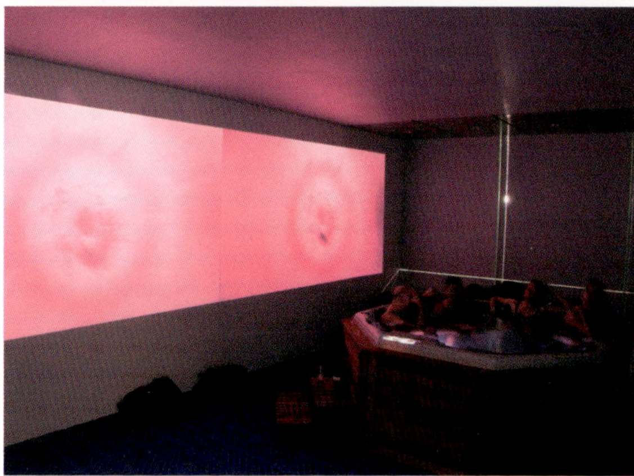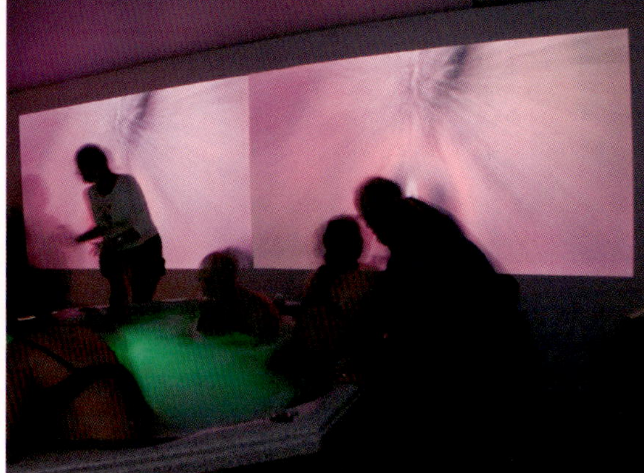

Wet Social Sculpture
2006
installation details
portable spa, pool chemicals, bathrobes, video projection, whale song

Jae Hoon Lee

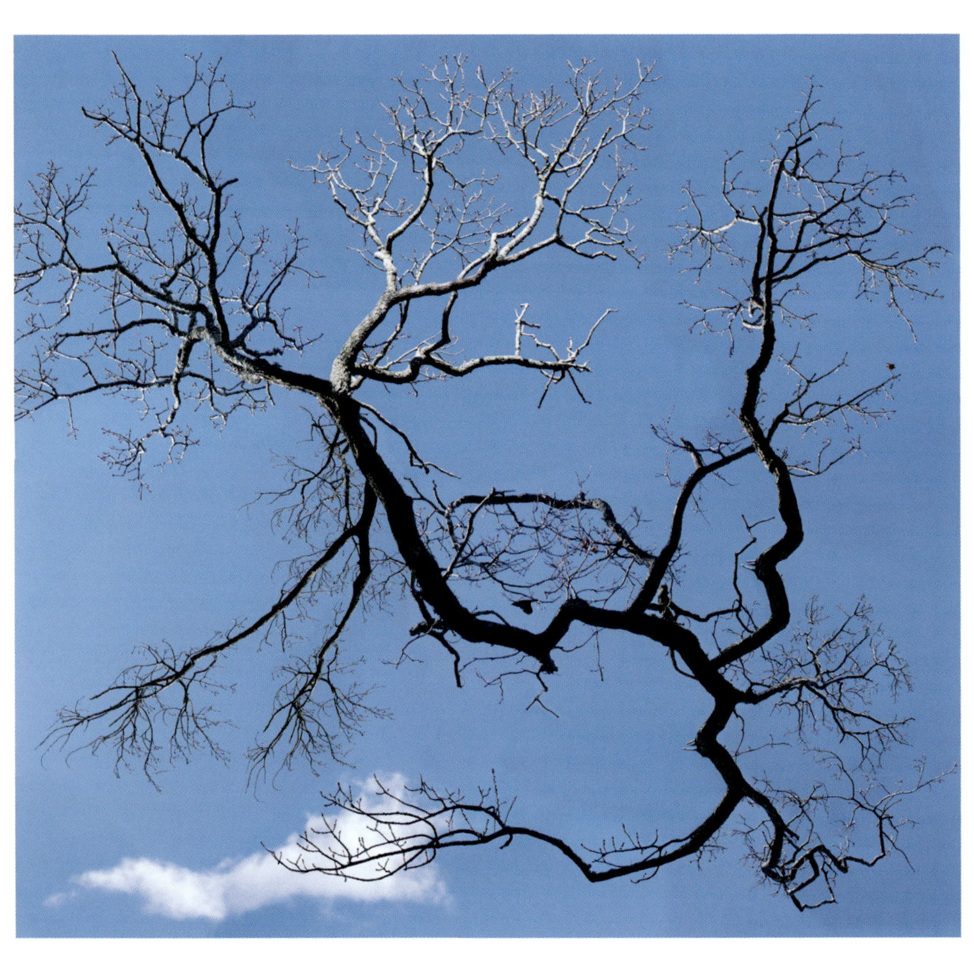

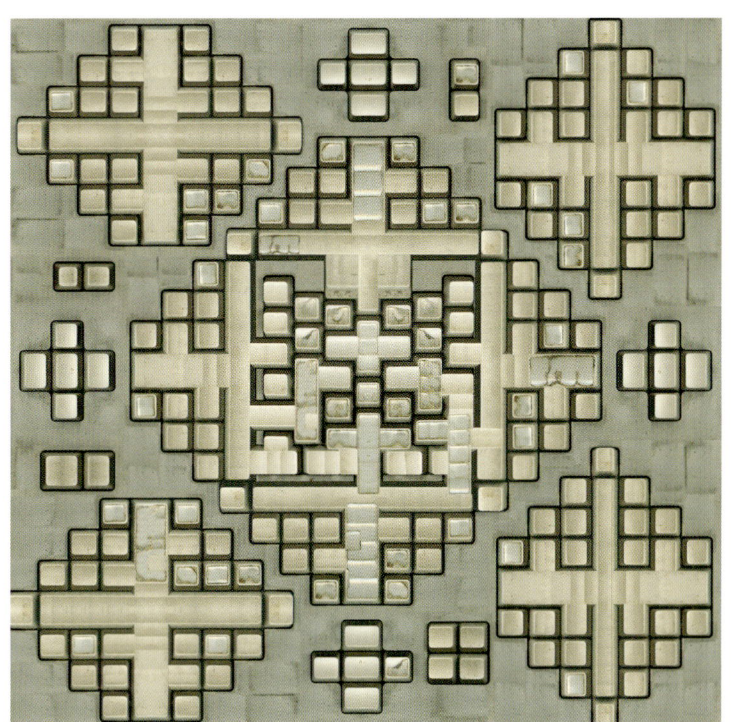

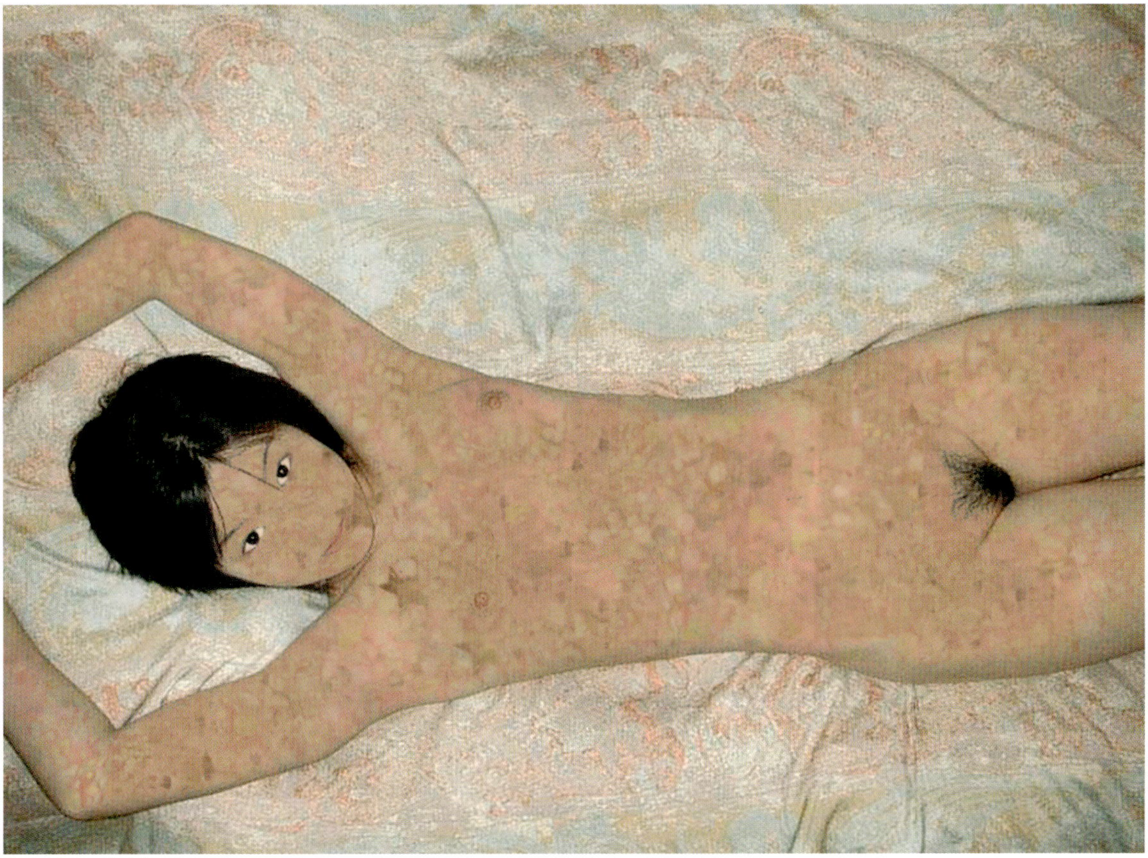

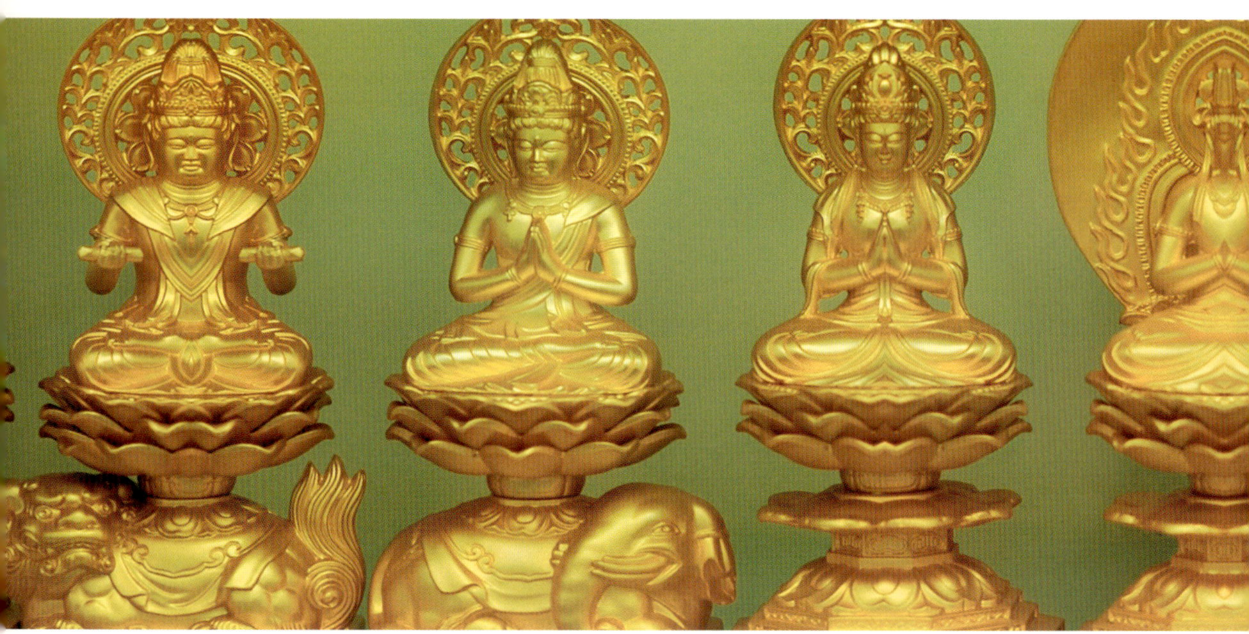

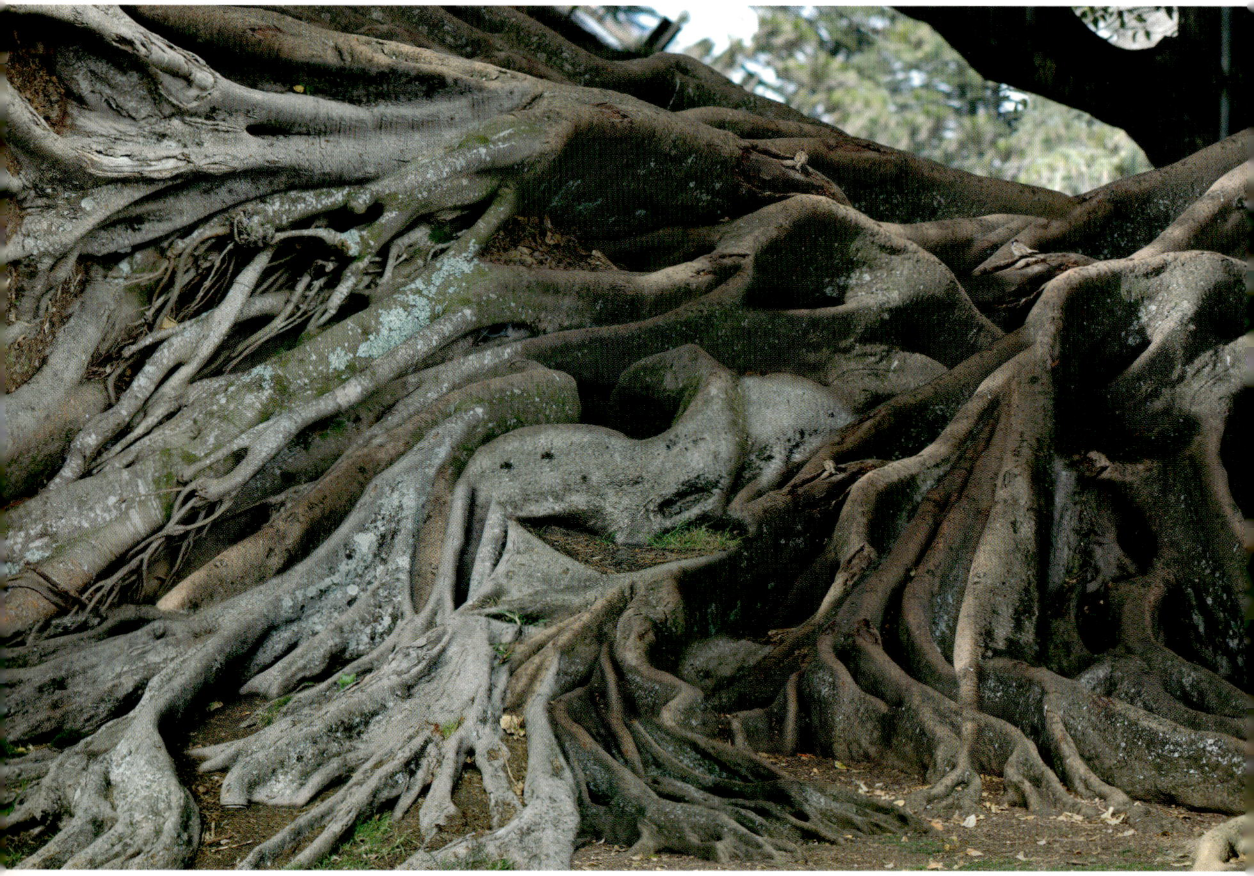

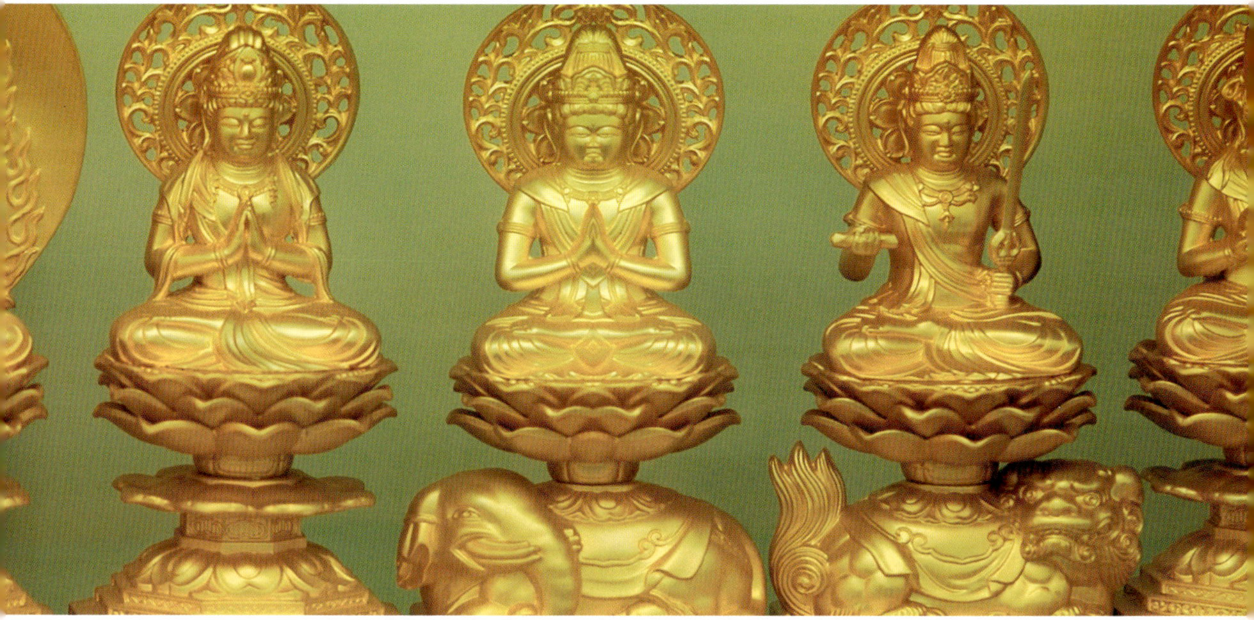

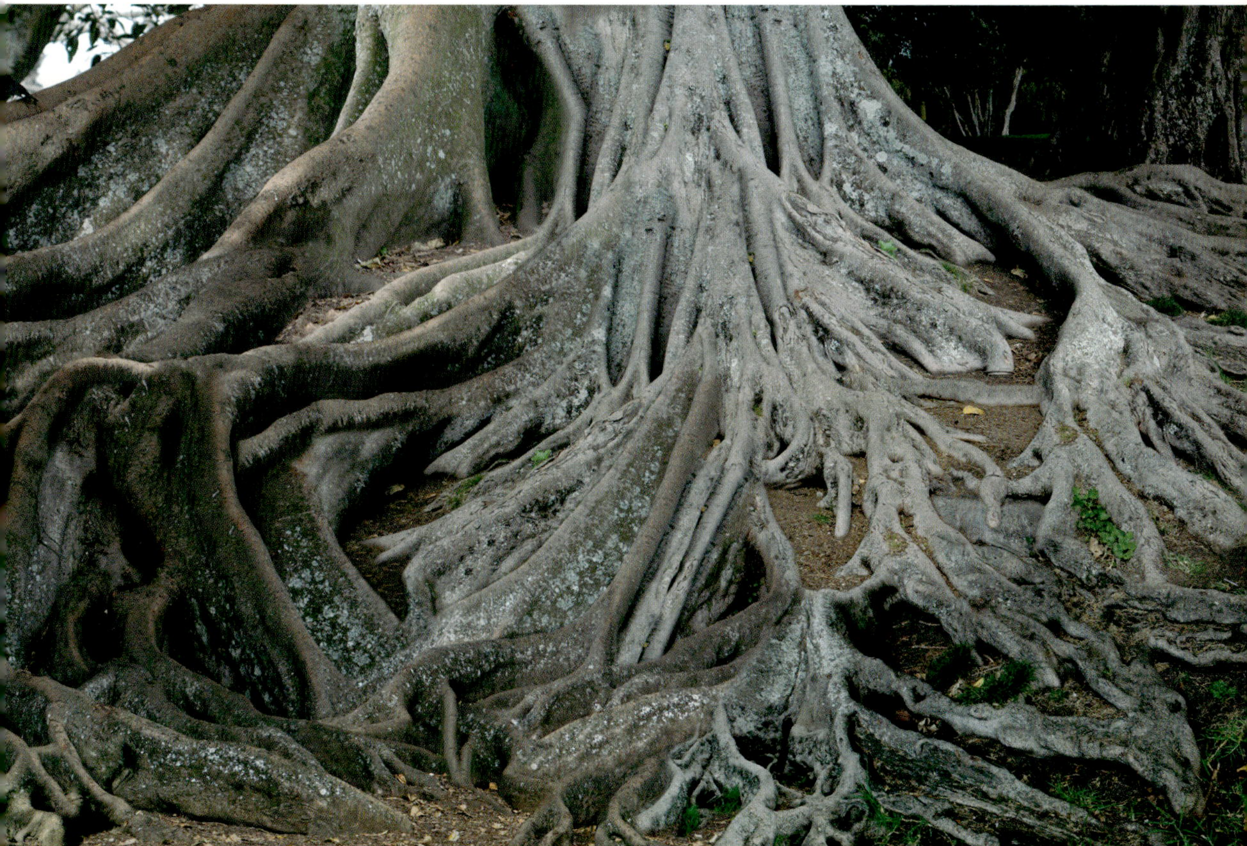

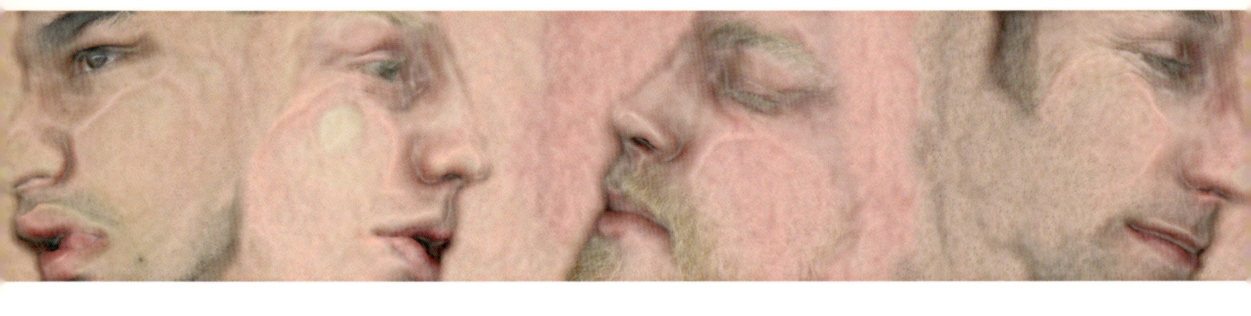

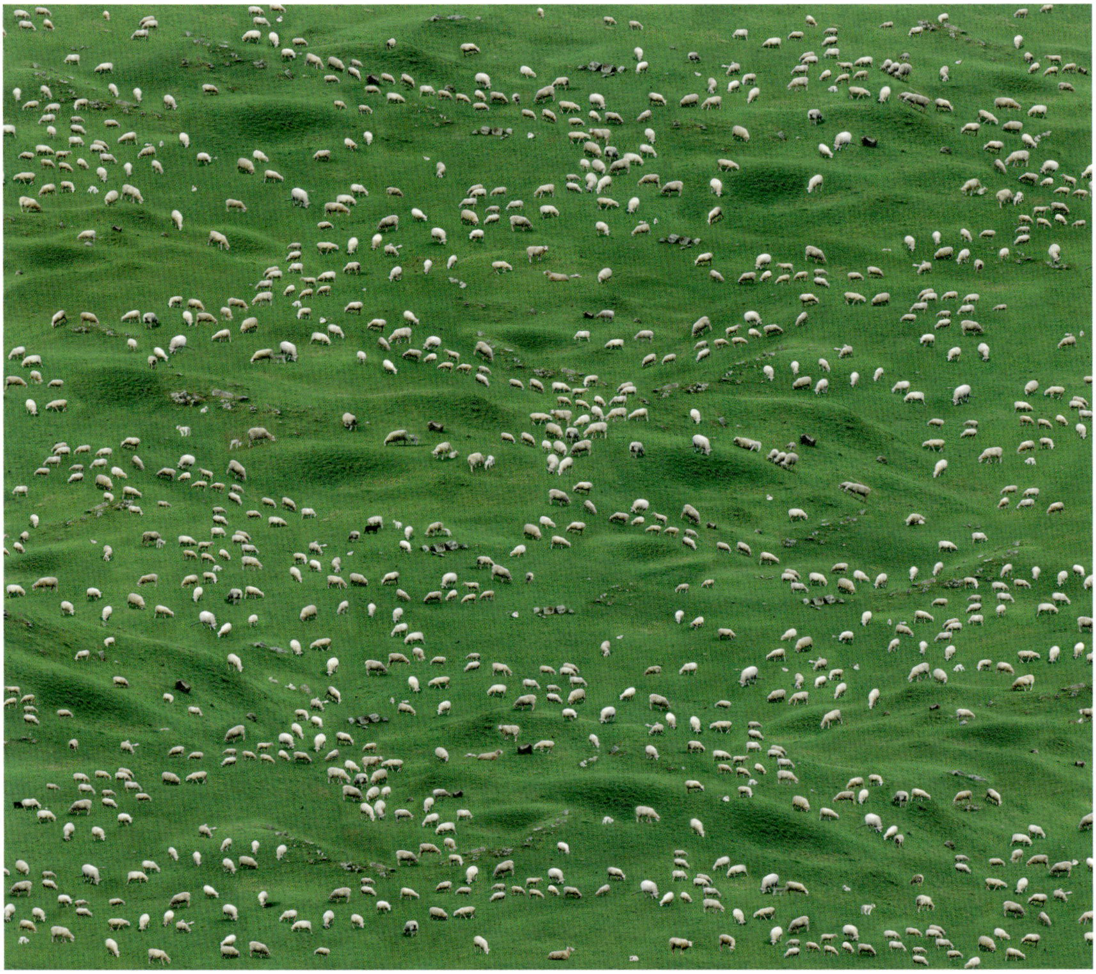

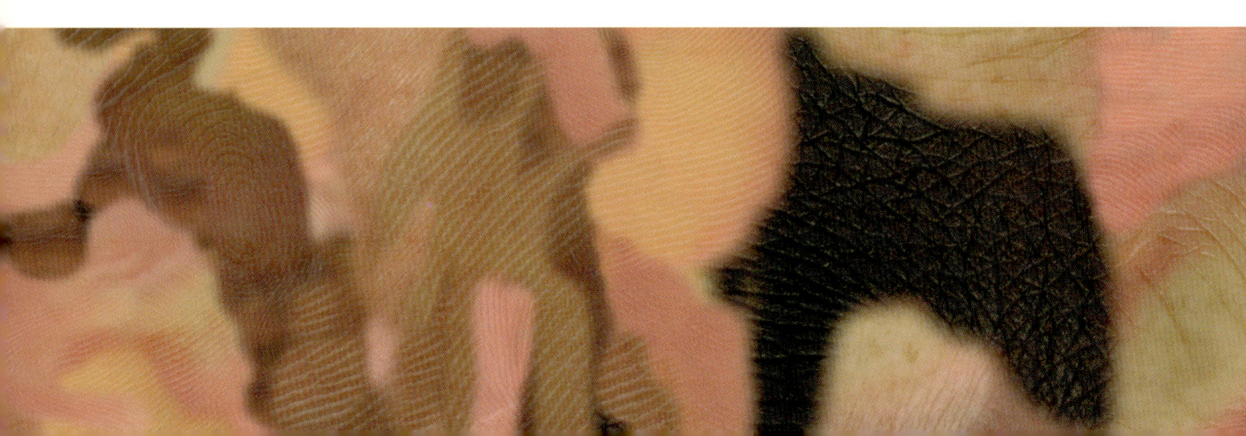

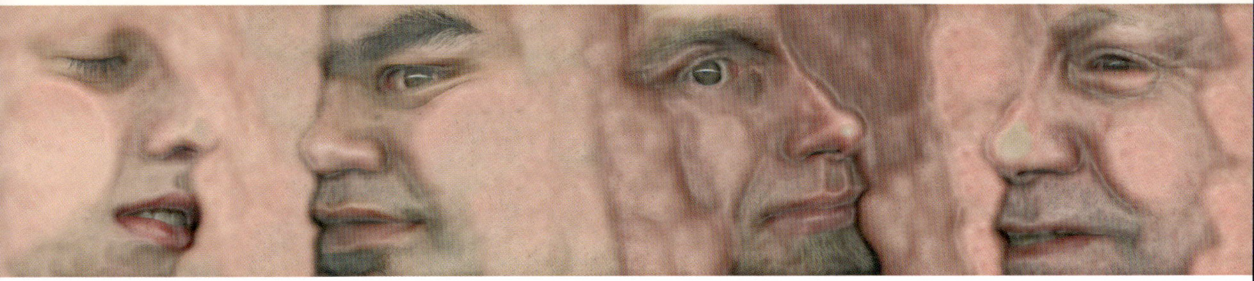

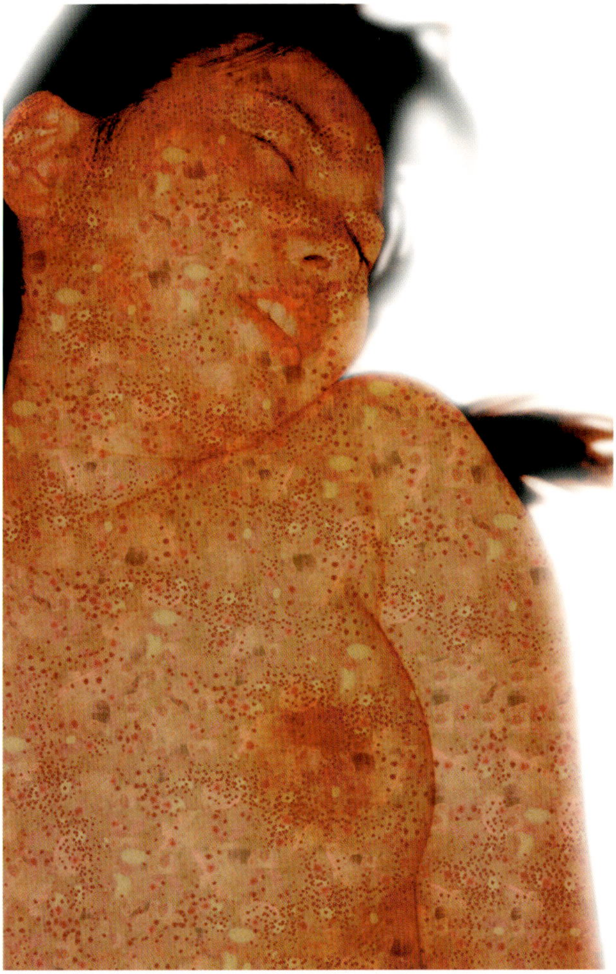

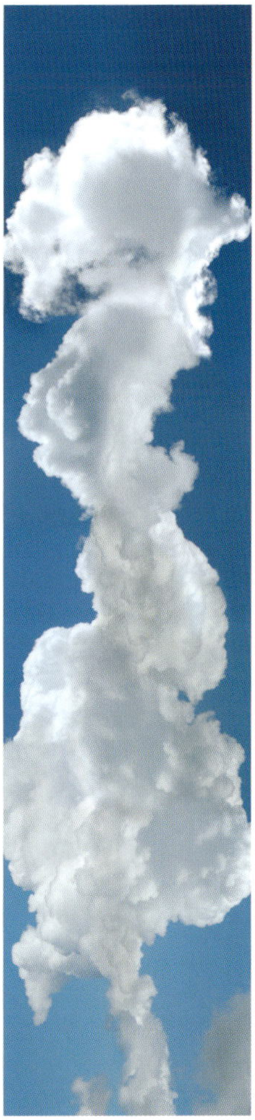

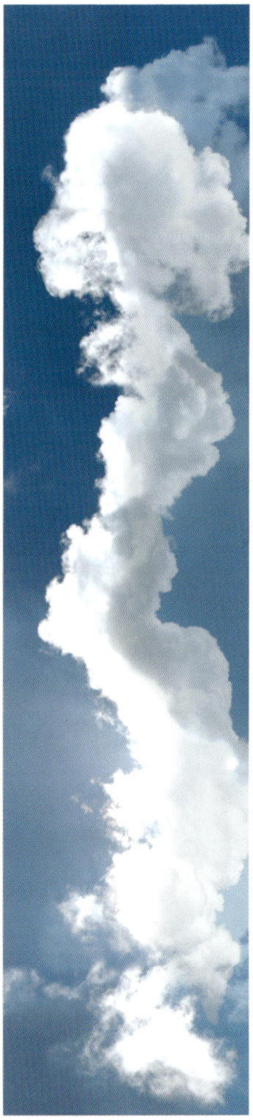

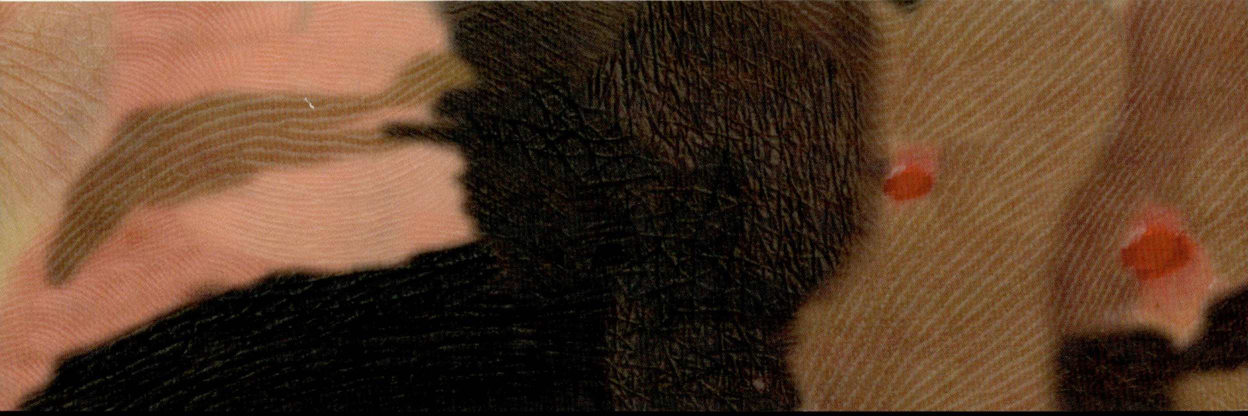

Sean Kerr

104

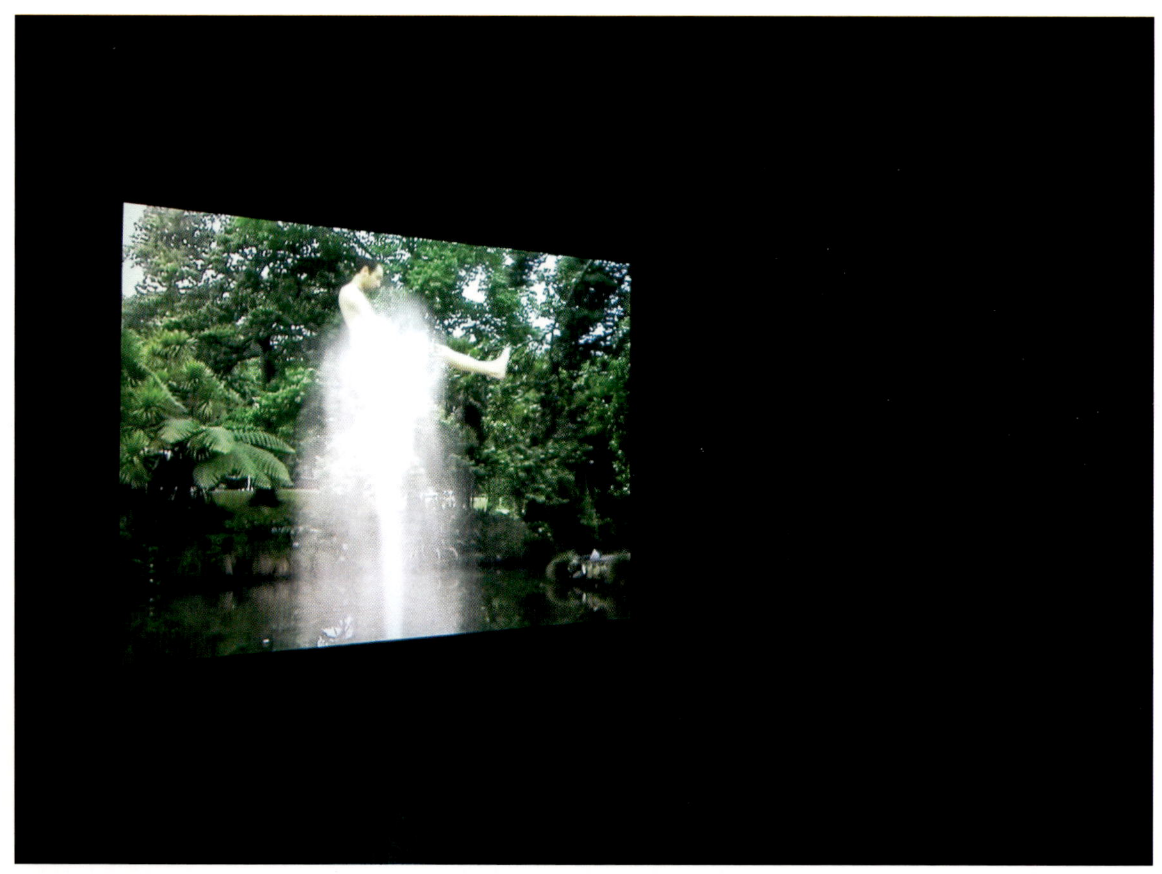

Fountain, from the series 'Super Natural'
2004
single DVD projection
Courtesy of Michael Lett

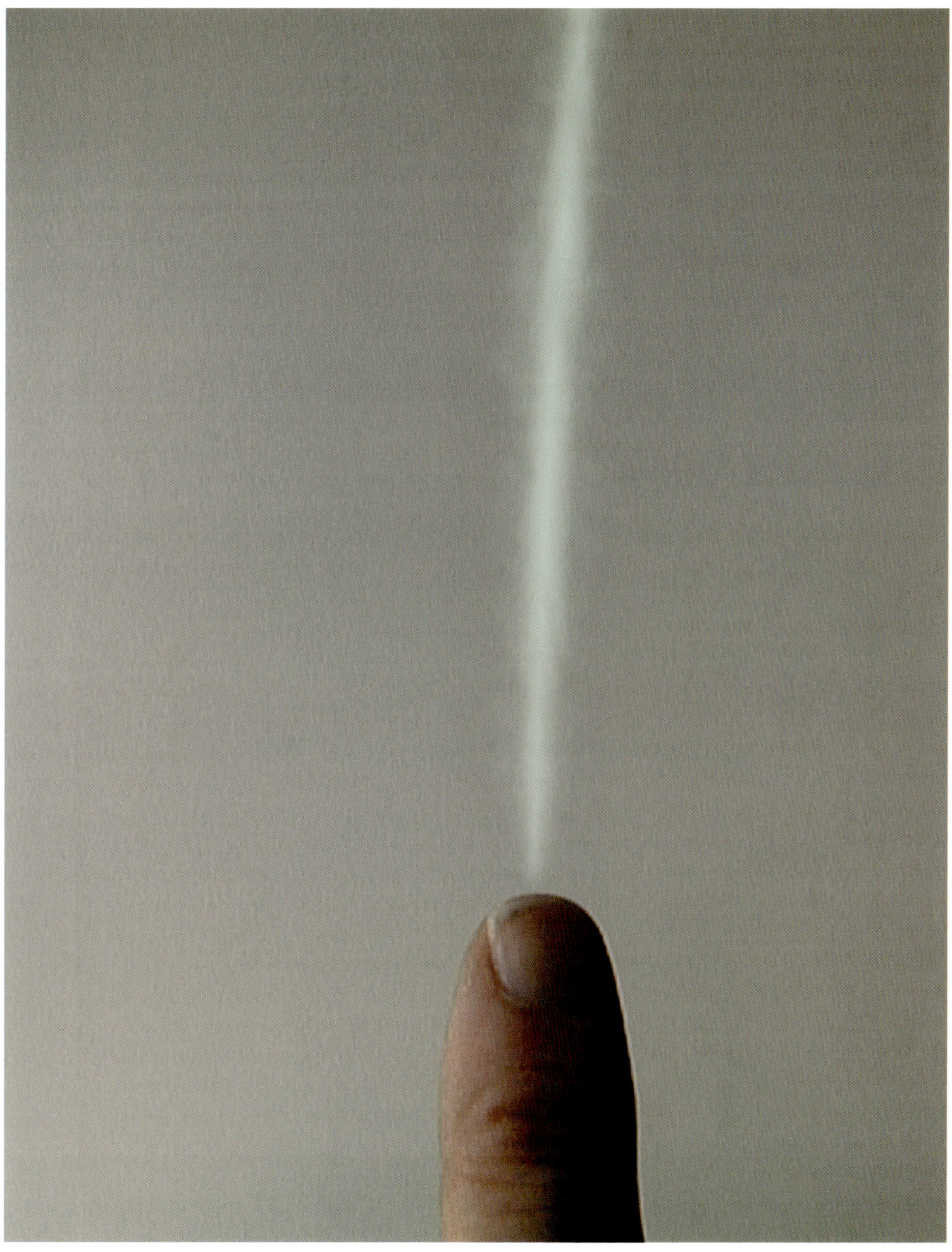

Gold Finger, from the series 'Super Natural'
2005
single DVD monitor (on its side)
Courtesy of Michael Lett

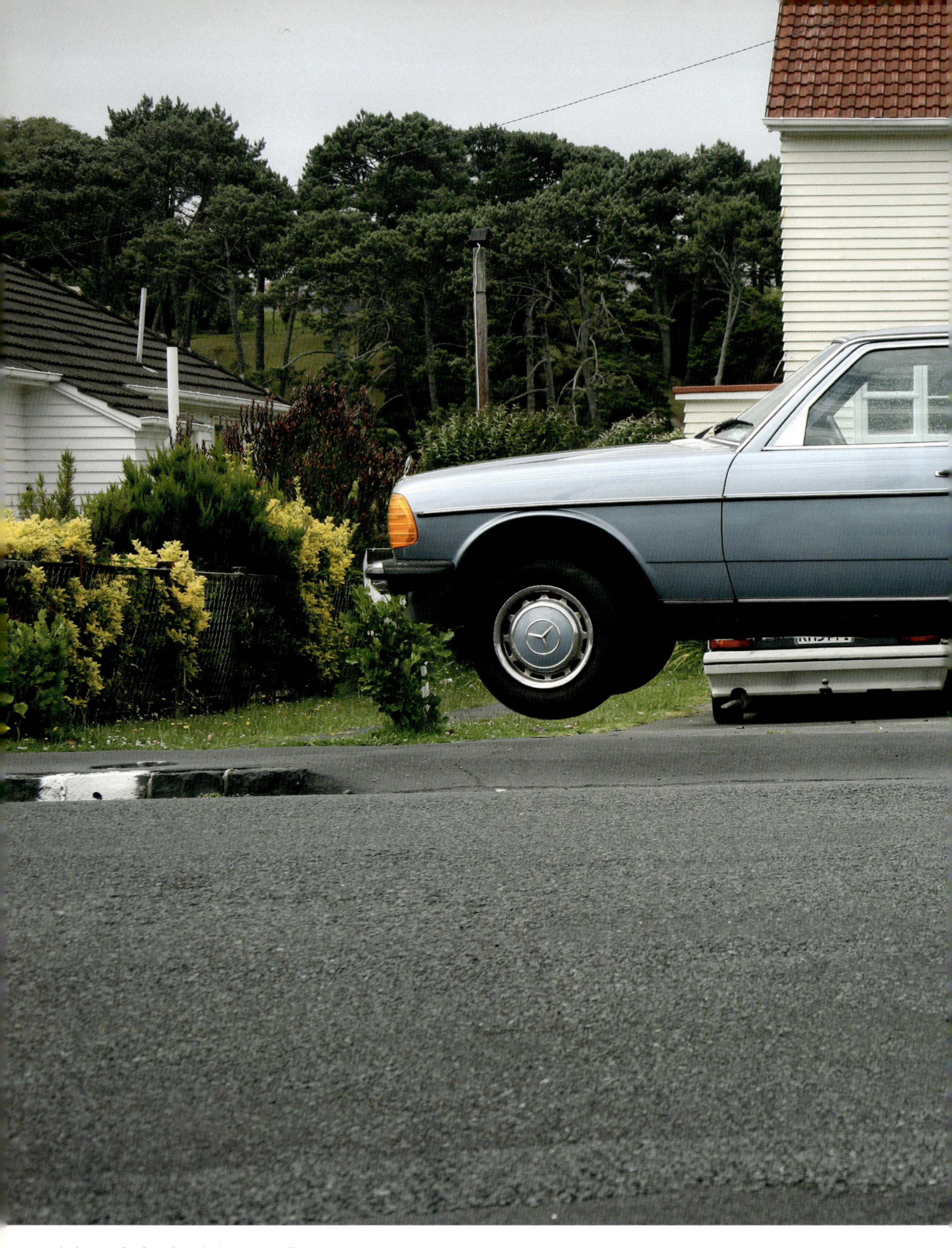

Levitating Mercedes, from the series 'Super Natural'
2007
photograph
Courtesy of Michael Lett

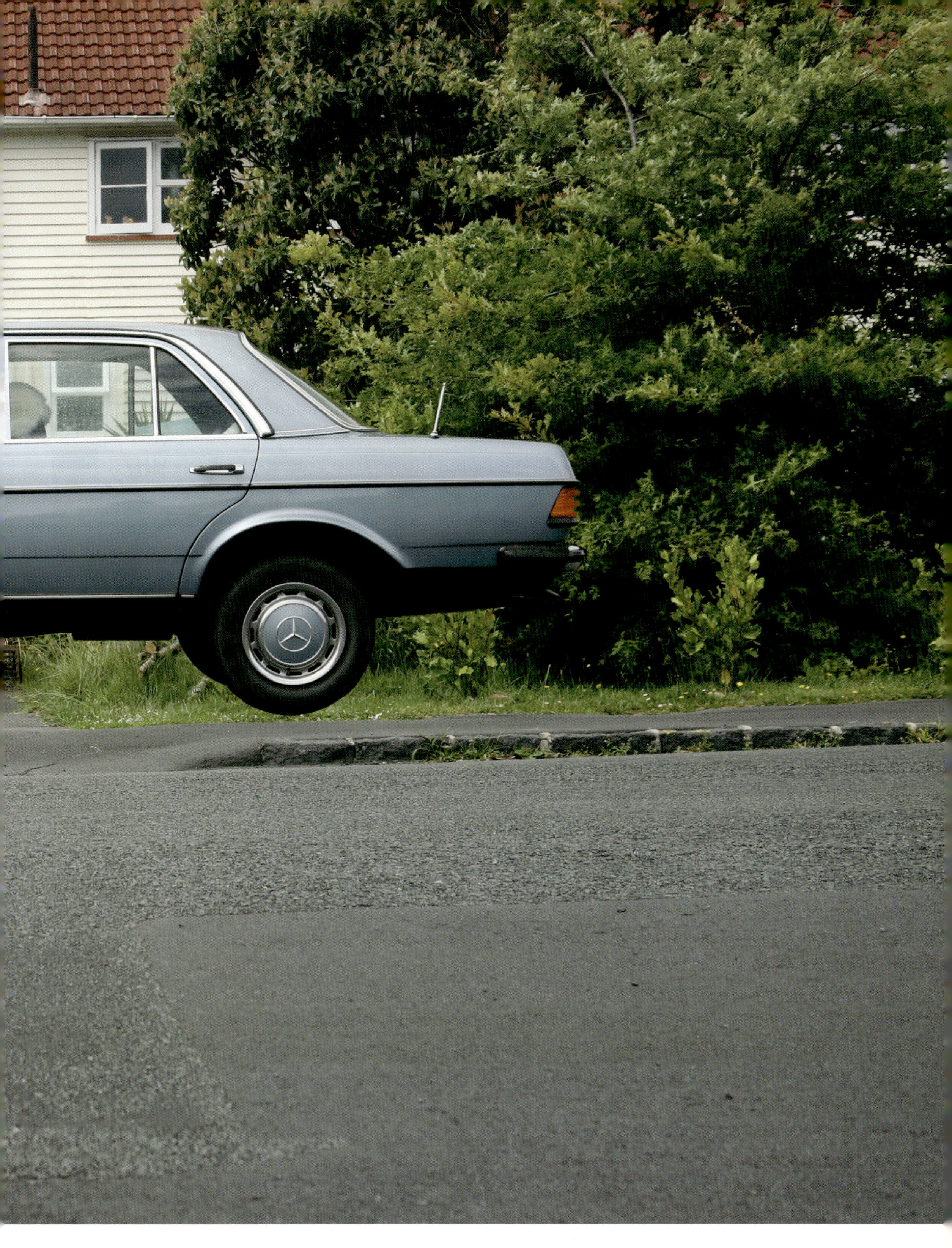

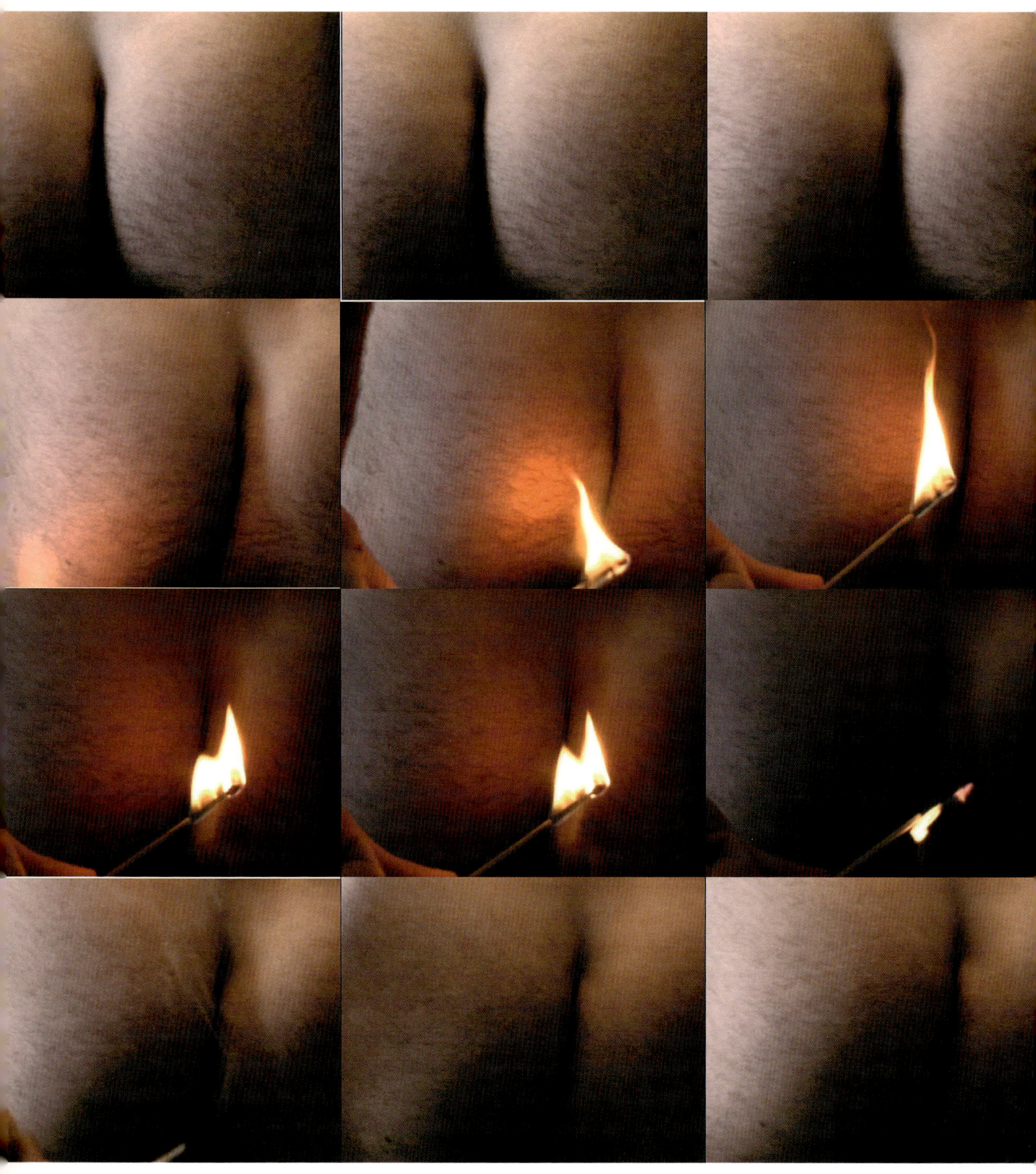

Performance Video 26 – Lighting Farts, from the series 'Super Natural'
2006
single DVD projection
Courtesy of Michael Lett

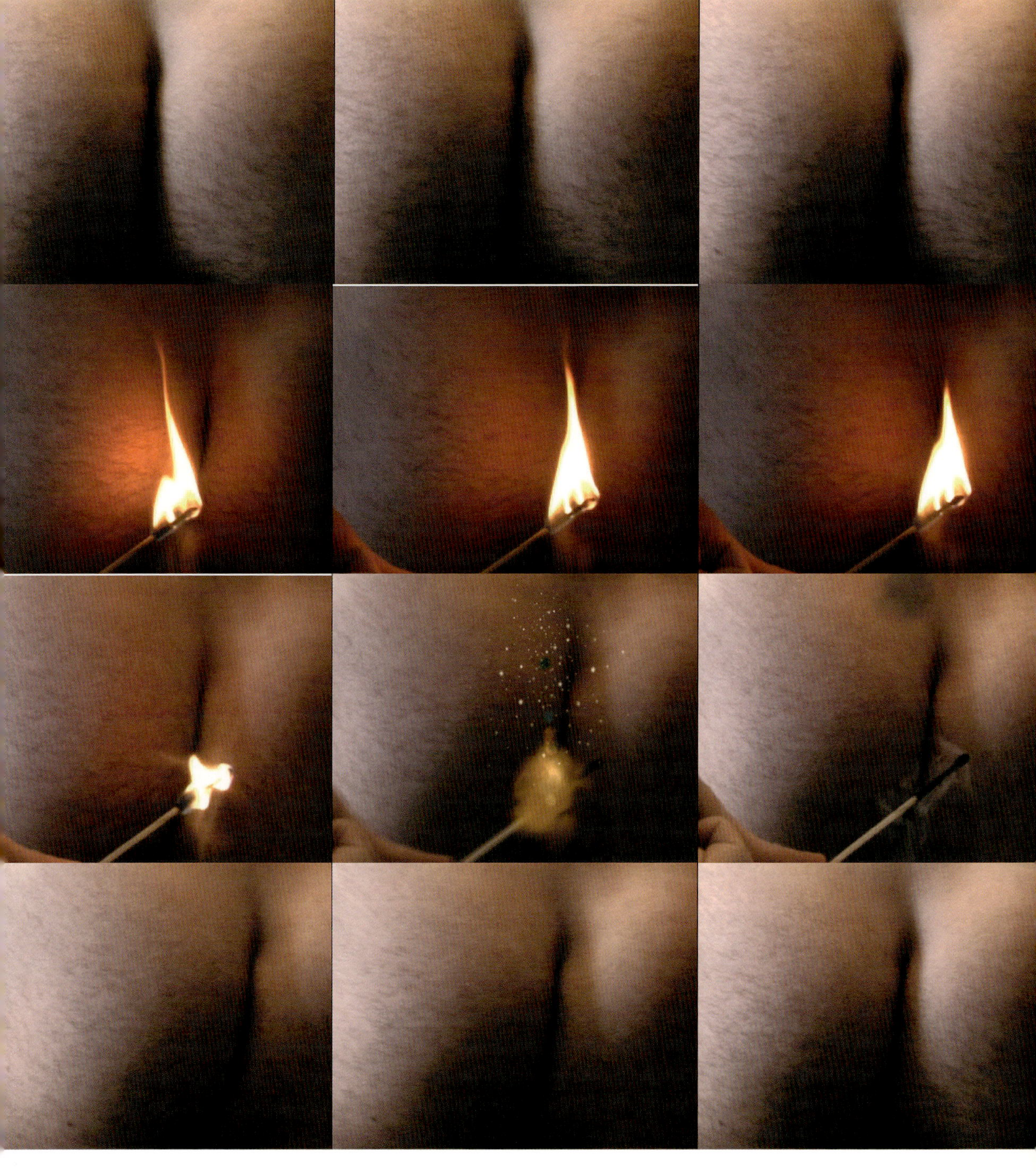

Simon Denny

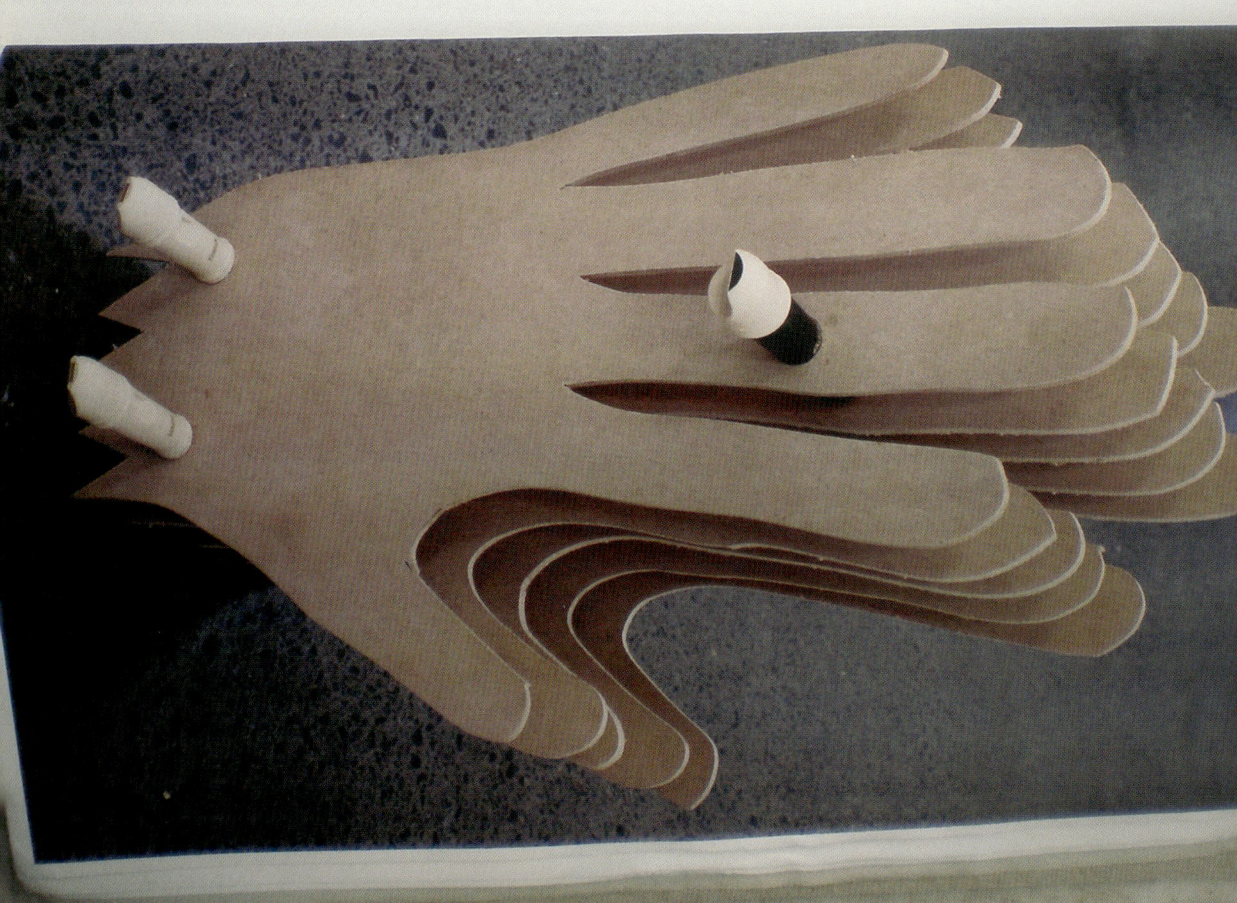

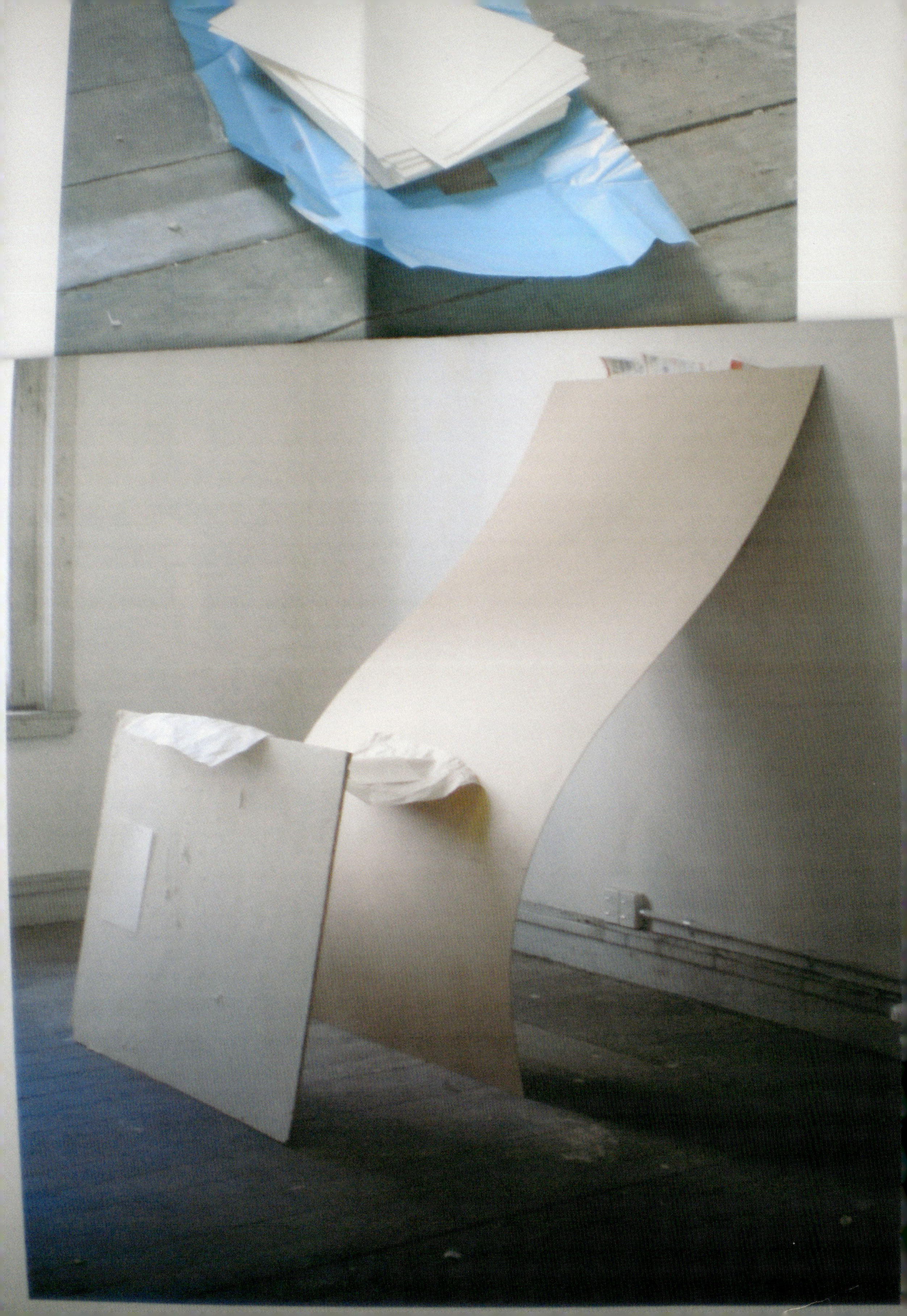

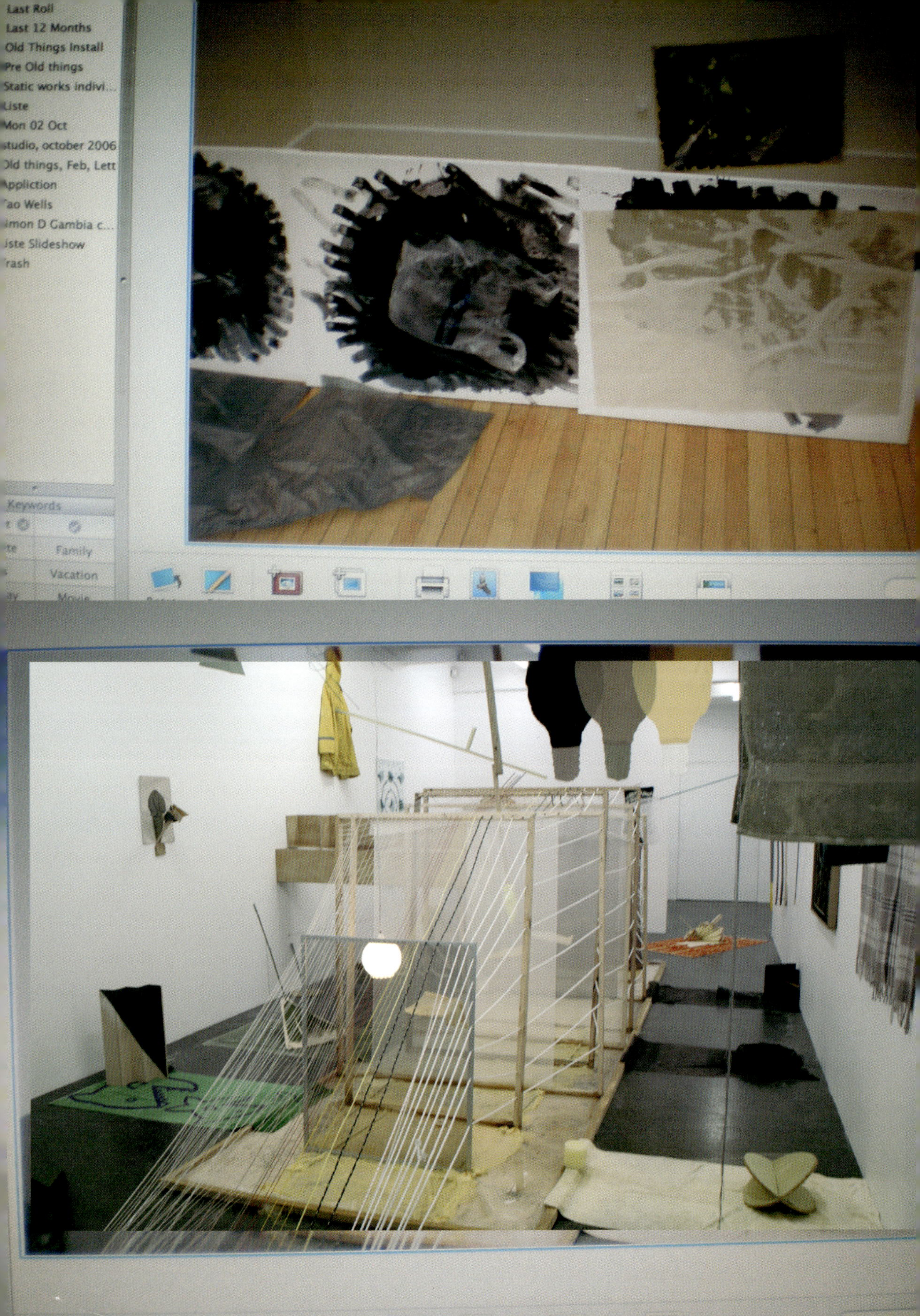

Last Roll
Last 12 Months
Old Things Install
Pre Old things
Static works indivi...
Liste
Mon 02 Oct
studio, october 2006
Old things, Feb, Lett
Appliction
Tao Wells
imon D Gambia c...
iste Slideshow
Trash
Keywords
Family
Vacation
Movie

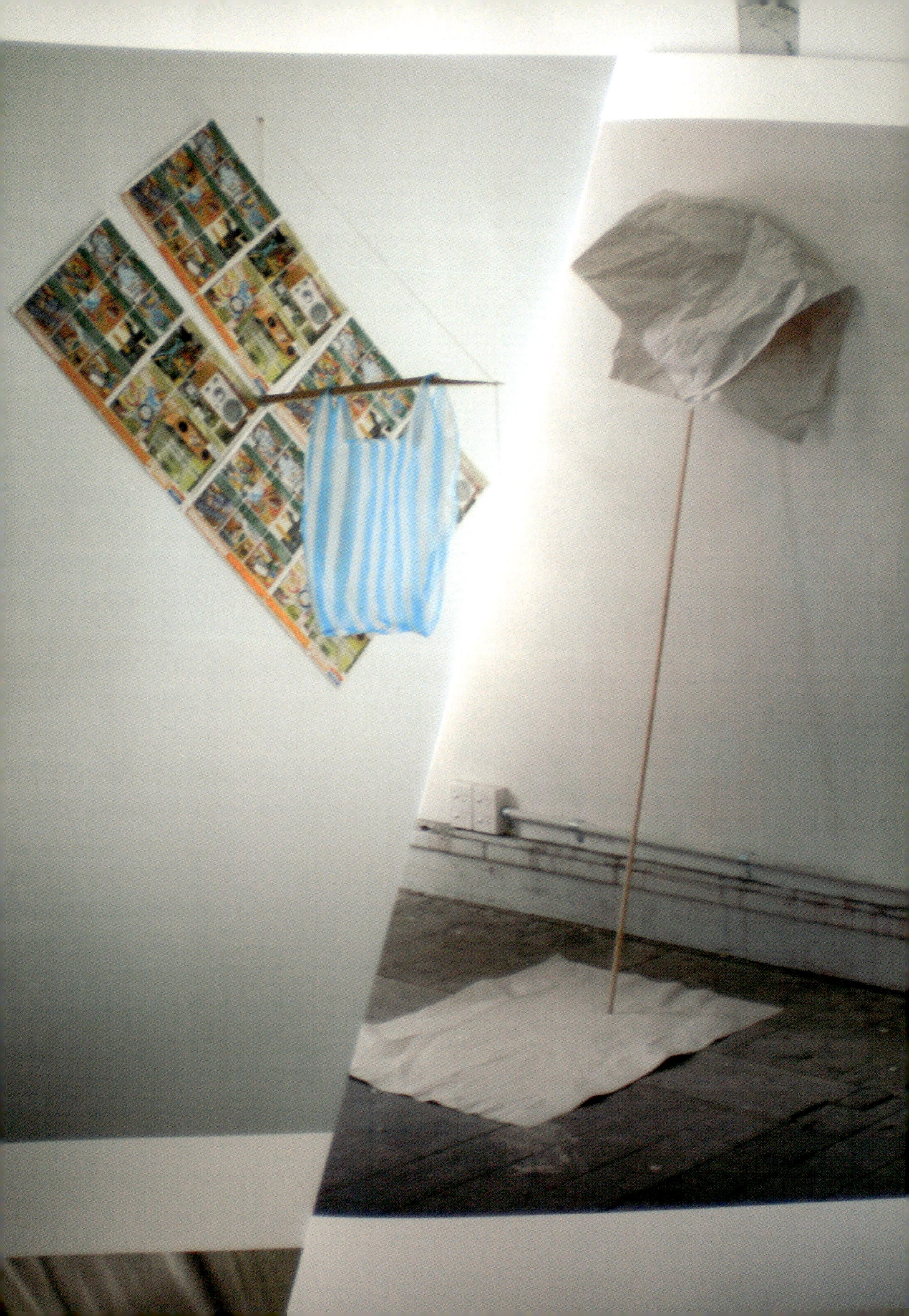

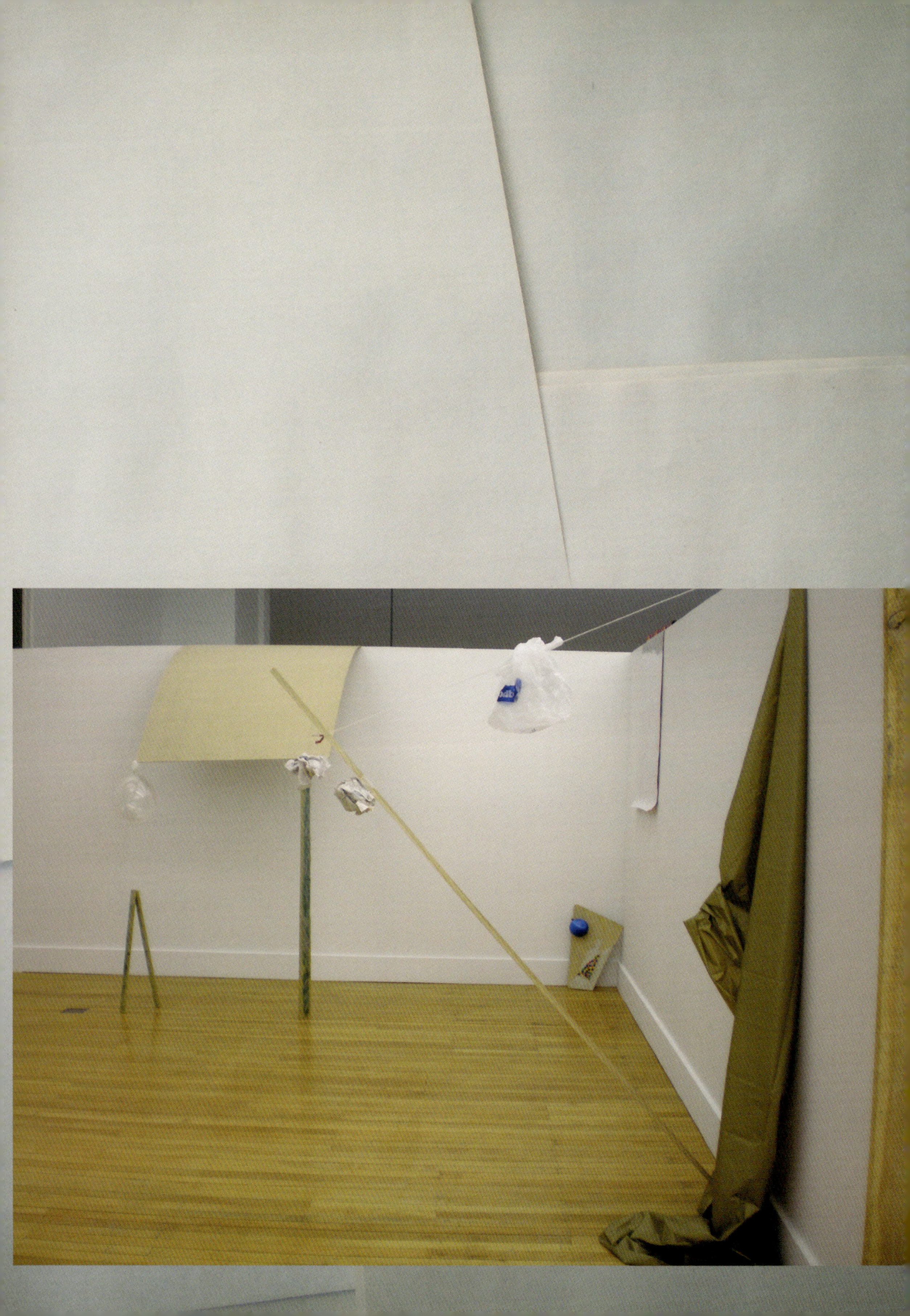

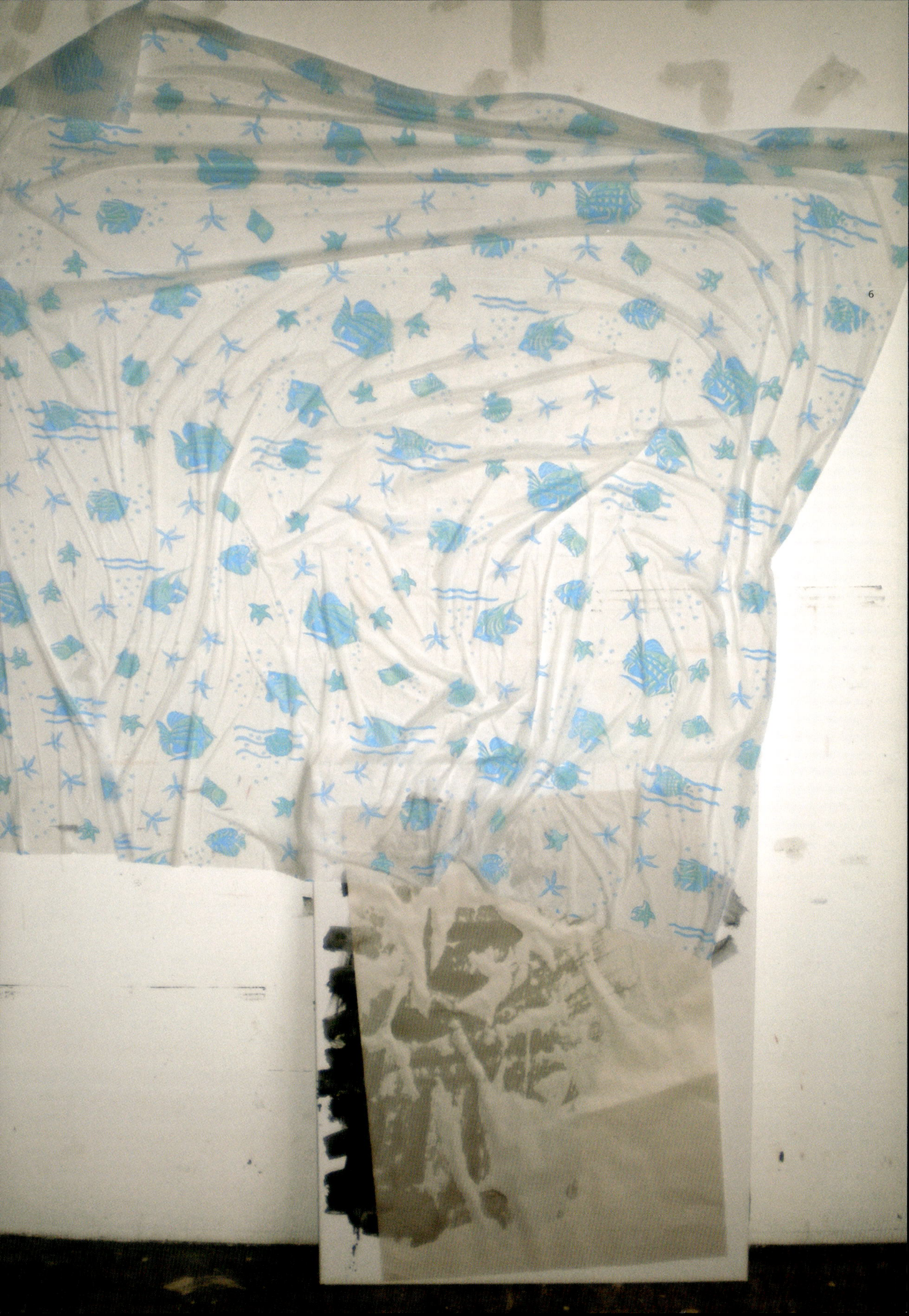

6

John Reynolds

116

Four Walls, Three Layers, Two Marks, One Light, 2006 (detail), acrylic paint and oil paint marker on gallery walls, plus one naked 200 watt light bulb, installed at Auckland Art Gallery

117

Untitled (with Patrick Reynolds), 2006, digital image

118–119

Last Evenings on Earth, 2006 (detail), oil and acrylic paint and graphite on canvas, 3 x 5.4 metres

120–121

Cloud, 2006, silver enamel paint marker on 7,073 canvases, installed in the NSW Gallery foyer at the 2006 Biennale of Sydney, approx. 50 running meters by 8 meters high

All photos: Patrick Reynolds

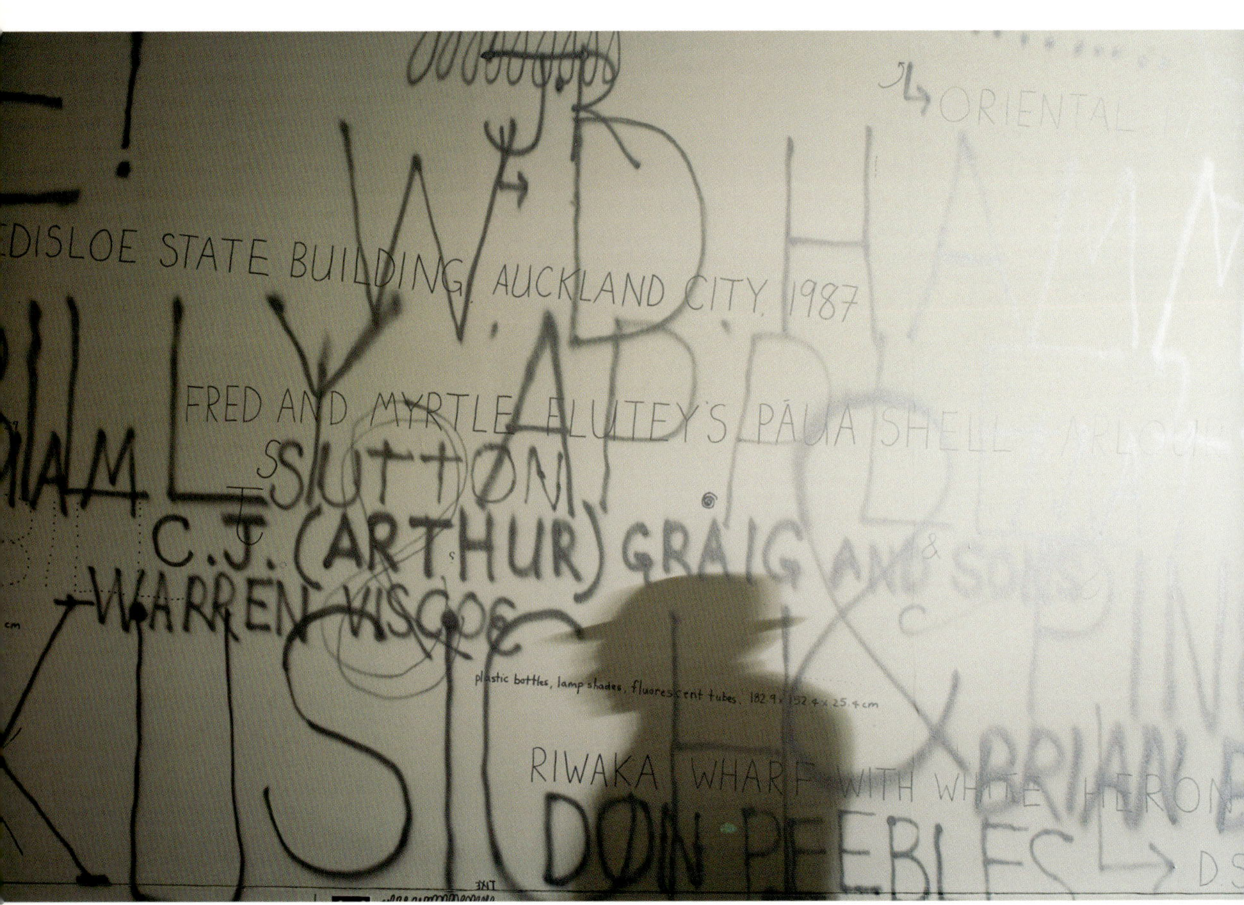

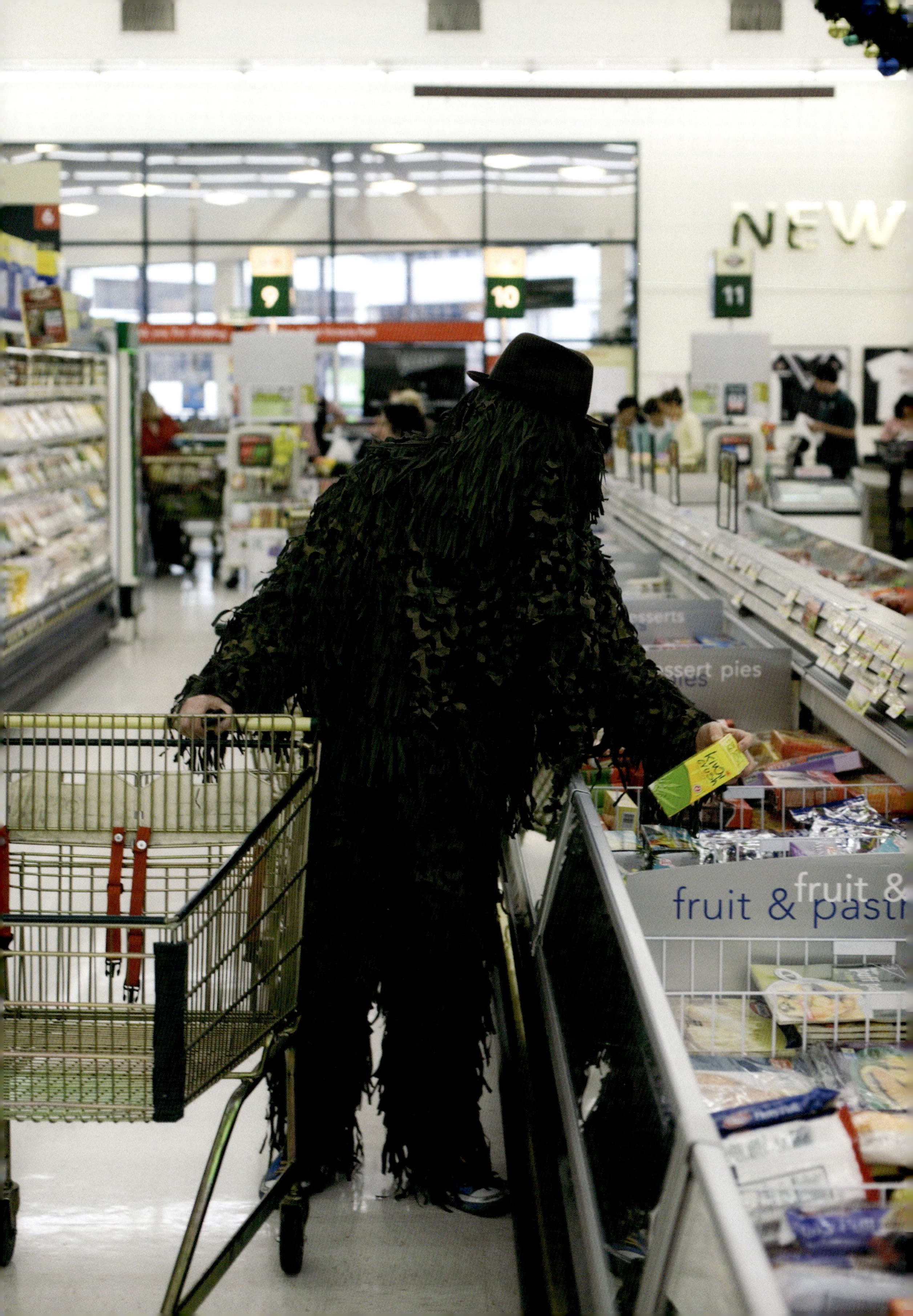

NEW
9
10
11
desserts
essert pies
ies
fruit &
fruit & past

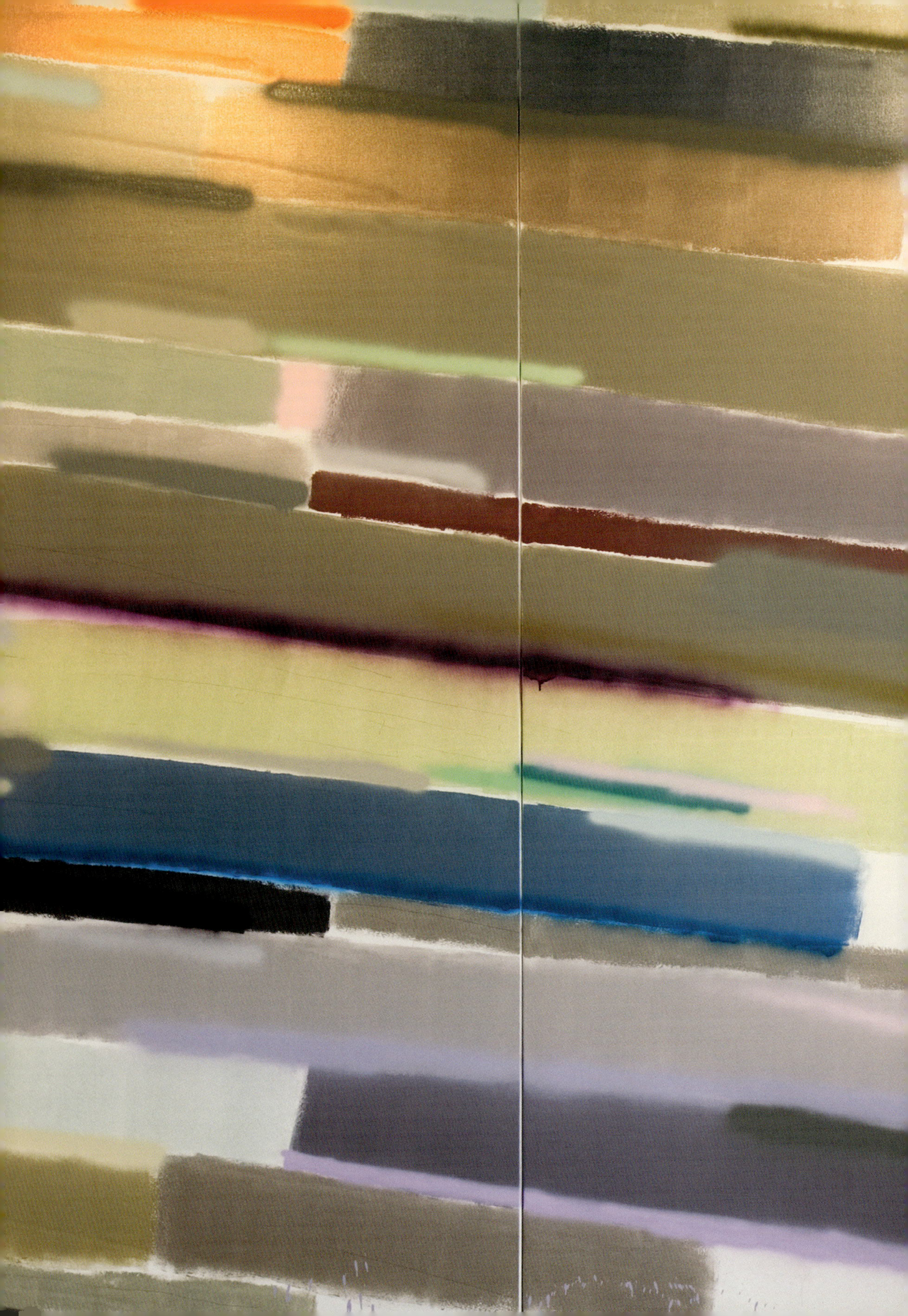

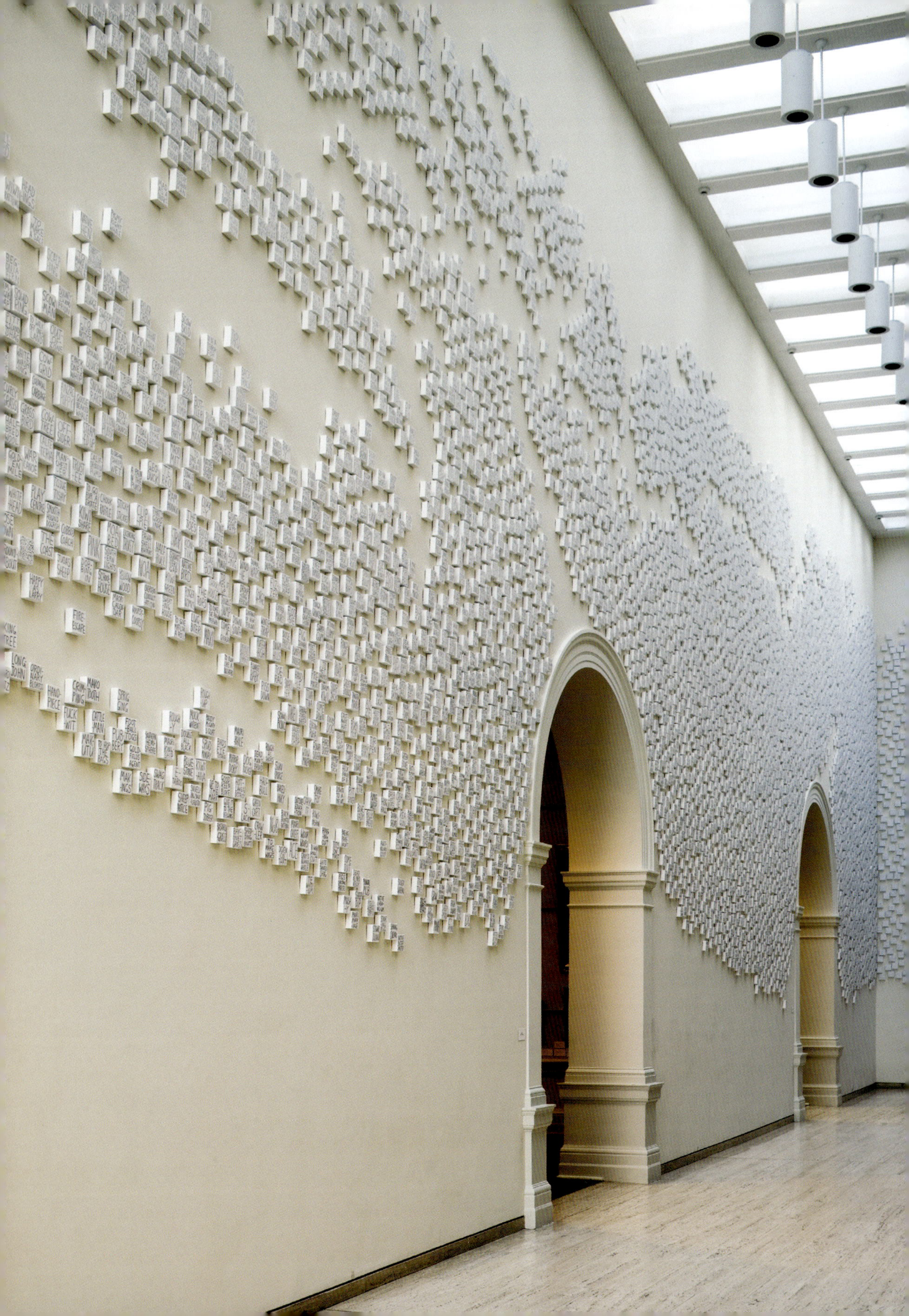

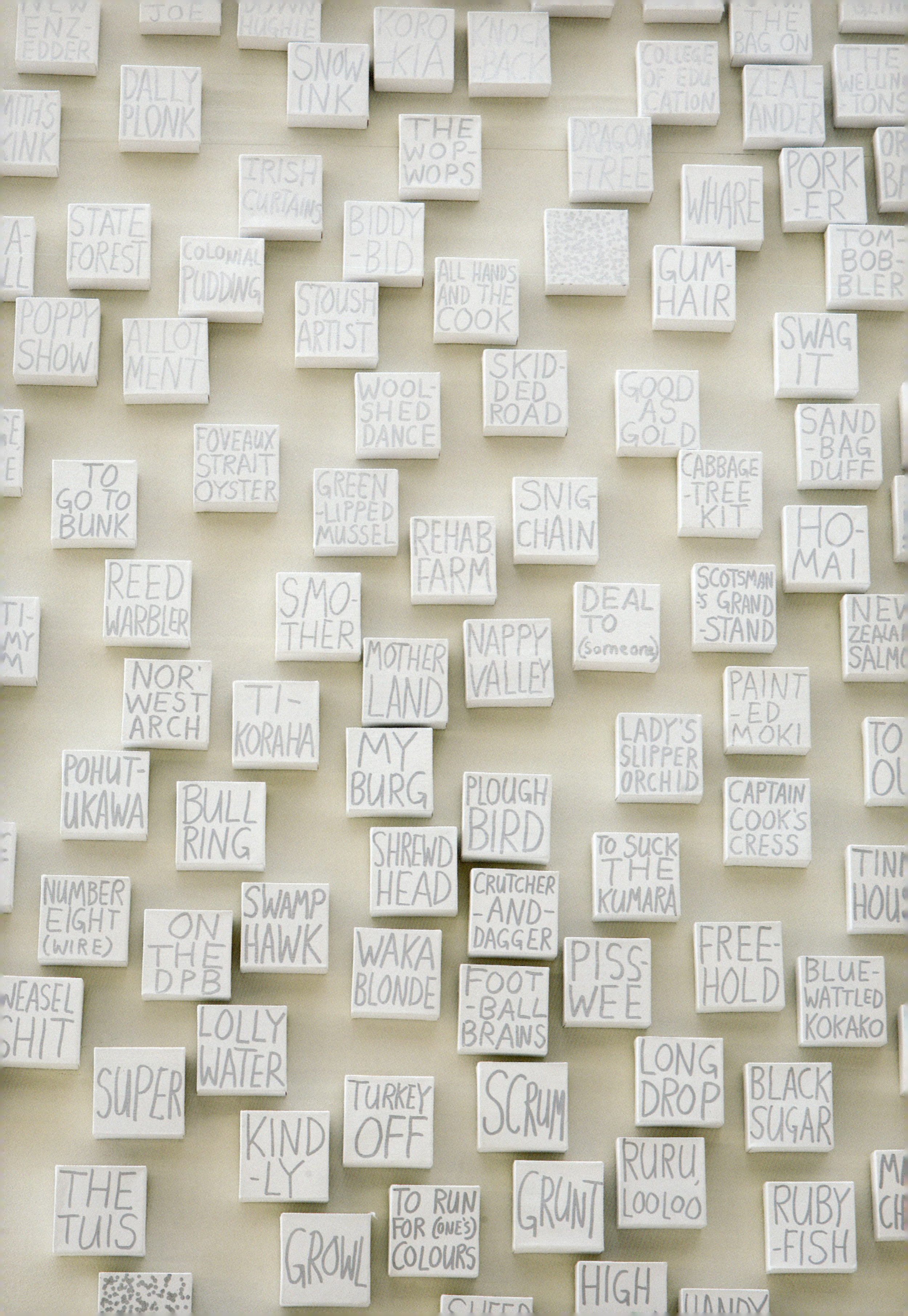

NEW ENZ-EDDER

JOE

DOWN HUGHIE

KORO-KIA

KNOCK-BACK

COLLEGE OF EDU-CATION

THE BAG ON

THE WELLING-TONS

NEW ZEAL-ANDER

SMITH'S KINK

DALLY PLONK

SNOW INK

THE WOP-WOPS

DRAGON-TREE

PORK-ER

IRISH CURTAINS

BIDDY-BID

WHARE

TOM-BOB-BLER

STATE FOREST

COLONIAL PUDDING

STOUSH ARTIST

ALL HANDS AND THE COOK

GUM-HAIR

POPPY SHOW

ALLOT-MENT

SWAG IT

WOOL-SHED DANCE

SKID-DED ROAD

GOOD AS GOLD

SAND-BAG DUFF

FOVEAUX STRAIT OYSTER

TO GO TO BUNK

GREEN-LIPPED MUSSEL

REHAB FARM

SNIG-CHAIN

CABBAGE-TREE-KIT

HO-MAI

TI-MY-M

REED WARBLER

SMO-THER

MOTHER LAND

NAPPY VALLEY

DEAL TO (someone)

SCOTSMAN'S GRAND-STAND

NEW ZEALAND SALMON

NOR'WEST ARCH

TI-KORAHA

MY BURG

LADY'S SLIPPER ORCHID

PAINT-ED MOKI

TO OU

POHUT-UKAWA

BULL RING

PLOUGH BIRD

CAPTAIN COOK'S CRESS

NUMBER EIGHT (WIRE)

ON THE DPB

SWAMP HAWK

SHREWD HEAD

CRUTCHER-AND-DAGGER

TO SUCK THE KUMARA

TINN HOUS

WEASEL SHIT

LOLLY WATER

WAKA BLONDE

FOOT-BALL BRAINS

PISS-WEE

FREE-HOLD

BLUE-WATTLED KOKAKO

SUPER

TURKEY OFF

SCRUM

LONG DROP

BLACK SUGAR

KIND-LY

THE TUIS

GROWL

TO RUN FOR (ONE'S) COLOURS

GRUNT

RURU, LOOLOO

RUBY-FISH

HIGH

Francis Upritchard

122

Green Man, 2005, ceramic vase, modelling material, paint, 26 × 13 × 13cm, photograph by Larry Lamay. Courtesy of Andrea Rosen Gallery, New York

Amulet, 2006, plastic and string, 1 × 7 × 6cm, photograph by Andy Keate. Courtesy of Kate MacGarry, London

Bone Rings, 2006, bone, 4 × 6 × 6cm, photograph by Andy Keate. Courtesy of Kate MacGarry, London

Green Dog Urn, 2003, ceramic and modelling material, photograph by the artist. Courtesy of Ivan Anthony, Auckland

123

Human Problems, 2004, leather bottle, clay, suede, marbles, string, modelling material and found jewellery, 32 × 13 × 7cm, photograph by Andy Keate. Courtesy of Kate MacGarry, London

124

No Name i (Ancestral Box), 2004, box, modelling material, feather, metal case, string, 21.5 × 24 × 2cm, photograph by Tom Powell. Courtesy of Salon 94, New York

125

No Name ii (Ancestral Box), 2004, box, modelling material, feather, string, 18 × 21.5 × 2cm, photograph by Tom Powell. Courtesy of Salon 94, New York

126

Pointing (Balata Figure), 2004, balata (natural rubber), 47 × 37 × 13cm, photograph by Christopher Burke. Courtesy of Andrea Rosen Gallery, New York

127

Thinker (Balata Figure), 2005, balata (natural rubber), 23 × 24 × 12cm, photograph by Christopher Burke. Courtesy of Andrea Rosen Gallery, New York

The layout of these pages is based on the book *Human Problems*, designed by James Goggin, Practise, published by Kate MacGarry, London and Veenman Publishers, Rotterdam.

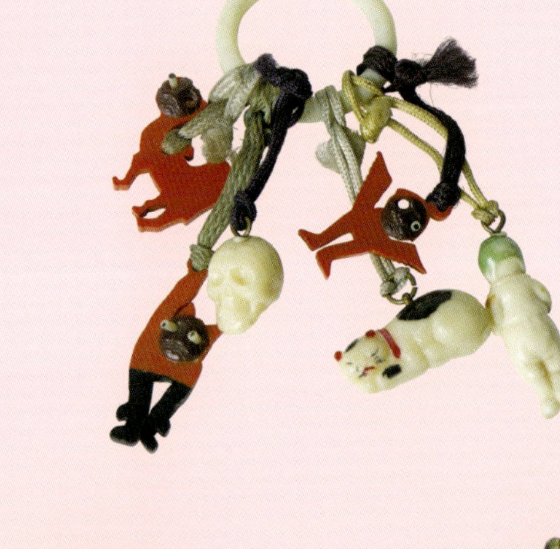

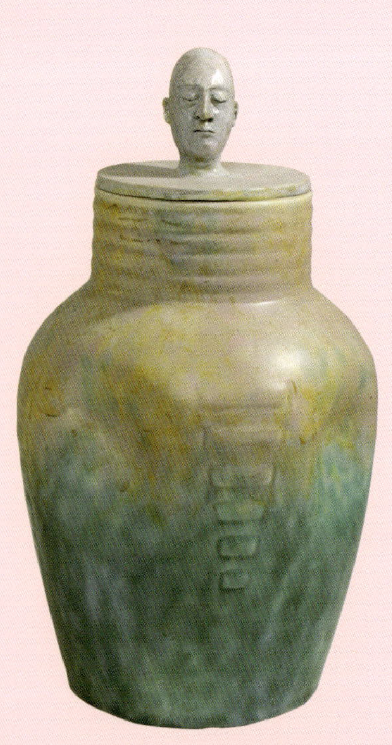

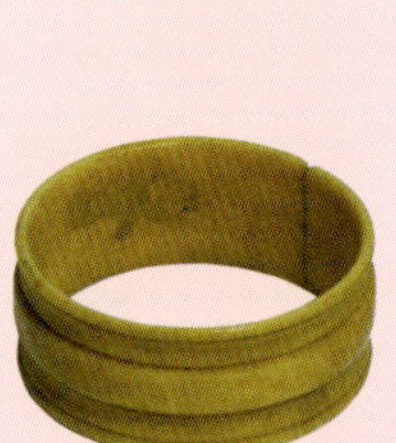

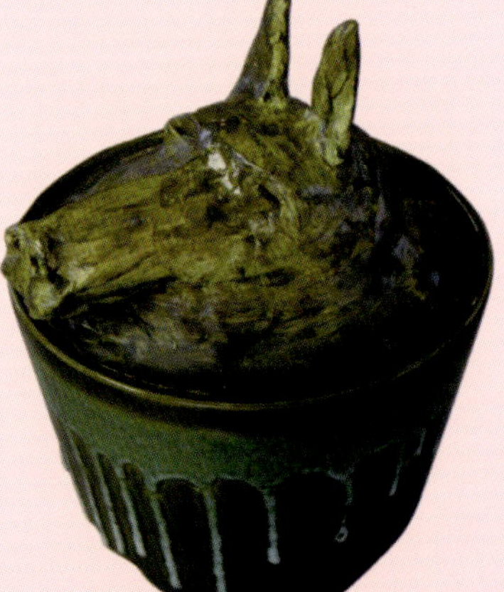

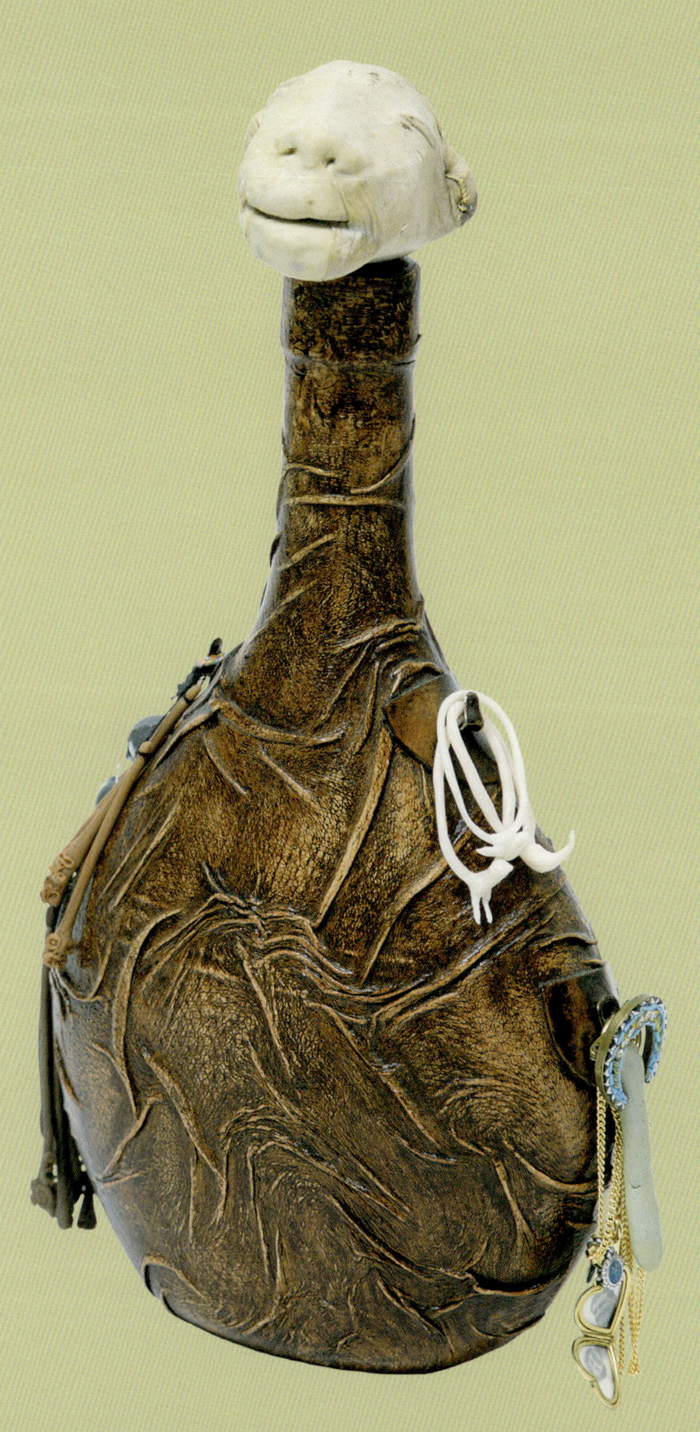

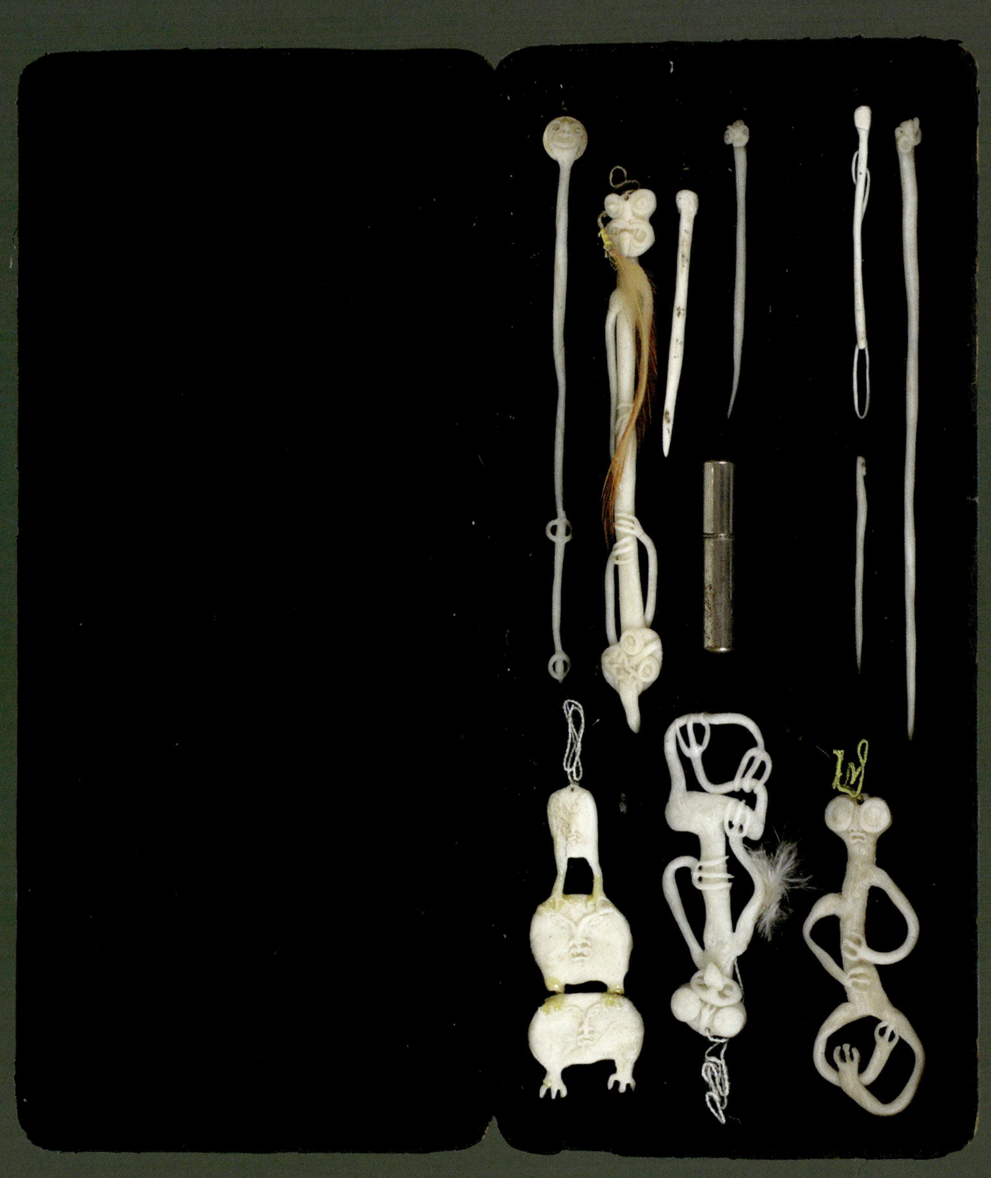

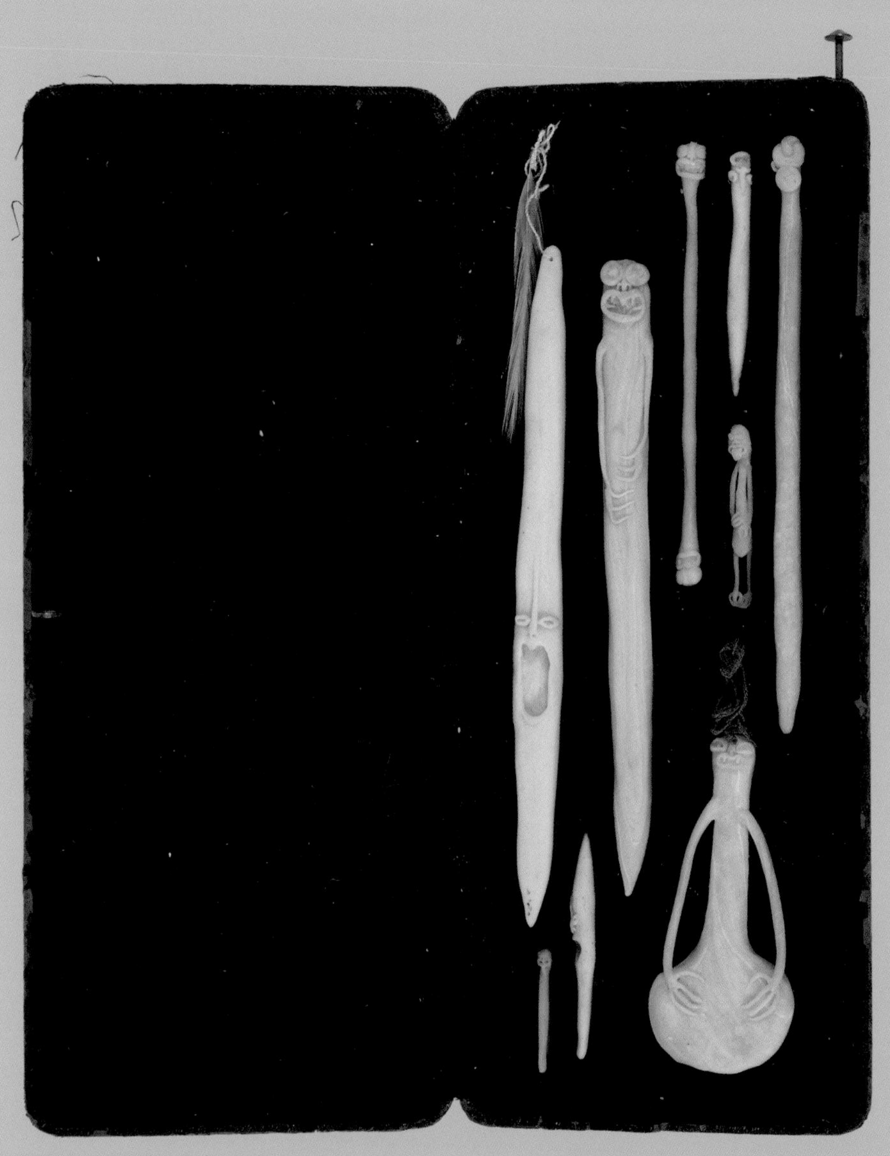

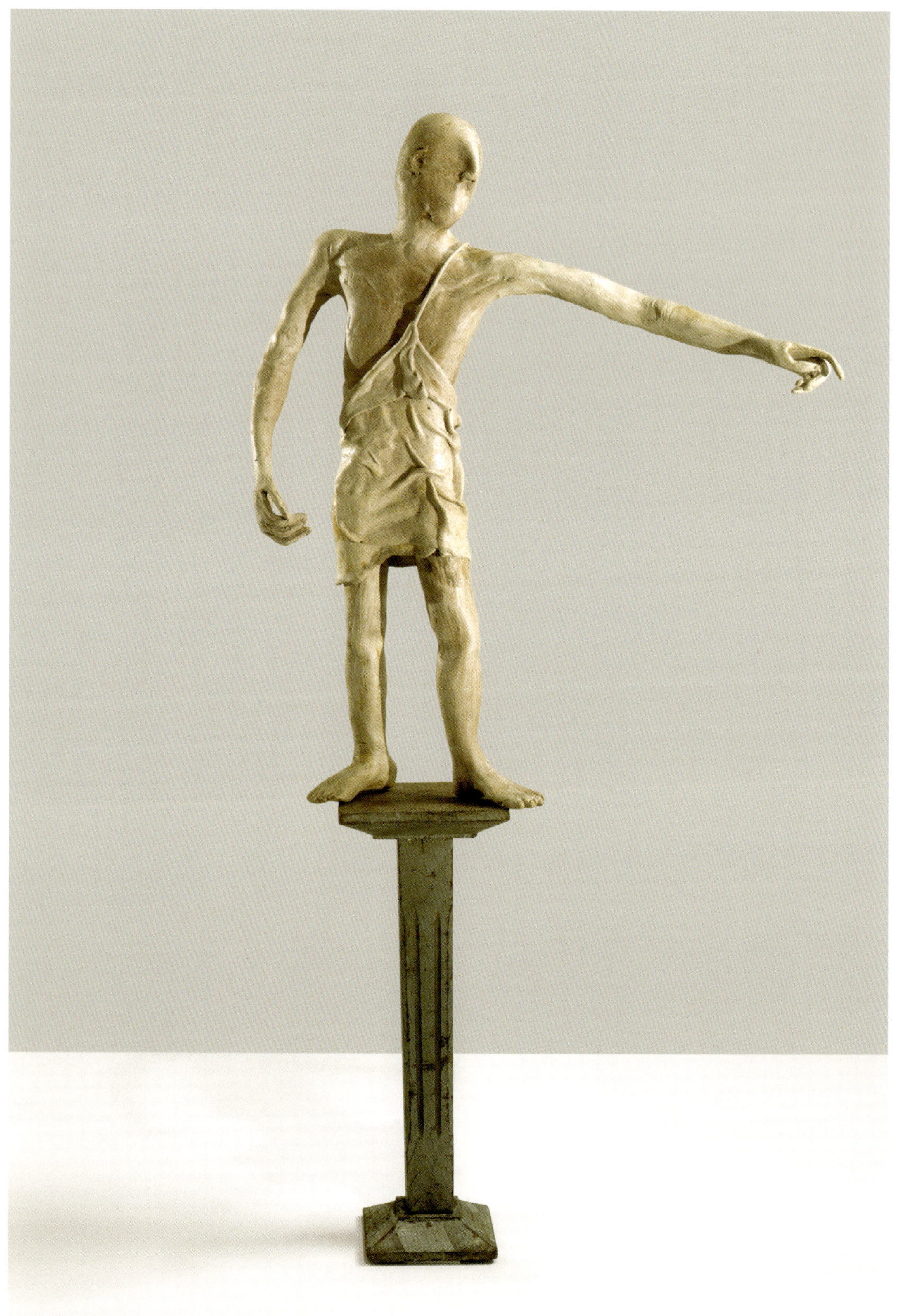

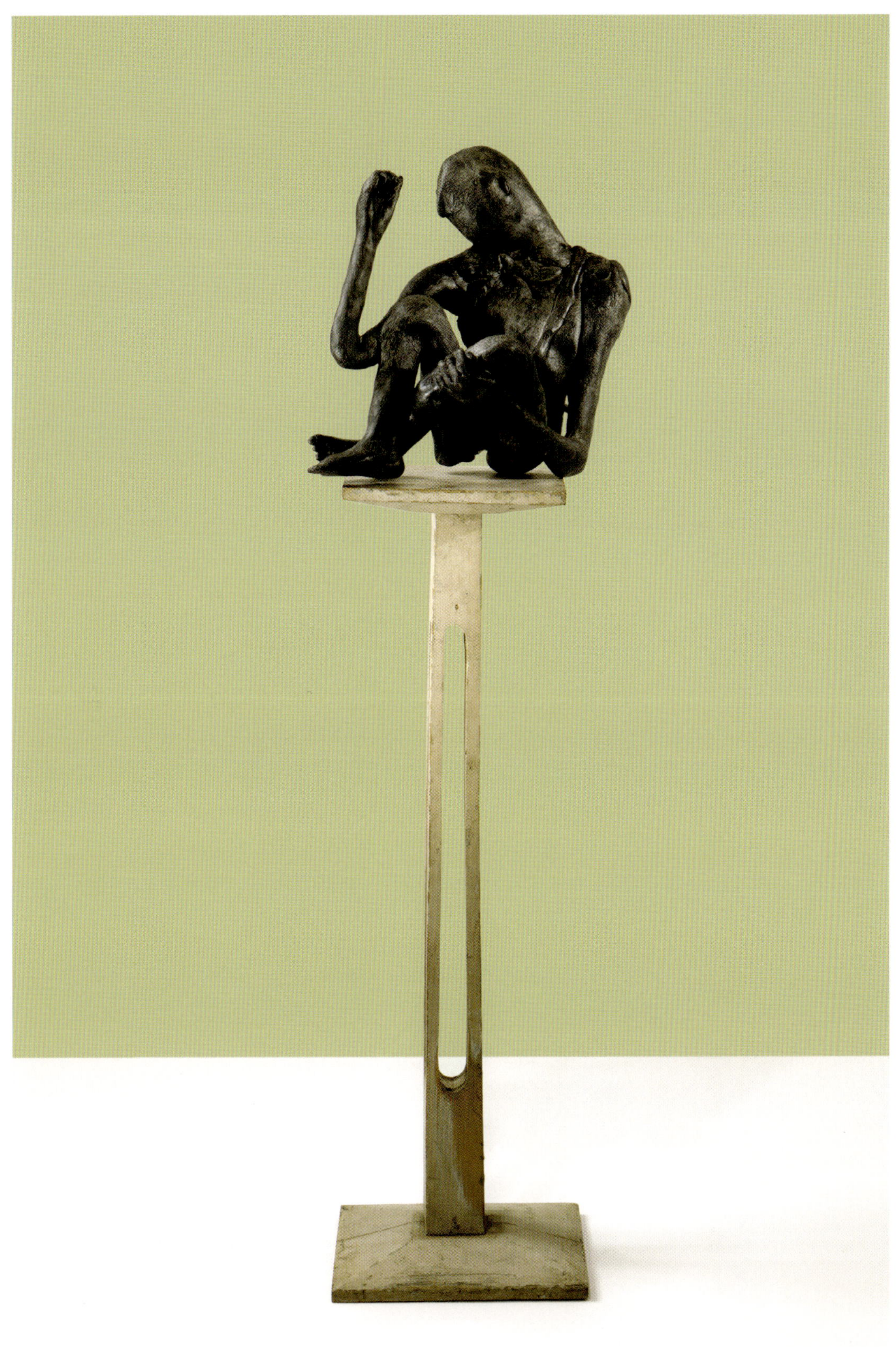

Eve Armstrong

128–129

Arrangement: tug, found packaging materials, found carpet underlay, packing tape in 'Eve Armstrong – ROAM', Artspace, Auckland, New Zealand, 2005. Photo: Richard Orjis

130–131

Row 1, left to right:

Trading Table flyers (detail) from *How to Hold a Trading Table, A Manual for Beginners,* self-published artist's book, 2004

Arrangement: sprawl (detail), cardboard, packing tape, found objects in 'A Tale of Two Cities: Busan-Seoul/Seoul-Busan', Busan Biennale, 2006

Trading Table, held as part of 'Eve Armstrong – ROAM' at Artspace, Auckland, 2005. Photo: Conor Clarke

Row 2, left to right:

Robot Head (detail) in *Cardboard Box Adaptives*, self-published artist's book, 2004

Lakeside Leisure Kit (detail) in 'Likes the Outdoors', Ramp Gallery, WINTEC, Hamilton, 2005

Backdrop, packing tape, photographs on vinyl adhesive, timber and plywood. Commissioned for SCAPE 2006, Christchurch Art Gallery Te Puna O Waiwhetu, 2006

Handheld Adaptives Kiosk (detail), found objects, kiosk, information brochures, packing tape, linoleum in 'The Bed You Lie In', Artspace, Auckland, 2004

Row 3, left to right:

Arrangement: sprawl (detail), cardboard, packing tape, found objects in 'A Tale of Two Cities: Busan-Seoul/Seoul-Busan', Busan Biennale, 2006

Arrangement, photograph, 2004

Hum & Haw, photographs on adhesive vinyl and packing tape on found object, found materials and objects, packing tape, 2007

Arrangement: stack (detail), found packaging materials, found carpet underlay, packing tape in 'Eve Armstrong – ROAM', Artspace, Auckland, 2005. Photo: Richard Orjis

132–133

Rise, photographs, packing tape, masking tape and acrylic paint on cardboard, 2007

All works courtesy of the artist and Michael Lett

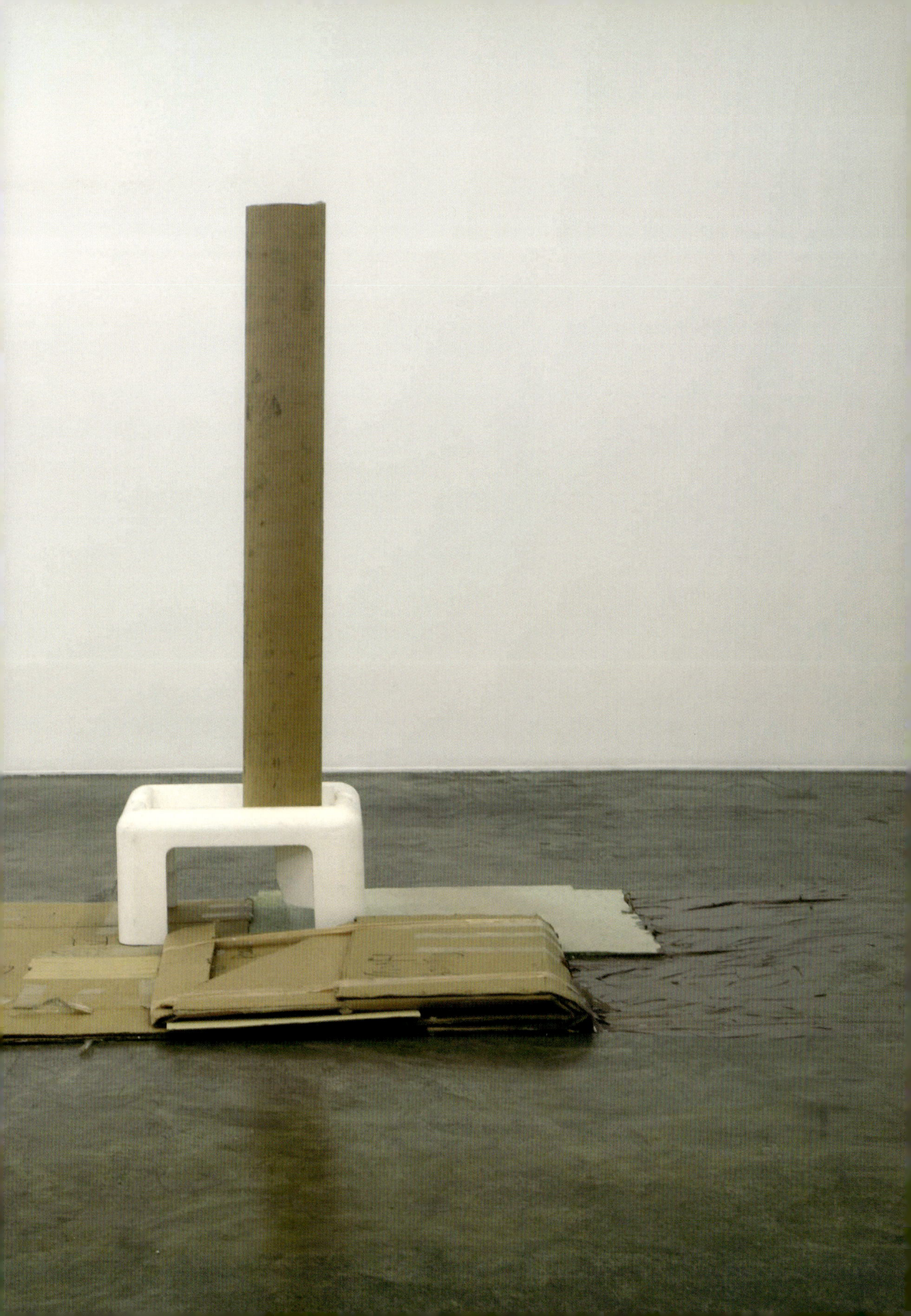

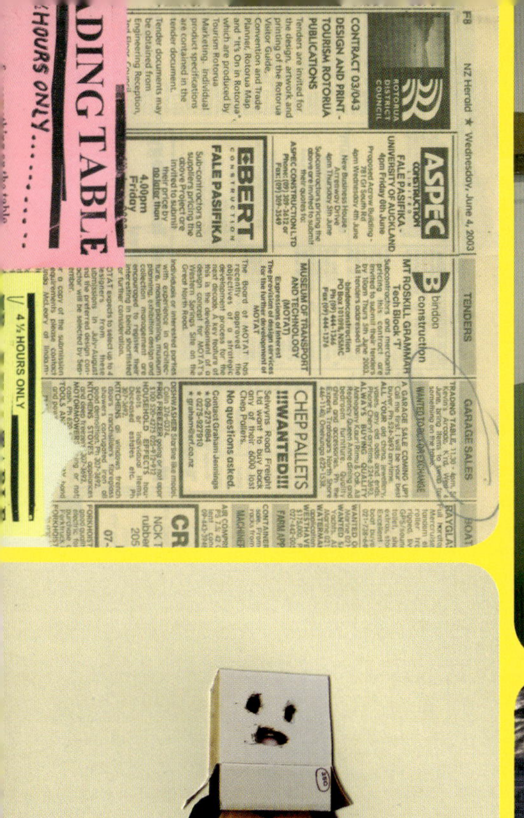
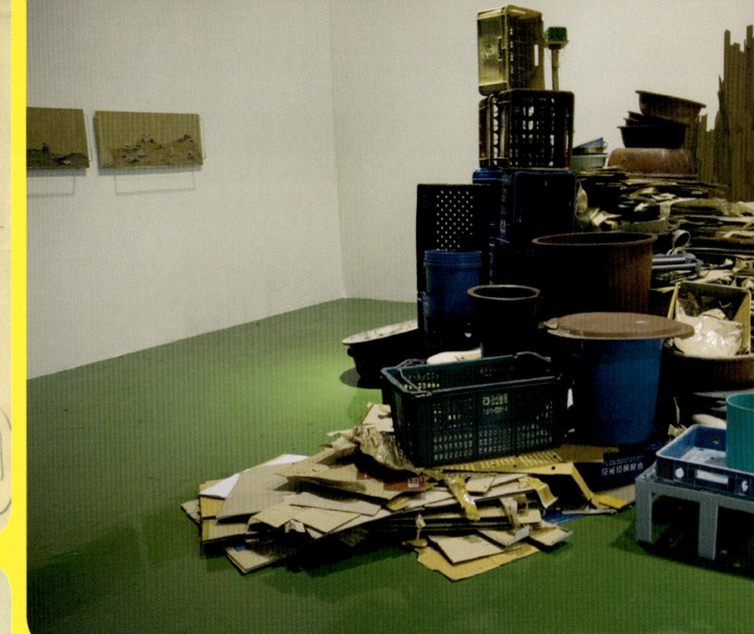
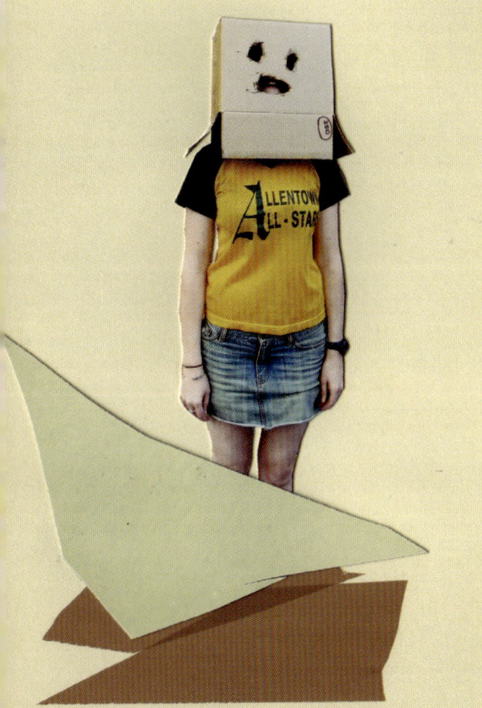
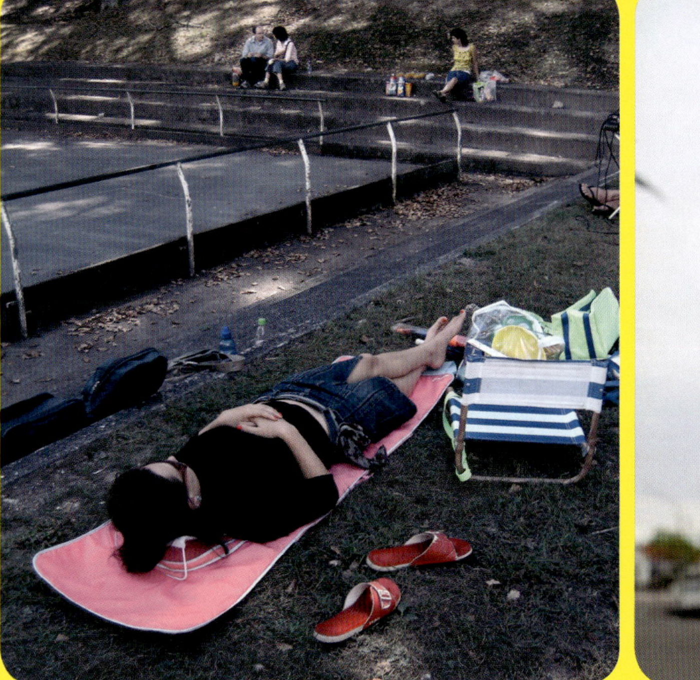
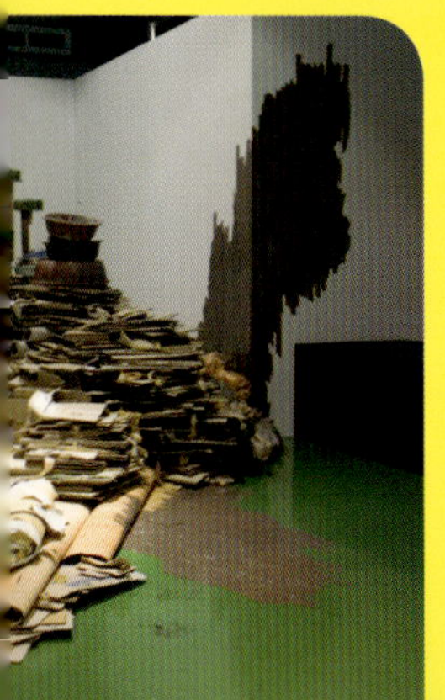
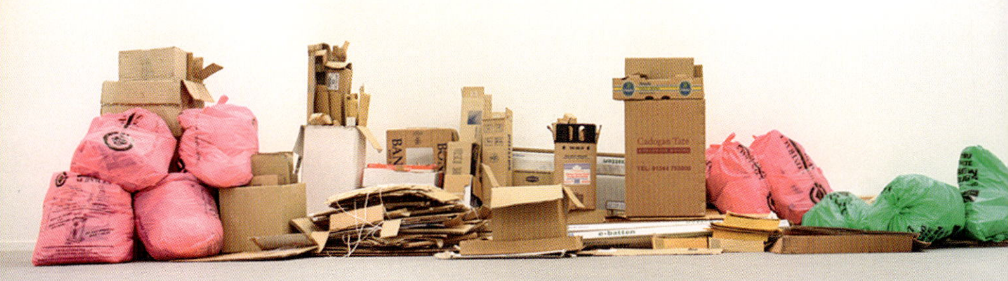

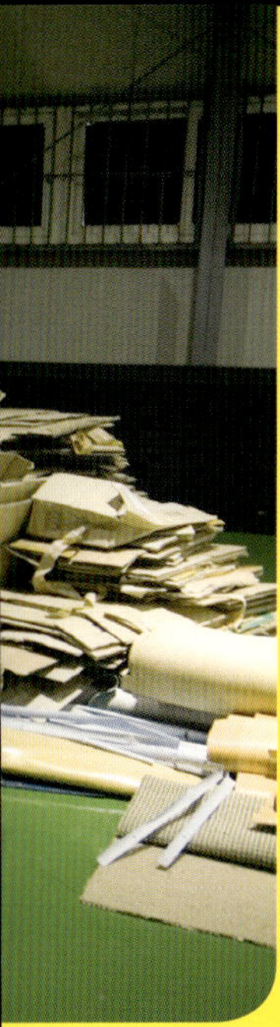

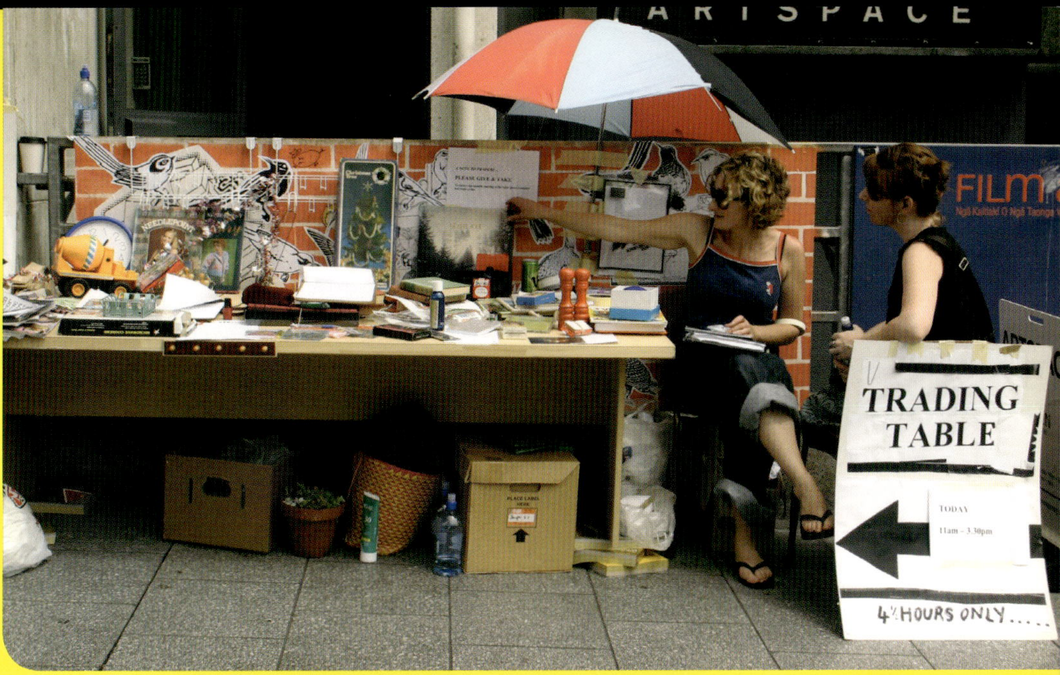

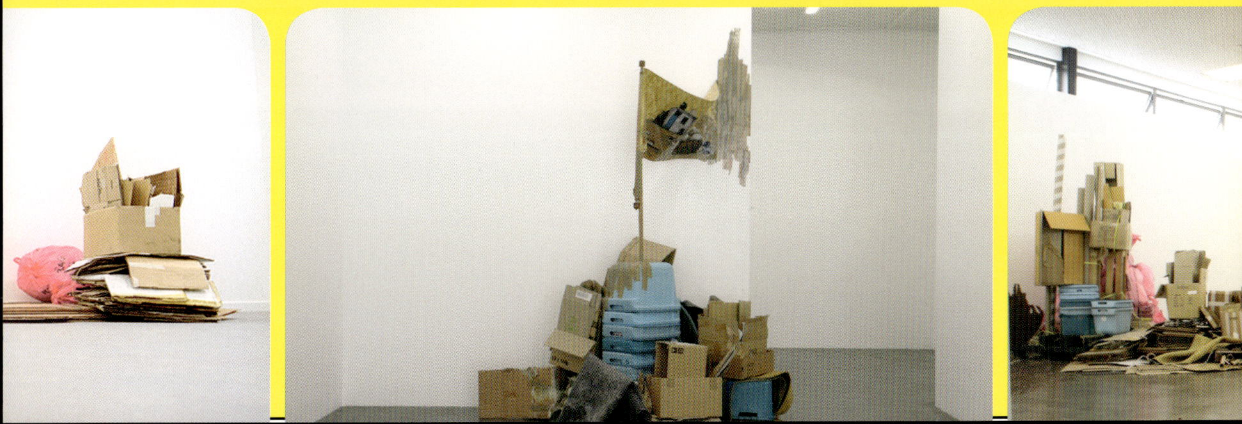
ARTSPACE
TRADING
TABLE
TODAY
11am – 3.30pm
4½ HOURS ONLY.....
FILM
OT DEP

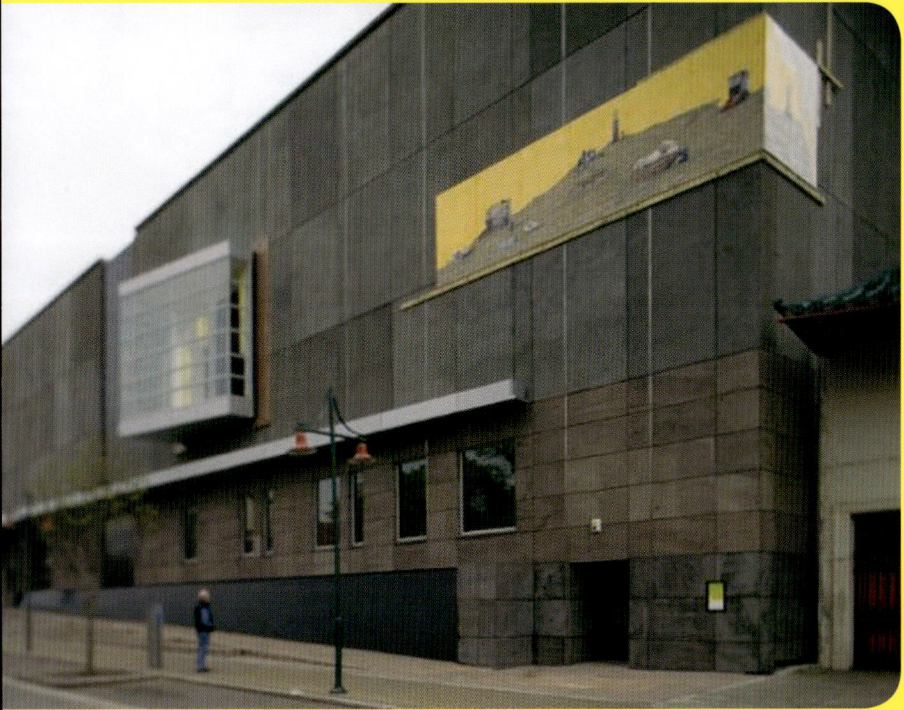

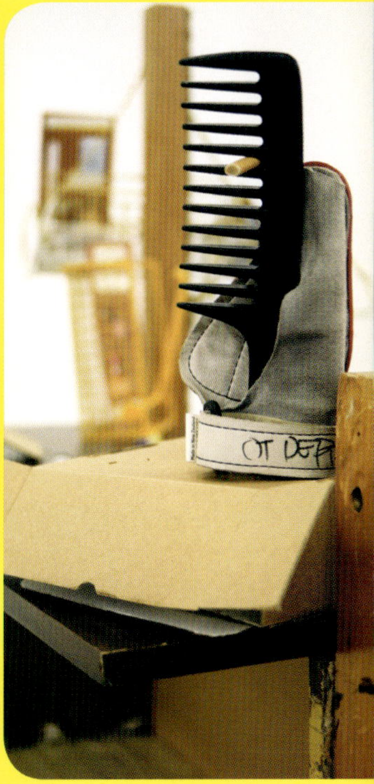

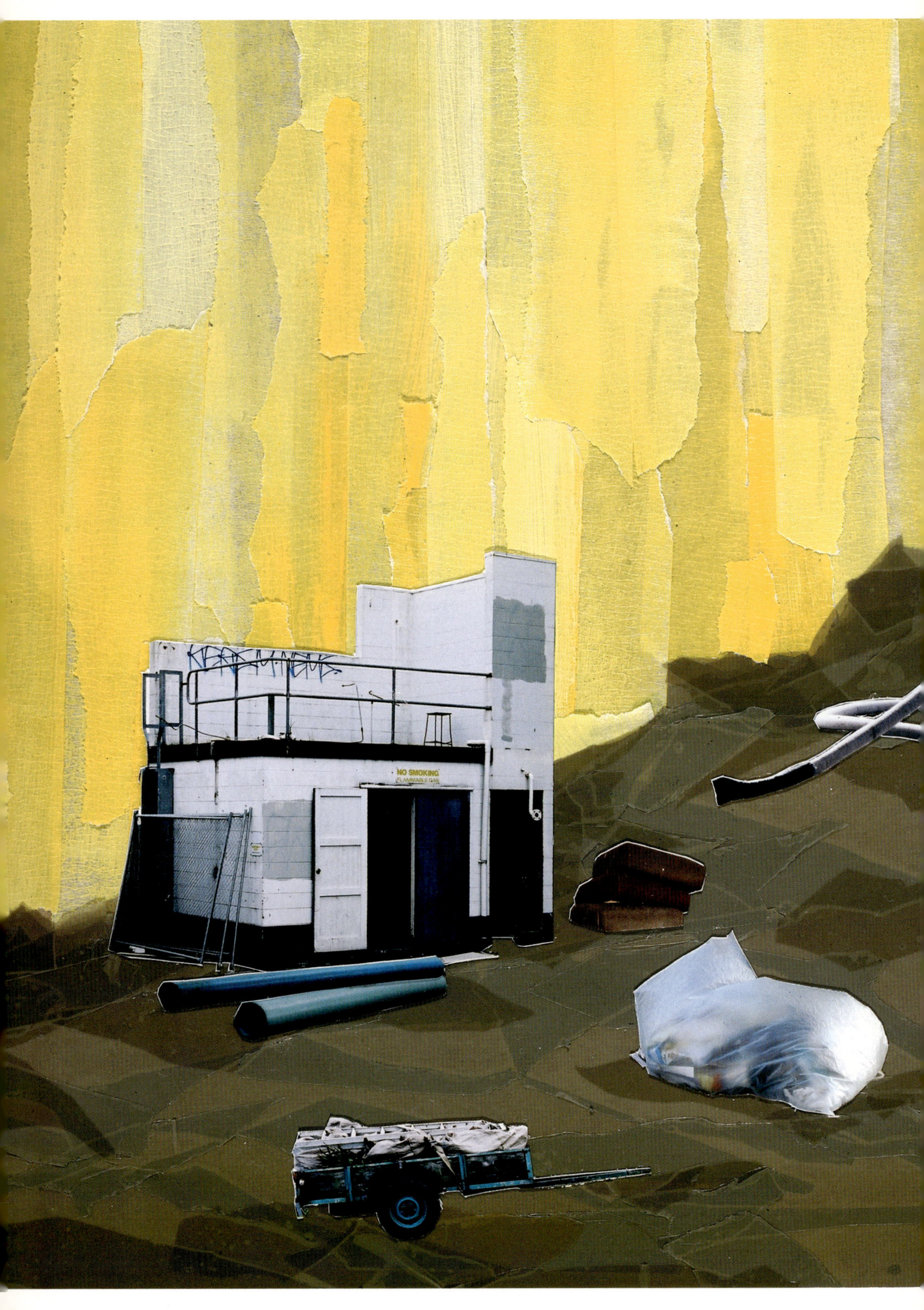

NO SMOKING
FLAMMABLE GAS

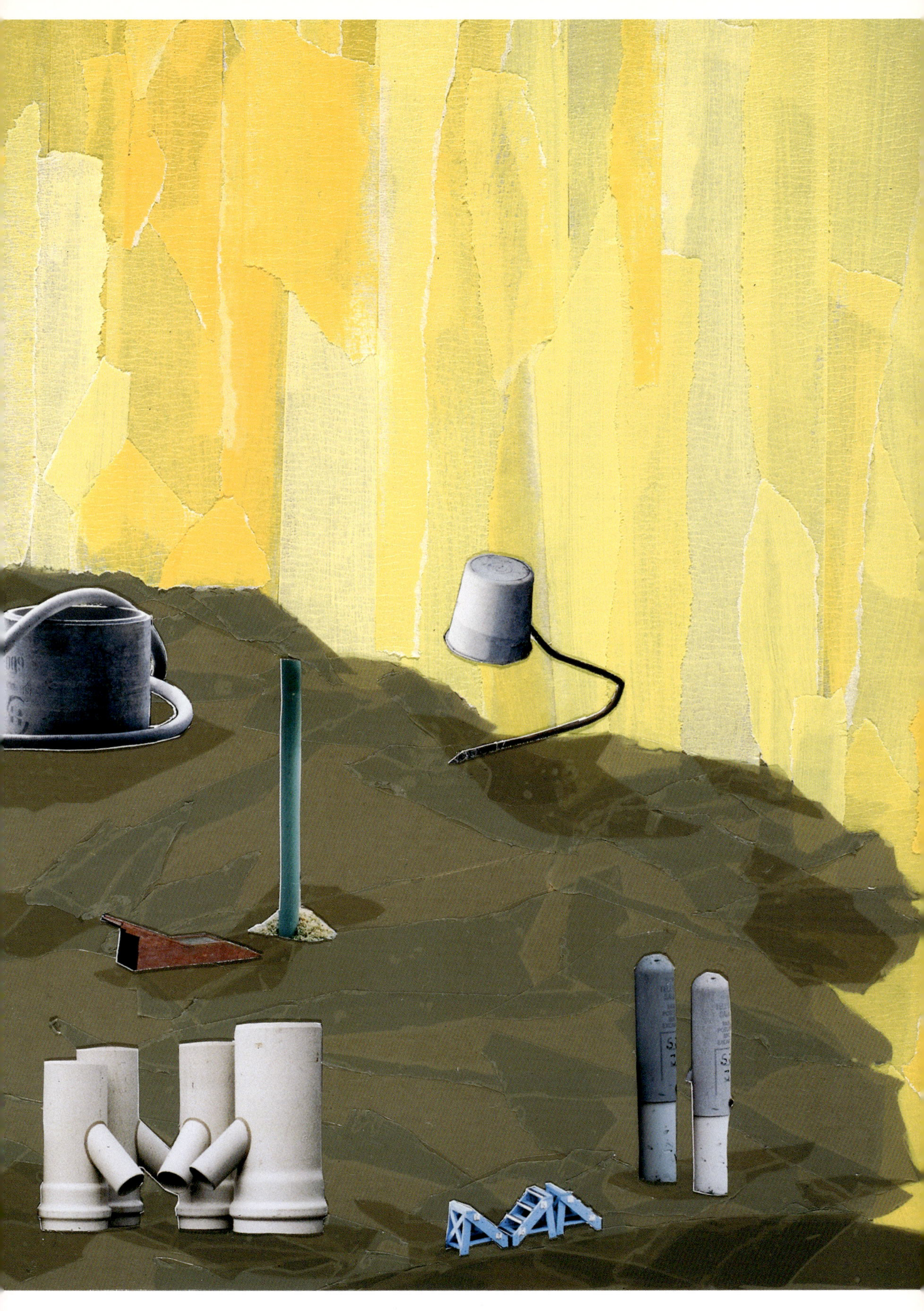

Saskia Leek

134	135	136	137	138	139
Milk Air System 2007 280 x 360mm oil on board	*Strait Arrows* 1997 280 x 360mm oil on board	*Like Sleep in Fog* 2007 280 x 360mm oil on board	*Sinker Park* 2007 280 x 360mm oil on board	*Mystic Eyes* 2007 280 x 360mm oil on board	*Lady Head* 2007 285 x 385mm oil on board

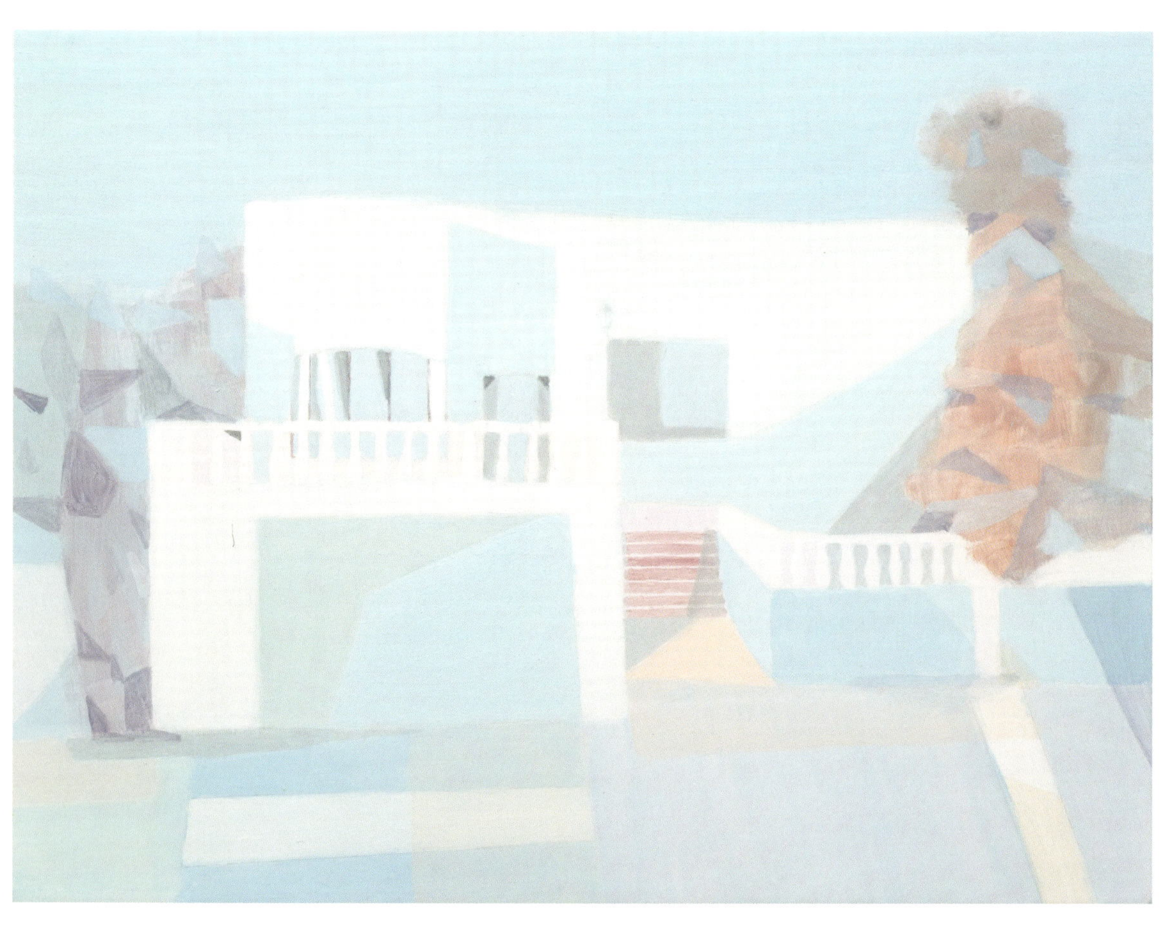

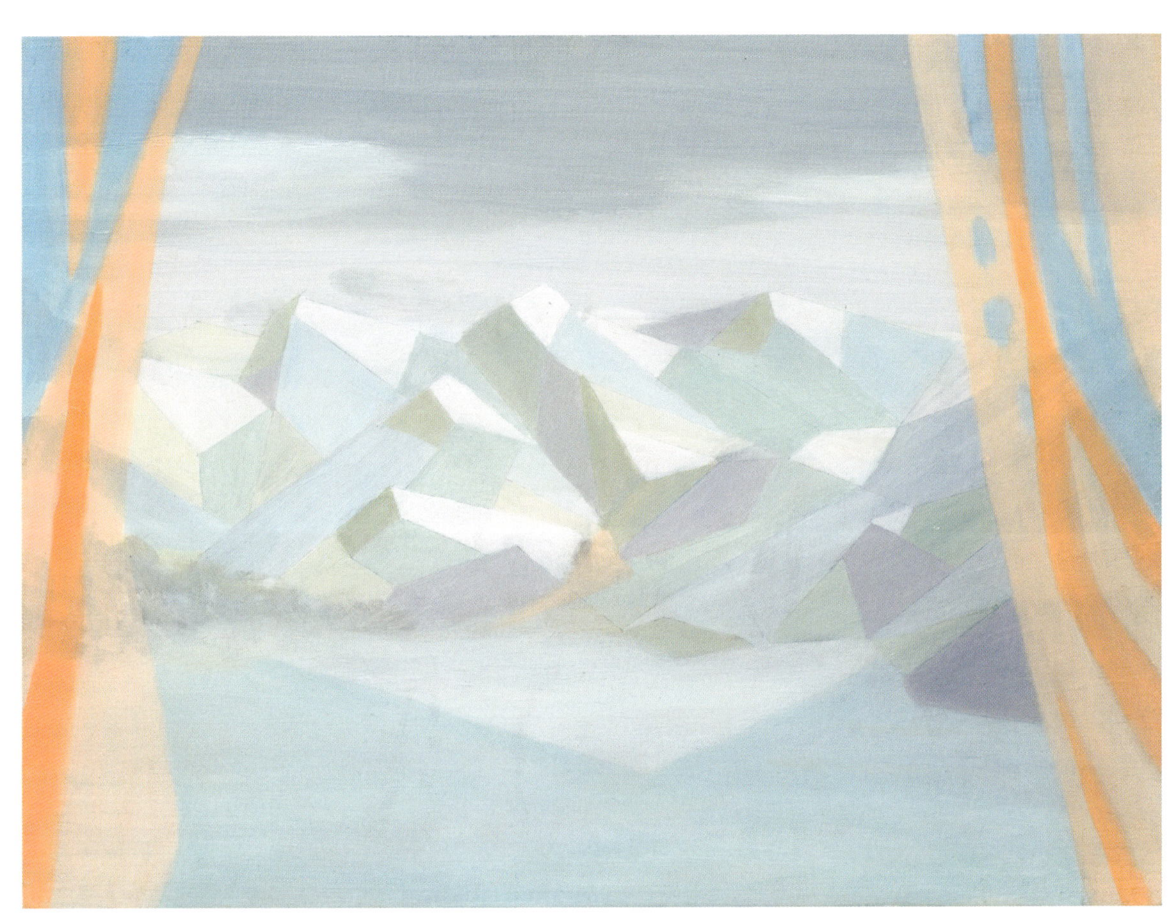

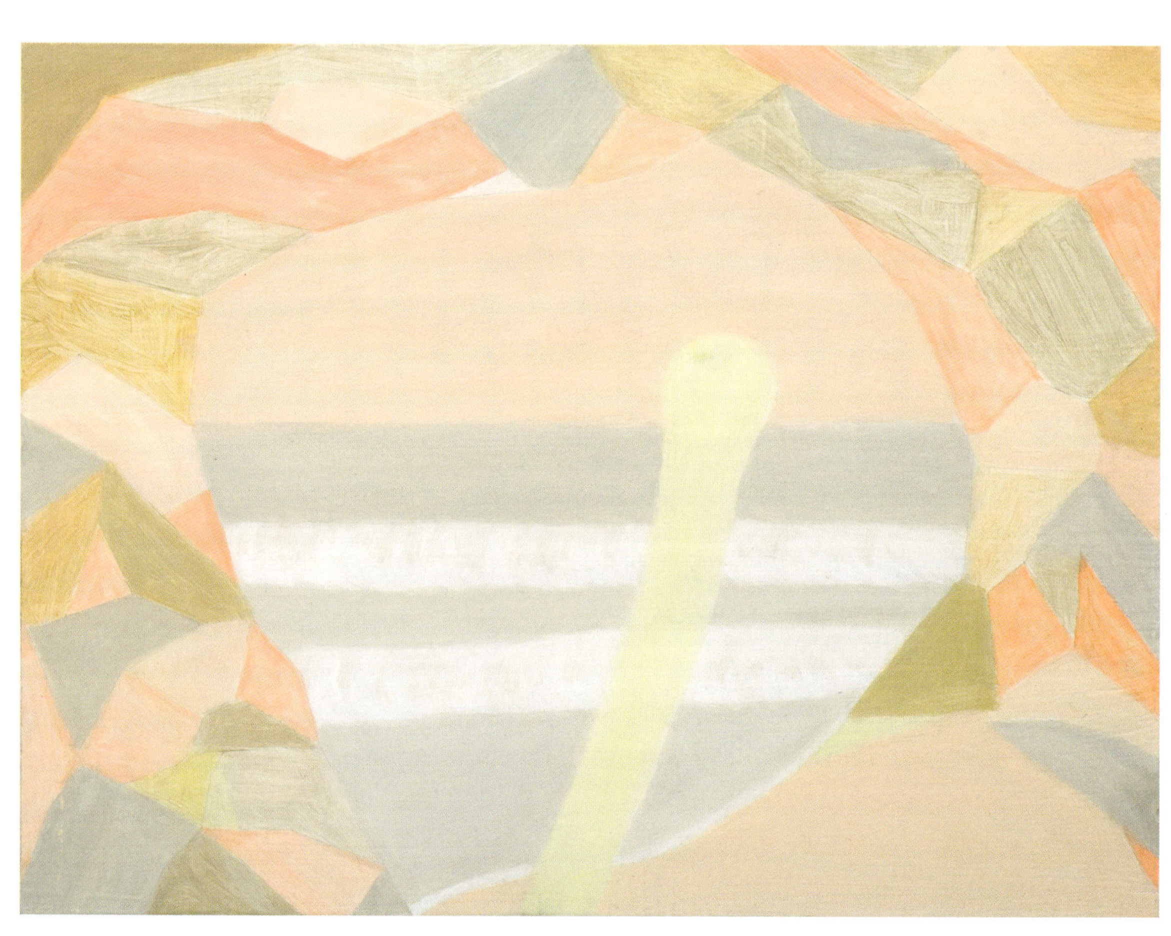

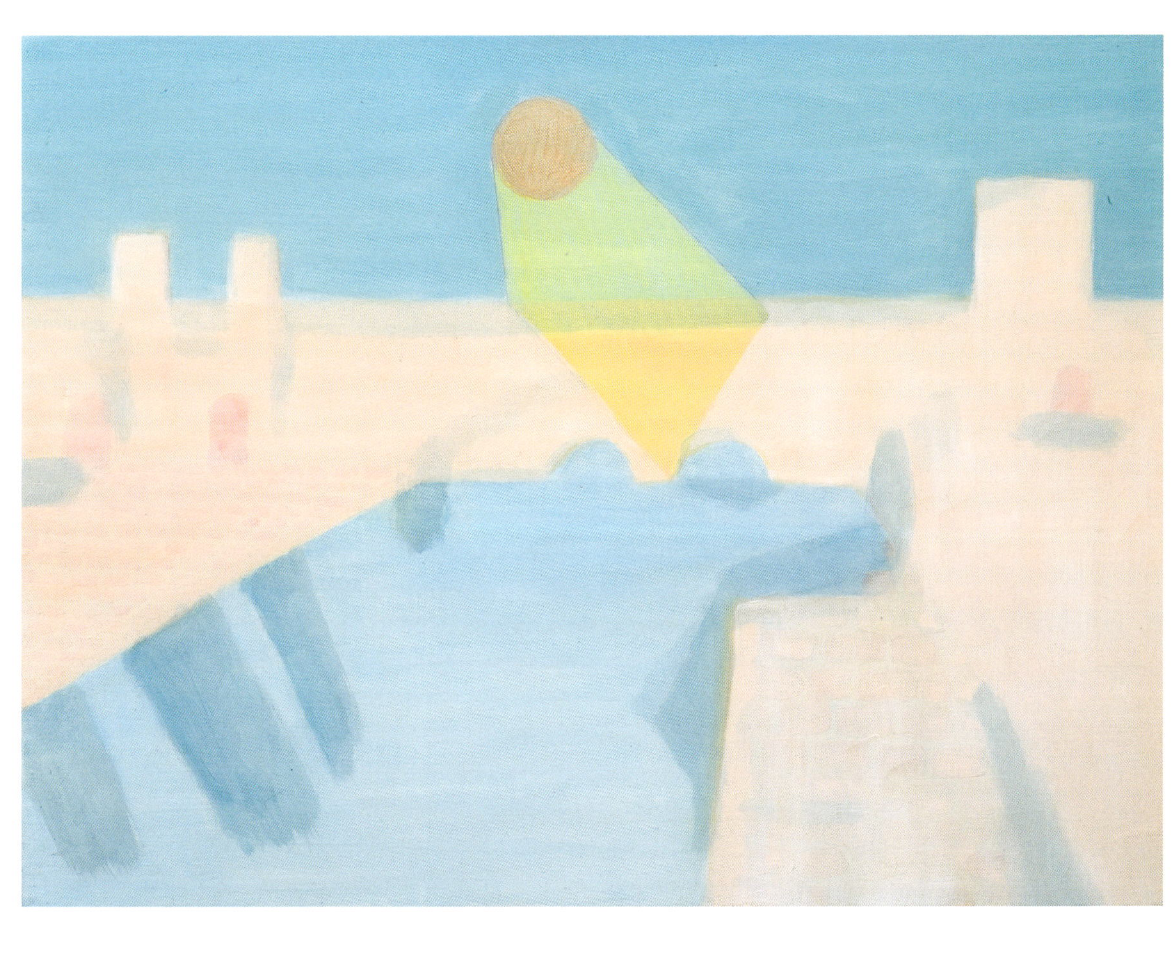

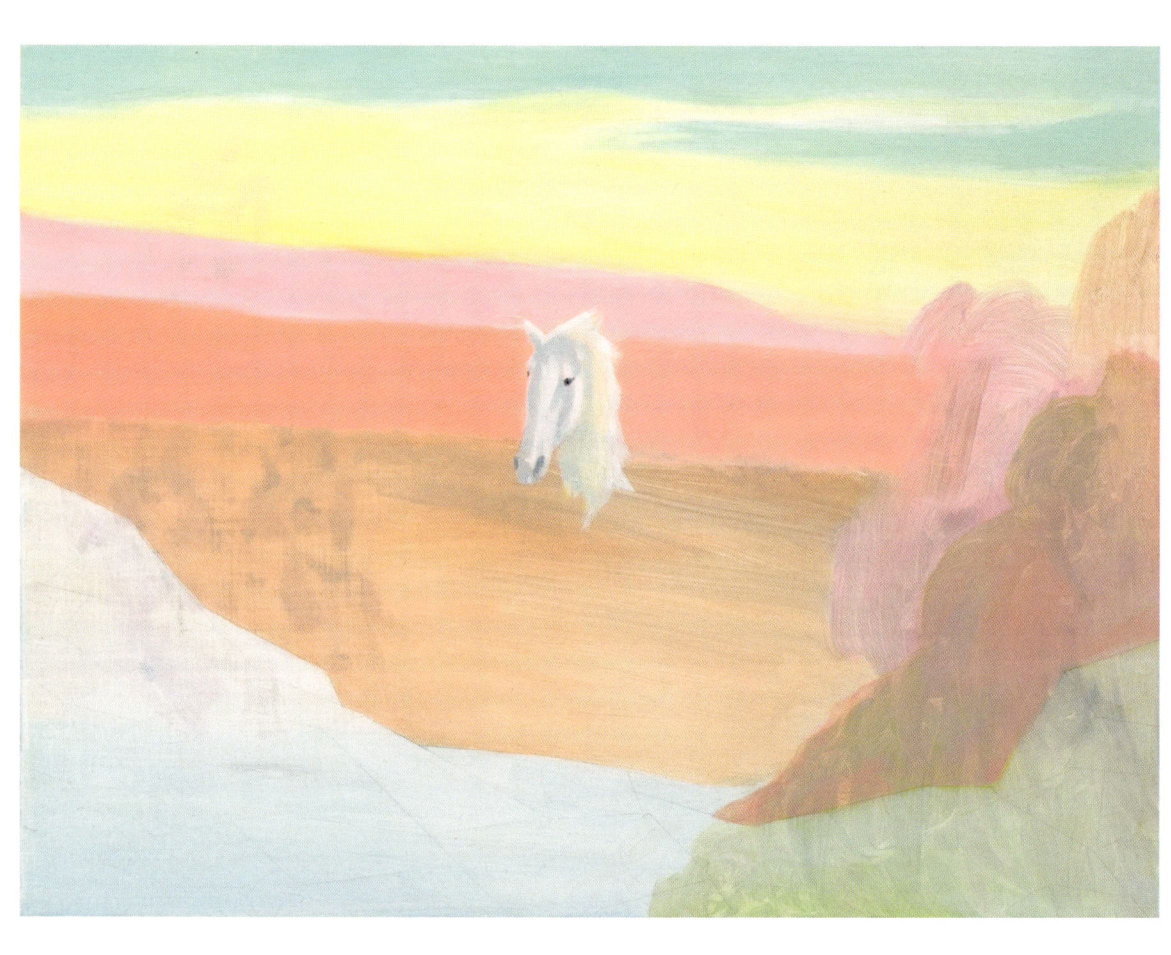

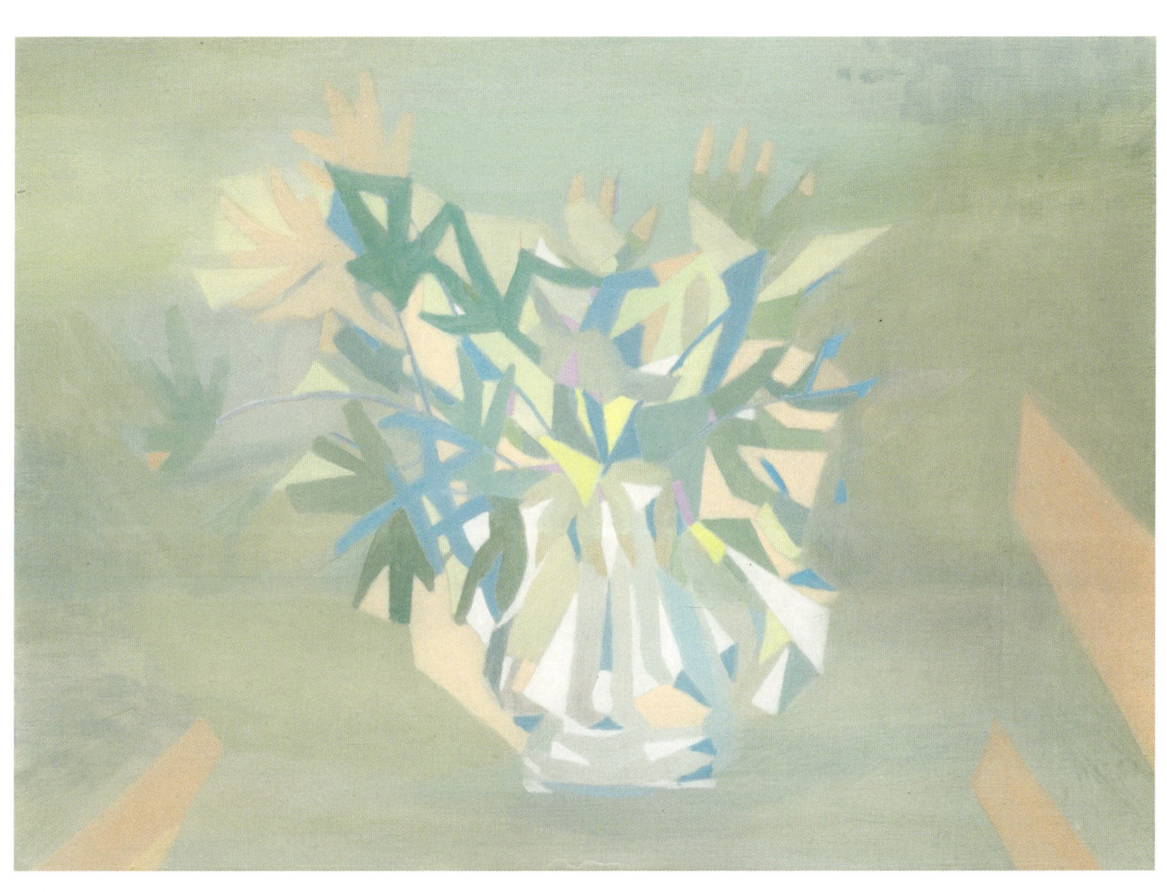

Fiona Amundsen

Lynn Mall City, Auckland, 26/03/2006, 6.25 (Three Shadows)

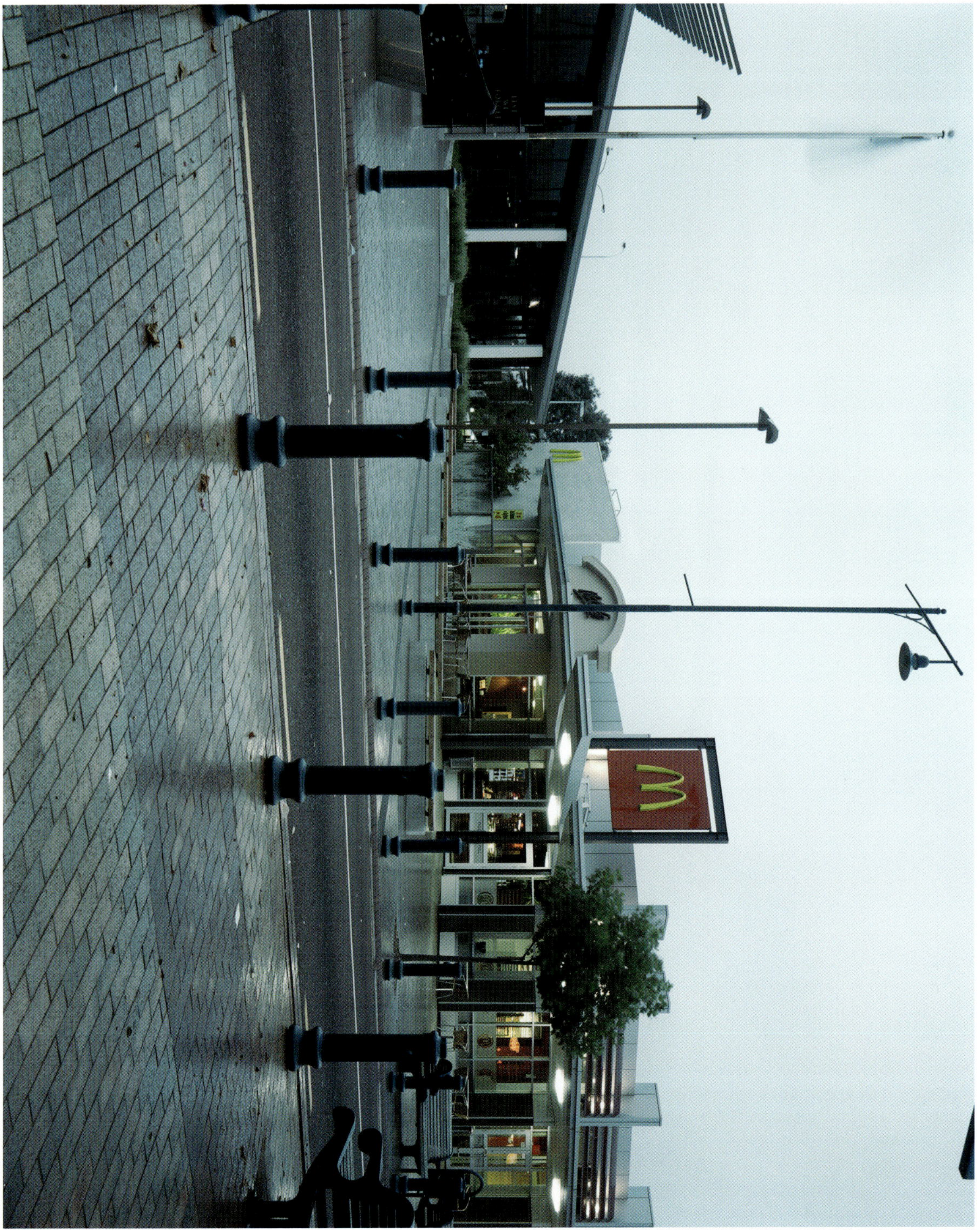

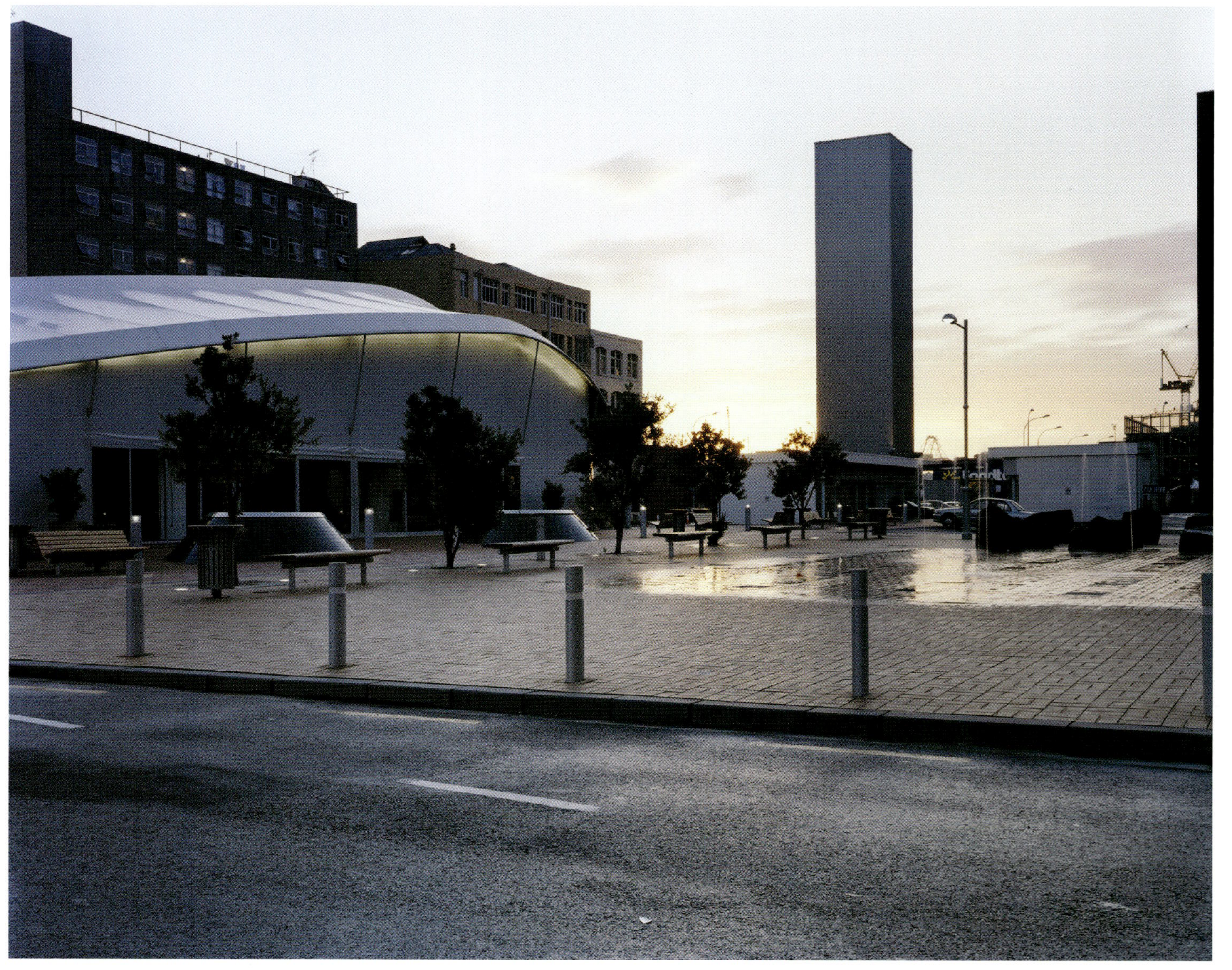

Galway Street (facing East), Auckland, 17/09/2006, 6.33 (Wet Paving Stones)

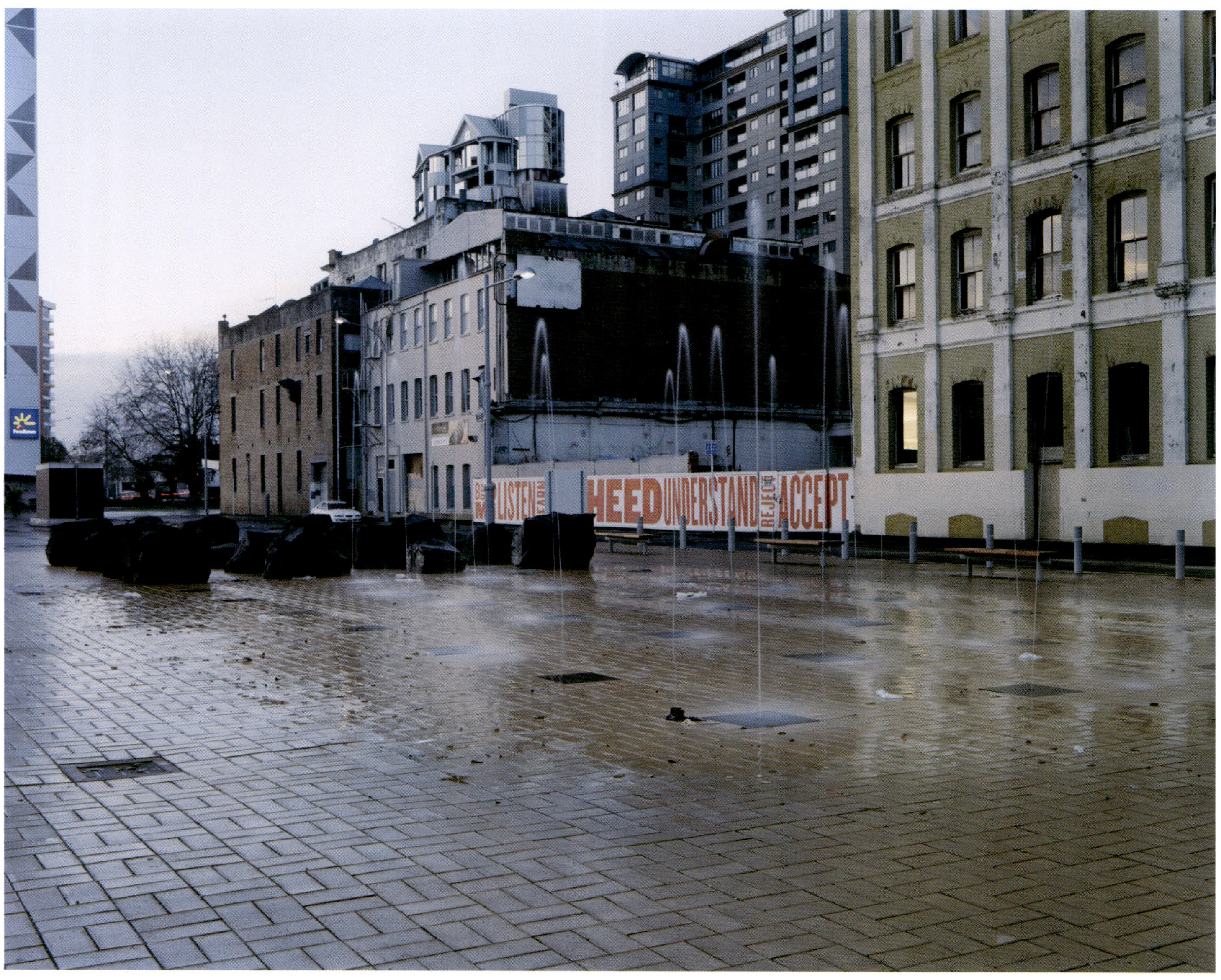

Galway Street (facing North), Auckland, 25/09/2006, 6.45 (Golden Window)

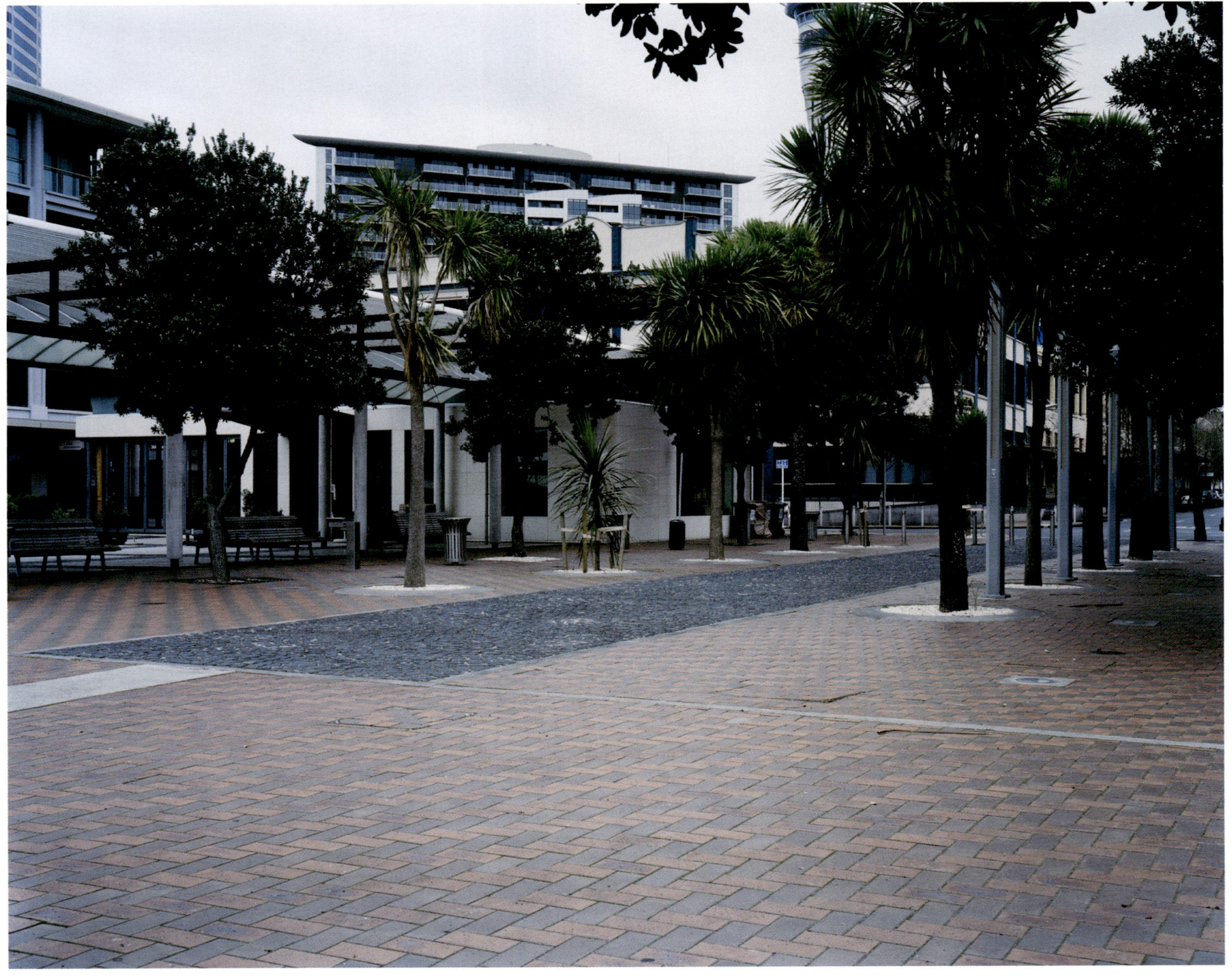

Market Square, Auckland, 15/09/2006, 6.38 (Leaf Pattern)

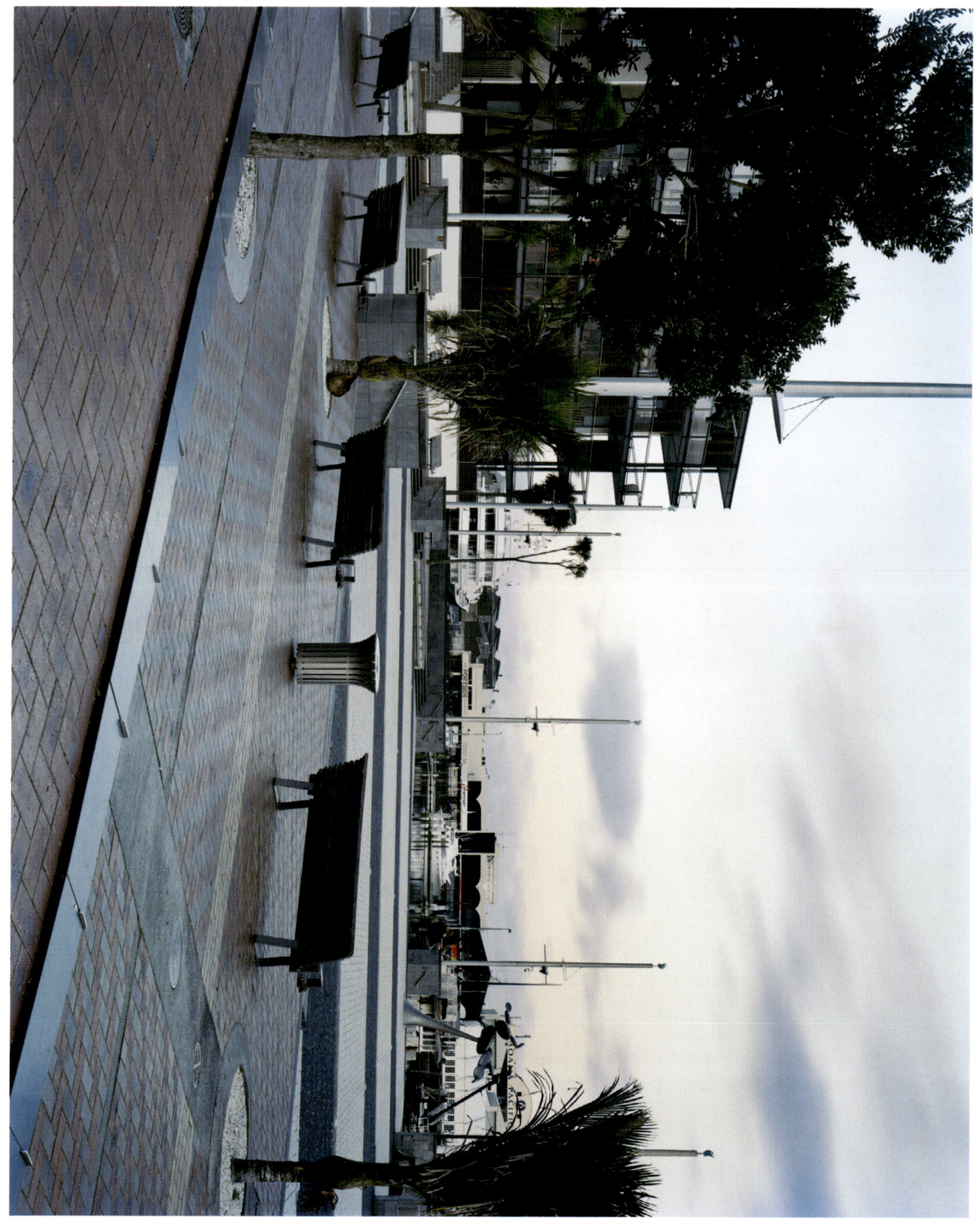

Waitemata Plaza, Auckland, 24/09/2006, 6.40 (Flare)

Michael Parekowhai

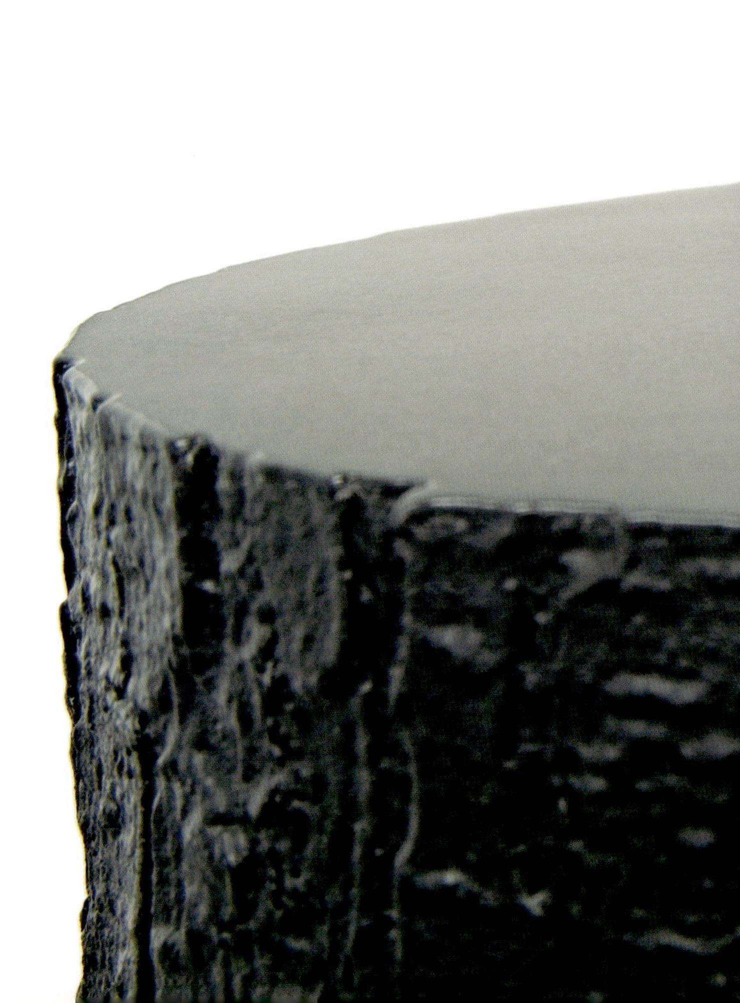

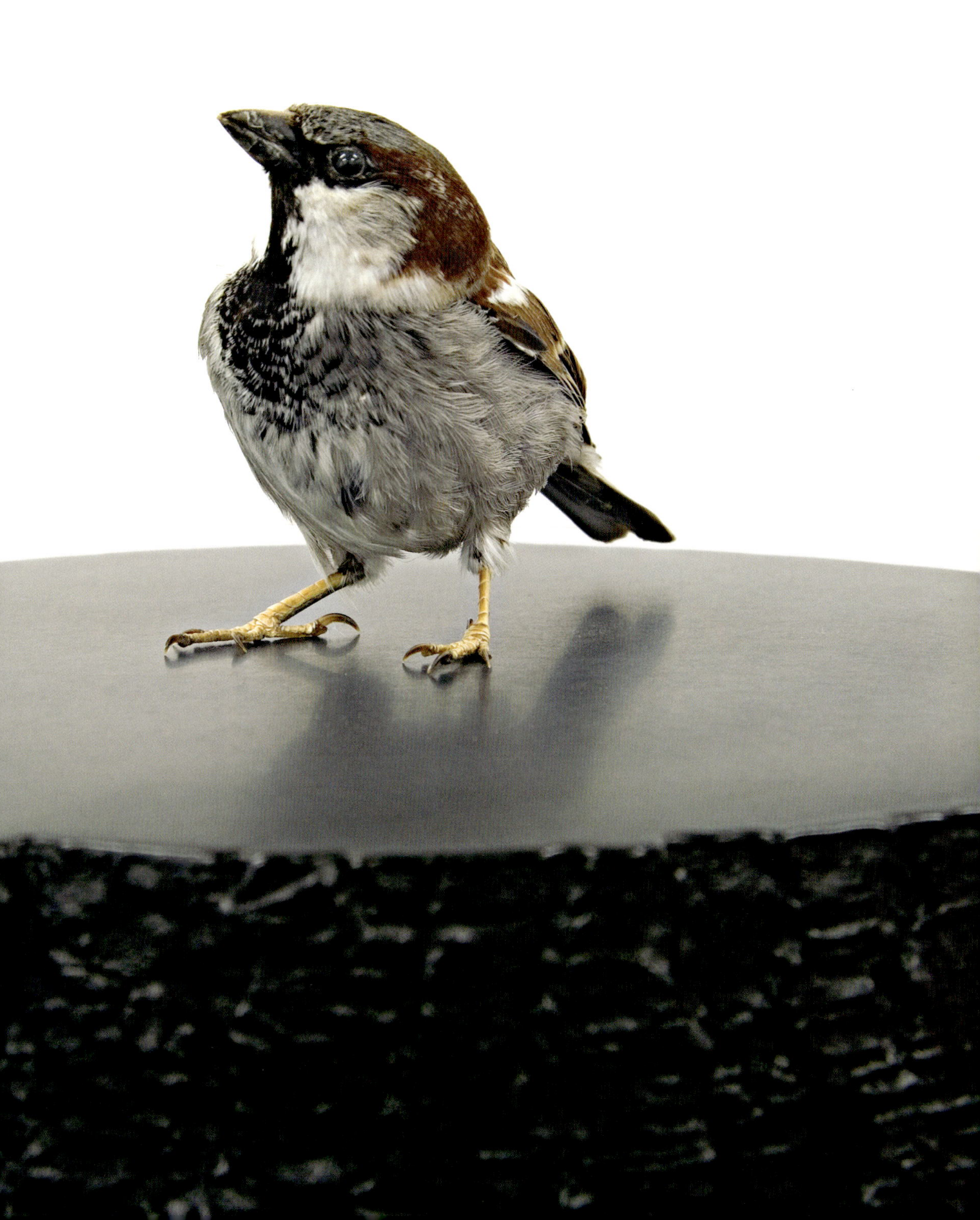

Billy Apple™

A History of the Brand

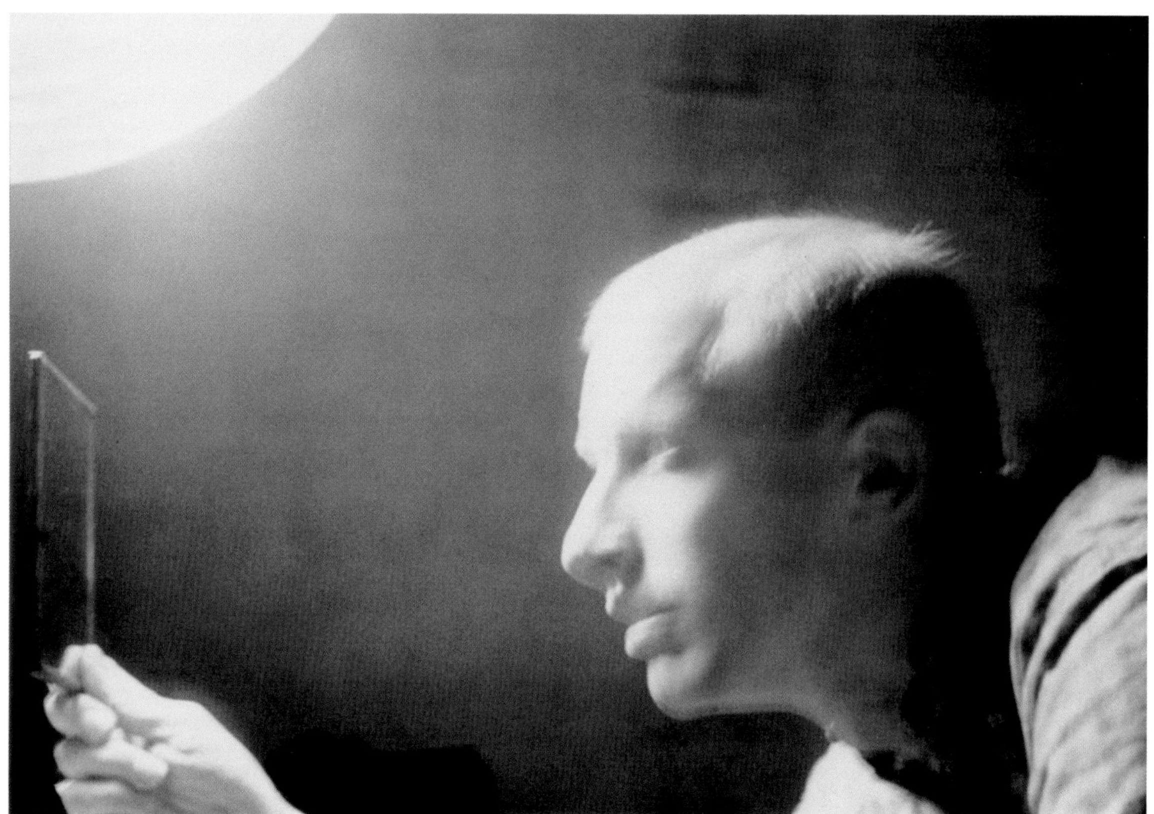

Barrie Bates, *Billy Apple Bleaching with Lady Clairol Instant Crème Whip, November 1962*

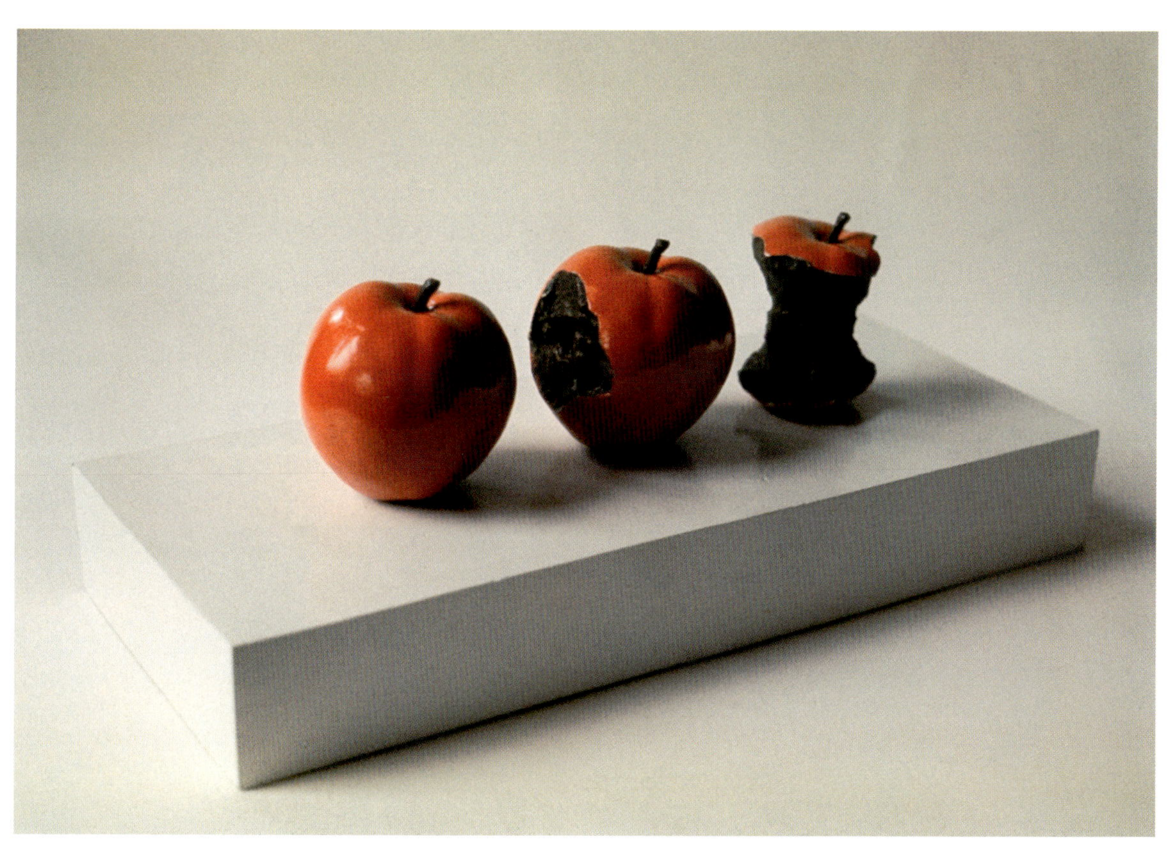

2 Minutes, 33 Seconds (Red), 1962. Painted bronze. Private collection, New Jersey.
Exhibited in *Apple Sees Red: Live Stills*, 1963, Gallery One, London

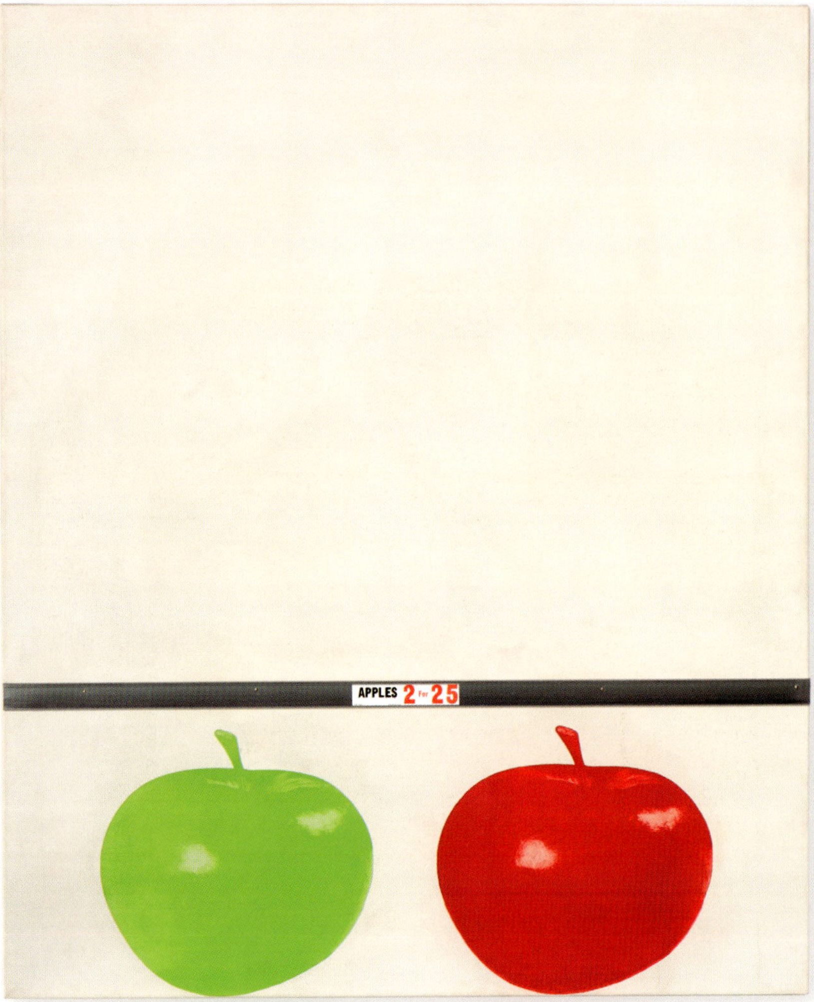

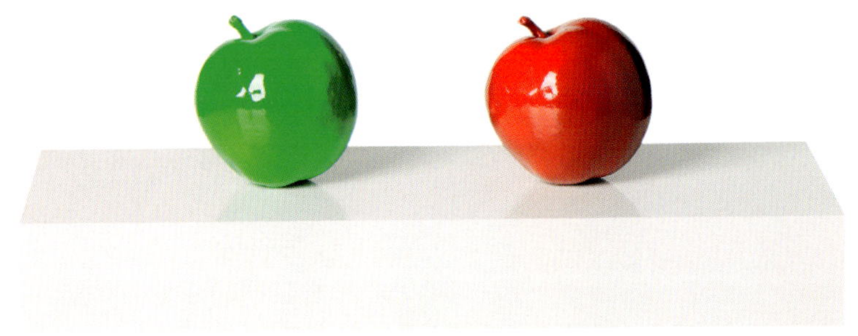

Apples, 2 for 25¢, 1962-1964. Offset lithograph on canvas with aluminum strip and printed plastic label. Collection of Museum of New Zealand Te Papa Tongarewa. First exhibited as *Green/Red Apples For Sale*, 1962 in *Apple Sees Red: Live Stills*, 1963, Gallery One, London. Later modified and retitled for *American Supermarket*, 1964, Bianchini Gallery, New York and Gallerie Il Segno, Rome, 1965

Apples (Green and Red), 1962. Painted bronze. Collection of Museum of New Zealand Te Papa Tongarewa

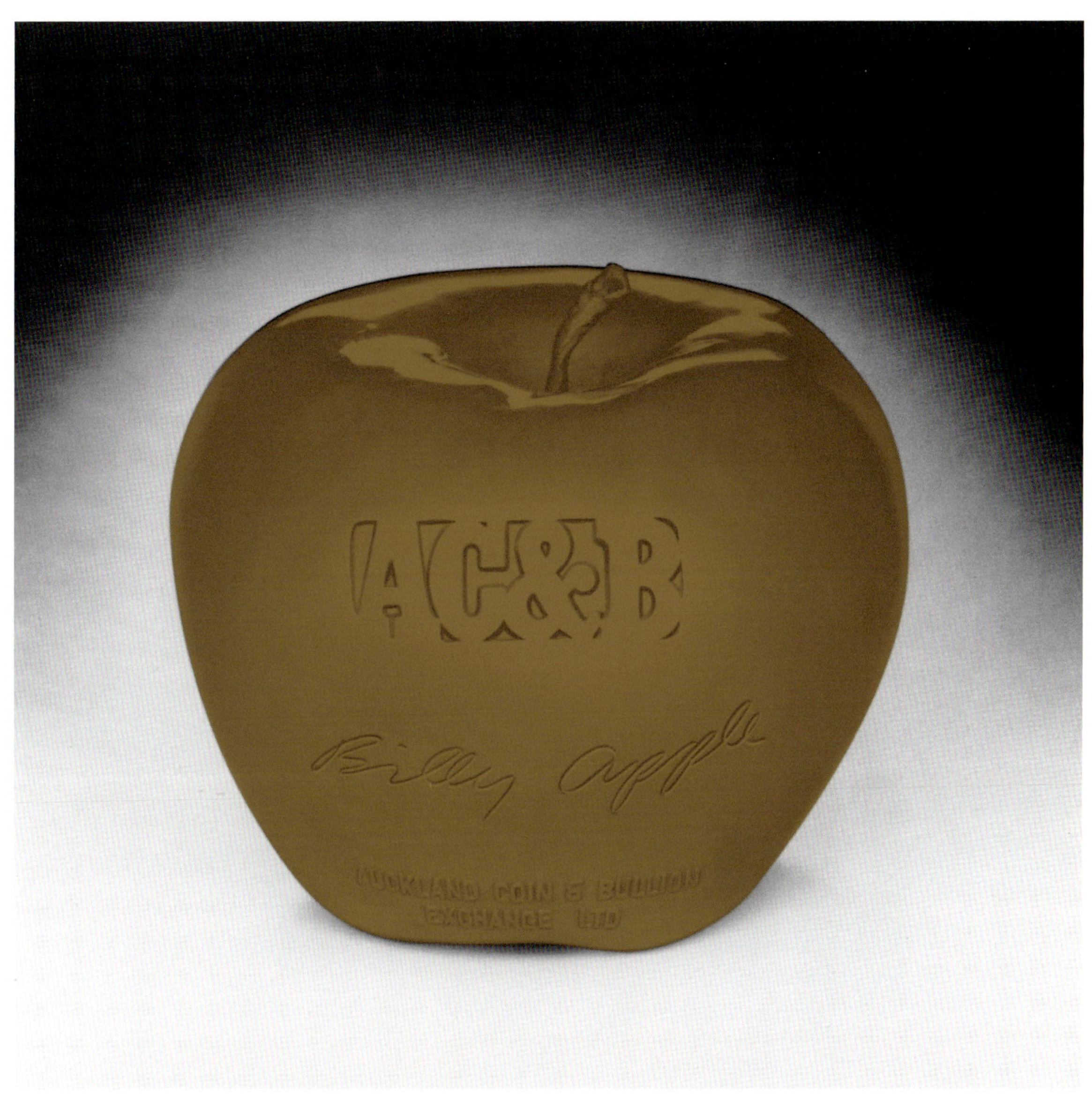

The Golden Apple, 1983. 103.599 ounces of pure gold. Private collection, Auckland.
Exhibited in *Apple Turns to Gold*, 1983, Auckland Coin and Bullion Exchange, Auckland

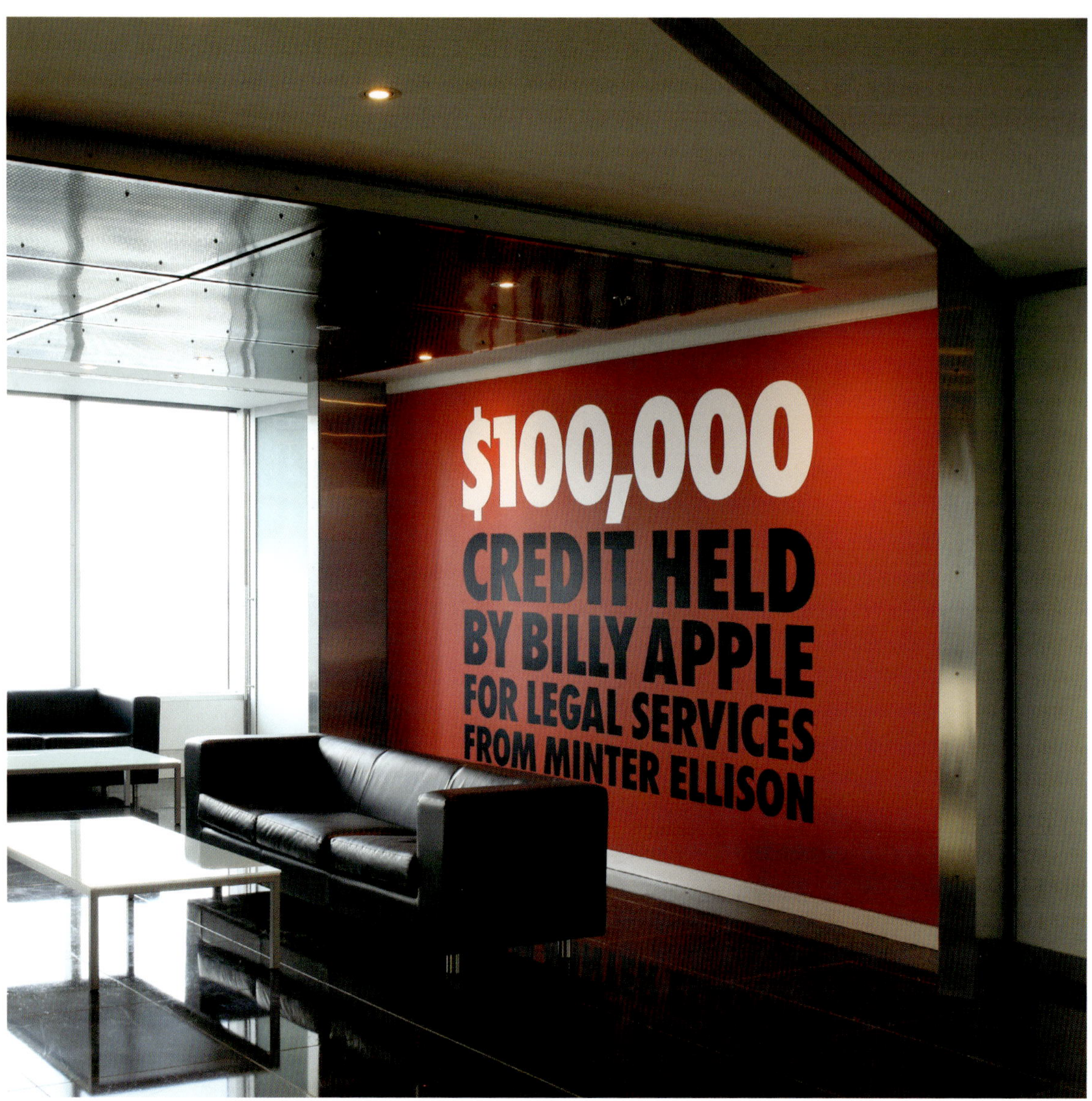

$100,000 *Credit Held*, 2005. Commissioned wall painting. Acrylic and vinyl text.
Collection of Minter Ellison Rudd Watts, Auckland

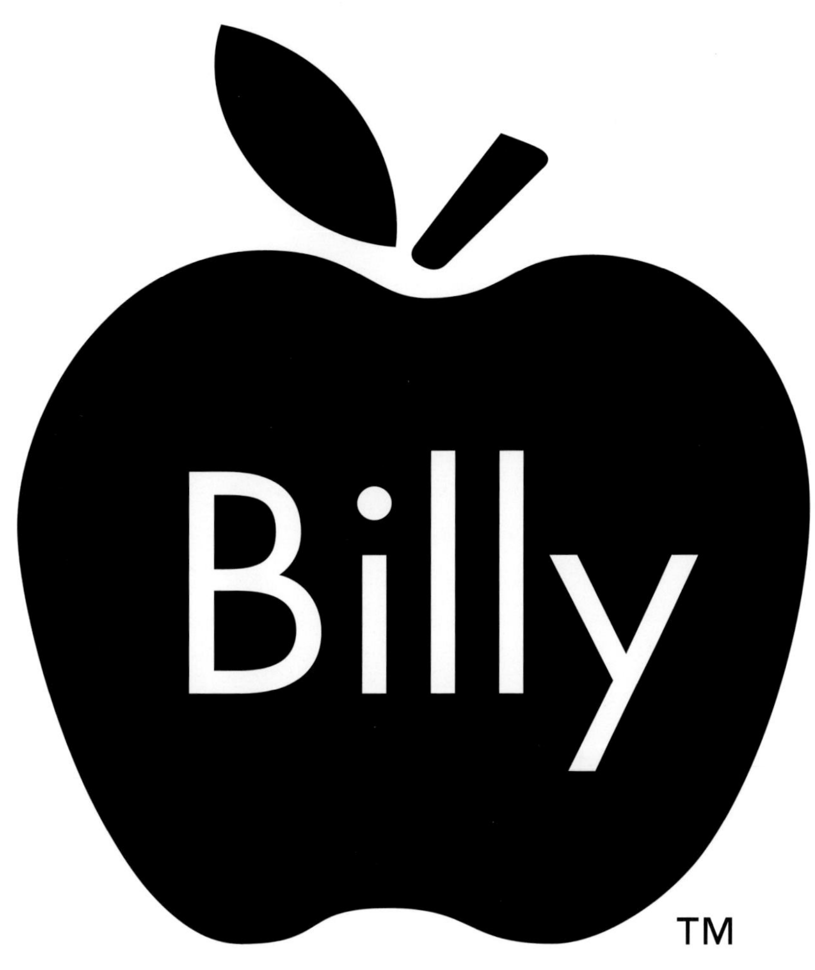

Trade Marked 29 March 2007

Yuk King Tan

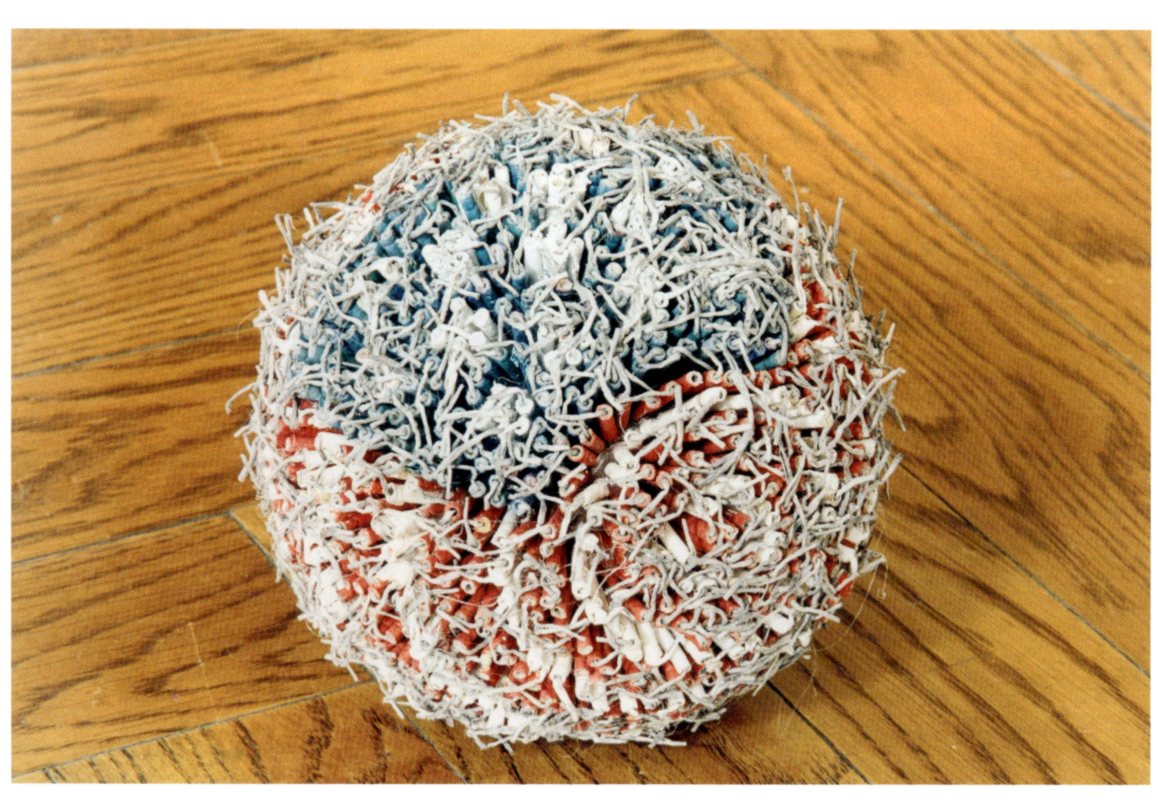

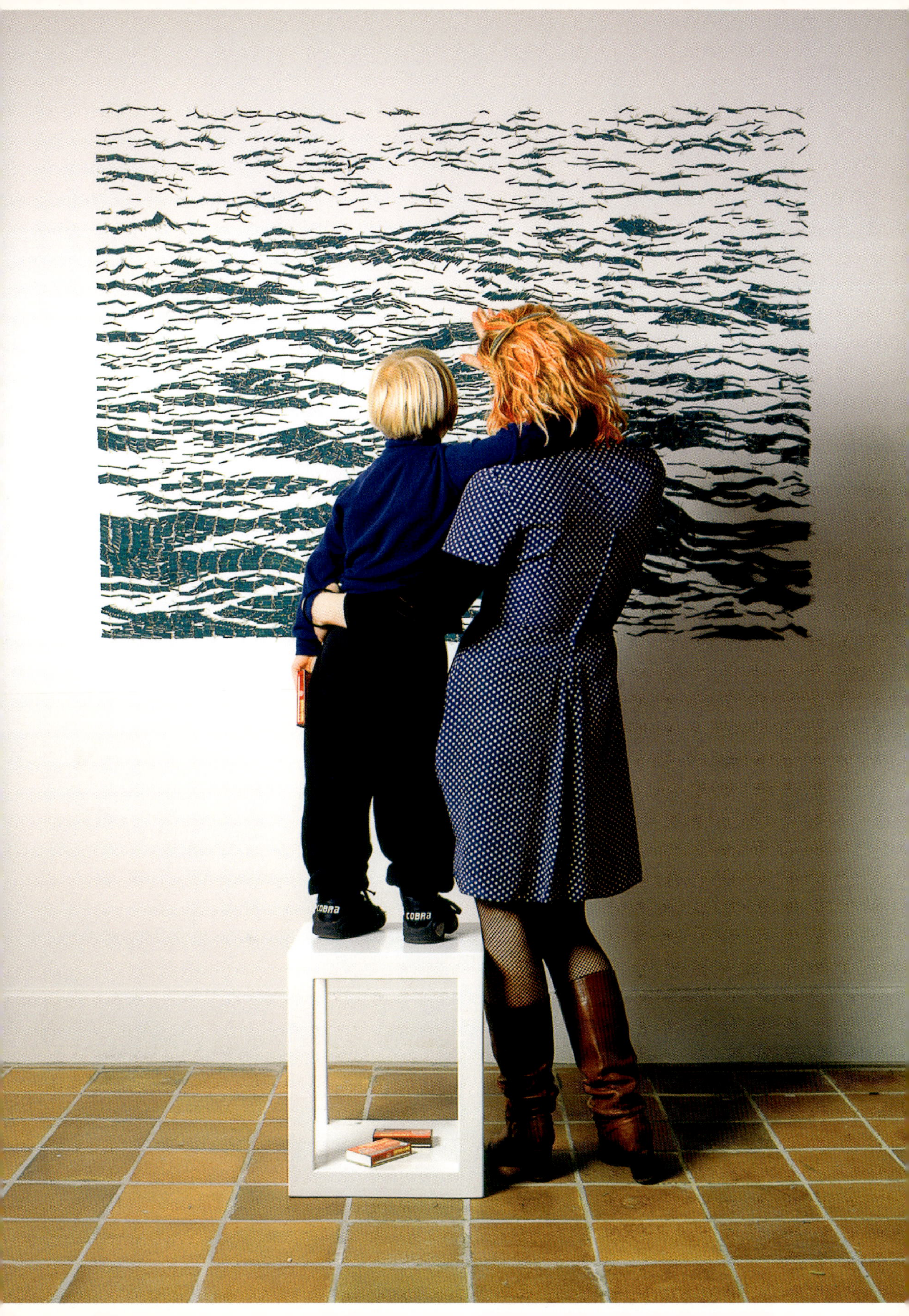

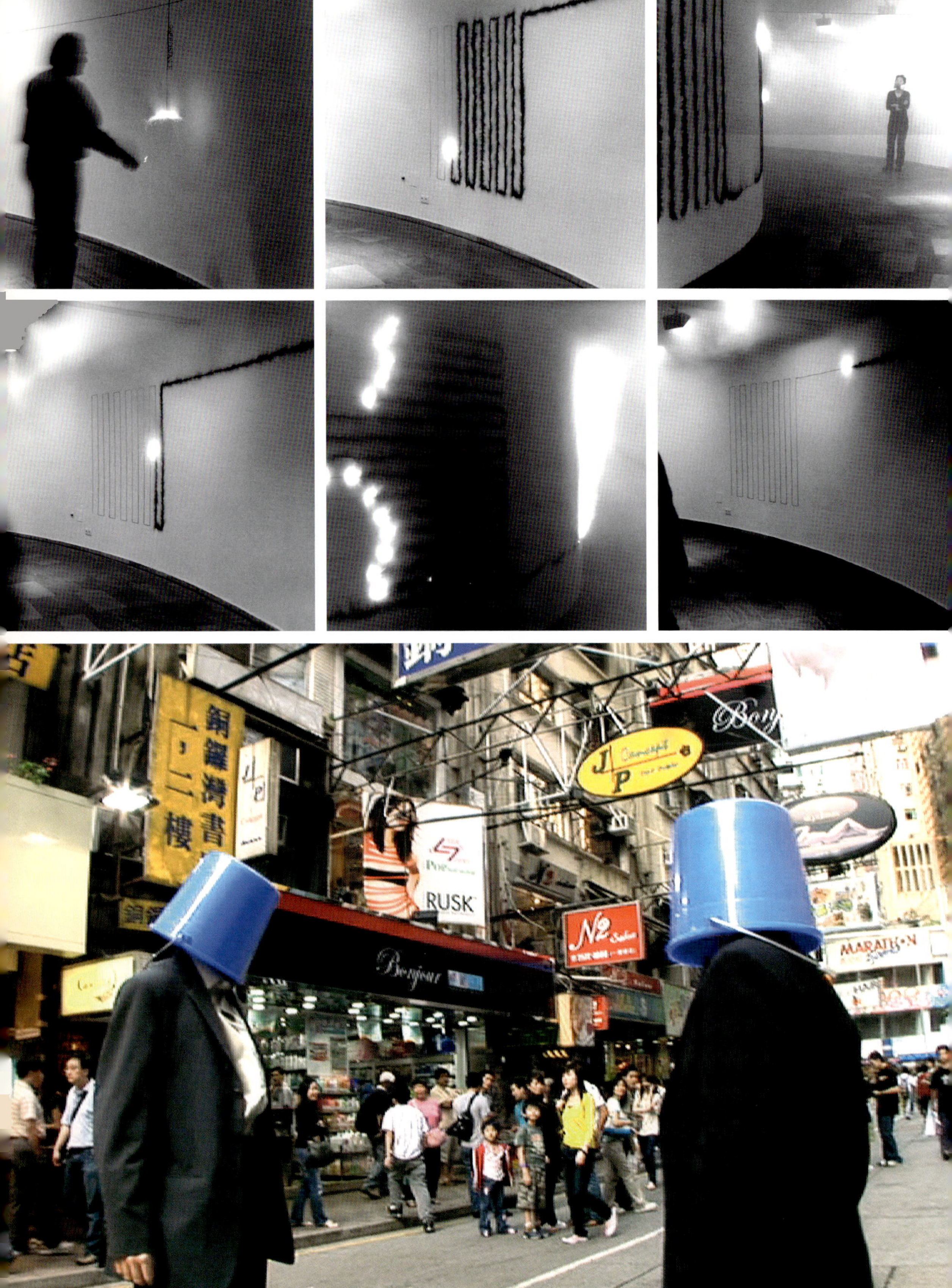

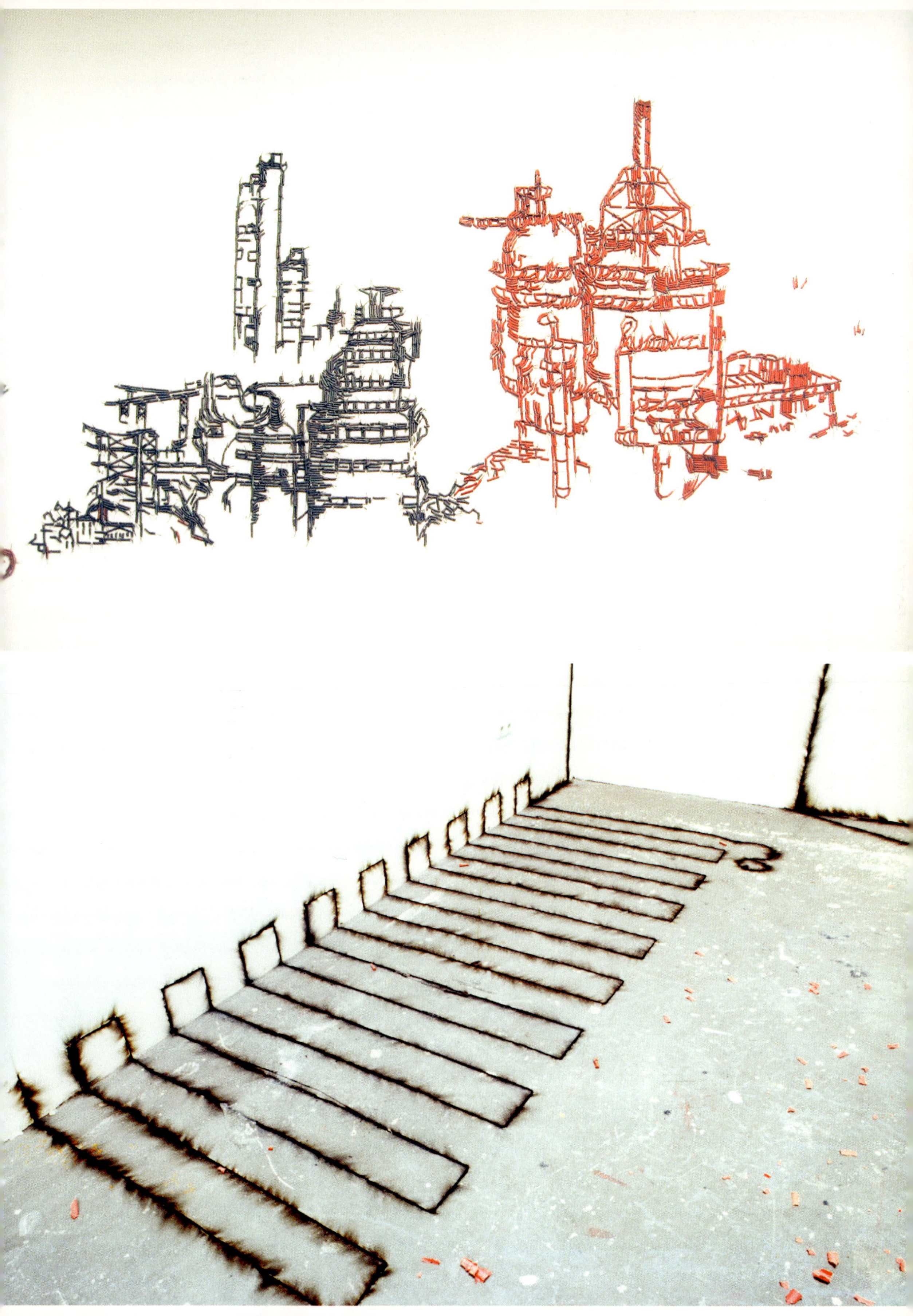

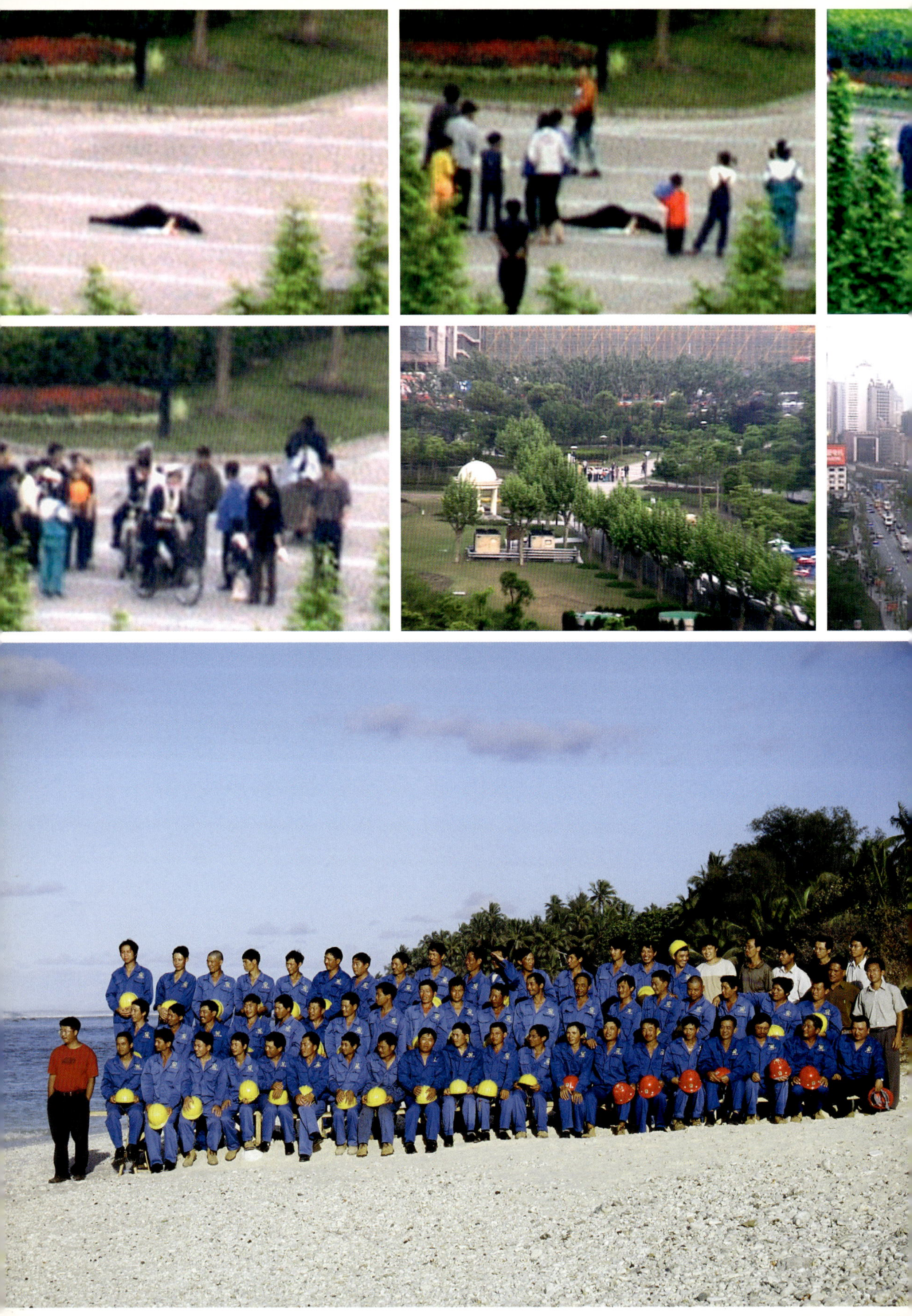

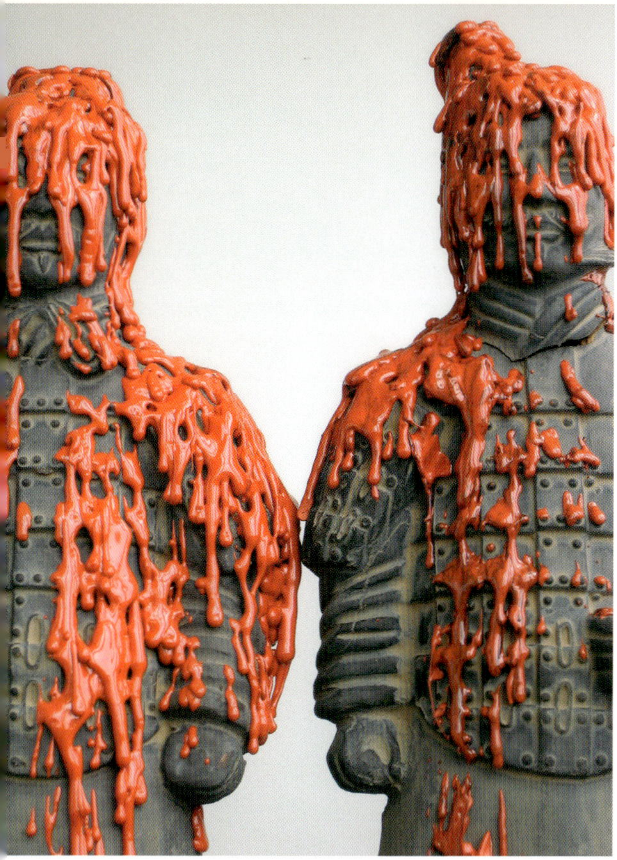

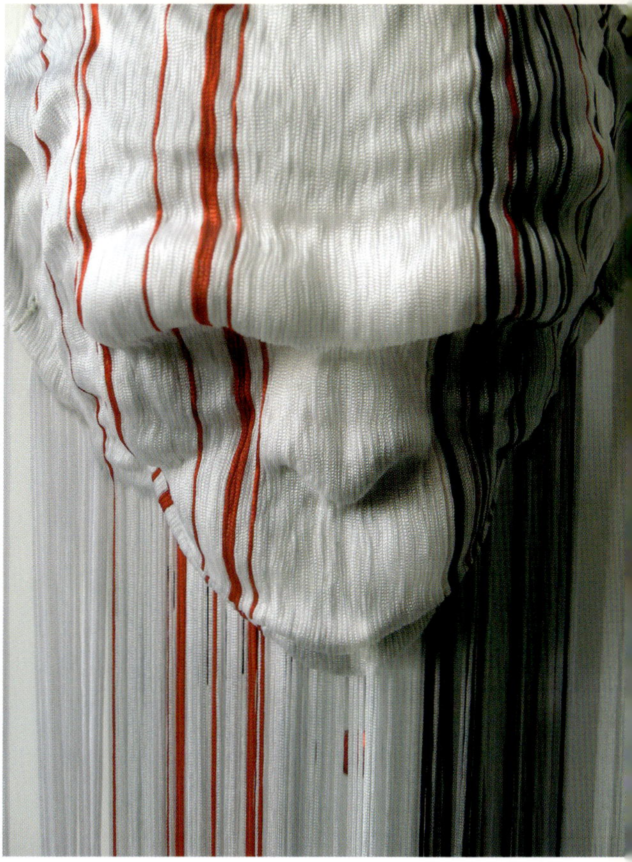

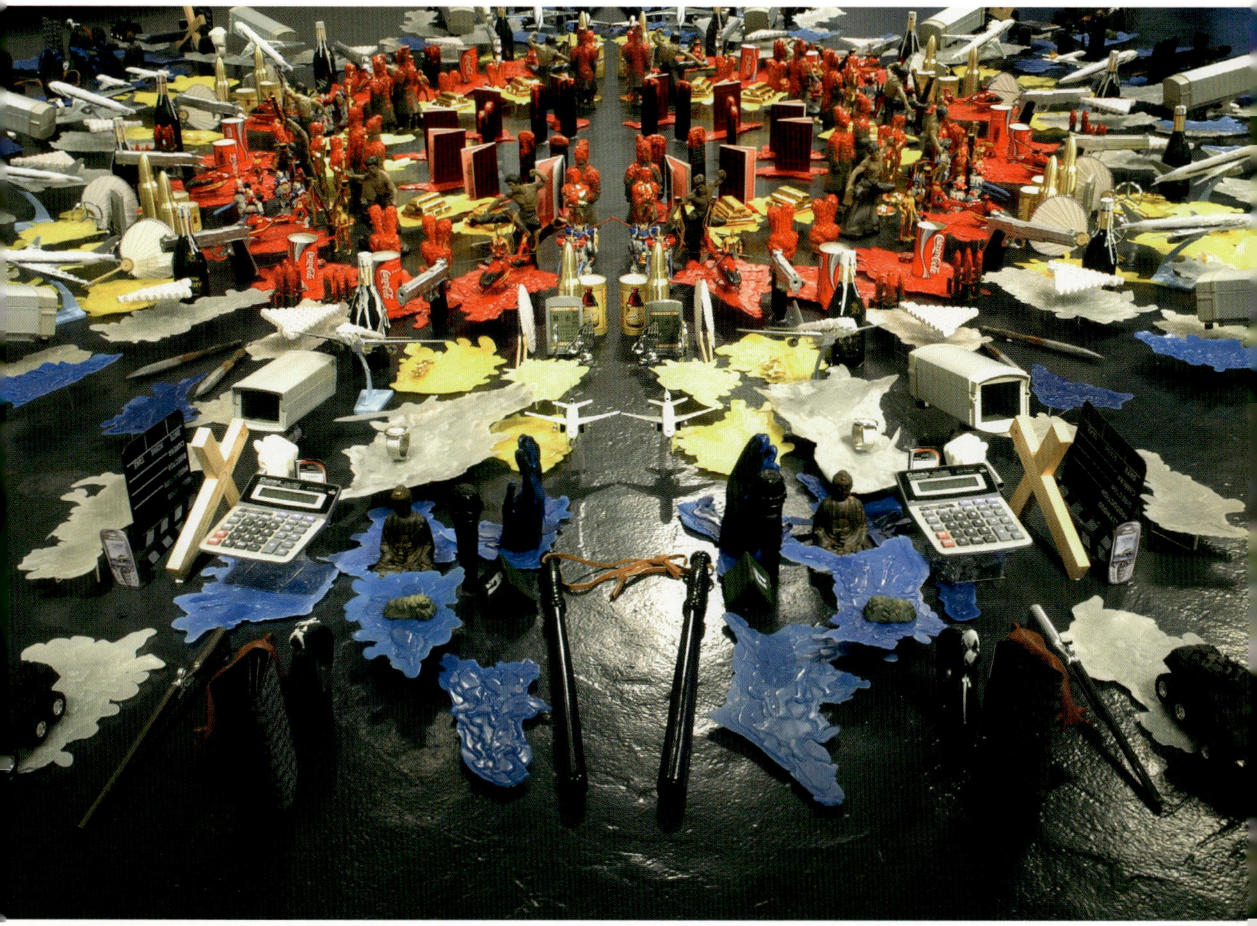

Andrew McLeod

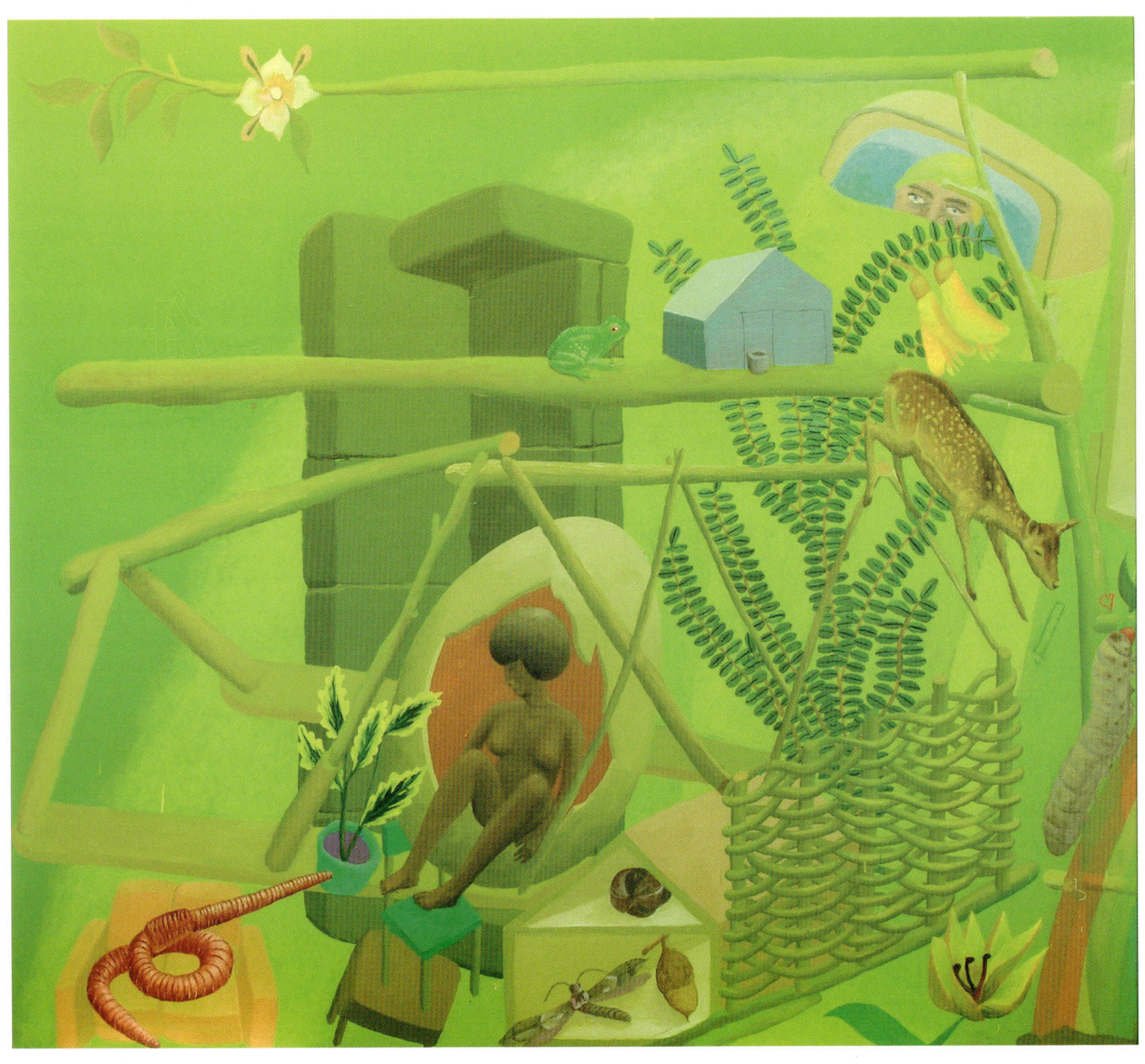

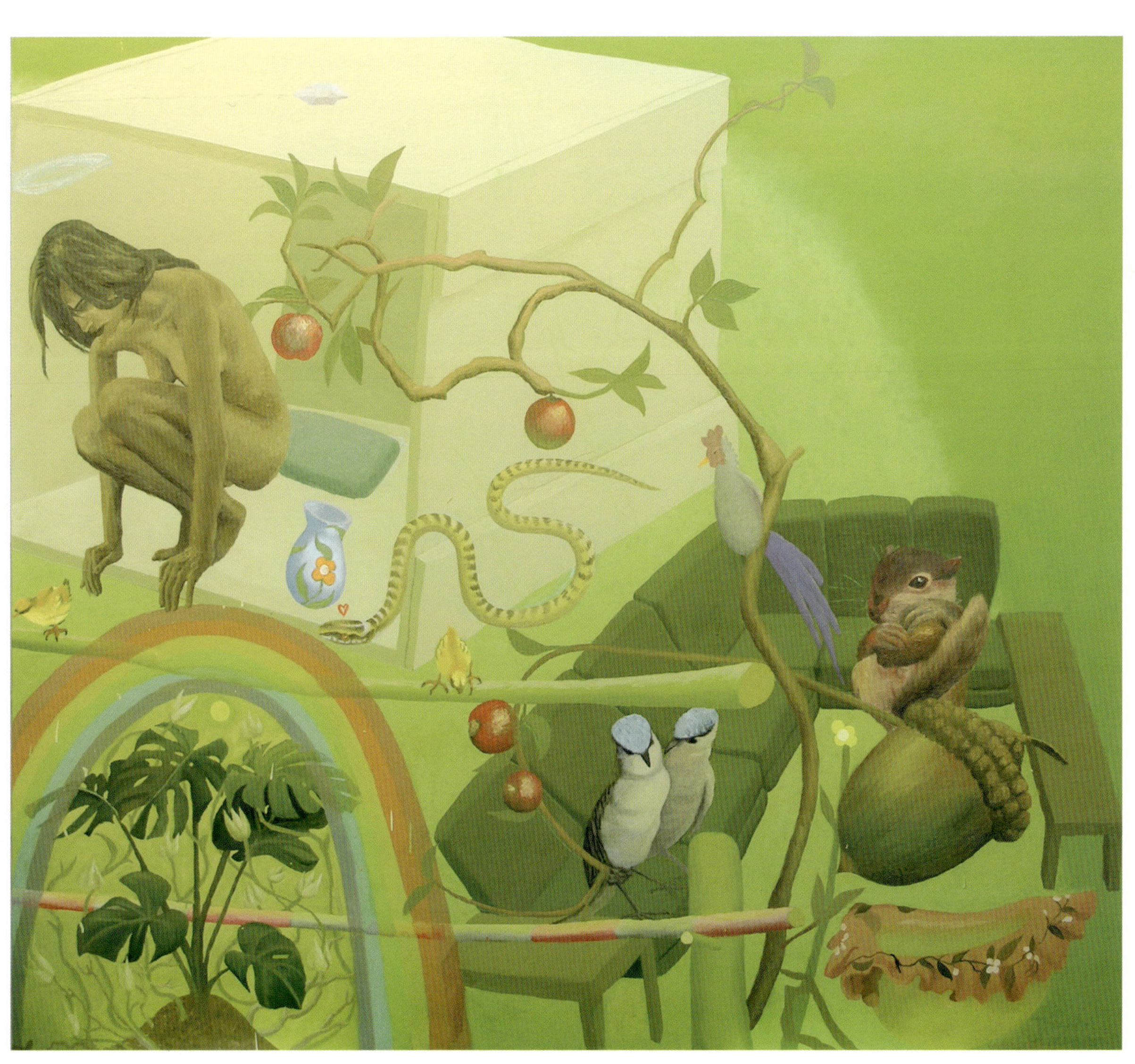

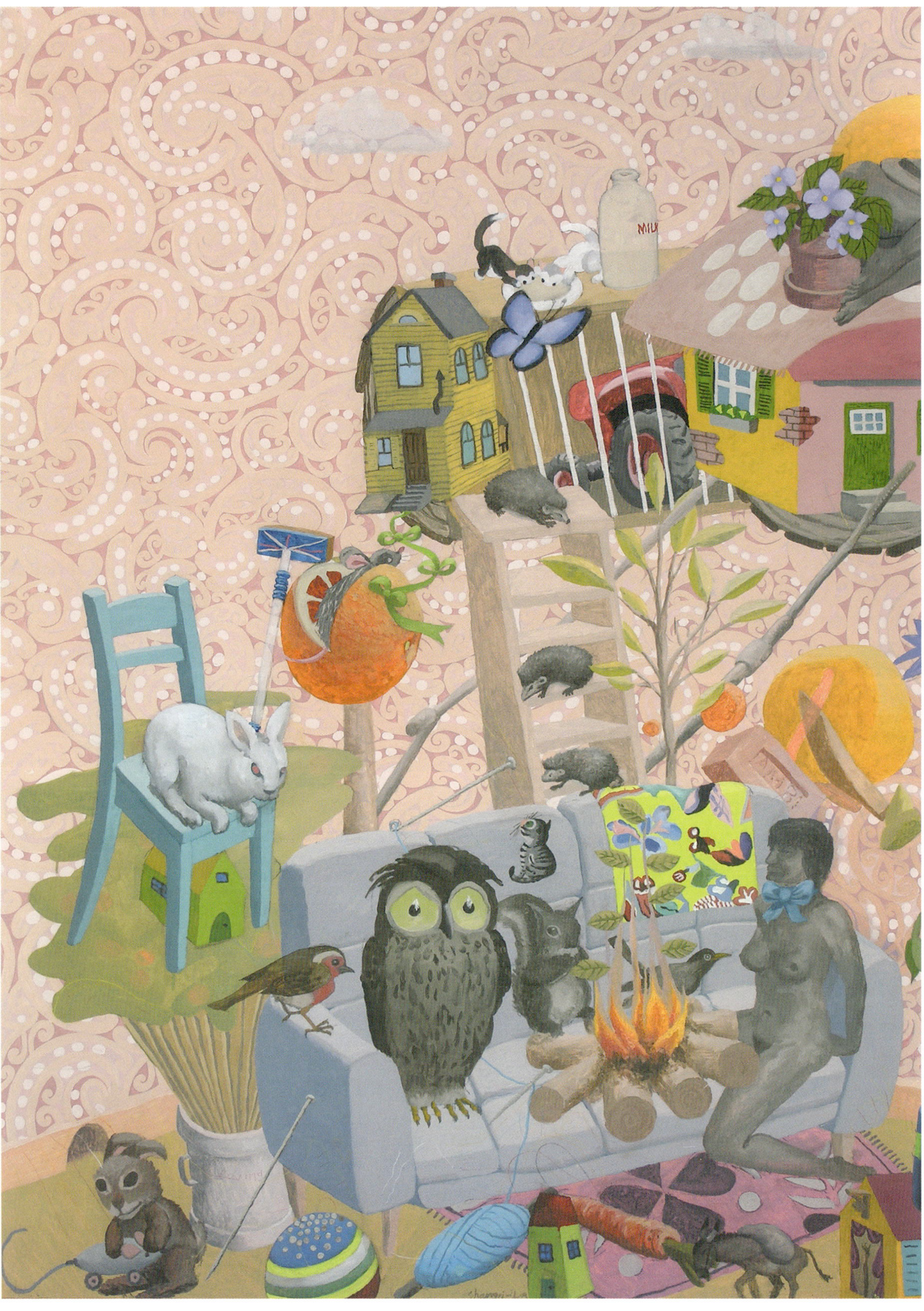

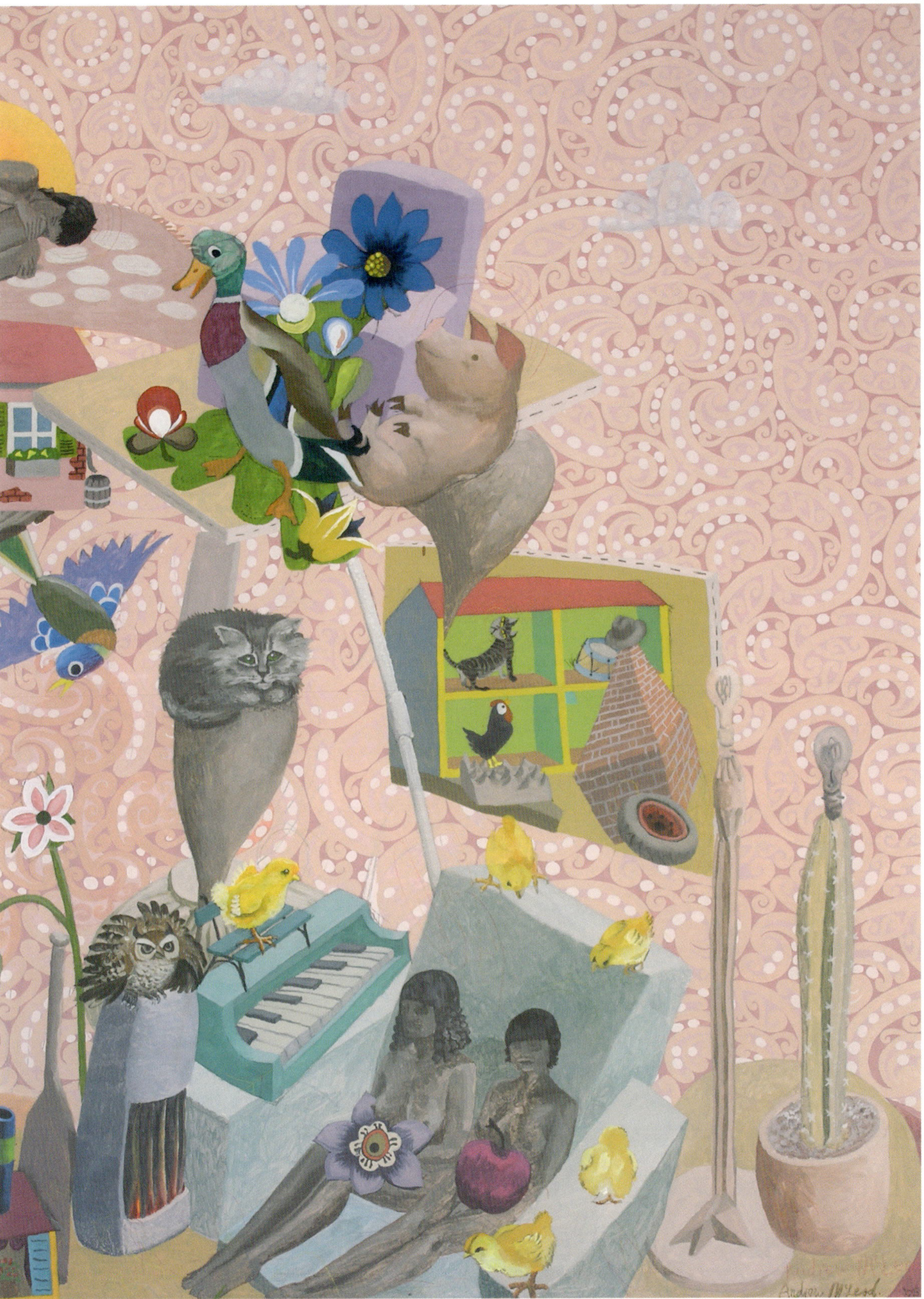

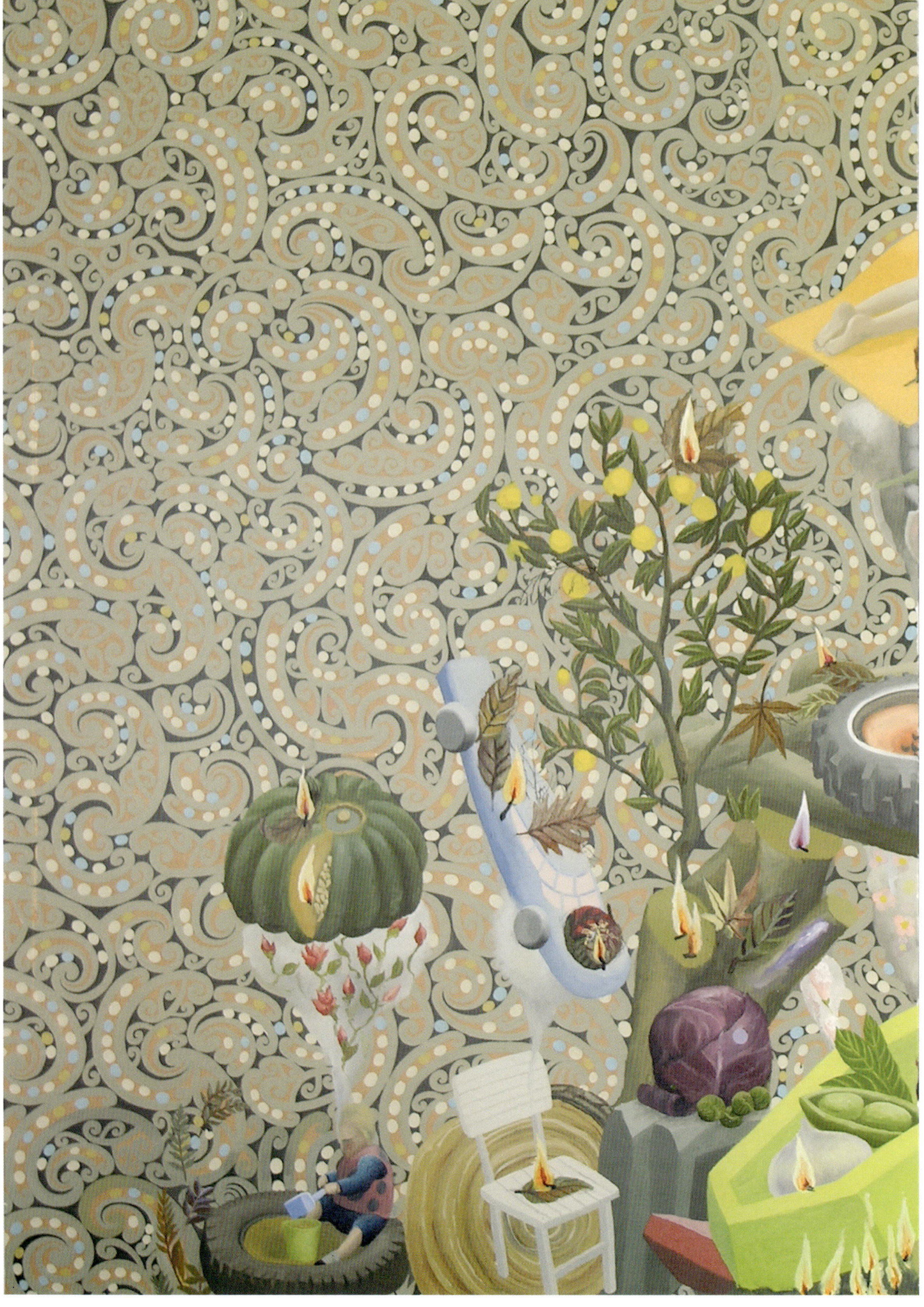

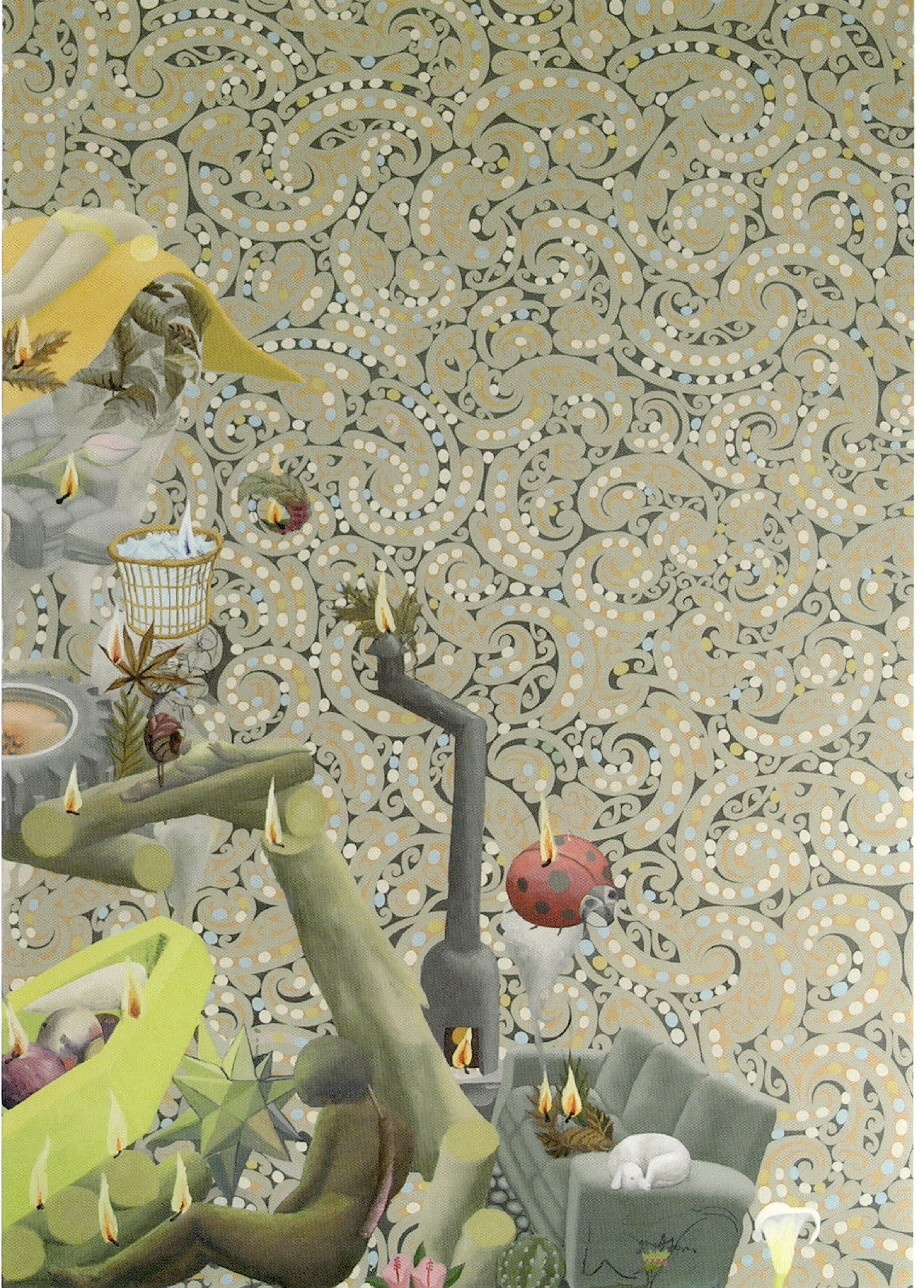

Judy Darragh

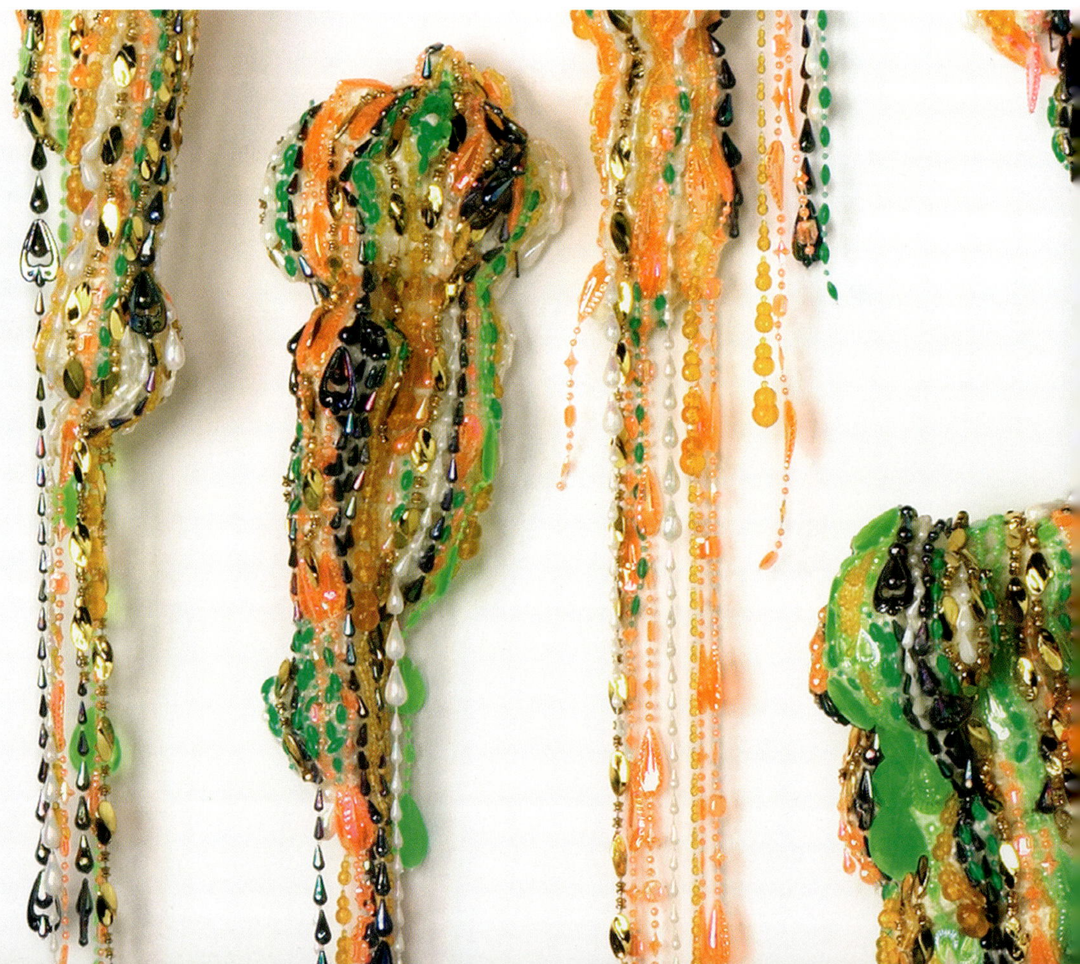

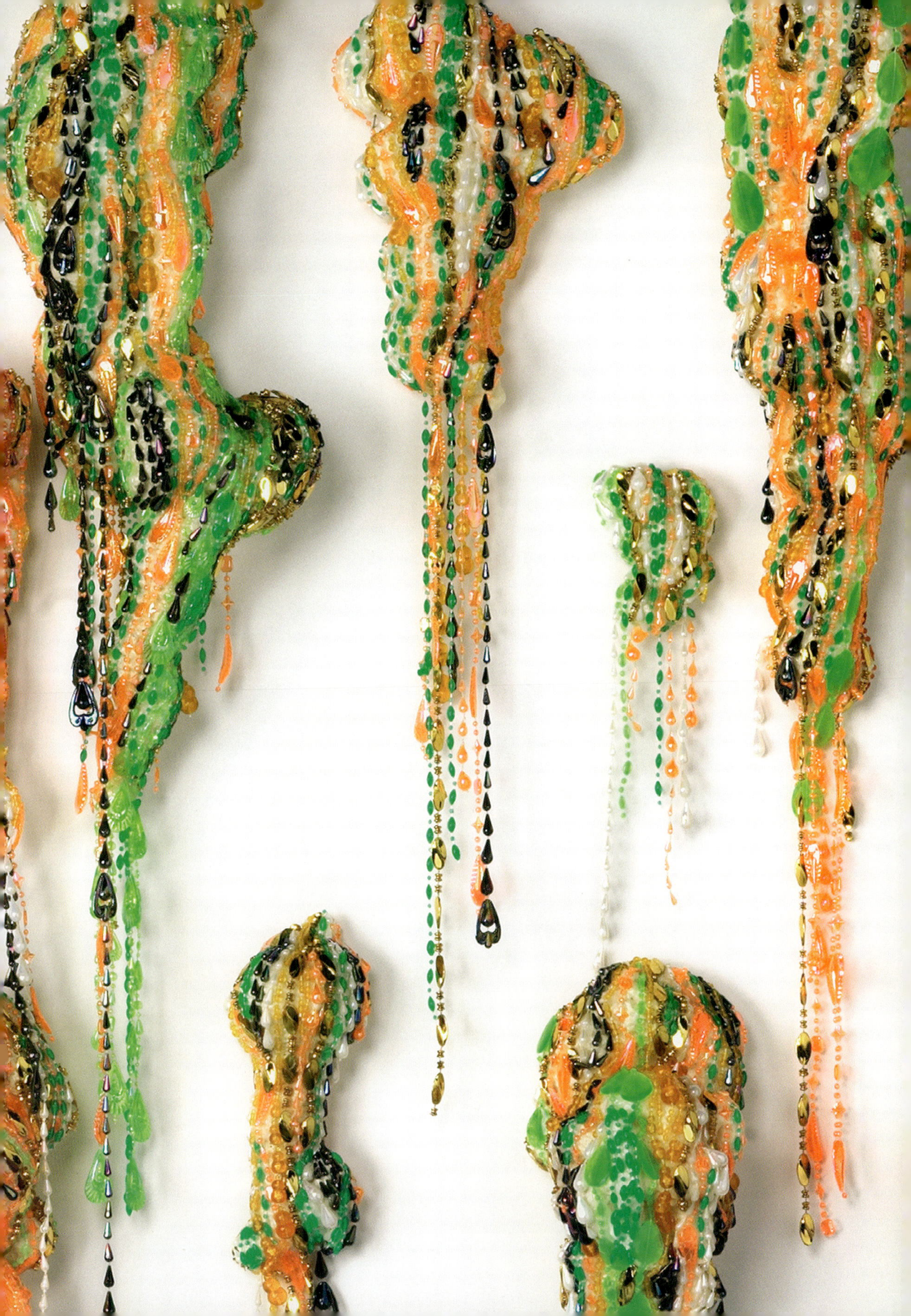

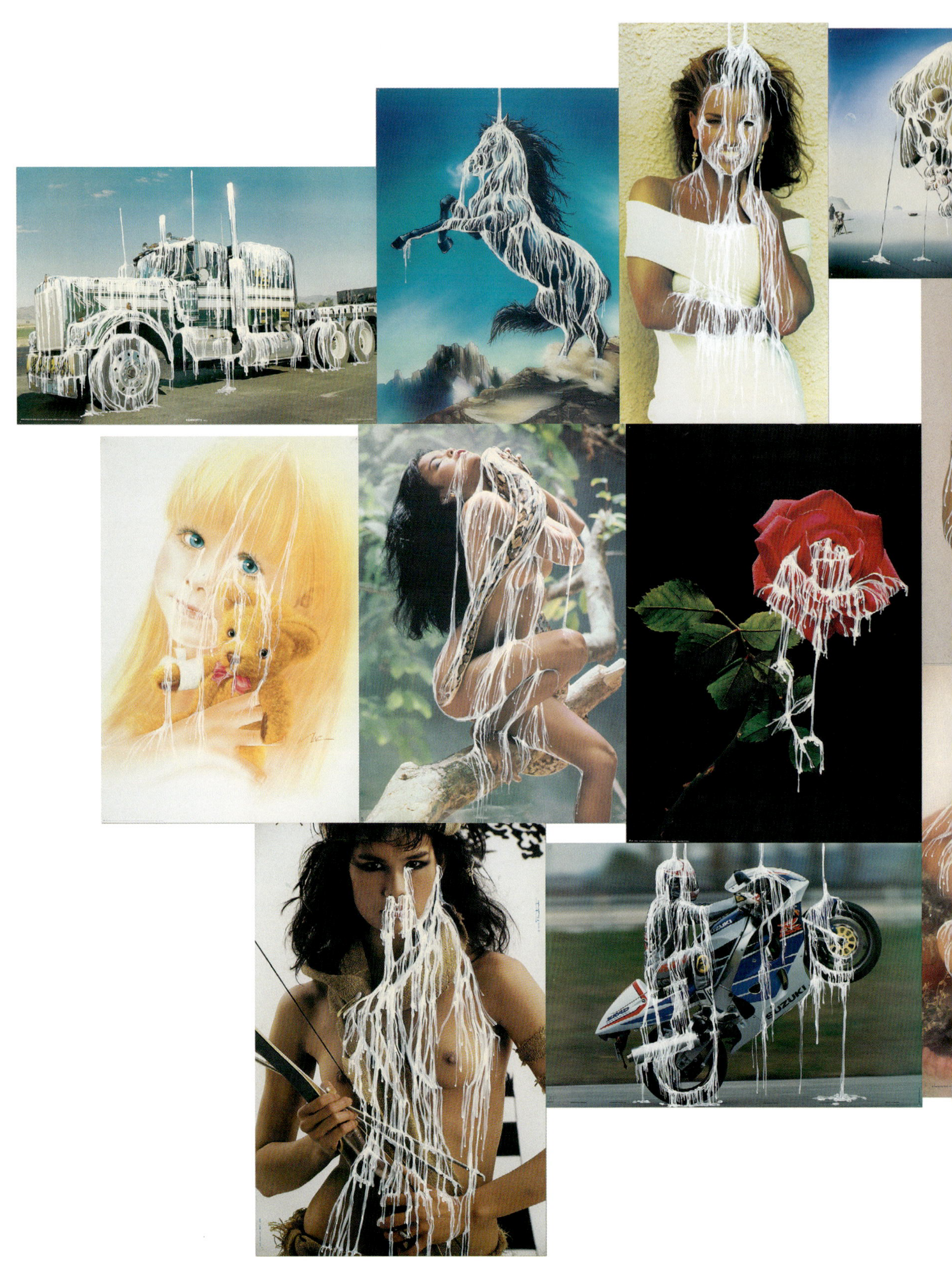

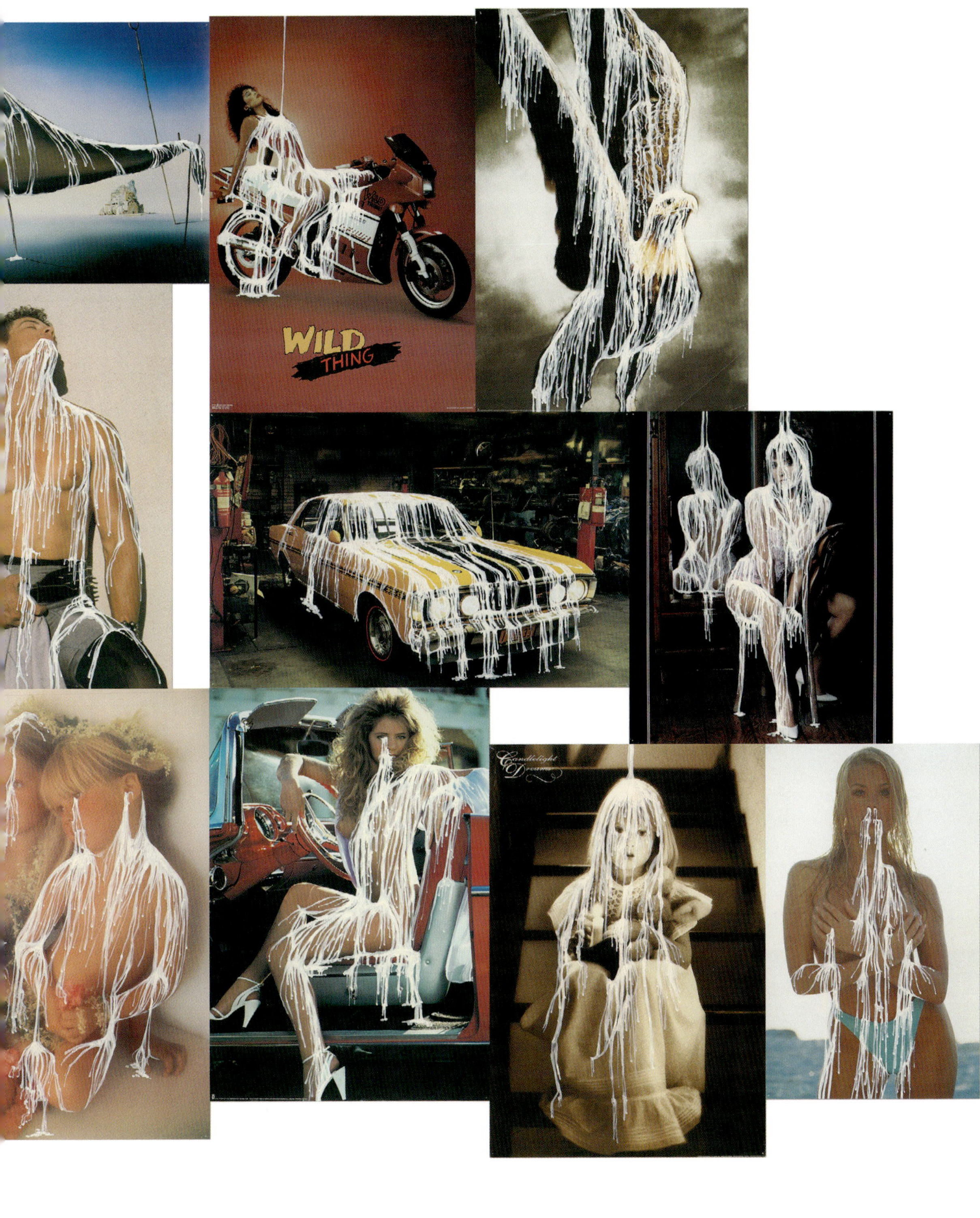
WILD
THING
Candlelight
Dreams

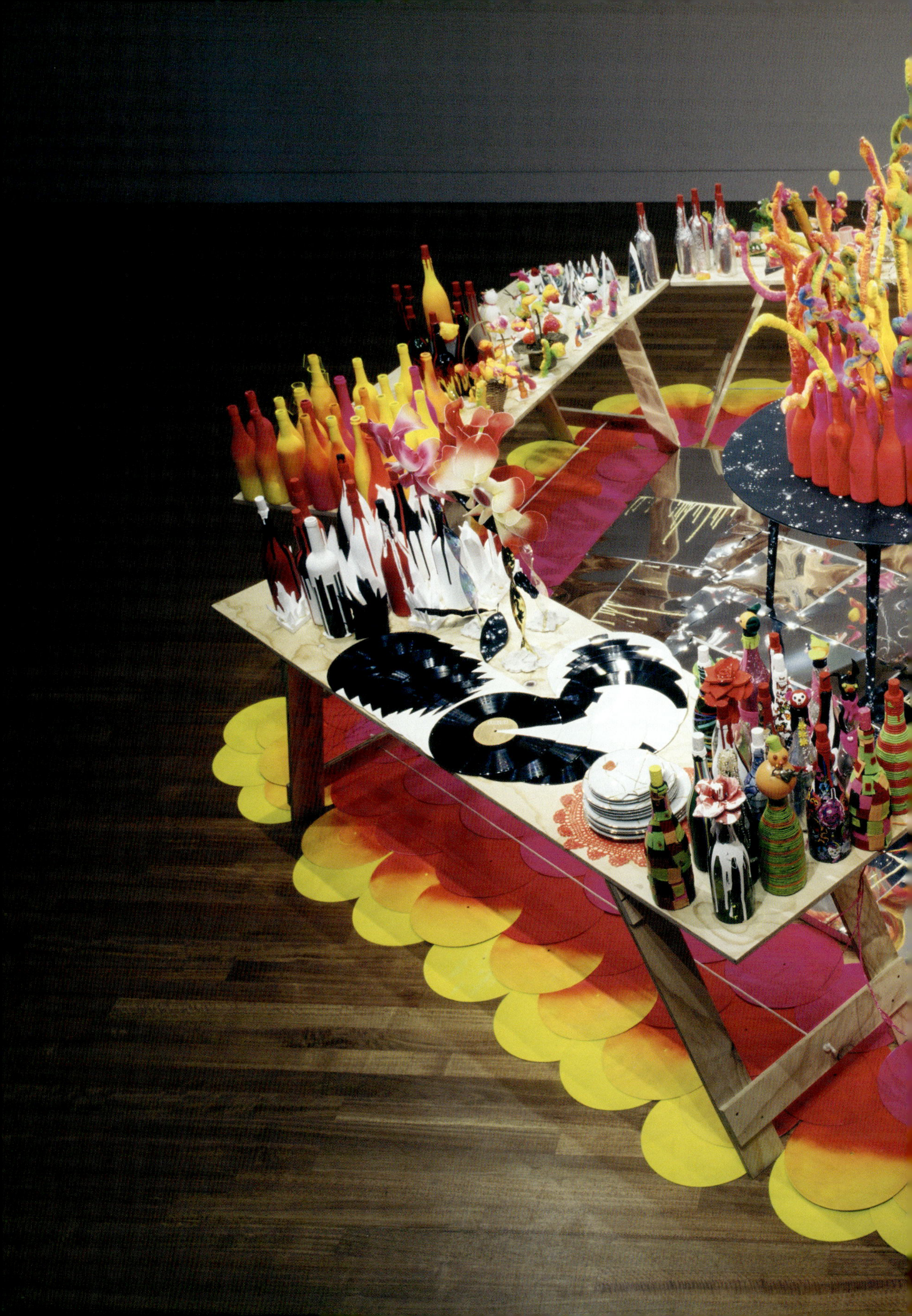

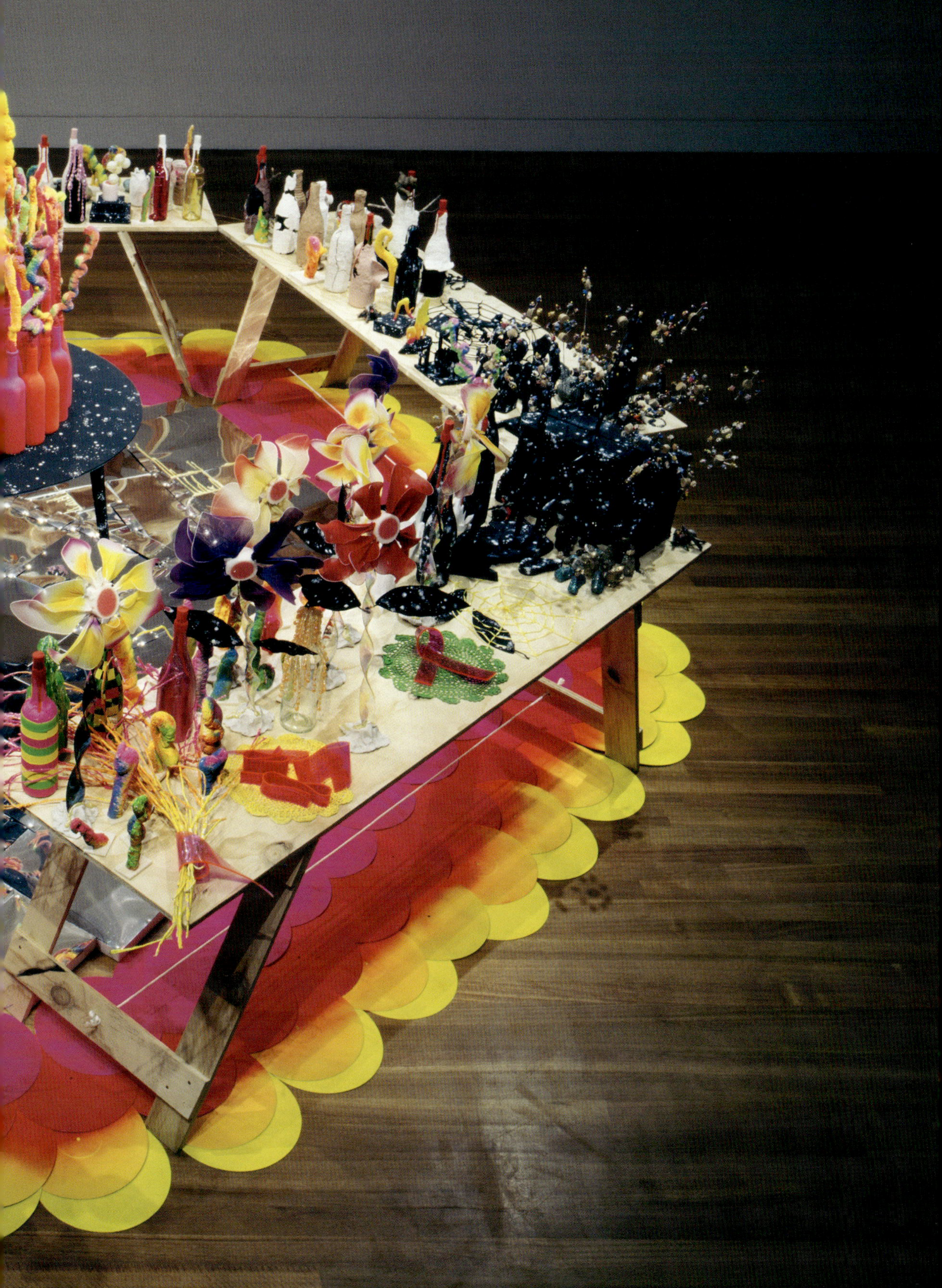

Rohan Wealleans

Tatunka, 2006
Dunedin Public Art Gallery

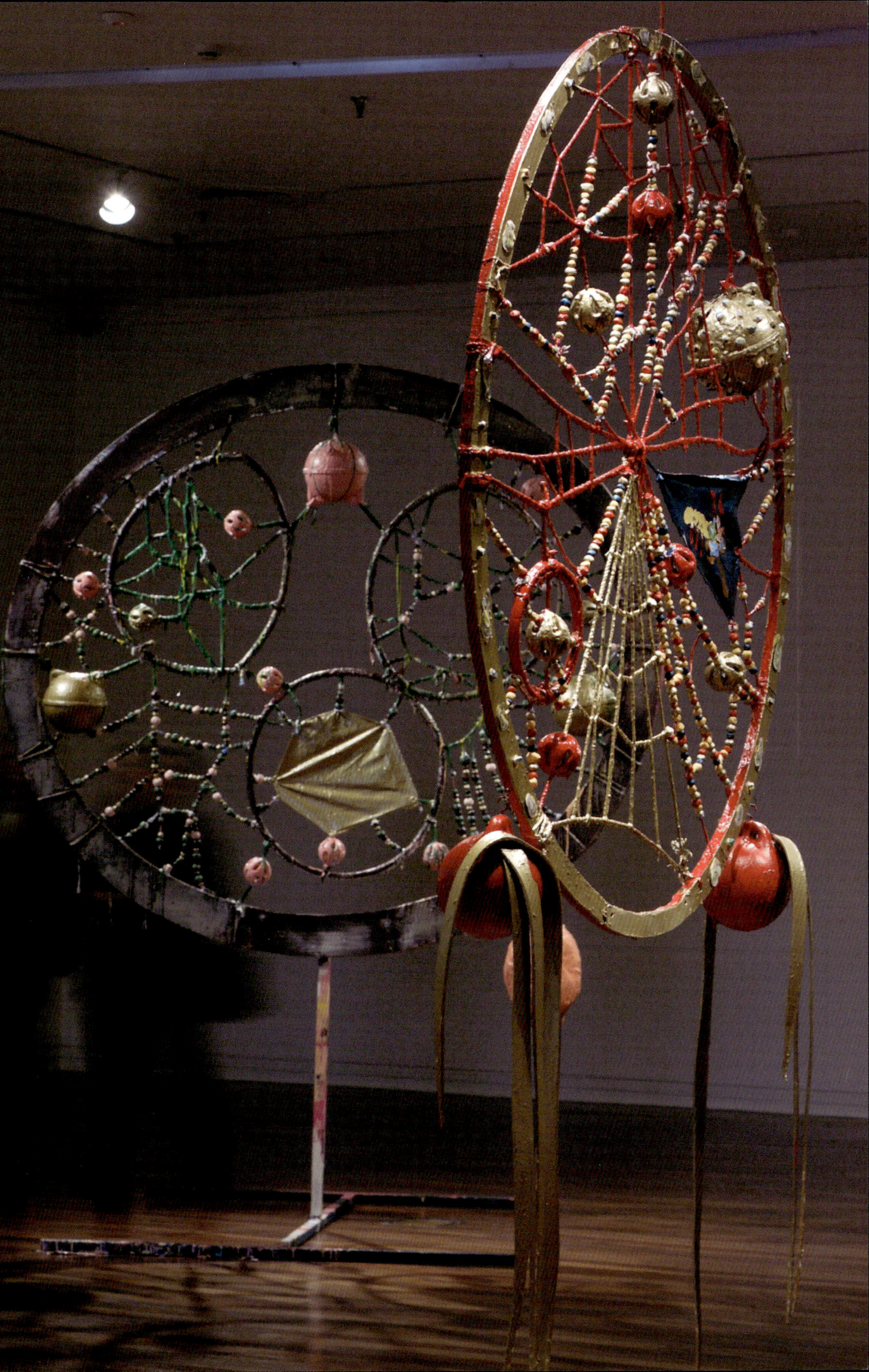

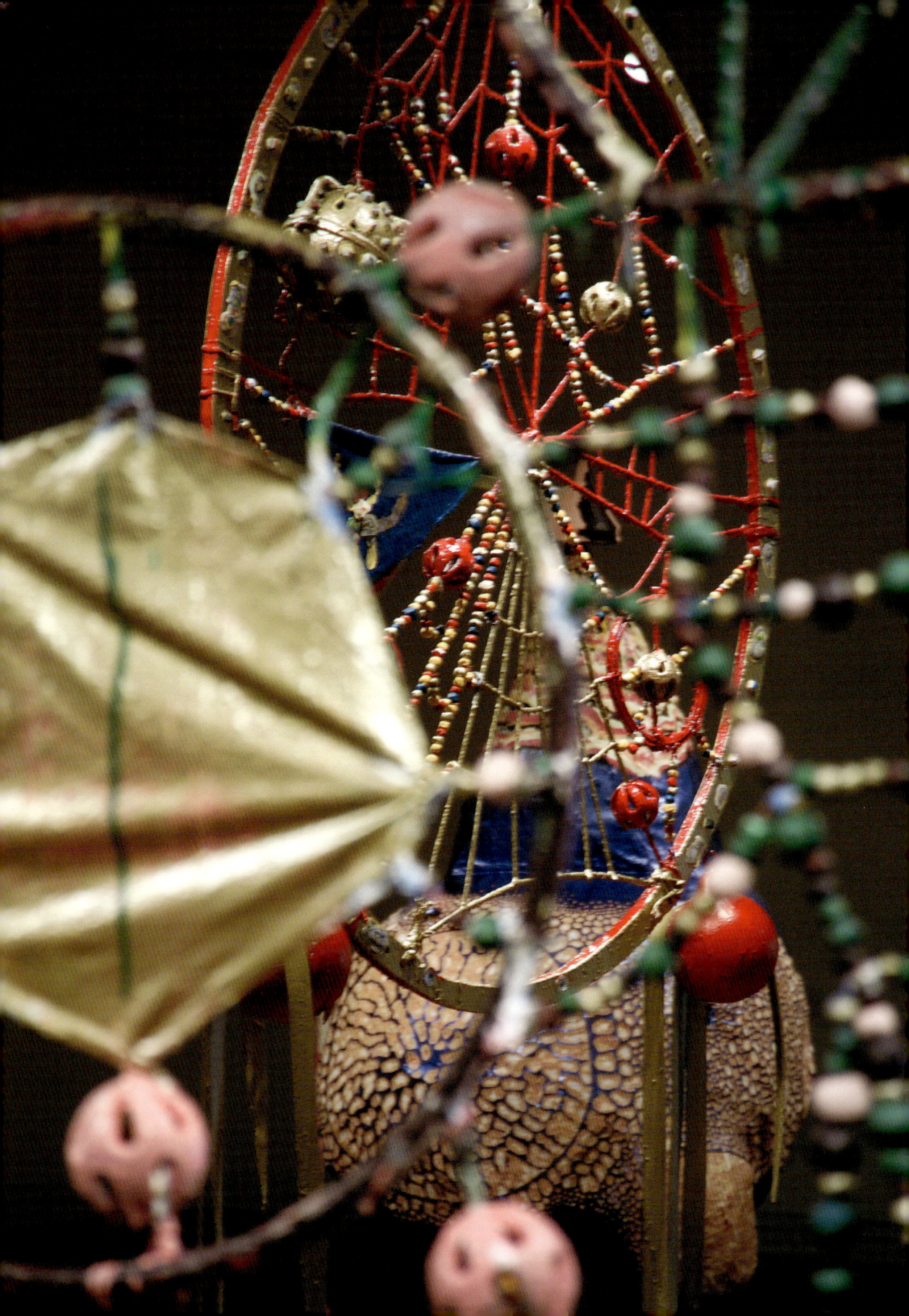

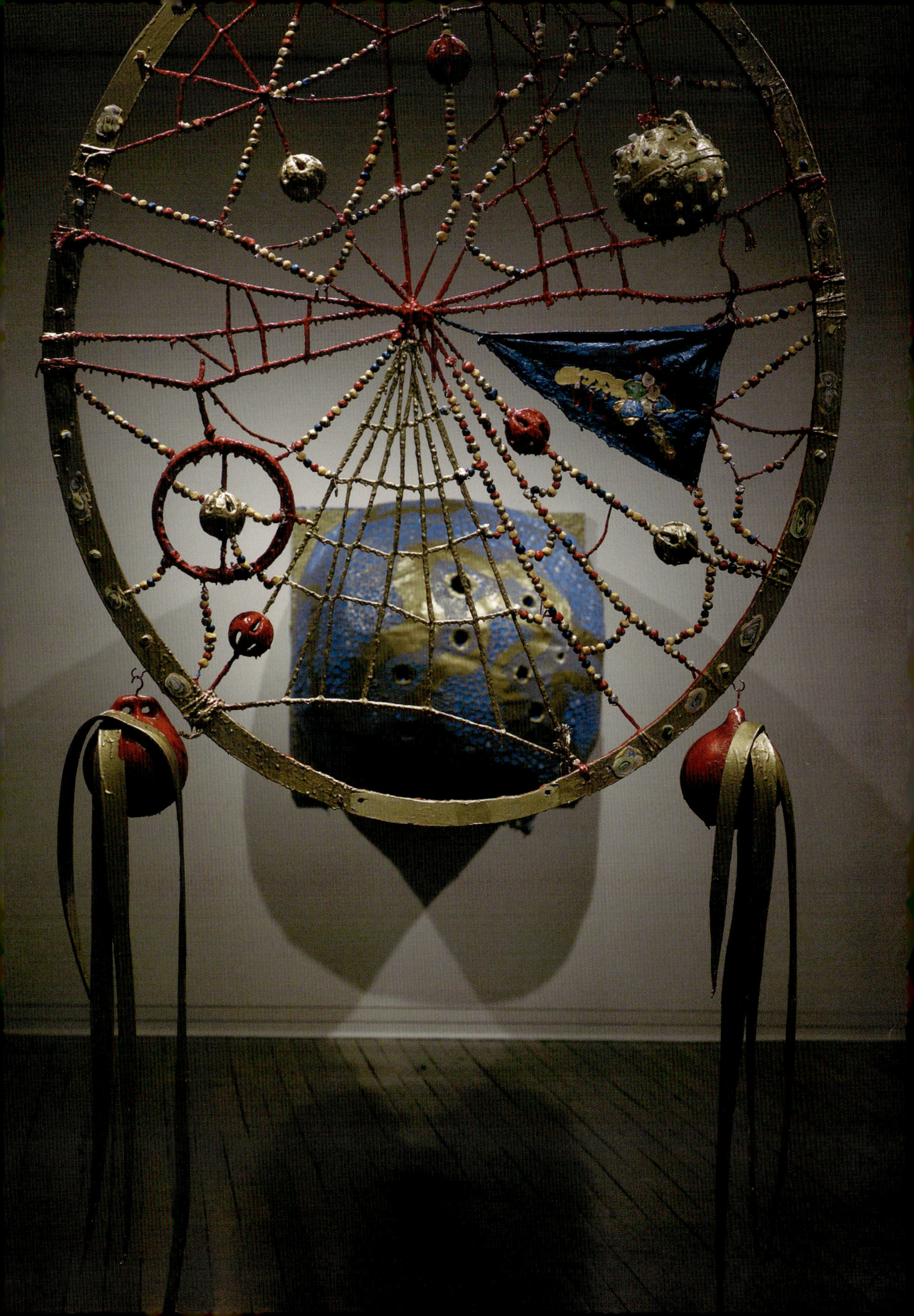

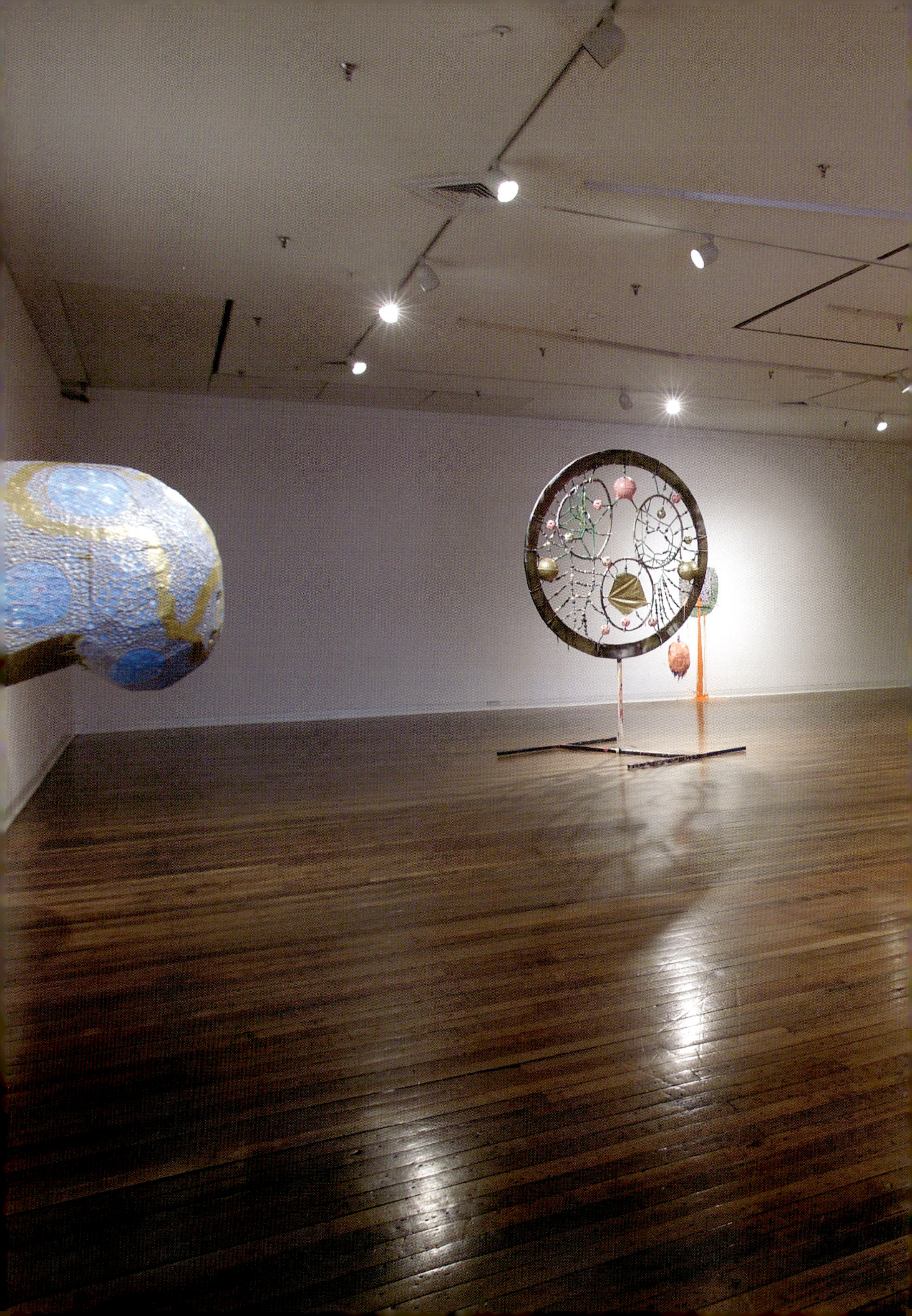

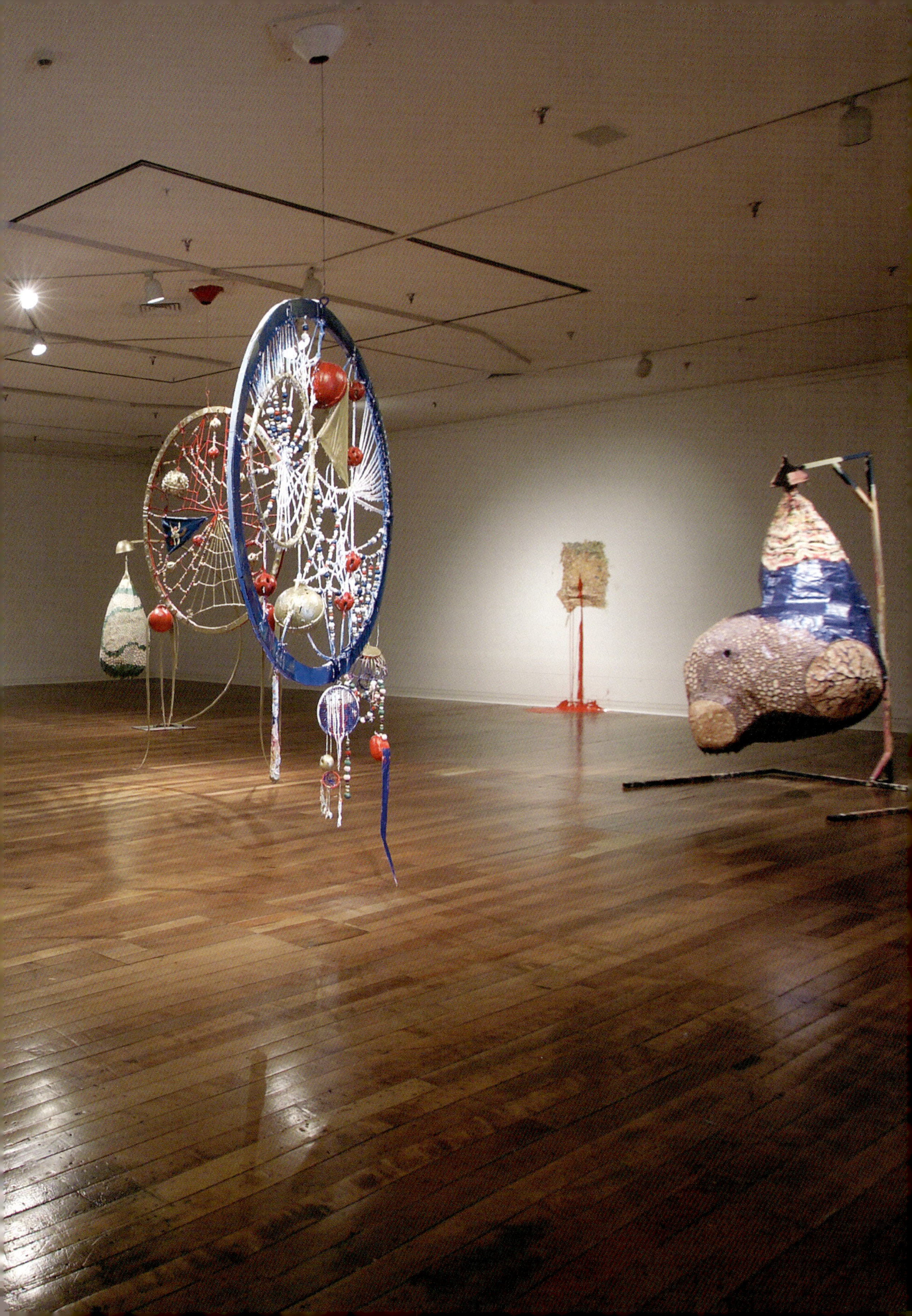

Ack

182–187

Peter Robinson

Ack (detail)
Ack I
Ack II

all works 2006

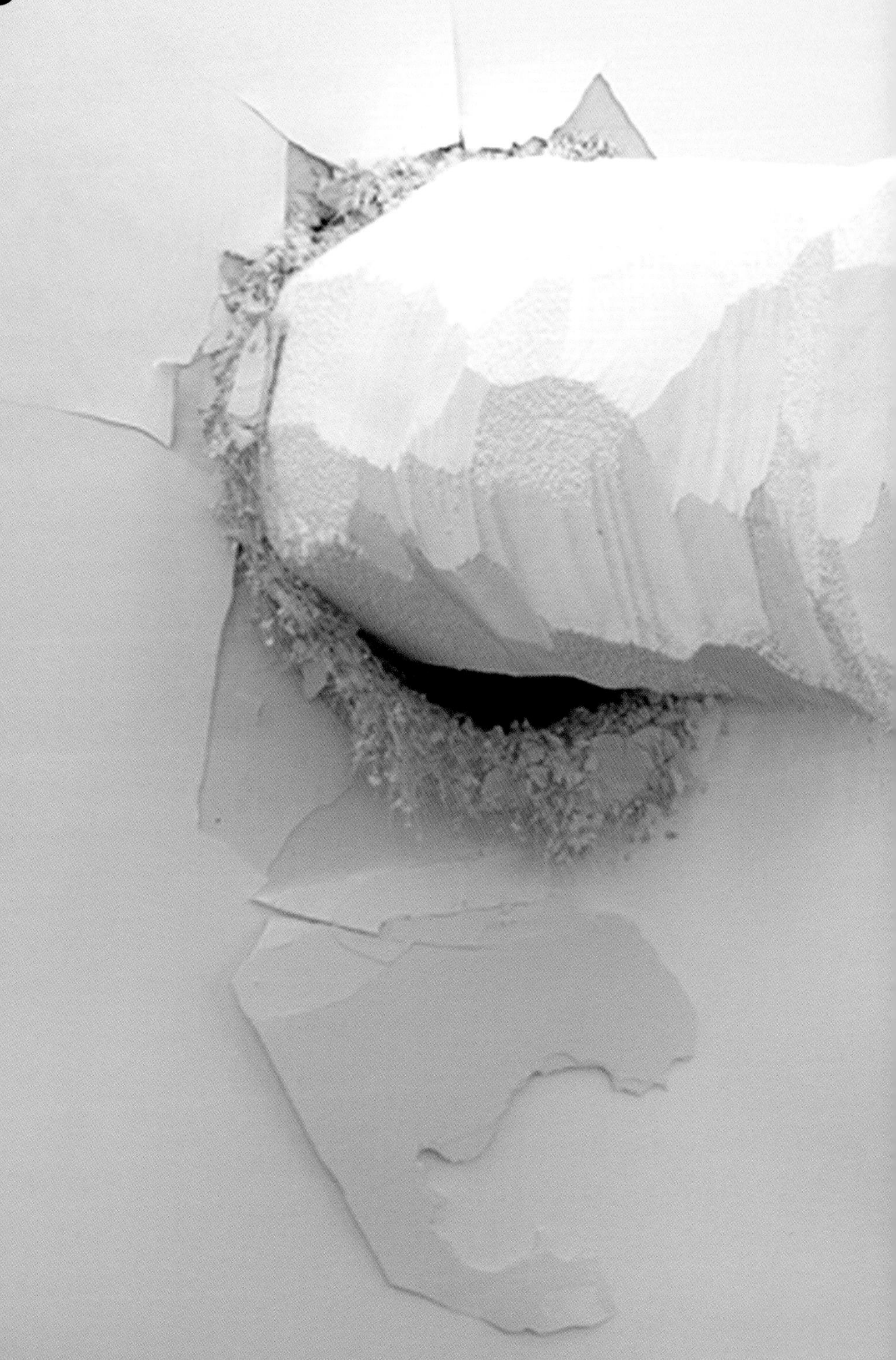

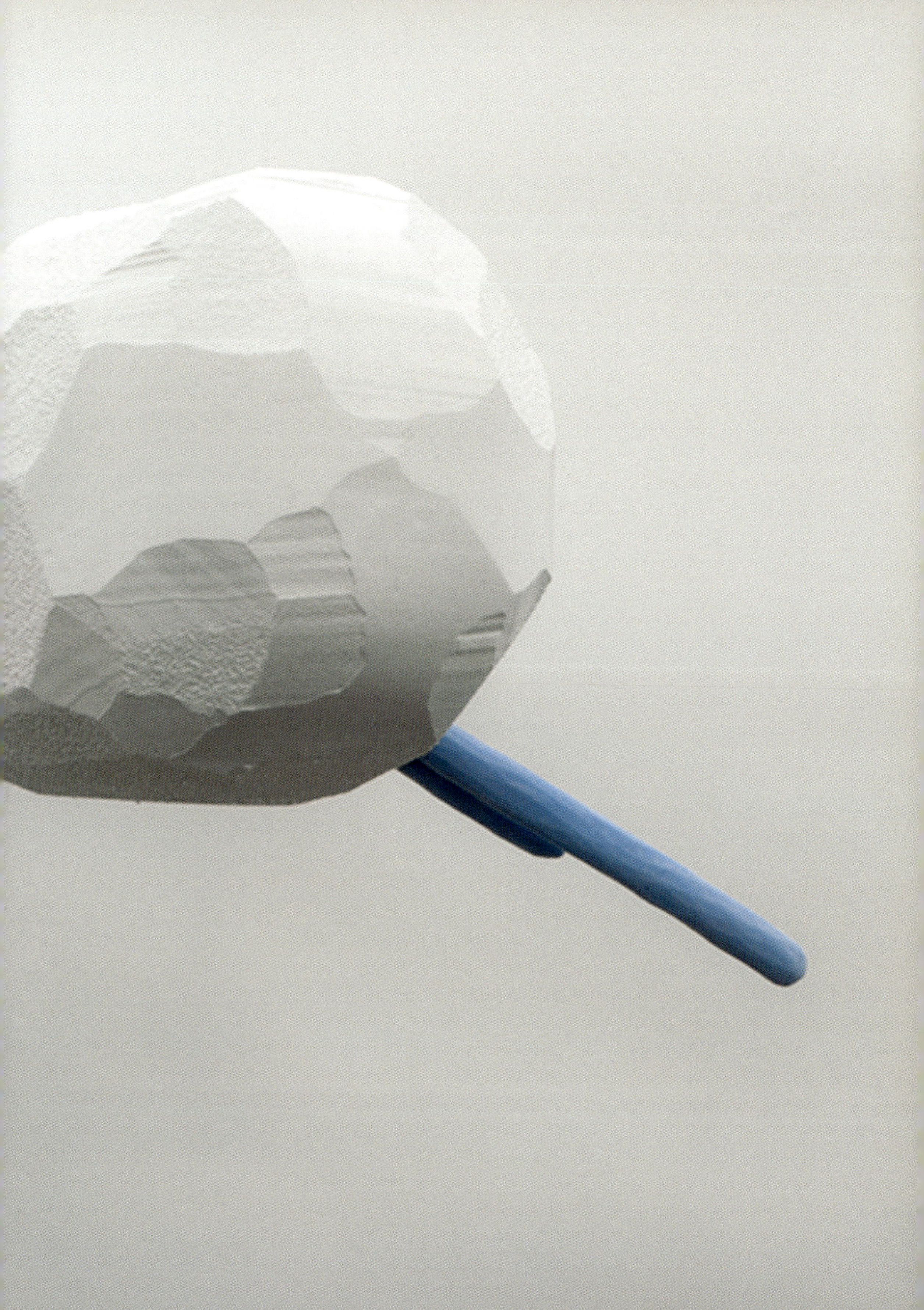

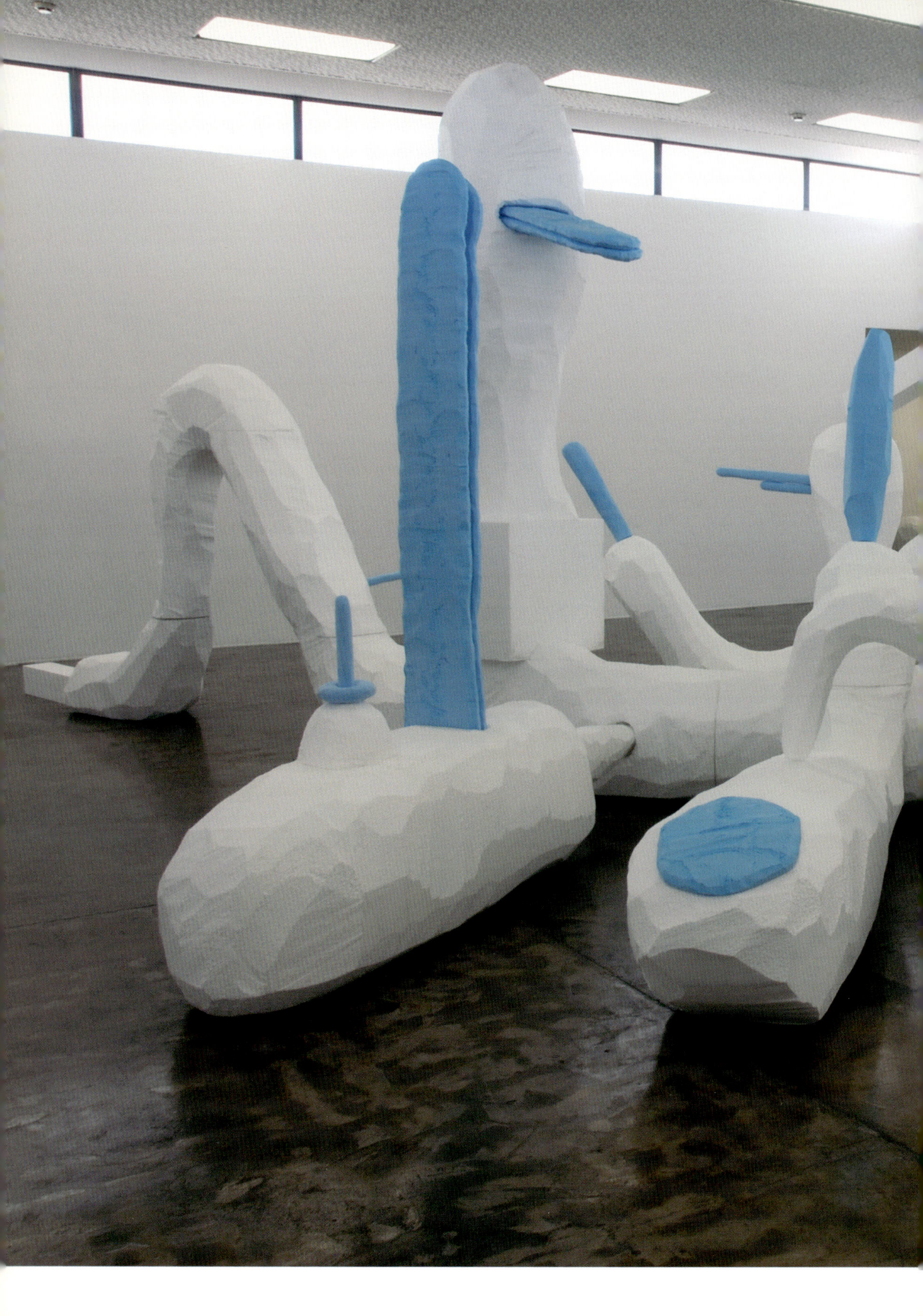

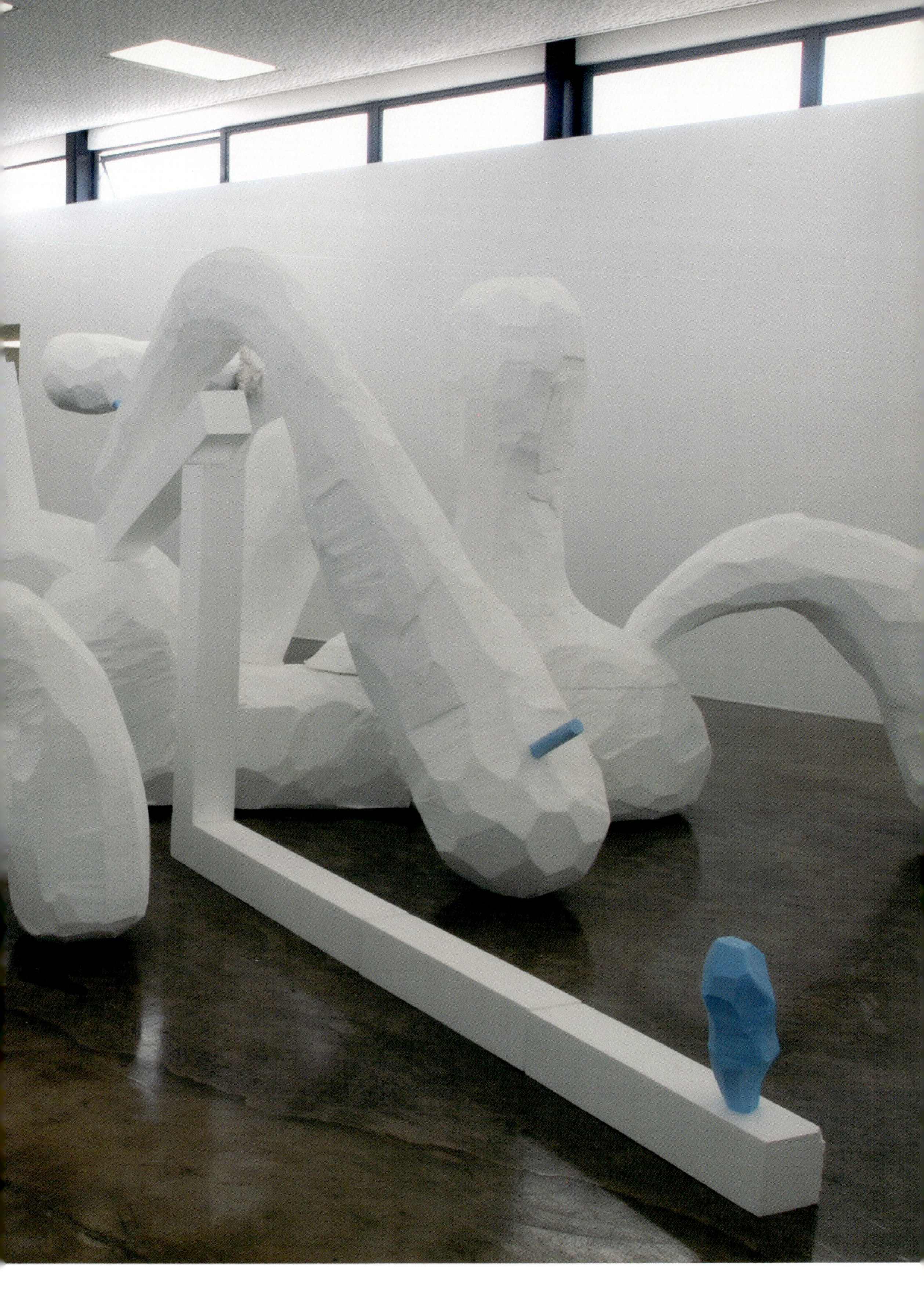

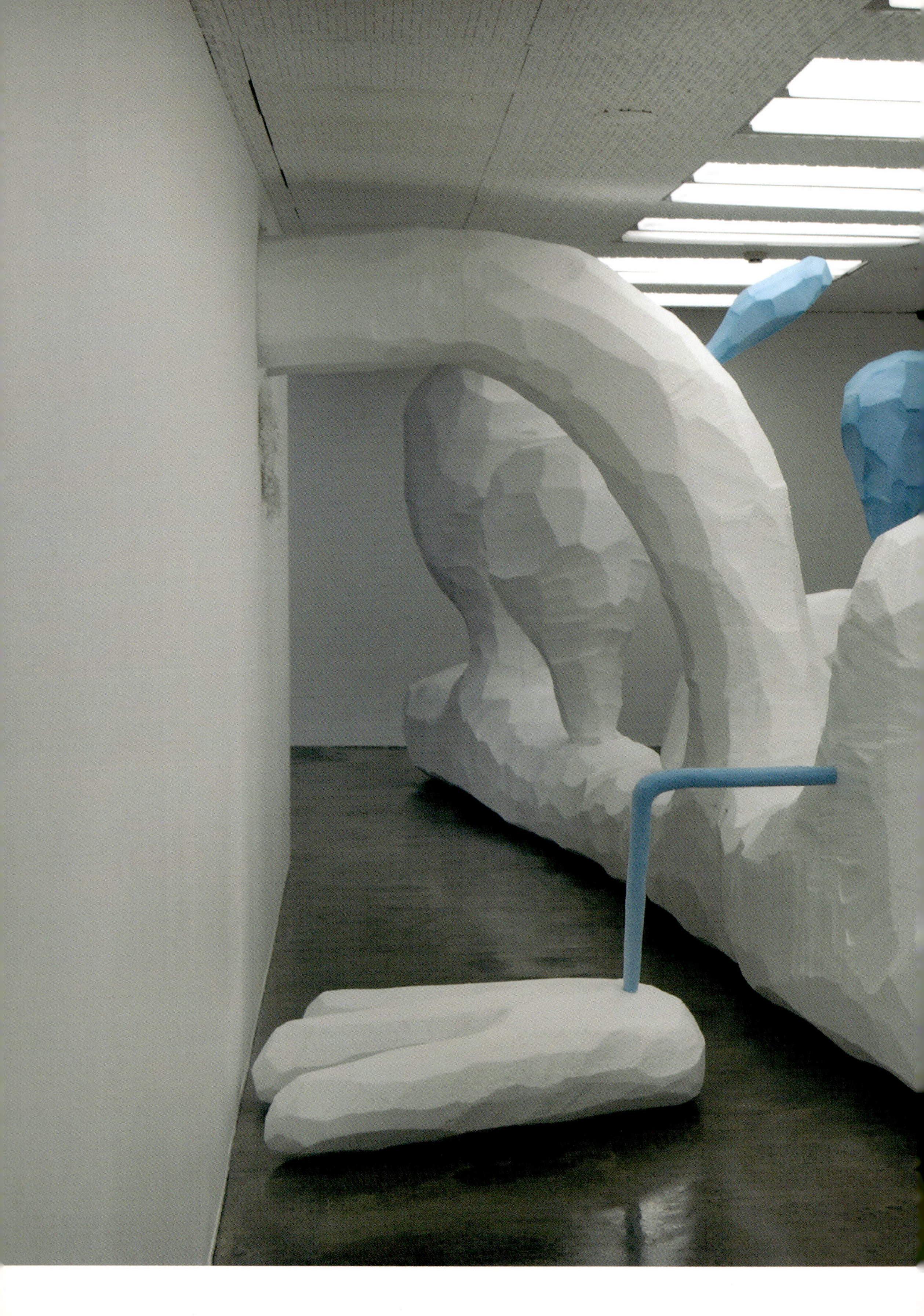

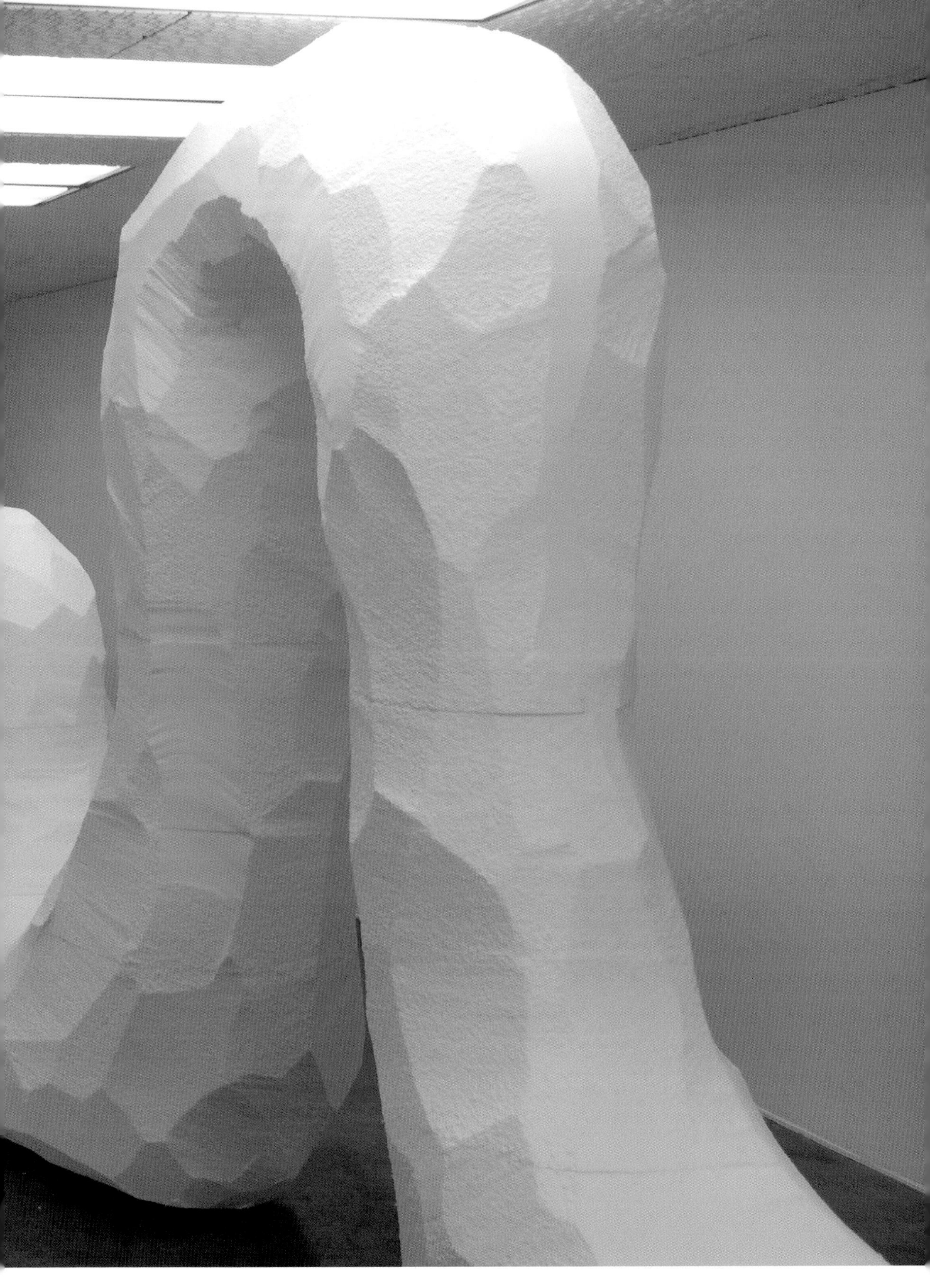

Artists' biographies

It's difficult to map the world when it is automated. There is a moment when the map becomes an abstract painting, which becomes a tennis court. Where the perspective is shoved backwards and the object couldn't even be used for ping-pong. I wonder if they would invent a Zamboni for a tennis court? There are numerous moments when Andrew Barber could have crossed the street but instead it was better to stay in Rm103 and make an artist run space with Nick Spratt. He now seems to have crossed the street. Or did he just lock himself out?

I'm not sure where the ideas came from, they seemed to be so wrong, but where did it all go wrong and why if they were wrong from the beginning would they then be made with the perfect materials? With beautiful materials of cedar stretcher bars, linen canvas then gesso and paint, a perfect mistake is completed. What was it that Kippenberger used to say, "Never try and correct a misunderstanding. You'll never get them to understand what you meant and more importantly from the misunderstanding you will arrive at a far more interesting place."

In a perfect world wrong ideas would work and artists would have their own action figures. *Andrew Barber breaks a leg* is not only a theatrical desire for success, but also a hope for some bodily damage done while in the heat of a anti-heroic act. For Barber that was just crossing the street.

Brian Butler

Born in 1978.
Lives and works in Auckland, Aotearoa New Zealand.

Solo exhibitions:
2007 – *Andrew Barber: Andrew Barber*, Gambia Castle, Auckland; *90% & untitled* (with John Reynolds), Ledge, Ramp Gallery, WINTEC, Hamilton.
2006 – *Andrew Barber*, N.O.T., Toowoomba, Queensland, Australia; *Danish Designs: gone bust, lost forever…*, Dep_art_ment, Auckland.
2005 – *Andrew Barber*, rm103, Auckland.
2004 – *Andrew Barber Breaks a Leg*, Canary Gallery, Auckland; *you can take the boy out of the _____ but you can't take the _____ out of the boy*, rm103; *Ship of Fools* (in collaboration with Paula Booker), Canary Gallery.

Selected group exhibitions:
2006 – *Carry On* (collaboration with Nicholas Spratt, Kylie Duncan and Kirsten Dryburgh), Next Wave Festival, Melbourne; *Month of April: exhibition in four parts*, Canary Gallery; *Painting of the Future* (with Stephen Bram), Canary Gallery; *Headway*, Artspace, Auckland; *one god, no masters*, Hamish McKay Gallery, Wellington.
2005 – *Duets II* (collaboration with Sriwhana Spong and with Lisa Benson), rm103; *Fifty-nine Metres Squared* (with Ben Buchanan, Bjorn Houtman, Steve Kay and Jeena Shin), Canary Gallery.
2004 – *Waterworks*, rm103; *rm Service*, Enjoy Public Art Gallery, Wellington; *Duets*, Ramp Gallery.
2003 – *cheap l.p.* (with Clinton Watkins and Bjorn Houtman), rm103; *Images of Desire*, Winston Hotel, Amsterdam.

Bibliography:
Ben Curnow (ed.), *New New Zealand Art*, Canary Gallery, Auckland and MOP, Sydney, 2003.
John Hurrell, 'A Good Team: Andrew Barber and John Reynolds at Ledge Gallery' on *Artbash* weblog, 3 March 2007.
Tessa Laird (ed.), *Nights of our Lives*, rm103, Auckland, 2005.
David Levinson, 'Andrew Barber: Washroom' in *Lumiere Reader*, August 2006.
'Fresh Paint' in *Urbis* 33, 2006.

Andrew Mcleod

"The incursions of text into the picture space is like a perambulating disembodied ghost leaving trails of words." (Margreta Chance, *Largess*)

Andrew McLeod's work is like a can of worms. Once the lid's off there is a searing sense that those slippery, wriggly manifestations are getting away on you. His prolific practice encompasses drawings, paintings, prints and books, each blurring into the next, jetsam compiled as an alluring insight into the artist's observations, both real and imagined. They are a private world made public. It's like stepping ever-so-slightly into a dream-like psychosis where surreal musings and realist inserts collide to create a cacophony of tones and narratives, leaving the viewer wandering around in a techno-colour dream world.

McLeod's work exists on the cusp of a dream-state and neurotic episode. There is a sense that the artist's discombobulated view of society, coupled with some rainbow-drenched mindscapes, seems to be an exploration of his place in the world. Margreta Chance writes that McLeod uses architectural plans and models to create a space where desire and longing can be played out. This desire is manifest in a saturated, meticulous urban garden that the artist tills with many tools over and over. A process of sprouting and growing, where bursting bulbs and singing birds sit alongside women bound with rope laid delicately – a Garden of Eden where capitalist grime rises to the surface. His work is a meeting place for the dreamer and the cynic to sit together, legs crossed, examining the master plan.

Danae Mossman

Andrew McLeod

Born in 1976.
Lives and works in Auckland, Aotearoa New Zealand.

Selected solo exhibitions:
2006 – *Good Works*, Ivan Anthony Gallery, Auckland; *New Works*, Peter McLeavey Gallery, Wellington, and Brooke|Gifford Gallery, Christchurch.
2005 – *New Works*, Peter McLeavey Gallery; *The Palace of Access*, Ivan Anthony Gallery.
2004 – *New Works*, Peter McLeavey Gallery.
2003 – *Theater of the Indigent*, Ivan Anthony Gallery.
2002 – *Largess*, Ivan Anthony Gallery; *Parabasis Snowwhite*, Snowwhite Gallery, UNITEC, Auckland.
2001 – *Interior Monologue*, Ivan Anthony Gallery.
2000 – *Tama-Kainga*, Ivan Anthony Gallery; *New Paintings*, Peter McLeavey Gallery.

Selected group exhibitions:
2006 – *How to Live Together: 27th Bienal de São Paulo*, Brazil; *54321 Artists' Projects*, Auckland Art Gallery Toi o Tamaki; *Accommodate*, St Paul St Gallery, AUT, Auckland.
2005 – *Otherworld*, Gertrude Contemporary Art Spaces, Melbourne; *New Works* (with Richard Killeen), Brooke|Gifford Gallery.
2004 – *Public/Private: 2nd Auckland Triennial*, Auckland Art Gallery Toi o Tamaki.
2003 – *Money for Nothing*, Artspace, Auckland.
2001 – *After Killeen: social observation in recent art*, Artspace, Auckland.
1999 – *Only the Lonely*, Artspace, Auckland; *Cleaning Up* (with Brendon Wilkinson), Peter McLeavey Gallery; *New New Zealanders*, Ray Hughes Gallery, Sydney.

Selected bibliography:
Margreta Chance, 'Logging in: the walled gardens of Andrew McLeod' in *Largess*, Artspace, Auckland, 2005.
Tessa Laird, 'Art's Young Dream' in *New Zealand Listener*, 4-10 December 2004.
Andrew McLeod, *Art Morality for Children*, 2006.
Andrew McLeod, *Good Proof*, 2005.
Andrew McLeod, *Shh Shh Shangri-la*, 2005.
Andrew McLeod, *Silver Arrow*, 2003.
Andrew McLeod, *Summer Drawings*, 2007.
Andrew McLeod and Liz Maw, *Parabiosis*, 2004.
Anna Miles, *After Killeen: social observation in recent art*, Artspace, Auckland, 2002.
Justin Paton, 'Revenge of the Nerd' in *New Zealand Listener*, 31 July 1999.
Gwynneth Porter, 'Where the mind goes, so it grows' in *Largess*, Artspace, 2005.

Ani O'Neill

Ani O'Neill

Remember those friendship books you passed around as kids to get to know the inner-most secrets (as far as a pre-pubescent teenager might have) of those around you? I got something like this by chain-email from Ani O'Neill recently with a list of 36 questions with the title 'getting to know your friends and family'. The most telling, and the most related to her work, was the question 'What would you like to accomplish before you die?' Her answer was simply to 'pass on lots of goodness that will be remembered, and passed on and on…'. I saw this as a key to understanding O'Neill's work.

Bright, bold bursts of soda pop coloured yarns have fizzed across gallery walls, embodied many forms and occupied a multitude of spaces. There is an evident pop aesthetic, yet Ani mines the gap between pop and craft. Craft with a deep South Pacific flavour is the basis of her work. The kind learned over time with loved ones, passed on to Ani through her Rarotongan relatives. Ani weaves her home-spun practice with a generous openness that warms viewers instantly.

For example, *The Buddy System* is a work that saw the artist spend day after day in the gallery with friends as co-buddies, teaching visitors how to crochet woollen flowers (as well as making many herself). The lush garden grew daily as visitors contributed to the installation, each flower then attached to the wall, resulting in a web-like network of relationships. With every flower drawn to the next by a chain stem of green wool, the wall was a supernova of social connectivity, ready to mail out to unsuspecting friends and families of the makers at the end of the exhibition.

It is this generosity that has seen Ani weave a complex practice that can soften even the most ardent of white cube spaces to make them social and brimming with joy and a lounge-like ease. In this sense I have no doubt that Ani will, as she hopes, pass on lots of goodness through her work that will be remembered by those who have experienced it.

Danae Mossman

Born in 1971.
Lives and works in Auckland, Aotearoa New Zealand and Rarotonga, Cook Islands.

Selected solo exhibitions:
2006 – *The Buddy System*, ARC one gallery, Melbourne Commonwealth Games Festival.
2005 – *Fresh Eke*, Waikato Museum of Art and History, Hamilton.
2003-2004 – *The Buddy System*, Te Manawa, Palmerston North, and Art in General, New York.
2002 – *ei line*, Sue Crockford Gallery, Auckland.
2001 – *Doodles*, Lord Mori Gallery, Los Angeles.

Selected group exhibitions:
2006 – *Islanded: contemporary art from New Zealand, Singapore and Taiwan*, Adam Art Gallery, Victoria University of Wellington, and Substation, Singapore; *Pasifika Styles*, Cambridge University Museum of Anthropology and Archeology.
2004 – 9th Festival of Pacific Arts, Belau.
2003 – *Liquid Sea*, MCA, Sydney.
2002 – SCAPE 2002 Art and Industry Biennial, Christchurch; *The Tomorrow People*, Lord Mori Gallery, Los Angeles, and The Physics Room, Christchurch.
2001 – Bright *Paradise: 1st Auckland Triennial*, Auckland Art Gallery Toi o Tamaki.
2000 – *Agents of Change: 12th Biennale of Sydney* (three performances with Lisa Reihana and Pacific Sisters); Biennale of Noumea, Tjibaou Centre for Contemporary Art.

Bibliography:
Elizabeth Caughey and John Gow, *Contemporary New Zealand Artists Vol. 4*, David Bateman, Auckland, 2005.
Robert Leonard, 'Ani O'Neill' in Jo Spark and Jonathan Watkins (eds.), *Everyday: 11th Bienniale of Sydney*, Sydney, 1998.
William McAloon, 'Kia Ora Tolls Here: Elam sculpture in the telephone exchange' in *Art New Zealand 70*, 1994.
Priscilla Pitts, *Contemporary New Zealand Sculpture: themes and issues*, David Bateman, Auckland, 1998.
Priscilla Pitts and Allan Smith (eds.), *The Nervous System: artists explore images and identities in crisis*, Govett-Brewster Art Gallery, New Plymouth, and City Gallery, Wellington, 1995.
Gwynneth Porter, *Doodles*, Lord Mori Gallery and Sue Crockford Gallery, 2002.
Allan Smith, *Bright Paradise: 1st Auckland Triennial*, Auckland Art Gallery Toi o Tamaki, 2001.
Lisa Taouma, *Cottage Industry*, City Gallery, Wellington, 1997.
Jim Vivieaere, 'Waka Collective' in *Present Encounters: The Second Asia-Pacific Triennial of Contemporary Art*, Queensland Art Gallery, Brisbane, 1996.
Bernida Webb, 'Ani O'Neill' in Ewen McDonald (ed.), *Agents of Change: 12th Biennale of Sydney*, 2001.

Bill Culbert

Bill Culbert

I think of Bill Culbert as what French filmmaker Agnès Varda would call a latter-day gleaner, someone who has inherited the rights of those who were allowed to pick over the remains of the harvest or, updating this for the 21st century, someone who has learnt to survive on the leftovers of consumer society. Like any good gleaner, he haunts those havens of the unwanted – rubbish dumps, recycling stations and remaindered bins – to retrieve an assortment of empty containers, broken tools and bargain-basement fittings, to reprieve them from their obsolescence. This is no random accumulation, nor a pathological acquisitiveness but rather a joyous recognition of their other, non-utilitarian potential. This, in Culbert's terms, is their capacity to serve as vessels of and vehicles for light. Literally, he makes things over as simple apparatuses that capture, reflect, emit and carry that immaterial substance, for no other reason than to give visual pleasure. I like the idea that Culbert works in the wake of use, turning the spin-offs of progress – filaments of neon, fluorescent tubes and Tupperware – into art, that ultimate signifier of uselessness. In so doing he reverses the logic of capital to give us something that is both incandescent and free.

Christina Barton

Born in 1935.
Lives and works in London and France.

Selected solo exhibitions:
2006 – *Bill Culbert*, Sue Crockford Gallery, Auckland.
2005 – *Bill Culbert*, Galerie Catherine Issert, St Paul de Vence.
2004 – *Light Wine Things*, Dunedin Public Art Gallery; *Daylight and Nightlight*, Roslyn Oxley9 Gallery, Sydney.
2003 – *Bill Culbert*, Auckland Art Gallery Toi o Tamaki.
2002 – *Bill Culbert*, Centre d'Arts Plastiques, St-Fons, Lyon, France.
1998 – *Lightworks*, Govett-Brewster Art Gallery, New Plymouth.
1984 – *Staircase Project*, ICA, London.
1977 – Serpentine Gallery, London.

Selected group exhibitions:
2006 – *High Tide: currents in contemporary New Zealand and Australian art*, Zacheta National Gallery of Art, Warsaw, Poland, and Contemporary Art Centre, Vilnius, Lithuania.
2004 – *Telecom Prospect 2004: new art New Zealand*, City Gallery, Wellington.
2002 – *Second Asia-Pacific Triennial of Contemporary Art*, Queensland Art Gallery, Brisbane.
1999 – *Toi Toi Toi: three generations of New Zealand artists*, Art Museum Fridericianum, Kassel, Germany, and Auckland Art Gallery Toi o Tamaki.
1983 – *The Sculpture Show*, Serpentine and Hayward Gallery, London.

Selected bibliography:
Yves Abrioux, *Bill Culbert*, Centre d'Arts Plastiques, St-Fons, Lyon, France, 2002.
Richard Kalina, 'Report from Downunder: down under no more', *Art in America*, April 2005.
Magda Kardasz, Simon Rees, *High Tide: new currents in art from Australia and New Zealand*, Contemporary Art Centre, Vilnius and Zacheta National Gallery of Art, Warsaw, 2006.
William McAloon, *Home and Away: contemporary Australian and New Zealand art from the Chartwell Collection*, Auckland Art Gallery Toi o Tamaki, 1999.
Justin Paton, *Light Wine Things*, Dunedin Public Art Gallery, 2004.

If a painter from fifteenth-century Venice had travelled from Europe halfway round the world to Aotearoa New Zealand, the results might look a lot like Bill Hammond's painting *Traffic Cop Bay* – a vision of New Zealand as a chain of smoky islands ruled by gangs of aristocratic birds.

Courtly beauty is the overall effect, but step closer and the details have you hooked. Hammond's bird-people rest on a razor's edge of otherness and identification. With their track-pants and tattoos, they seem to stand for the presence of humans in this place. At the same time, they evoke the cold-eyed otherness of nature. This tension is also there in Hammond's curving lines, half-way between a cut and a caress. And it's there especially in the way the birds stare endlessly at some unseen horizon. The effect of this staring, across a decade of paintings, is to build up a mighty suspense – like the electric calm inside a fort before the enemy arrives.

Who are they waiting on, though? What do they see? Of the many answers, the most telling reels us right in to Hammond's dark historical drama. The birds are looking ahead to the very future we viewers now inhabit. Though Hammond is best known for these recent 'history paintings', he spent the first half of his career painting 'modern life'. With their jagged spaces and skin-problem colours, his paintings of the 1980s are unforgettable anatomies of a hyped-up, stressed-out decade. Place them alongside his evocations of the deeper past and what you have is an astonishing account of New Zealand's history, connecting the dead calm of the past to the frantic noise of the present. This is why a painting as beautiful as *Traffic Cop Bay* also manages to emanate such foreboding. The birds can see us coming.

Justin Paton

Born in 1947.
Lives and works in Lyttelton, Aotearoa New Zealand.

Selected solo exhibitions:
2007 – *Predator Rock*, Ivan Anthony Gallery, Auckland.
2006 – *Ancestral*, Ivan Anthony Gallery.
1999-2000 – *Bill Hammond: 23 big pictures*, Dunedin Public Art Gallery, and Auckland Art Gallery Toi o Tamaki.
1999 – *Melting Moments*, Brooke|Gifford Gallery, Christchurch.
1998 – *Blood Bin, Sin Bin*, Gregory Flint Gallery, Auckland, Brooke|Gifford Gallery, and Peter McLeavey Gallery, Wellington.

Selected group exhibitions:
2005 – *Small World, Big Town: contemporary art from Te Papa*, City Gallery, Wellington.
2004 – *Coming Home in the Dark*, Christchurch Art Gallery Te Puna o Waiwhetu.
1999 – *Third Asia-Pacific Triennial of Contemporary Art*, Queensland Art Gallery, Brisbane.
1998 – *Dream Collectors*, Museum of New Zealand, Te Papa Tongarewa, Wellington, Auckland Art Gallery Toi o Tamaki and Dunedin Public Art Gallery; *Skywriters and Earthmovers*, Art Annex, McDougall Art Gallery, Christchurch.
1995 – *Hangover*, Waikato Museum of Art and History, Hamilton, Govett-Brewster Art Gallery, New Plymouth, Robert McDougall Art Gallery, and Dunedin Public Art Gallery.
1992 – *Headlands: thinking through New Zealand art*, Museum of Contemporary Art, Sydney, and Te Papa Tongarewa Museum of New Zealand, Wellington.

Selected bibliography:
Jim Barr and Mary Barr, 'Endangered species' in *Distance Looks Our Way: ten artists from New Zealand*, Distance Looks Our Way Trust, Wellington, 1992.
Alexa Johnston and Ian Wedde, *Dream Collectors: one hundred years of art in New Zealand*, Te Papa Press, and Auckland Art Gallery Toi o Tamaki, 1998.
Gregory O'Brien, *Lands and Deeds: profiles of contemporary New Zealand painters*, Godwit Publishing, Auckland, 1996.
Justin Paton, 'Low Job' in *Art New Zealand* 80, 1996.
Gwynneth Porter and Priscilla Pitts (eds), *Bill Hammond: 23 big pictures*, Dunedin Public Art Gallery, 2000.
Allan Smith, 'Bill Hammond Paints New Zealand' in *Art Asia Pacific* 23, 1999.

Billy Apple

What's in a name? It is a question that haunts and
conditions the work of Billy Apple. You see, Billy
Apple was born Barrie Bates in 1935 in Auckland,
New Zealand. But in November 1962 he dramatically
abandoned 'Bates' and took up the name 'Billy
Apple', marking the occasion by dyeing his hair and
documenting the whole procedure as an art work.
By this stage he was in London, having finished his
studies at the Royal College of Art, and was poised to
launch himself as an artist.

His first solo exhibition (Gallery One, 1963) publicised
his re-branding by presenting a range of works
designed to show off his new identity. They included
a series of photo-portraits, taken by the celebrity
photographer Robert Freeman, that presented
the artist like any new product, and various
representations of apples – some printed on canvas,
others cast in bronze – that underlined the artist's
uncanny objectification.

Apple continued to play with his name after he moved
to New York in 1964, adding his particular spin to the
emergent Pop Art scene; and back in New Zealand in
the economically heady days of the late 1980s. Right
now he is working with New Zealand's HortResearch
scientists and American apple growers on a new
premium variety apple cultivar: the 'Billy Apple',
which will be marketed in a worldwide campaign in
partnership with Saatchi & Saatchi. Their idea is to
produce a new apple with real art credentials, using
Apple's brand to add cultural capital.

So a simple gesture has become a highly marketable
commodity. With unnerving persistence and
exemplary production skills, Apple proves the fate of
the individual in an era of mass consumption. Floating
sign and insistent brand, he is categorically an artist
for our time.

Christina Barton

Billy Apple

NZ/USA
Born 1935, re-branded 1962

Selected solo exhibitions:
2007 – *Trade Marked*, Sue Crockford Gallery, Auckland.
2006 – *Severe Tropical Storm 9301 Irma*, Te Tuhi, Auckland.
2005 – *History of the Brand*, Sue Crockford Gallery, Auckland.
2003 – *Four Decades, 1962-2002*, Hamish McKay Gallery, Wellington.
1991 – *As Good as Gold: Art Transactions 1981-91*, Wellington City
Art Gallery touring exhibition.
1984 – *Selected Works 1962-74*, Leo Castelli Gallery, New York.
1980 – *Censure*, Leo Castelli Gallery and Charles Cowles Gallery,
New York.
1977, 1978 – *Extension of the Given*, Leo Castelli Gallery, New York.
1976 – *-/+ 38* (with Jerry Vis), 112 Greene Street Gallery, New York.
1975 – *Two Subtractions*, Auckland City Art Gallery.
1974 – *From Barrie Bates to Billy Apple 1961-74*, Serpentine Gallery,
London; *Five Subtractive Connections*, The Clocktower, New York.
1972 – *An Audiotape Work to be Heard in Total Darkness* (with
Annea Lockwood), Holly Soloman, 98 Greene St Loft, New York.
1970 – *Neon Transformation*, Apple, 161 West 23rd Street, New York.
1967 – *UFOs*, Howard Wise Gallery, New York.
1965 – *Apples to Xerox*, Bianchini Gallery, New York.
1963 – *Motion Picture Meets the Apple*, Institute of Contemporary
Arts, London; *Apple Sees Red: Live Stills*, Gallery One, London.

Selected group exhibitions:
2004 – *Território Livre*, XXVI Bienal de São Paulo, São Paolo.
2003 – *American Supermarket*, Andy Warhol Museum, Pittsburgh.
2002 – *Shopping: A Century of Art and Consumer Culture*, Schirn
Kunsthalle, Frankfurt and Tate Liverpool.
1999 – *Global Conceptualism: Points of Origin 1950s-1980s*, Queens
Museum of Art, New York touring exhibition; *Toi Toi Toi: Three
Generations of Artists from New Zealand*, Museum Fridericianum,
Kassel; *Kronos + Kairos: Über die Zeit in der Zeitgenössischen Kunst*,
Museum Fridericianum, Kassel.
1982 – *Vision in Disbelief: The 4th Biennale of Sydney*, Art Gallery of
New South Wales, Sydney.
1981 – *Alternatives in Retrospect*, New Museum, New York.
1964 – *American Supermarket*, Bianchini Gallery, New York.
1963 – *Gallery One: Ten Years*, Gallery One, London.

Selected bibliography:
Christina Barton, 'Who is Billy Apple? The Artist After the Death
of the Subject', *Reading Room 1*, 2007.
Wystan Curnow, 'Blond Ambition: Billy Apple', *Artscribe 89*,
Nov/Dec 1991.
Mary Delahoyd, *Alternatives in Retrospect: A Historical Overview,
1969-1975*, The New Museum, New York, 1981.
Lucy Lippard, *Pop Art*, Frederick A Praeger, New York, 1966.
Lucy Lippard, *Six Years: The Dematerialization of the Art Object*,
Frederick A Praeger, New York, 1973.
Terry Smith, 'Peripheries in Motion: Conceptualism and
Conceptual Art in Australia and New Zealand' in *Global
Conceptualism: Points of Origin 1950s-1980s*, Queens Museum of
Art, New York, 1999.

Dane Mitchell

THE CURSE OF ART

Here's the thing... according to my logic a curse
rendered as a process is first an idea, confirmed by
belief, undertaken by an agent, then propelled into
physical space and time. There it meets you – the
recipient. For it to work you need to cycle backwards:
receive a physical sign, suspend *disbelief*, seek agency
and locate the idea.

This process mirrors aspects of conceptual art making
and its reception, uncomfortably seating artist and
sorcerer in the same room. Both believe in the ability
of the idea to translate into physical form and space.
This circuitous route between artist-viewer/sorcerer-
recipient from which form, agency and idea are
produced and received, has a blind spot in the middle
called belief. Both parties must *believe* if the action is
going to take effect.

Like the two probabilities in Dane Mitchell's set
diagram 'help and hinder' their intersection does not
necessarily provide a solution. The subset of 'help
and hinder', like our circular curse, could merely
provoke a question without action – the route short-
circuiting... Fortunately Mitchell has foreseen a way
out of existential inaction and provided a help-line
active during the course of its reception. While you
ponder whether to believe a subset can be formed
from the mutual probabilities of help and hindrance,
consider seeking agency. Will you trust its advice and
capability? How will the curse be lifted? What is being
cursed, the idea of the publication, or its pages? I leave
you, tenderly, within this process. *The curse of art.*

Natasha Conland

Dane Mitchell

Born in 1976.
Lives and works in Auckland, Aotearoa New Zealand.

Selected solo exhibitions:
2006 – *The Shelter or A Fear of the Touch of the Unknown;* A Gentil
Carioca, Rio de Janeiro; *Thresholds*, Litmus Project, Massey
University, Wellington; *The Consequences of Inaction*, Starkwhite,
Auckland.
2005 – *Present Surface of Tell*, The Physics Room, Christchurch.
2004 – *Analise*, A Gentil Carioca; *Direct Line*, Small Gallery,
CalArts, Los Angeles.
2003 – *From The Dust Archive*, Starkwhite.

Selected group exhibitions:
2006 – *Local Transit*, Artists Space, New York; *Trans Versa*, Museo
de Arte Contemporaneo, Santiago, Chile; *Don't Misbehave!: SCAPE
2006 Biennial of Art in Public Space,* Christchurch; *Archiving Fever*,
Adam Art Gallery, Victoria University of Wellington; *Bartertown*,
Uplands Gallery, Melbourne; *High Anxiety*, Loose Projects, Sydney.
2005 – *Vanishing Point: representing the invisible*, Starkwhite.
2004 – *Remember New Zealand*, 26th Bienal de São Paulo; *Infiltrate*,
The Substation, Singapore; *History Now*, Te Tuhi, Auckland;
Cuckooborough, West Space, Melbourne; *New New Zealand Art*,
MOP Gallery, Sydney.

Selected bibliography:
Jim Barr and Mary Barr, 'Shelf Life' in *The Shelter or A Fear of
the Touch of the Unknown*, A Gentil Carioca and Ramp Press,
Hamilton, 2006.
Emily Cormack, 'Self Help' in *Don't Misbehave!: SCAPE 2006
Biennial of Art in Public Space*, Christchurch.
Louise Garrett and Emily Cormack, *Present Surface of Tell*, The
Physics Room and Ramp Press, 2005.
Charlotte Huddleston, *Linked: connectivity and exchange*, Govett-
Brewster Art Gallery, New Plymouth, 2006.
Sally McIntyre, 'Dane Mitchell' in *Flash Art International*, vol.
XXXVIII, no. 244, October 2005.
Gwynneth Porter, 'Instructions for Assembly' in *The Shelter or A
Fear of the Touch of the Unknown*, published by A Gentil Carioca
and Ramp Press, 2006.

Daniel Malone

BASE EARTH

The co-dependency between the constructive and the destructive is strong. Rip it down and start again. Daniel Malone has explored both impulses in his work which, even at its most sculptural, has its feet planted in action/performance. Malone is attracted to objects or symbols where not only multiple readings are at play, but where there is a degree of collision or paradox in the mix, as evidenced by his interest in bricks – as a tool for building or a transformative weapon when thrown in protest.

For a recent season of performance at the Govett-Brewster Art Gallery, Malone falls down the gallery stairs. When his fall stops, he picks himself up, makes his way to the top and falls again, and again, and again. In Santiago Chile, he digs a cooking pit in the earth (in Maori this is called a hangi) on the side of the street, where he cooks/fires sweet-potato shaped forms made from the earth and clay. Kumara/sweet potato, being one of the staple crops of the first Pacific settlers of Aotearoa/New Zealand, with botanical lineage in South America, have been used within anthropological hypotheses to prove patterns of migration. At the Singapore Biennial, in *Steal This Smile! :)*, Malone harnesses the energies of volunteers in an attempt to levitate City Hall, where annual meetings of the IMF and World Bank take place, through communal thought-power (a re-staging of an event led by American icon Abbie Hoffman who attempted to do the same in the 1960s with the Pentagon in Washington).

Malone draws upon social, political and cultural contexts of place, often folding in layers of reference to prior art practice. His work could be seen to investigate the interrelationship between objects and their systems of production and consumption with a seriously provocative playfulness that is refreshing and destabilising in equal measures.

Heather Galbraith

Daniel Malone

Born 1970, Taumarunui, Aotearoa New Zealand.
Lives and works in Warsaw, Poland.

Selected solo exhibitions:
2007 – *Coals To Newcastle (Brick (Out) House)*, Maitland Gallery Sculpture Park, Newcastle, Australia; *Uprising / Downrising*, Kordegarda Gallery, Warsaw.
2006 – *You Say Camote / I Say Kumara / Camote / Sweet Potato (Let's Call The Whole Thing Off)*, Galeria Metropolitana / South Project, Santiago, Chile.
2004 – *Mythopoeia: there and back again*, New Zealand Film Archive, Wellington.
2003 – *malone@artspace*, Artspace, Auckland.
1999 – *N.E.W.S.*, China Art Objects Galleries, Los Angeles; *Why Not Sneeze?*, Experimental Art Foundation, Adelaide, Australia.

Selected group exhibitions:
2007 – *Turbulence: 3rd Auckland Triennial* (collaboration with The Long March and Kah Bee Chow), Auckland Art Gallery Toi o Tamaki.
2006 – Singapore Biennale; *Don't Misbehave!: SCAPE 2006 Biennial of Art in Public Space*, Christchurch; *Local Transit*, Artists Space, New York; *High Tide: currents in contemporary Australian and New Zealand art*, Zacheta National Gallery of Art, Warsaw, Poland, and Contemporary Art Centre, Vilnius, Lithuania.
2004 – *Reason and Emotion: 2004 Biennale of Sydney*; *Remember New Zealand*, 26th Bienal de São Paulo.
2002 – *Tomorrow People*, Lord Mori Gallery, Los Angeles, and The Physics Room, Christchurch; *+64*, Kunstlerhaus Bethanien, Berlin.

Selected biography:
Jonathan Bywater, *Da Nile is Not a River in Africa*, UNITEC, Auckland, 2000.
Jonathan Bywater, 'Daniel Malone is feeling himself,' *New Zealand Listener*, 22-28 January 2003.
Isabel Carlos, *On Reason and Emotion: 2004 Biennale of Sydney*, 2004.
Deborah Cain, 'Whitefella Cleaning?: topographies in translation' in *SITE 25*, 2006.
Tina Engels-Schwarzpaul, 'Frontiers of Shame and Repulsion' in *Interstices: a journal of architecture and related arts 4*, 2005.
Daniel Malone and Gwynneth Porter, 'Perfect Pitch' in *Log Illustrated #13*, 2001.
Gwynneth Porter, 'The East is a Career' in *Log Illustrated #2*, 1998.
MAL/ONE/PRACTICE, interactive CD-Rom catalogue raisonné of works, 1991-2006.
malone@artspace, Teststrip Micrograph, Auckland, 2003.

RAG PICKERS

The art and occupation of the rag pick is a noble one; one lost to the corporatisation of recycling and a disposable world. That's not to say they have disappeared completely, they live among us though you might think they have all fled to take different forms. Spinning gold from the waste of society it is said that the drunken emperor turns into a rag picker. Somewhere between Simone Martini's famous fresco of Condottiere Guidoriccio da Fogliano, Manet's *Ragpicker* and Gordon Matta-Clark's *Food*, Eve Armstrong's work manifests itself and its transfiguration. Trash heaps are the mounds of sculptural evidence of a human existence. To transcend the waste of life, to transmute it, is an act of the alchemical, the act of an artist. Here's where the rag picker spins gold from packing tape, where desire is formed from the cast-offs or the recycled.

When we no longer want it, what do we do with it? When we want it, how do we get what we want when we think we have nothing? How do we negotiate it, how do we trade it? What is it that we can exchange? There is always something we can convert, something we have that you want, a comb, a plant, a shirt, a book, a lighter, a record, a song, a map, a candy, a skill, a thought, a story. It's an empowering experience.

Brian Butler

Eve Armstrong

Born in 1978.
Lives and works in Auckland, Aotearoa New Zealand.

Selected solo exhibitions:
2006 – *SLIPs: small local improvement projects*, Enjoy Public Art Gallery, Wellington.
2005 – *ROAM*, Artspace, Auckland.
2004 – *Book Bonanza*, rm103, Auckland.
2000 – *The Process of Breaking*, Gallery 203, Nelson.

Selected group exhibitions:
2007 – *Turbulence: 3rd Auckland Triennial*, Auckland Art Gallery Toi o Tamaki.
2006 – *Don't Misbehave! SCAPE 2006 Biennial of Art in Public Space*, Christchurch; *A Tale of Two Cities: Busan-Seoul/Seoul-Busan*, Busan Biennale, Busan, Korea.
2005 – *Likes The Outdoors*, Ramp Gallery, WINTEC, Hamilton.
2004 – *The Auckland Project* (with Louisa Bufardeci) in *Public/Private: 2nd Auckland Triennial*, George Fraser Gallery, University of Auckland.
2003 – *The Habitat Project* (collaboration with Gaelen McDonald), rm103; *A4 Work Exchange*, Kunsthochscule Weissensee Berlin.

Selected bibliography:
Eve Armstrong, *How To Hold a Trading Table: a manual for beginners*, August 2004.
Sarah Farrar, 'Reality Technicians: everyday sorcery in installation art in New Zealand' in *Artlink*, vol. 26, # 2.
Sue Gardiner, 'Everyone is an artist' in *Art News New Zealand*, May 2006.
Tessa Laird, 'Inorganic Collections' in *New Zealand Listener*, 18-24 March 2006.
Allan Smith, 'Stacks on the mill, more on still: Eve Armstrong and a short history of heaps, stacks and piles' in *Volume 1*, Artspace, Auckland, 2007.
Andrew Paul Wood, 'Invading Your Space' in *New Zealand Listener*, 4-10 November 2006.

Fiona Amundsen

Fiona Amundsen

Fiona Amundsen's photographs of un-populated 'generic' urban and suburban sites employ a strict methodology: the same camera and lens are used, the composition and time of shooting is consistent. While the works appear to have a sense of uniformity, this slowly collapses as detail within the images emerge. We are required to look, and look again. Fiona Amundsen's practice critically engages with conceptual art, documentary and anthropology. Through her disciplined process of making the artist seeks to remove the possibility of chance, or the inclusion of overtly emotional, theatrical or romantic content.

Works are made in series, e.g. 'Modern' (1999) – images of empty motorways taken from over-bridges; 'Pedestrian' (2000) – parks, play grounds, sports fields, courts and pools; 'Time Trials' (2001) – speedway tracks; 'Wooden' (2002) – rural pony clubs practice rings; and 'Garden Place' (2003/4 and 2006/7) – public squares. Immediately apparent is the banality of the sites. Whether in New Zealand, Australia, Japan, all these sites are designed for human use, yet they are depicted sans occupants.

This tangible absence of people heightens the potentiality for action, places emphasis on the concrete structures and draws our attention to small anomalies (a soggy newspaper, a blown light bulb). Their starkness brings to mind literary and cinematic depictions of 'abandoned' cities, such as in *The Day of the Triffids*, or *The Quiet Earth*, except here, nothing major is out of place, no cars have been upturned or windows smashed; a strong sense of unease results. Reinforced through the titling of each photograph is the non-visible presence of Amundsen at work; location, date and time of the image (always early morning 6.53, 7.05, 7.47).

Most recently, with 'Garden Place', Amundsen has begun to loosen the strictness of her methodology, employing what she calls 'a sort of sloppiness which manifests in the *filling-up* of the frame.' The angles of her shots are becoming more oblique and her titling ever so slightly more elaborate. Small inconsistencies are welcomed; a flag is blurred by motion, a light hits the camera lens bleaching a treetop, and a golden reflection tenderly animates a facade.

Heather Galbraith

Born in 1973.
Lives and works in Auckland, Aotearoa New Zealand.

Selected solo exhibitions:
2006 – *Garden Place*, Roger Williams Contemporary, Auckland, and McNamara Gallery, Wanganui.
2004 – *Time Trials*, Canberra Contemporary Art Space; *Garden Place*, Ramp Gallery, WINTEC, Hamilton.
2003 – *Time Trials*, The Physics Room, Christchurch; *Wooden*, West Space, Melbourne.

Selected group exhibitions:
2007 – *Telecom Prospect 2007: new art New Zealand*, City Gallery, Wellington.
2005 – *Contemporary New Zealand Photographers*, Starkwhite, Auckland; *Trust Waikato National Contemporary Art Award*, Waikato Museum of Art and History, Hamilton.
2002 – *Slow Release: recent photography from New Zealand*, Heide Museum of Modern Art, Melbourne.

Bibliography:
Cassandra Barnett, 'Stranger Than Kindness: works from Garden Place' in *Architecture New Zealand*, no. 1, 2007.
Christina Barton, 'Finding the pattern: the photographs of Fiona Amundsen' in *Art New Zealand* 118, 2006.
Emma Bugden, 'You and Me and Everyone We Know' in *Artlink*, vol. 26, no. 2, 2006.
Anthony Byrt, 'Fiona Amundsen' in Lara Strongman (ed.), *Contemporary New Zealand Photographers*, Mountain View Publishing, Wellington, 2005.
Anthony Byrt, 'Empty Fragments of a Missing Subject' in Fiona Amundsen, *Wooden*, Auckland, 2002.
Hanna Scott, 'From the Series Gastronome' in *The Velvet Rickshaw / A Ramp Magazine*, April 2004.
Zara Stanhope, *Slow Release: recent photography from New Zealand*, Heide Museum of Modern Art, Melbourne, 2002.

A TRINKET IS A CHARM FOR TRADE

To describe these objects as curiosities seems a shame. They sustain so much oxymoronic potency that curiosity simply does not express enough. Despite the best of psychoanalytic and post-colonial writing, there is resounding inexplicability in what makes us curious, but it's often what makes us pick something up off the table. Alive in the work is the politics of transformation unique to the trade in colonial cultures, however, culture is often domesticated in her work. For something curious is typically something strange rather than familiar, and Francis Upritchard's objects are often familiar. They convey the intimacy of something transformed from trinket into jewellery; beast to furniture; or museum piece to utility.

Upritchard's peculiar achievement is in rearranging the order of things and displacing their relative values. So that a hand-made gourd with an animal stretching out of its neck generates a simultaneously comic and despairing effect, bedecked in jewels and amulets for luck. The *trick* of her trade is in recasting an old jug into a sacred vessel. Yet far from a resplendent metamorphosis, Upritchard's objects appear to carry their awkward and impoverished beginnings with them into glorious display. Her process mirrors the fundamentals of second-hand trade, where value (both economic and cultural) is set in the eye of the beholder. The disowned becomes re-owned and the tension of the object lies in this semi-transition from broken to fixed, old to new. It's not quite clear whether the new owner has made a healthy repair for these things in the context of art, but carefully she procures the savage together with the charming from the ordinary.

Natasha Conland

Born in 1976.
Lives and works in London.

Selected solo exhibitions:
2006 – *Francis Upritchard*, Kate MacGarry, London.
2005 –*Francis Upritchard*, Andrea Rosen Gallery, New York; solo project for Salon 94, New York; *Francis Upritchard*, The Bakery, Annet Gelink Gallery, Amsterdam; *Doomed, Doomed, All Doomed*, Artspace, Auckland.
2004 – Camden Arts Centre, London.
2003 – *Francis Upritchard*, Kate MacGarry; *New Work*, Ivan Anthony Gallery, Auckland.
2001 – *Ich Dien*, Ivan Anthony Gallery.

Selected group exhibitions:
2006 – *Le Nouveau Siécle*, Museum Van Loon, Amsterdam; *The Walters Prize 2006*, Auckland Art Gallery Toi o Tamaki; *Around The World In Eighty Days*, South London Gallery.
2005 – *The Way We Work Now*, Camden Arts Centre.
2004 – *The Secret History of Clay*, Tate Liverpool; *New Blood*, The Saatchi Gallery, London.
2003 – *Becks Futures*, ICA London, Southampton City Art Gallery, and CCA Glasgow; *Lost Collection*, Laing Gallery, Newcastle; *Picture Room*, Gasworks, London.

Selected bibliography:
Louisa Buck, 'Francis Upritchard' in *The Art Newspaper*, August 2003.
Michael Glover, 'Francis Upritchard' in *The Independent Review*, July 2003.
Derek Henderson, 'The empire strikes back', i-D *Magazine* 52, March 2005.
Matthew Hyland and Jamie King, *Doomed, Doomed, All Doomed*, Artspace, Auckland, 2005.
Ben Seymour, 'The Bart Wells Gang' in *Frieze* #66, March 2002.
Francis Upritchard, *Human Problems*, Veenman and Kate MacGarry, London, 2006.
File Notes #04: Francis Upritchard, Camden Arts Centre, January-April 2004.
'Future Greats' in *ArtReview*, December 2005.

Jae Hoon Lee

Jae Hoon Lee

Again and again and again. Jae Hoon Lee is a master of repetition, his winding videos circling an idea over and again to build to a visual rhythm. *One Hundred Faces* (2002) merged computer scans of the skin from one hundred people encountered over the period of a year—friends and strangers alike—to create a moving loop of digitally stitched-together bodies. *One Hundred Faces* breaks down individual features into a seething but somehow still meditative mosh-pit.

and...and...and.... Lee has previously documented his own body in a series of scans; day after day to build an imperfect expanse of skin, scars, bruises and wrinkles. Interested in the Eastern philosophy of Taoism, particularly in relation to his treatment of materials, Lee has written: 'water is formless because it takes shape depending on the vessel that contains it... we construct the body fluidly like water'. Bodies, as Lee sees it, are disassembled, deterritorialized, and up for transformation.

So is nature. Jae Hoon Lee's similar treatment of the outdoors – leaves, sheep, the ground, clouds – creates comprehensive maps tracing non-existent environments. The forensic gaze of his camera or scanner seeks out connections between the most humble of materials, and renders them dizzyingly compulsive.

Mirror image. This relentless tracking has recently extended to capturing images of computers, turning the recording device back on itself. *Salvation* (2006) cobbles together the keyboards of various old computers, buttons upon buttons, to create the motherboard of all machines. The stains and marks of overuse are clearly visible, bringing us back again, once more, to the body and its ever-present residues.

Emma Bugden

Born in 1973.
Lives and works in Auckland, Aotearoa New Zealand.

Selected solo exhibitions:
2005 – *Alchemy of the Land*, Starkwhite, Auckland.
2004 – *Translucent*, Window, Auckland.
2003 – *Skin Projection*, Ramp Gallery, WINTEC, Hamilton.
2000 – *Transform*, George Fraser Gallery, University of Auckland.

Selected group exhibitions:
2006 – *Asia Pacific Documentary and Video Festival*, Performance Space, Asia-Australia Arts Centre, Sydney; *Open Late*, Institute of Modern Art, Brisbane; *Asian Traffic Hong Kong*, Hong Kong Arts and Cultural Centre.
2005 – *Square2*, City Gallery, Wellington; *Hotbed*, Dunedin Public Art Gallery; *Asian Traffic Singapore*, Esplanade, Singapore; *Asian Traffic Beijing*, Today Art Museum, Beijing; *Asian Traffic Shanghai*, Zendai Museum of Modern Art, Shanghai.
2004 – *Break/Shift*, Govett-Brewster Art Gallery, New Plymouth; *Greenhouse*, Frankfurter Welle, Frankfurt, Germany; *Code NZ*, Canvas International Art, Amsterdam; *Asian Traffic*, Gallery 4A, Sydney, Australia; *Black box*, Australian Centre for Photography, Sydney; *Bin-Bang-it-o-yo?*, Chang-Dong Gallery, Seoul.
2003 – *Pressing Flesh*, Auckland Art Gallery Toi o Tamaki; *Electric Power*, Han-Jeon Plaza Gallery, Seoul, Korea; *UpFront*, The Foyer Art Project, AK03, Auckland.
2002 – *A Tossing of Experimental Shorts*, Cinema Cube, Seoul, Korea; *The Future of Auckland*, Artspace, Auckland.
2001 – *Alive!*, Adam Art Gallery, Victoria University of Wellington; *Flesh and Fruity: new artists 2001*, Artspace, Auckland.

Bibliography:
Andrew Clifford, 'Falling Free' in *The Physics Room Annual*, The Physics Room, Christchurch, 2004.
Sue Gardiner, 'Heavens Above' in *Art News New Zealand*, Summer 2006.
Tessa Laird, 'Fantastic Planet' in *New Zealand Listener*, 16-22 April 2005.
Anna Miles and Robert Leonard, *Flesh and Fruity: new artists 2001*, Artspace, Auckland, 2001.

Jim Speers

Jim Speers

The two bodies of work represented in these pages, stills from the 3-channel film work *Akropolis* (2006) and the poster work *ab* (2007), give an introduction to the multi-faceted practice of Jim Speers, which also includes sculptural objects and large-scale installations. Speers is drawn to architecture, images and objects that have become repositories for attitude and aspiration (whether this is socio-economic, political, or nationalistic). Editing is a crucial part of the film-making process, and the analogy extends to all of Speers' practice: the assembly of discordant objects, images, or sequences as a proposition for a refreshed suite of meanings.

ab (which stands for 'a billion') floats above a solarised image of the architecture of the Hubble Telescope, a symbol of how our technological prowess has boosted our knowledge of far-off-terrain, yet also a symbol of how little we actually know. Instead we invent and embellish science 'fact' with our own fictions, legends, and tales to enable a more tangible (and comforting) visualization.

In Greek 'Akro' means high and 'polis' city – the word evolved to describe a high part of a town or city which was special, sacred and fortified. In Vilnius, Lithuania, 'Akropolis' is a vast one-stop-shop retail centre, with an ice rink at its core. Here retail is the new sacred, the site for commune and battle. *Akropolis* juxtaposes scenes of a soccer team waiting for foe in the middle of the ice rink, bored, bemused and cold; two dog walkers meet in snow, their conversation mute, their dogs' playful fighting more animated and expressive that their gestures. A monologue from a historian proudly tells of the brave (and sole) Lithuanian fighter pilot to fly for the Royal Air Force during the Battle of Britain in WWII. He congratulates Speers on the high proportion of New Zealand pilots who flew for the Allied force during the same battle. A conversation in a café between two critical and informed young men (one Finnish and one Lithuanian) centres on the complex series of border conflicts, political allegiances and occupations that have shaped their respective nations. Like the soccer players, (and Speers), these two men have never fought in a war, yet with the current proliferation of wars and conflicts 'in play', their awareness of the complex machinations of the past gives some modicum of hope for the future.

Heather Galbraith

Born in 1970.
Lives and works in Auckland, Aotearoa New Zealand.

Selected solo exhibitions:
2006 – *Bluebird*, Jensen Gallery, Auckland.
2005 – *Plans for a New Island*, Jensen Gallery; *Ghost Trail Services*, Kunstverein, Ludwigsburg, Germany; *Raider Lodge*, St Paul St Gallery, AUT, Auckland.
2001 – *Brazil is Fine, Jeffrey*, Hocken Library, Dunedin, and Forrester Gallery, Oamaru.
2000 – *Tiffany's Kyoto*, Artspace, Auckland.
1999 – *Sister City, No Sound*, Jensen Gallery.
1997 – *Cigarettes and Real Estate*, Manawatu Art Gallery, Palmerston North.
1995 – *Mutterlistig*, Teststrip, Auckland.

Selected group exhibitions:
2007 – *Video Block 3*, Peng! raum für kunst, Mannheim, Germany.
2006 – *High Tide: currents in contemporary Australian and New Zealand art*, Zacheta National Gallery of Art, Warsaw, Poland, and Contemporary Art Centre, Vilnius, Lithuania.
2005 – *Happy Birthday to New*, Auckland Art Gallery Toi o Tamaki.
2004 – *Gridlock: cities, structures, spaces*, Govett-Brewster Art Gallery, New Plymouth; *Remember New Zealand*, 26th Bienal de São Paulo.
2003 – *Slow Light*, Gus Fisher Gallery, University of Auckland; *Lightworks*, Pataka, Porirua.
2001 – *Feature: art, life and cinema*, Govett-Brewster Art Gallery; *Prospect 2001*, City Gallery, Wellington; *Multistylus Programme*, Auckland Art Gallery Toi o Tamaki; *Southern Lights*, Dunedin Public Art Gallery.
2000 – *The Crystal Chain Gang: prismatic geometry in recent art*, Auckland Art Gallery Toi o Tamaki.
1999 – *Nostalgia for the Future*, Artspace, Auckland.
1998 – *Every Day: 11th Biennale of Sydney*; *Folklore: the New Zealanders*, Artspace, Auckland, and Sarjeant Gallery, Wanganui.
1997 – *Signs of the Times*, City Gallery, Wellington; *Light Show*, Manawatu Art Gallery, Palmerston North.

Bibliography:
Stella Brennan, *Nostalgia for the Future*, Artspace, Auckland, 1999.
Robert Leonard (ed.), *Communicating at an Unknown Rate*, Waikato Museum, Hamilton and Artspace, Auckland, 2002.
Raimundas Malasauskas, 'High Tide' in *ArtUS*, Issue 16, January/Feburary 2007.
William McAloon. 'Jim Speers' in *Art Asia Pacific* 23, 2000.
Allan Smith, *The Crystal Chain Gang: prismatic geometry in recent art*, Auckland Art Gallery Toi o Tamaki, 2000.

John Reynolds

Dots, dashes, dragged lines overlay and abut, building a shimmering field of mark and colour. While Reynolds primarily works within painting and drawing, these media are employed in investigations of orchestral richness and architectural/spatial sensitivity. He moves from producing small canvases and works on paper to vast wall paintings, and site-responsive installations, such as the levitating Cloud at the 2006 Sydney Biennial, where 7073 small square white canvases – each with a silver text taken from The *Oxford Dictionary of New Zealand English* (1997) – floated 'surround-sound' around the walls of a space at the Art Gallery of New South Wales, NZ vernacular 'colonising' the site.

Reynolds' work keys in and contributes to international investigations while being firmly located in Aotearoa/New Zealand and the Pacific. He plays with visual and aural language, isolating and repeating forms, components, or texts to test possibilities of resonance and explore the fertile ground of understanding and misunderstanding. Two recent 'open air' interventions have taken place in a sculpture park on the site of Oceana Gold goldmine in Otago, New Zealand; *Snow Tussock* (2003) and *Golden Spaniard* (2006-7) create landforms and punctuate them with strategic planting of unsung native plants. While there is a very distinctive 'touch' to John Reynolds's work, he constantly surprises, seduces and destabilizes.

Back-handed compliments can sometimes be at play when the work of artists with lengthy art-making careers are discussed: prolific = verbose; eminent = ego needs stroking; senior = still here; quirky = socially inept. Not one of these subtexts ring true with John Reynolds. To prolific, eminent, senior (and influential), quirky, you can add lightening-quick-of-wit, a dab hand with a pencil/brush/oil stick or marker, ever-generous and constantly curious. He makes it look easy, which we all know, it sure ain't.

Heather Galbraith

John Reynolds

Born in 1956.
Lives and works in Auckland, Aotearoa New Zealand.

Selected solo exhibitions:
2006 – *Last Evenings on Earth and Alien Hand Paintings*, Sue Crockford Gallery, Auckland.
2005 – *I gotta use words when I talk to you*, Sue Crockford Gallery; *Painting is easy…*, Peter McLeavey Gallery, Wellington.
2004 – *Einstein Sings Nirvana*, Sue Crockford Gallery.
2003 – *I'm Doing Nothing Wrong*, Sue Crockford Gallery.
2002 – *HEVN*, Adam Art Gallery, Victoria University of Wellington.
2001 – *K' Rd To Kingdom Come*, Govett-Brewster Gallery, New Plymouth; *Antipodes*, Sue Crockford Gallery; *Harry Human Heights*, Artspace, Auckland.

Selected group exhibitions:
2006 – *54321 Auckland Artists' Projects*, Auckland Art Gallery Toi o Tamaki; *Zones of Contact: 15th Biennale of Sydney*.
2004 – *Vacancy*, Te Tuhi, Auckland.
2003 – *Nine Lives*, Auckland Art Gallery Toi o Tamaki.
2002 – *2002 Walters Prize*, Auckland Art Gallery Toi o Tamaki.
1995 – *A Very Peculiar Practice: aspects of recent New Zealand painting*, City Gallery, Wellington.
1992 – *New Works 1992: five New Zealand artists*, National Art Gallery, Wellington; *Headlands: thinking through New Zealand art*, Museum of Contemporary Art, Sydney.
1989 – *After McCahon: some recent configurations in art*, Auckland City Art Gallery, Auckland.

Selected bibliography:
Mary Barr (ed.), *Headlands: thinking through New Zealand art*, Museum of Contemporary Art, Sydney, 1992.
Christina Barton, *After McCahon: some recent configurations in art*, Auckland City Art Gallery, 1989.
Greg Burke and Robert Leonard, *SUMWHR*, Artspace, Auckland and Govett-Brewster Art Gallery, New Plymouth, 2002.
Allan Smith, *A very peculiar practice*, City Gallery, Wellington, 1995.
Allan Smith, 'John Reynolds' in *Home and Away: contemporary Australian and New Zealand art from the Chartwell Collection*, David Bateman and Auckland Art Gallery Toi o Tamaki, Auckland, 1999.

THE PRETENDER: "I LOVE YOU BECAUSE YOU ARE YOU, AND ONLY YOU".

Judy Darragh has a genuine interest in fakery. Never afraid of artifice, instead she indulges it, continuing to remind us of that issue of popular concern and pleasure – that art is a series of clever tricks. So it stands to reason that the tricks of her trade have been the deployment of such insincere implausible articles as plastic flowers, fluorescent paint, bogus craft, fake jewels, cheap sleaze, and kitsch copies of fine art. What's more, these items are brought together in excess in her sculptural assemblages with camp exultation.

There is still something excellent about seeing paint, looking like cum, drip down a stack of old wine bottles. The titillation (if there is any) is not due to its verisimilitude – porn doesn't need that – it's knowing it's fake and taking it anyway. The preposterous try-hard, the fool, has a way of reminding us more poignantly of the real.

Very often with Darragh her constructions are an homage to something that has lost its cool, its contemporaneity, its mojo. Her recognition of kitsch is precisely at this level. She understands when something has lost its ability to be taken (god-forbid) seriously. Cleverly, her revival most recently of Judy Chicago's iconic *Dinner Party* cues us to consider the decay of feminism in contemporary art. Darragh's rendition of the *Dinner Party* is radically camp and decadent, reminiscent of the after-party; a collection of broken pieces fiercely made-good. If feminism can become kitsch so can democracy, environmentalism and… love? Ultimately, Darragh's work in the territory of tack strikes at the core of the contemporary genuine: "I'd like to love you but I can't love".

Natasha Conland

Judy Darragh

Born in 1957.
Lives and works in Auckland, Aotearoa New Zealand.

Selected solo exhibitions:
2006 – *Arts Society*, Te Tuhi, Auckland; *Selected Works Selected*, Roger Williams Contemporary, Auckland; *Night / Fall*, Ramp Gallery, WINTEC, Hamilton; *Frozen Flood*, Dunedin Public Art Gallery.
2004 – *So… you made it?*, Te Papa Tongarewa, Museum of New Zealand, Wellington.
2001 – *Motherboard*, rm401, Auckland.
2000 – *One Wonders*, Anna Bibby Gallery, Auckland.
1999 – *Sunspots*, Artspace, Auckland.
1998 – *Love Songs 'til Midnight*, The Physics Room, Christchurch; *Cube'n'Dice*, Fiat Lux, Auckland.
1997 – *365 Daze*, Jonathan Smart Gallery, Christchurch.
1996 – *Universal Drapes*, Teststrip, Auckland; *a Floral Extravaganza* (collaboration with Ani O'Neill), Auckland Art Gallery Toi o Tamaki, Dowse Art Gallery, Wellington, and Bath House Art Gallery, Rotorua.

Selected group exhibitions:
2005 – *Highchair: New Zealand artists on childhood*, Auckland Art Gallery Toi o Tamaki, and St Paul St Gallery, AUT, Auckland; *Remember New Zealand*, 26th Bienal de São Paulo.
2004 – *Telecom Prospect 2004: new art New Zealand*, City Gallery Wellington.
2001 – *Still Life*, Adam Art Gallery, Victoria University of Wellington; *Fabrications*, Dunedin Public Art Gallery.
2000 – *Drive*, Govett-Brewster Gallery, New Plymouth.
1999 – *Out of the Ordinary*, Auckland Art Gallery Toi o Tamaki; *Wonderlands*, Govett-Brewster Gallery; *Papermake*, Modern Art Inc, London.
1997 – *Sharp and Shiny*, Govett-Brewster Gallery.
1995 – *Hangover*, Waikato Museum, Hamilton, Dunedin Public Art Gallery, and Robert McDougall Art Gallery, Christchurch.
1994 – *Stop Making Sense*, City Gallery, Wellington.

Selected bibliography:
Paula Booker, *Arts Society*, Te Tuhi and Clouds, Auckland, 2006.
Trish Clark and Wystan Curnow (eds.), *Pleasures and Dangers*, Moët and Chandon Art Foundation and Longman Paul, 1992.
Natasha Conland (ed.), *So… you made it?*, Te Papa Press, Wellington, 2005.
Gwynneth Porter, 'Judy Darragh talks to Gwynneth Porter' in Robert Leonard and Lara Strongman (eds.), *Hangover*, Dunedin Public Art Gallery and Waikato Museum of Art and History, 1995.
Gwynneth Porter, 'Crimes of Boredom' in *365 Daze*, Jonathan Smart Gallery, 1997.

Judy Millar

Judy Millar

They rise up every three years on traffic islands and vacant lots – makeshift wooden hoardings that carry promises and putdowns in the run-up to a general election. Typically, they're no sooner raised than defaced or demolished, only to be patched up the next day. It might seem a long way from these shantytown structures to the abstract paintings of Judy Millar, except that Millar's new paintings hang on their own temporary hoardings. Angled awkwardly across galleries, they swing her paintings off the wall and aggressively into 'our' space. Meanwhile, in the spaces *inside* Millar's paintings, there's a corresponding sense of trouble massing, of things blocked, torn, whipped about. In early 2006, Millar's rollercoaster brushstrokes (ragstrokes, to be precise) gave way to fingermarks blindly raked through dark paint, like the afterimage of someone clawing up a mud bank. It wasn't Pollock that came to mind, but the churned surfaces of Gutai paintings. The same urgency inhabits her new series *Something nothing*, where Millar releases cloudbursts of black strokes that seem to censor the colour underneath, and wipes ragged holes into fields of ash-coloured paint. Ultra-thin acrylic gives all this action a sealed, 'virtual' look, as if we're watching televised images shredded in mid-transmission. It makes sense that Millar's two major encounters of 2006 were with the Prado's Spanish paintings and their 'spectrum of black', and Robert Fisk's wrenching history of conflict and counter-conflict, *The Great War for Civilization*. It's too often assumed that to engage with 'current events' painters must depict them directly. But Millar shows how painting can remain alert to wider tremors, even while – especially while – remaining abstract. Which is what makes the sight of her paintings up on wooden hoardings so resonant – a makeshift but determined proclamation of painting's place in the thick of things.

Justin Paton

Born in 1957.
Lives and works in Auckland, Aotearoa New Zealand, and Berlin.

Selected solo exhibitions:
2006 – *Something, Nothing*, 64zero3, Christchurch.
2005 – *I Will, Should, Can, Must, May, Would Like to Express*, Auckland Art Gallery Toi o Tamaki, Auckland; *Here Eyes Are Hell*, Galerie Mark Müller, Zurich; *Flammpunkt* (with Sophia Schama), Spielhaus Morrison Galerie, Berlin; *Veils, Trails and Horses Tails*, Bartley Nees Gallery, Wellington.
2004 – *The Shooting Gallery*, Ramp Gallery, WINTEC, Hamilton; *I'd Like Painting*, Gow Langsford Gallery, Auckland.
2003 – *I is She as You to Me*, Dunedin Public Art Gallery.
2002 – *The Shape of a Curve*, Gow Langsford Gallery, Sydney.
2000 – *Stable Violet, Permanent Sunset*, Bartley Nees Gallery.
1997 – *Solid Body*, Auckland Art Gallery Toi o Tamaki.

Selected group exhibitions:
2007 – *Telecom Prospect 2007: new art New Zealand*, City Gallery, Wellington.
2005 – *Devil's Puchbowl*, Chris Grimes Gallery, Los Angeles.
2004 – *IS/NZ*, Kunstverein Kreis Ludwigsburg, Ludwigsburg, Germany.
2003 – *Fragmente des Paradieses*, Kunsthalle Palazzo, Liestal, Switzerland.
2002 – *Past Presents*, Te Papa Tongarewa Museum of New Zealand, Wellington; *Memos For The Next Millennium*, Gus Fisher Gallery, University of Auckland; *Spieglein, Spieglein and der Wand...*, Mark Müller Gallery, Zurich.
1999 – *Leap of Faith*, Govett-Brewster Art Gallery, New Plymouth.
1996 – *The Second Asia-Pacific Triennial*, Queensland Art Gallery, Brisbane.
1994 – *Parallel Lines: Gordon Walters in context*, Auckland City Art Gallery.

Selected bibliography:
Anthony Byrt, *Sticky*, Ramp Press, WINTEC, Hamilton, and Whitecliffe College of Arts and Design, Auckland, 2004.
Robert Leonard, *Judy Millar: I will, should, can, must, may, would like to express*, Auckland Art Galley Toi o Tamaki, 2005.
Justin Paton, *I is She as You to Me*, Dunedin Public Art Gallery, 2003.
Peter Shand, *The Contingency of Vision*, Suter Gallery, Nelson, 2001.
Allan Smith, 'The Past and Future Perfect' in *Art/Text* 50, 1995.

Julian Dashper

Julian Dashper

Julian Dashper has spent the last 25 or so years grappling with the challenge of being an artist who has chosen to work globally but base himself peripherally in New Zealand. This has allowed him the unique perspective of attending to an internationalist art history from a distance, enabling him to devise strategies to work around his geographical isolation while simultaneously articulating its effects.

One outcome of this has been to draw attention to his non-appearance in the annals of mainstream art history, firstly by doing his own stock-taking – *Untitled (CV 1979-2007)* is his extensive resumé (29 pages at last count) which he exhibits on the gallery wall as an actual artwork – and secondly, by continually reminding the old world of his existence (*Future Call, 1994/2007*). This latter has the artist, like an irrepressible ghost, repeatedly ringing galleries from the other side of the world but always requiring the telephone remains unanswered, because of course, in New Zealand, it is already tomorrow.

While such works draw attention to the mechanics of the art world and the systems that connect it, they also emphatically reiterate where Dashper is based and what he has done to work with that fact. Moving effortlessly between media – painting, sculpture, recorded sound, moving image – he makes a virtue out of distance, laying claim to second-hand history, to reposition himself in a new time and space. His may be a fragile foothold, poised as it is at the edge, but it leaves an impression nonetheless.

Christina Barton

Julian Dashper was born in Auckland, New Zealand in 1960. He has been exhibiting regularly throughout New Zealand since 1980, Australia and Europe since 1992 and across America since 2001. In 2001 Dashper was based as an artist in residence at the Chinati Foundation in Marfa, Texas (www.chinati.org) funded by a senior Fulbright fellowship. Dashper's work from the last 25 years has just been the subject of a major touring retrospective in America, curated by Christopher Cook and David Raskin.

Dashper's work focuses on the histories, theories and more general or popular ideas of abstraction (in particular abstract painting), conceptualism and minimalism as a working methodology. The geographical positioning of New Zealand globally and how this country receives and disseminates visual information is also a core subject in Dashper's work. His practice manifests itself in various forms, including paintings, unique photographs of paintings, found objects which he infuses with abstract images, various multiples plus limited edition CD and 12" polycarbonate recordings of impromptu performances he has been involved with or heavily orchestrated.

Dashper is represented in all the major public collections in New Zealand, the MCA in Sydney, the Ludwig Forum für Internationale Kunst in Aachen, Germany, the Sheldon Memorial Art Gallery in Lincoln, Nebraska, the Ulrich Museum of Art in Wichita, Kansas and the Stedelijk Museum in Amsterdam.

Dashper lives in Auckland and travels regularly.

Maddie Leach

Maddie Leach

What is the thread that binds Maddie Leach's practice? Is it the fact that she makes and appropriates real things that people use, or that her process entails working with tradespeople and technicians, or that she invites participation, real and imagined? Or is it her playful negotiation of the distance between lived places and the spaces of art; or her tender replaying of minimalist agendas? Yes, of course. But there is something more, and it is rather harder to pin down.

If I can articulate this inchoate thought, it is that Leach lays claim to the horizontal, to that plane of extension that operates in one, utterly earthbound, dimension. Steering away from the vertical impulse of traditional sculpture, she sets the stage for activities that are all the more engagingly human. There is no transcendent spirit here, only gravity working, to bring down trees and rain, tax moving bodies, cast boats aground.

This trajectory doesn't stop things dead. Quite the opposite, it sends them on linear paths that map out spaces of vastly varying dimensions: from the shuffle of feet across a dancefloor, or the movement of wood from one stack to another, to the lumbering path of a ship making its way out of a harbour, or, further still, across the expanse of an ocean. There is an elegant pathos here. Leach's passages lack purpose; there is transport but no reason. By exploiting a worldly circuitry, she may have found the still point in the system's endless crossings.

Christina Barton

Born in 1970.
Lives and works in Wellington, Aotearoa New Zealand.

Selected solo exhibitions:
2006 – *My Blue Peninsula*, Te Papa Tongarewa Museum of New Zealand, Wellington.
2005 – *Show 14: a cord of wood (or how to light a dark corner)*, Show, Wellington.
2004 – *Take Me Down to Your Dance Floor*, Dunedin Public Art Gallery.
2003 – *Dear Dancer*, Enjoy Public Art Gallery, Wellington.
2002 – *Gallery Six: the ice rink and the lilac ship*, Waikato Museum of Art and History, Hamilton.
2001 – *Gallery Seven (10000 Metres)*, City Gallery, Wellington.
1999 – *Gallery 4*, Manawatu Art Gallery, Palmerston North; *At Home* as part of *Oblique*, Otira Township, Westland.
1997 – *Unearthly Stranger*, The Honeymoon Suite, Dunedin.

Selected group exhibitions:
2006 – *Trans Versa*, Museo de Arte Contemporaneo, Santiago, Chile; *High Tide: currents in contemporary Australian and New Zealand art*, Zacheta National Gallery of Art, Warsaw, Poland, and Contemporary Art Centre, Vilnius, Lithuania.
2005 – *Linked: connectivity and exchange*, Govett-Brewster Art Gallery, New Plymouth; *Breathing Space*, The Physics Room, Christchurch.
2004 – *Vacation: projection series 7*, Govett-Brewster Art Gallery; *Telecom Prospect 2004: new art New Zealand*, City Gallery Wellington.
2001 – *Parallel Worlds*, Centre for Contemporary Photography, Melbourne, and Adam Art Gallery, Victoria University of Wellington.
2000 – *Sister Spaces*, Southern Exposure, San Francisco.

Selected bibliography:
Christina Barton, 'Out of The Deep: Gallery Six by Maddie Leach' in *Gallery Six: The Ice Rink and The Lilac Ship* catalogue, Wellington, 2004.
Marcus Moore, 'Platforms of Distance: The Art of Maddie Leach' in *Art New Zealand* 111, 2004.
John di Stefano, 'Ice and Space: Maddie Leach and VJ Rex' in *Art Asia Pacific* 42, 2004.
Justin Paton, 'Floortime' in *Take Me Down to Your Dance Floor*, Wellington, 2005.
Priscilla Pitts, *Contemporary New Zealand Sculpture: themes and issues*, David Bateman, Auckland, 1998.

Michael Parekowhai

"Call it the Trojan Horse effect. Since the early 1990s Michael Parekowhai has explored metaphors of defence under the cover of glossy, toy land surfaces."
(Justin Paton, *Frieze*)

Call him an artful dodger, call him the double agent, there are many ways to set the stage for Michael Parekowhai and his swift manoeuvring. His work glistens and gleams right in your eye with its factory finish. You need only to bust away from the glare to see how straight he's actually playing it. He's showing up the art world's tendency for pigeonholing, dodging categorisation by utilising mediums as signifiers and offering multiple entry points through each.

His practice has rolled out kitsets on steroids, taxidermied rabbits and sparrows, framed portraits of stiff floral bouquets, light-boxes patterned with reappropriated traditional Maori designs, custom-built guitars (which were used to perform Englebert Humperdink's classic song *Ten Guitars*, which topped Maori music charts in the 1960s, at the opening of the exhibition of the same name), an immaculately slick black Steinway concert grand piano inlaid with Paua shell and adorned with carved roses and arum lilies, giant childhood games, and the list gets longer. In any case, his work has unerringly high production values, and even if the medium slips effortlessly from one thing to the next – the artful dodge – the narrative elements remain constant.

With a twist of humour, Parekowhai reappropriates cultural signifiers and stereotypes, riffing off New Zealand's colonial history, the commodification of childhood, environmental politics and consumerism. He has also delved into art historical references, taking the canon's popular phrases by the horns and wrestling them around a little. Cultural identity, politics and popular culture are just a few strings to his bow, which he loads with arrows, one after the other, firing at the constantly moving target.

Danae Mossman

Michael Parekowhai

Born in 1968.
Lives and works in Auckland, Aotearoa New Zealand.

Selected solo exhibitions:
2006 – *Eerst me fiets (First my bicycle)*, Roslyn Oxley9 Gallery, Sydney.
2005 – *Driving Mr. Albert*, Michael Lett, Auckland.
2004 – *The Consolation of Philosophy – Piko nei te matenga*, Govett-Brewster Art Gallery, New Plymouth.
2001 – *Patriot: Ten Guitars*, The Andy Warhol Museum, Pittsburgh.
1999-2000 – *Patriot: Ten Guitars*, Artspace, Auckland, Third Asia-Pacific Triennial, Queensland Art Gallery, Brisbane, City Gallery, Wellington, Govett-Brewster Art Gallery, and Dunedin Public Art Gallery, Dunedin.
1994 – *Kiss the Baby Goodbye*, Govett-Brewster Art Gallery, and Waikato Museum of Art and History, Hamilton.

Selected group exhibitions:
2006 – Fifth *Asia-Pacific Triennial of Contemporary Art*, Queensland Art Gallery, Brisbane; *Beaufort Inside*, PMMK, Museum of Modern Art, Ostend, Belgium; *High Tide: currents in contemporary Australian and New Zealand art*, Zacheta National Gallery of Art, Warsaw, Poland, and Contemporary Art Centre, Vilnius, Lithuania.
2004 – *A Grain of Dust A Drop of Water: 5th Gwangju Biennale*, Korea; *Paradise Now?*, Asia Pacific Society, New York.
2002 – *(The World May Be) Fantastic: 14th Biennale of Sydney*.
2001 – *Techno Maori*, City Gallery, Wellington; *Bright Paradise: 1st Auckland Triennial*, Auckland Art Gallery Toi o Tamaki.
2000 – *Flight Patterns*, Museum of Contemporary Art, Los Angeles.
1995 – *Cultural Safety*, Waikato Museum of Art and History, Hamilton, City Gallery, Wellington, Ludwig Forum, Aachen, Frankfurter Kunstverein, Frankfurt, and Dunedin Public Art Gallery.
1992 – *Headlands: thinking through New Zealand art*, Museum of New Zealand Te Papa Tongarewa, Wellington, Museum of Contemporary Art, Sydney, Australia.
1990 – *Choice!*, Artspace, Auckland.

Selected bibliography:
Gregory Burke, 'Michael Parekowhai' in *Art/Text* 69, May-July 2000.
Gregory Burke, *Cultural Safety*, Frankfurter Kunstverein and City Gallery, Wellington, 1995.
Connie Butler, 'West of Everything' in *Parkett* 57, 1999.
Robert Leonard and Lara Strongman, *Kiss the Baby Goodbye*, Govett-Brewster Art Gallery and Waikato Museum of Art and History, 1994.
Michael Parekowhai, The Andy Warhol Museum, Pittsburgh, 2002.

Mladen Bizumic

Mladen Bizumic

Right now Mladen Bizumic is based in Berlin. He is working on a project for the Freud Museum in Vienna where he will install a vitrine of architectural fragments from Viennese buildings. These will be accompanied by two commissioned works: a piano piece composed by his girlfriend and a 'psychoanalytic poem' written by his mother, a psychologist. The project nicely articulates Bizumic's practice. Local material – the built environment of Vienna – will find its way into a museum, reframed as a self-consciously 'historical' display, which, in turn, will be translated and abstracted in both highly structured and oddly arbitrary ways. For which is the musical note that figures the sound of a built form? What is the 'unconscious' of rubble that can be put into a poem?

Bizumic's work always has a sophisticated finish, a guise that suggests a keen analytical intelligence. One could put it down to his European inheritance. But if one probes appearances the logic snags on what is a decidedly absurdist streak. Maybe this comes from his Central European background, which positions him a little off-kilter and therefore suits his adopted home, New Zealand. In projects, here, he has imagined extending the Guggenheim franchise to an east coast resort town in the central North Island; and staging a biennale in tourist-friendly Fiji. His supporting presentations are always impeccable, but their impulse is deflationary, not of the settings he works with, but rather of the overbearing ambitions of the global culture industry. Like a New World Walter Benjamin, he sees New Zealand as modernity's final frontier, treating this place as an ideal setting from which to ponder its ruins; somewhere, perhaps, for new beginnings.

Christina Barton

Born in 1976.
Lives and works in Berlin, Germany and Auckland, Aotearoa New Zealand.

Selected solo exhibitions:
2007 – *How If: A Translation in III Acts*, Kuenstlerhaus Bethanien, and Program, Berlin.
2006 – *The Crystal Memorial*, Charim Galerie, Vienna; *Superstructure Doubled* (with Øystein Aasan), Korridor, Berlin.
2005 – *Cafe Wittgenstein*, Sue Crockford Gallery, Auckland; *event. horizon.black.hole*, Dunedin Public Art Gallery.
2004 – *Aipotu: Love Will Tear Us Apart (again)*, Hocken Library Gallery, Dunedin.
2003 – *Fiji Biennale Pavilions*, Govett-Brewster Art Gallery, New Plymouth; *event.horizon*, Ramp Gallery, Hamilton.
2002 – *A Beautiful Afterlife*, Auckland Art Gallery Toi o Tamaki; Untitled (Tauranga Guggenheim), Artspace, Auckland.

Selected group exhibitions:
2007 – 2nd Moscow Biennale.
2006 – *A Tale of Two Cities, Café 1*, Busan Biennale, Korea; *High Tide: New Currents in Art from Australia and New Zealand*, Zacheta National Museum of Art, Warsaw, Poland, and Contemporary Art Centre, Vilnius, Lithuania; *Don't Misbehave!: SCAPE 2006 Biennial of Art in Public Space*, Christchurch.
2005 – *Re: Modern*, Kuenstlerhaus, Vienna; *Small World, Big Town: Contemporary Art from Te Papa*, City Gallery, Wellington.
2004 – *We Are the World*, Chelsea Art Museum, New York; *Break/ Shift*, Govett-Brewster Art Gallery.
2001 – *Bright Paradise: 1st Auckland Triennial*.

Selected bibliography:
Marc Gloede, 'The Axis Powers' in *How If: A Translation in III Acts*, Program, Berlin, 2007.
Magda Kardasz, 'Upside Down' in *High Tide*, Zacheta Narodowa Galeria Sztuki, Warsaw, 2006.
Tessa Laird, 'Occhio alla Nuova Zelanda' in *Case Da Abitare*, June 2005.
Natasha Conland - 'Passing Through: A Base in New Zealand Art' in *Broadsheet*, June-August 2005.
Cassandra Barnett and Grant Matheson, 'Ride on Time: Recent Works by Mladen Bizumic' in *The Velvet Rickshaw – A Ramp Magazine*, April 2004
Simon Rees, 'Pacific Trade and Exchange' in *Fiji Biennale Pavilions*, Govett-Brewster Art Gallery, 2004.

Peter Robinson

At a talk recently for the exhibition *Ack*, by Peter Robinson at Auckland's Artspace, vigorous debate ensued between members of the audience largely about the formal qualities of the pieces. Towards the end of the discussion, I ventured a remark about the sexual nature of the exhibition. Heads turned to look at me, most etched with a polite distaste or disbelief. Clearly, no one saw the work in that light.

Huh? I was confused. I returned to the show later to check. No, there it was, a giant white protrusion poking through from one room to the next, inserting itself through architectural structures with wanton abandon. It was large, audacious, and exuberantly physical. It was also visceral and gloriously, bodily, potent. A monument carved from pristine white polystyrene, *Ack* was as assured within the space as I have ever seen from Robinson. An artist who has, over the years, variously attacked and tackled the heady topics of biculturalism, world conflicts, the art world as marketplace, and the universe itself, Robinson's most recent works have moved away from the slickness of the early 2000s back into a more raw execution. However, these latest works appear less concerned with the world outside and more concerned with innards. Like a science experiment gone wrong, *Ack*, and other recent projects such as *The Humours*, resemble a splurge-fest of bodily functions and internal organs, rendered as chaotic yet exquisite sculptural forms.

Emma Bugden

Peter Robinson

Born in 1966.
Lives and works in Auckland, Aotearoa New Zealand.

Selected solo exhibitions:
2007 – *Polyglot*, Sue Crockford Gallery, Auckland.
2006 – *Ack*, Artspace, Auckland; *The Humours*, Dunedin Public Art Gallery.
2005 – *Three colours* (with Gordon Bennett), Institute of Modern Art, Brisbane, and Heide Museum, Melbourne.
2002 – *Black Holes Suck And So Do I*, Kapinos Galerie für Zeitgenössische Kunst, Berlin.
2001 – *Cipher*, 5th Gallery, Dublin; *Divine Comedy*, Govett-Brewster Art Gallery, New Plymouth.
2000 – *No reading allowed here*, Kapinos Galerie für Zeitgenössische Kunst; *The end of the Twentieth Century*, Peter McLeavey Gallery, Wellington.

Selected group exhibitions:
2006 – *Walters Prize*, Auckland Art Gallery Toi o Tamaki.
2004 – *Termite Art Against White Elephant: actual behaviour of drawing*, Museo Colecciones ICO, Madrid.
2003 –*The Sky is the Limit*, Kunstverein, Langenhagen.
2002 – *Iconoclash*, ZKM, Karlsruhe, Germany; *Centre of Attraction: 8th Baltic Triennale of International Art*, Vilnius; *Media City Seoul*, Museum of Modern Art, Seoul; *Rest In Space*, Kunstnerhus Oslo.
2001 – *bi-polar*, 49th Venice Biennale, New Zealand Pavilion, Museo di Sant'Apollonia, Venice; *Superman in Bed – Collection Schürmann Kunst der Gegenwart und Fotografie*, Museum am Ostwall, Dortmund, Germany; *...troubler l'écho du temps, oeuvres de la collection*, Musée d'Art Contemporain de Lyon.
2000 – *Continental Shift*, Ludwig Forum für Internationale Kunst, Aachen (toured to Bonnefantenmuseum, Maastricht, Stadsgalerij, Heerlen, The Netherlands, and Musée d'Art Moderne, Lüttich, Belgium); *Heimat Kunst*, Haus der Kulturen der Welt, Berlin.
1999 – *Kunstwelten im Dialog*, Museum Ludwig, Köln; *Toi Toi Toi: three generations of artists from New Zealand*, Museum Fridericianum, Kassel, and Auckland Art Gallery Toi o Tamaki.

Selected Bibliography:
Gregory Burke, 'bi-polar: divine comedy and a demure portrait of the artist strip-searched', *bi-polar*, 49th Biennale di Venezia, Creative New Zealand, Wellington, 2001.
Gregory Burke, *Cultural Safety: contemporary art from New Zealand*, Frankfurter Kunstverein, Frankfurt am Main and City Gallery, Wellington, 1995.
Robert Leonard, 'Peter Robinson's Strategic Plan' in *Art Asia Pacific* 16, 1997.

Rohan Wealleans

Want to find out where the major tensions lie in
the landscape of contemporary painting? Then find
Rohan Wealleans and mark the spot – he's never far
from the fault-lines. A pakeha (white) painter who
has invented his own Pacific tribe, a male artist who
has recast themes and forms from the '70s Women's
Art Movement, and a maker of aggressively physical
objects who has shrewdly raided the 'post-object'
practices of performance and conceptual artists,
Wealleans takes histories and images previously
considered incompatible or antagonistic and feeds
them into his paintings with glee. 'Feeds' is the
right word, too, because there's an open-mouthed,
full-bellied look to the things he makes. With their
meaty sheen, sharp-toothed detailing and bulging
polychrome openings, the paintings are literally
hungry for our attention. Wealleans evolved the basic
look back in art school, when he began layering up
boards with hundreds of coats of house paint and
then took to this skin with a Stanley knife, revealing
exquisitely layered undercolours – the glorious guts of
painting. Lately he's performed these anatomy lessons
on forms that dangle hugely in open space, and the
results are lumpy, space-invading rebukes to the many
current abstract paintings that resemble screensavers
or high-end sneaker designs. What complicates their
weird allure is Wealleans's practice of entangling the
works in intricate fictions and back-stories, often
involving 'first contact' with some alien culture or
foreign realm. Eager to outflank expectations about
what he ought to make, Wealleans has claimed the
freedom to act up and act out – to paint from within
the worldview of a cartoon character, an outsider,
a beast, an extraterrestrial… In the process he has
made painting – the most familiar of art forms – into
something wonderfully alien.

Justin Paton

Rohan Wealleans

Born in 1977.
Lives and works in Auckland, Aotearoa New Zealand.

Selected solo exhibitions:
2006 – *Tatunka*, Dunedin Public Art Gallery; *In The Shadow of
the Beast*, Hocken Library, Dunedin; *I Got Urges*, Ivan Anthony
Gallery, Auckland.
2005 – *PEGD [Planet Earth Geology Department]*, Hamish McKay
Gallery, Wellington; *Rocococococo*, Ivan Anthony Gallery.
2004 – *Albino*, Ivan Anthony Gallery; *Different Strokes*, Hamish
McKay Gallery.
2003 – *In the Bush*, Hamish McKay Gallery; *The Paint Whisperer*,
Ivan Anthony Gallery.

Selected group exhibitions:
2006 – *Stolen Ritual*, Roslyn Oxley9 Gallery, Sydney; *Metaphysics of
Youth*, Fuoriso, Pascara, Italy.
2005 – *Hotbed*, Dunedin Public Art Gallery; *Snake Oil: recent
acquisitions*, Chartwell Collection, Auckland Art Gallery Toi o Tamaki.
2004 – *Remember New Zealand*, 26th Bienal de São Paulo.
2003 – *IKI Thanks for all the IKA*, Contemporary Art Centre,
Vilnius, Lithuania; *Waikato Contemporary Art Award*, Waikato
Museum of Art and History, Hamilton.
2002 – *Break*, Govett-Brewster Art Gallery, New Plymouth; *Flesh
and Fruity*, Artspace, Auckland.

Selected bibliography:
Jonathan Bywater, 'Exhibitions: Auckland' in *Art New Zealand*
111, 2004.
Sue Gardiner, 'Rohan Wealleans: winner of national
contemporary art award' in *Art Monthly*, December 2002.
Tessa Laird, 'The Best Art of 2004' in *New Zealand Listener*, 25-31
December 2004.
Tessa Laird, 'Pink Eye: is this whitefella dreaming?' in *Sweet #1*,
April, 2004.
Anna Miles, *Flesh and Fruity: new artists 2001*, Artspace,
Auckland, 2001.

Ronnie van Hout

Ronnie van Hout

KNOWING YOU KNOWING ME

Ronnie van Hout burst onto the New Zealand art scene in 1999 with his infamous performance, *Knowing Me*. In this ephemeral work van Hout spoke solely in a fake American accent (African American vernacular) for an entire year (1998-1999). He repeated this performance in 2000 whilst undertaking a Creative New Zealand artist residency in Rochester, New York, this time adopting an English (West Country) accent for the six month period of the residency.

Van Hout's ongoing interest in sham personalities and phony concepts of self and belonging is widely attributed to his culturally mixed parentage. His mother is native North American Iroquois and his father is Dutch African from Suriname.

His background also explains van Hout's reputation as something of an autodidact. Raised on a turkey farm in remote Piha and schooled entirely at home by his blind mother, he received no formal (or informal) art education. With little discernable knowledge of art history or any technical skill, he has relied on charm, wit and cunning to position himself as one of New Zealand's leading emerging artists.

At the Sydney Biennale in 2004, in addition to filling a room at the Museum of Contemporary Art with generic posters and body casts, van Hout masqueraded as Carsten Nicolai during the vernissage, having spent five months leading up to the event learning to speak German (with an East German accent). A highlight of the Biennale was van Hout's electrifying performance as Nicolai, complete with laptop and lasers, which took place on the steps of the Sydney Opera House.

I am who you want me to be.[1]

Tell me who I am.[2]

In interview in 2003, van Hout provided an astute summary of the issues he explores in his work. Here he describes the artist, himself, as an image that is created by its audience. With characteristic acuity, he simultaneously makes illusive reference to the granddaddy of New Zealand art with his repeated verbal motif, 'i am'.[3]

He may be an artist but van Hout won't cut it as a con artist. His best work reflects a fundamental desire in all of us to step into someone else's skin; a transformative urge that, in van Hout's case, paradoxically reveals a conspicuous craving for recognition.

Vals Leugen is a freelance art curator, writer and art consultant. He lives and sometimes works in Berlin, Germany.

1. Interview with L. Hubbard, 'The Real De-Coy', *Art Monthly*, February 2003, p.46.
2. Ibid, p.47.
3. Colin McCahon (1919-1987) was a prominent New Zealand artist (en.wikipedia.org).

Born in 1962.
Lives and works in Melbourne, Australia.

Selected solo exhibitions:
2006 – *Sleep Less*, Darren Knight Gallery, Sydney.
2005 – *Ersatz*, Kunstlerhaus Bethanien, Berlin; *Now + Then = Nothing*, Hamish McKay Gallery, Wellington; *The Disappearance*, Ivan Anthony Gallery, Auckland.
2004 – *I've Abandoned Me*, Dunedin Public Art Gallery, City Gallery, Wellington, Manawatu Art Gallery, Palmerston North, and Auckland Art Gallery Toi o Tamaki.
2003 – *No Exit Part 2*, The Physics Room, Christchurch.
2001 – *Only the Only*, Art Gallery of New South Wales, Sydney.
1999 – *Am I Talking To Me?*, International Studio Programme, New York.
1998 – *Nobody Knows*, Auckland Art Gallery Toi o Tamaki.
1997 – *Pre-Millennial: signs of the soon coming storm* (with Michael Stevenson), South Australian Centre of Contemporary Art, Adeleide.
1996 – *I'm OK*, Govett-Brewster Art Gallery, New Plymouth.

Selected group exhibitions:
2007 – *A Room Inside*, Ian Potter Museum of Art, Melbourne.
2006 – *High Tide: new currents in Art from Australia and New Zealand*, Zacheta National Gallery, Warsaw, Poland, and CAC Gallery, Vilnius, Lithuania; *Don't Misbehave!: 2006 SCAPE Biennial of Art in Public Space*, Christchurch; *Micro Macro City*, Australian Pavilion, 10th International Architecture Exhibition, La Biennale di Venezia, Venice.
2005 – *Das Unfassbare*, 2YK Gallerie, Berlin.
2004 – *Prospect 2004*, City Gallery, Wellington.
2002 – *Elvis Has Left the Building*, Kunstlerhaus Bethanien, Berlin, and Perth Institute of Contemporary Art; *If Nothing but Human*, Ian Potter Museum of Art.
2001 – *Bright Paradise: 1st Auckland Triennial*, Auckland Art Gallery Toi o Tamaki.
1999 – *Toi Toi Toi: three generations of artists from New Zealand*, Museum Friedericianum, Kassel and Auckland Art Gallery Toi o Tamaki.

Selected bibliography:
Dan Arps, 'I don't think much of myself, but I think about myself all the time' in *Natural Selection #1*, Summer, 2004.
Rachel Kent, *Masquerade: representation and the self in contemporary art*, Museum of Contemporary Art, Sydney, 2006.
Robert Leonard, 'Over-Impressed', art/text 57, May-July 1997.
Justin Paton, *I've Abandoned Me*, Dunedin Public Art Gallery, 2003.
Priscilla Pitts, *Contemporary New Zealand Sculpture: themes and issues*, David Bateman, Auckland, 1998.

Saskia Leek

MILK PAINTINGS

Even in cultures most renowned for the consumption of milk it appears to be losing popularity. Its fatty cholesterol-causing properties are scrutinised, and bovine associations considered indelicate. Doubtless in other places still, milk is strange and sumptuous, even a sign of prosperity. As we marginalise the fats and balance the proteins this cloudy comforting liquid comes closer to water than the western world likes to imagine – we could probably have it clear but we prefer its trademark opacity. Nonetheless nobody's crying over spilt milk, it's common enough and a little retrograde.

Consider Saskia Leek's small and standard format panels as milk paintings. Her art balances the proteins of the old and familiar without nostalgia. The experience is like looking through an opaque wash towards an almost decaying image – a painting that's not quite right. The image is set into a milky haze, the past underneath everyday spilt milk. This skim layer coats often inexplicably familiar scenes, sometimes based on Leek's collection of junk-shop paintings, sometimes illustrations, but all of the imagery is distilled to such an extent that a totally new object and sensibility is created. Her abstractions are a fusion of 1970s-inspired cubism in art and design and a paint variation of wood inlay; her figuration like so many hands attempting to reproduce their favourite cat or house in pigment, casein, oil, wool etc. Their strength is in reminding us of the common deception that we are improving our relation with the things that surround us, and the magic of making gems from stones.

Natasha Conland

Saskia Leek

Born in 1970.
Lives and works in Auckland, Aotearoa New Zealand.

Selected solo exhibitions:
2007 – *Tunnels, Nets and Holes*, Darren Knight Gallery, Sydney.
2006 – *Pictures of the Lumpen Sun*, Ivan Anthony Gallery, Auckland.
2005 – *Point of Vanishing*, Jack Hanley Gallery, San Francisco; *Putting to Sleep Fierce Beasts*, Darren Knight Gallery; *Drifters*, Govett-Brewster Art Gallery, New Plymouth, and Jonathan Smart Gallery, Christchurch.
2004 – *Secrets of Invisibility*, Ivan Anthony Gallery.
2003 – *Dare to Lose to Win*, Hamish McKay Gallery, Wellington.
2002 – *Forget the Dead You've Left*, Ivan Anthony Gallery, Govett–Brewster Art Gallery, and City Gallery, Wellington.
2000 – *Ghost Painting*, Dunedin Public Art Gallery.

Selected group exhibitions:
2006 – *A Spoonful Weighs a Ton*, Ian Potter Museum of Art, Melbourne; *Tall Tales and History Lessons*, Dunedin Public Art Gallery.
2005 – *Dealing Kindly With Insects in the Home*, Jack Hanley Gallery, San Francisco; *Home Sweet Home*, Dunedin Public Art Gallery; *World Famous in New Zealand*, Canberra Contemporary Art Space; *Small World, Big Town: contemporary art from Te Papa*, City Gallery, Wellington.
2004 – *Home Sweet Home*, National Gallery of Australia, Melbourne; *Some Forgotten Place*, Berkeley Art Museum, University of California.
2003 – *The Tomorrow People*, Lord Mori Gallery, Los Angeles.
2002 – *Past Presents*, Te Papa Tongarewa, Museum of New Zealand, Wellington.
2001 – *Bright Paradise: 1st Auckland Triennial*, Auckland Art Gallery Toi o Tamaki.
2000 – *In Glorious Dreams*, Govett-Brewster Art Gallery.

Selected bibliography:
Roger Boyce, 'Saskia Leek at Jonathan Smart' in *Art in America*, January 2007.
Jonathan Bywater, 'Saskia Leek: Ivan Anthony Gallery' in *Artforum*, Sept 2006.
Jonathan Bywater, 'What Now?' in *Art/Text* #53, 1998.
Natasha Conland, 'Saskia Leek: Drifters in Residence' in *Broadsheet* #35, March-May 2006.
Anna Miles, 'The World of Leek' in Visit 3, Govett-Brewster Art Gallery, 2005.
Justin Paton, *Ghost Painting*, Dunedin Public Art Gallery, 2000.
Gwynneth Porter, 'Among Other Things' in *Log Illustrated* #3, Summer, 1998.
Drifters, Govett-Brewster Art Gallery, 2006.

Sean Kerr

Sean Kerr is an artist with an interest in video games, the supernatural and digital manipulation. His interdisciplinary practice includes sound, installation, video and internet-based work, as well as collaborative and curatorial projects. A geek of low-tech computer games and graphics, Kerr has a penchant for minimal solutions as ludicrous as the archaic software he favours. The agency here is to strip things off to bare-simple and bounce off clichés. It is like choosing the lowest common denominator or turning back to analogue mode after video games' fusion of 3D animation, CG effects, architecture, artificial intelligence, sound effects, dramatic performances and storytelling have gone way too hyped. One can see him peering in with amazement and incredulity, yet indifferent anyway. Kerr is an adamant teaser whose deadpan puns and jokes, plainly regressive and childish – back to lighting farts and magic tricks – demand a complicit wit and playfulness. In sound, monotone is the norm; it has been suggested that his sound pieces should "be heard as abstract narratives". Subversive and critical, Kerr's works are a backlash to high technology, surveillance cameras or hyperbolic digital effects, offering instead straightforward illusions maximized with dexterous mind games. Levitating a Mercedes in New Zealand suburbia and native bush or a kiwi above the kitchen table – are these acts of the supernatural? It all depends on your belief system, digital proficiency or incisive sense of humour.

Mercedes Vicente

Sean Kerr

Born in 1968.
Lives and works in Auckland, Aotearoa New Zealand.

Selected solo exhibitions:
2006 – *light my fire*, Special, Auckland.
2005 – *Gameboy*, Michael Lett, Auckland.
2004 – *Move me no mountain*, Michael Lett.
2003 – *WTF*, rm103, Auckland.
2001 – STACKER, Artspace, Sydney; WHAM, Waikato Museum of Art and History, Hamilton; *DOT part IV*, Moving Image Centre, Auckland.
2000 – *minimalist massacre part 4*, Manawatu Art Gallery, Palmerston North; *abstractor*, City Gallery, Wellington; *the_abuser*, Blue Oyster Gallery, Dunedin.
1999 – *facetoface part 2, minimalist massacre*, The Physics Room, Christchurch.

Selected group exhibitions:
2006 – *Don't Misbehave!: SCAPE 2006 Biennale of Art in Public Space*, Christchurch.
2005 – *Square2*, City Gallery, Wellington.
2004 – *8ight-light of the pacific*, Kunsthal Hof88, Almelo, The Netherlands, and Matrix Art Project, Brussels; *Telecom Prospect 2004: new art New Zealand*, City Gallery, Wellington; *Ampersand*, High St Project, Christchurch; *Remember New Zealand*, 26th Bienal de São Paulo.
2003 – *Extended Play*, Govett-Brewster Art Gallery, New Plymouth; *Arcadia*, Govett-Brewster Art Gallery; *Arcadia [extra lives]*, Gus Fisher Gallery, University of Auckland; *DOT [the film]*, 35mm digital film, New Zealand Film Festival.
2002 – *UP*, Te Papa, Wellington; *Media City*, Seoul Biennale, Seoul Museum of Art, Seoul.
2001 – *Prospect 2001*, City Gallery, Wellington; *Parallel Worlds*, CCP Melbourne, and Adam Art Gallery, Victoria University of Wellington.
2000 – *Rumble in the Bronx*, Wizards, Christchurch; *Sister Spaces*, Southern Exposure, San Francisco.

Bibliography:
Danny Butt, 'Do art-droids dream of...' in *Artlink*, vol. 21, no. 3, 2001.
Sean Kerr, 'The conversation' in *Media City*, Seoul Biennale, Seoul Museum of Art, 2002.
Simon Rees in *Extended Play*, Govett-Brewster Art Gallery, 2003.
Hanna Scott, *Arcadia*, Govett-Brewster Art Gallery, 2003.
Mitchell Whitelaw, STACKER, Artspace, Sydney, 2001.
Maria Walls, *minimalist massacre part 4*, Manawatu Art Gallery, 2000.

Simon Denny

I've often thought of Simon Denny's sculptural work as clusters. Like communities, clusters are about finding connections and similarities, gaining strength and legitimacy in being bound together. A recent work of Denny's that has stuck in my mind is *Untitled (static)*, comprising two objects: a plastic tablecloth and a woollen blanket. The plastic is pressed to the wall in a surface lick of static electricity; a blanket is dropped at the base of the wall, emphasising the transformative process. It's deceptively simple, leaving you room to cast your mind to the process to unravel its essence. Something like watching Jean-Luc Godard's *Weekend*, it takes a while to figure out how he got to that point – bordering on absurd, yet beguiling. The hanging is a critical action, as is the ongoing maintenance required (re-application every few days is needed). It is clear that it is not the objects, but the trace that is the key.

Denny draws objects together, arranging things, shifting them from the realm of formal concern into a kind of symbolic order. Spartan – with a wink to Arte Povera – objects lean, curve, bond and play in a poetic casualness (think lesserism not minimalism). Poor materials made rich through association, ready-mades ordered to life. The union is a residue of his actions. He acts as alchemist transferring mute objects into sculptures that relish the potentiality of materials and possible order. Like a pin-ball machine for the senses, his work requires a constant manoeuvring around with kinks and jinks 'til you hit something you connect with.

Taut with a formal tension, yet confident in its frayed edges, the amalgams are traction for the viewer to consider the performative aspect that drives the work. Denny's works pares back, offers up some breathing space. He is like a magpie with an eye for slippages and vantage points. He takes stock and intervenes with hawk-like precision, leaving only a trace to give the viewer some traction.

Danae Mossman

Simon Denny

Born in 1982.
Lives and works in Auckland, Aotearoa New Zealand.

Solo exhibitions:
2006 – *Old Entertainment System*, Window, University of Auckland; *Old Things*, Michael Lett, Auckland.
2005 – *Arranging Sympathies*, The Physics Room, Christchurch; *A Process of Bewilderment*, Enjoy Public Art Gallery, Wellington.

Selected group exhibitions:
2007 – *The Köln Show 2*, European Kunsthalle, Köln, Germany; *Moment Making*, Artspace, Auckland; *Prospect 2007: new New Zealand art*, City Gallery, Wellington.
2006 – *Break/Construct*, Govett-Brewster Art Gallery, New Plymouth; *Shift*, Galerie Grita Insam, Vienna; *54321 Performance Projects*, Auckland Art Gallery Toi o Tamaki; *Mostly Harmless: performance series*, Govett-Brewster Art Gallery; *Archiving Fever*, Adam Art Gallery, Victoria University of Wellington; *Don't Misbehave!: 2006 SCAPE Biennial of Art in Public Space*, Christchurch; *News is Also on Television* (performance with Tahi Moore), Michael Lett.
2005 – *They Who Would Eat the Fruit Must First Climb the Tree*, rm103, Auckland; *Project Space* (with Tahi Moore), rm103; *Tahi and Simon find the morning towards the border of bewilderment and begin construction*, George Fraser Gallery, University of Auckland.
2004 – *Left Di Right*, Special, Auckland; *Auckland Project in Public/ Private: 2nd Auckland Triennial*, George Fraser Gallery.
2002 – *Better Living* ,Te Tuhi, Auckland.

Selected bibliography:
Tessa Giblin, 'Staccato' in *Volume 2*, The Physics Room, 2005.
Tessa Laird, 'Pest Modernism' in *New Zealand Listener*, 3-9 September 2005.
Tessa Laird, 'Auckland's Young Generation of Rampant Maximalists' in *New Zealand Listener*, 18-24 March 2006.
Sally McIntyre, 'Simon Denny: Old Things' in *Art Asia Pacific 50*, 2006.
Tahi Moore, 'Making things old' in *Old Things*, Michael Lett, 2006.

Sriwhana Spong

Lost
Oh ye who tread the Narrow Way
By Tophet-flare to Judgement Day,
Be gentle when 'the heathen' pray
To Buddha at Kamakura!
(Rudyard Kipling)

Are you sure there are Lions, Tigers or Tuis? I don't know but I've just arrived and the sound of birds is deafening. The night is too black and the smell too potent, but I'm sure we are not alone. I'm sure the world has shrunk and the altars to the gods are made of checkerboard stakes, apples and incenses, plastic straws and gardenias, popcorn strands on an apple tree, or was it strands of cigarettes hanging in the pitch black at nightfall? I can't recall the bananas and golden bay leaves but I smell the incenses burning. I've been here, the ritual is too strong and the memory too close. Here we landed and I never left, the sound of the Cicada fills my head.

There was a party and I spun the memory of some other place and time, El Dia de los Muertos or Diwali, no, no it was just Auntie's summer afternoon tea, I can't remember. There were cocktails and songs, "Bali Ha'i" or was it "Shall We Dance?". Come in… come in, one more, just one more memory. Just a late Sunday afternoon reading Naguib Mahfouz, or was it Miguel Covarrubias? The Raja has left and the void must be felt, but then again my past is your future and your home is my land and your father is my brother and all I want is to go home to touch terra firma. Black and white, light and shadows, I lived it once and it was a happy time?

I offer this to you, with hope and a sense of hope and happiness, but if the truth were told I'm still not sure where I am or if you have been here. We pray, and pry and hope and then the empire is so far away.

Brian Butler

Sriwhana Spong

Born in 1979.
Lives and works in Auckland, Aotearoa New Zealand.

Selected solo exhibitions:
2006 – *Candlestick Park*, Anna Miles Gallery, Auckland.
2005 – *Muttnik*, Anna Miles Gallery.
2003 – *C'est la vie ma cherie*, Anna Miles Gallery.

Selected group exhibitions:
2007 – *Turbulence: 3rd Auckland Triennial*, Artspace.
2006 – *Don't Misbehave!: 2006 SCAPE Biennial of Art in Public Space*, Christchurch; Busan Biennale, Busan, Korea; *Happy Believers: 7th Werkleitz Biennale*, Halle; *2x2 Contemporary Projects*, City Gallery, Wellington; *Local Transit*, Artspace, Auckland; *Single Currency*, VCA, Melbourne; *Silver Clouds*, Next Wave Festival, Melbourne Festival of the Arts; *Earthly Delight*, Anna Miles Gallery; *An Unlikely Return to the Legend of Origins*, Sparwasser HQ, Berlin.
2005 – *Cultural Futures*, St Paul St Gallery, AUT, Auckland; *Waikato Contemporary Art Award*, Waikato Museum, Hamilton; *Playing Favourites*, Enjoy Public Art Gallery, Wellington; *World Famous in New Zealand*, CCAS, Canberra; *Possible Worlds*, 64zero3, Christchurch.
2004 – *Break/Shift*, Govett-Brewster Art Gallery, New Plymouth; *ACP Video Show*, Scott Donovan Gallery, Sydney; *The Greenhouse*, Frankfurter Welle, Frankfurt; *Industrial Light and Magic* (collaboration with Daniel Malone), rm103, Auckland.
2003 – *Dimensions Of*, High Street Project, Christchurch; *Flachwelt*, Capri Gallery, Berlin.

Selected bibliography:
Tessa Laird, 'My Life as a Goddess' in *Staple Magazine*, March/April 2004.
Tessa Laird, 'Love letters in the sand' in *New Zealand Listener*, 6-12 Aug 2005.
Laura Preston, '7 Days' in *Turbulence: 3rd Auckland Triennial*, Auckland Art Gallery Toi o Tamaki, 2007.
Laura Preston, 'Daytrip' in *Don't Misbehave!: SCAPE 2006 Biennial of Art in Public Space*, Christchurch, 2006.
Zara Stanhope, 'It ain't necessary so…' in *World Famous in New Zealand*, Canberra Contemporary Art Space, 2005.
Virginia Were, 'When Night Falls' in *Artnews NZ*, Summer, 2005.

Stella Brennan

Stella Brennan

Discursive and theoretical, Stella Brennan's practice loosely embraces video, sculpture and installation, and extends to curatorial projects and writings. Brennan enjoys excavating extraordinarily eclectic and obscure sources: rare documentary and science-fiction films, critical texts, or information sourced from the internet. They are cult stories of modernity's obsolete technological utopias, nostalgic tales of progress and urbanism that she salvages like a treasure dusted off from a second hand shop. Using syntax that presents, represents and reframes, her wry works resist interpretation. Her curiosity about early postmodern debates around architecture, the production and manipulation of knowledge and the hegemony of information technology, is aimed at finding forms of emancipation rather than succumbing to the seductions of postmodern consumerism. In spite of this her artefacts possess a fetishist materiality, embodying an ambivalence about this ineludable reality of our time. Her objects teeter on this brink: mesmerising ludicrous architectural spaces are fashioned out of consumer software, data projections and Styrofoam blocks; the interface of her iMac OS 9 desktop is rendered in painstaking needlepoint embroidery; meanwhile, visitors are invited to shower off and enjoy a steamy psychedelic spa pool experience in the gallery.

Mercedes Vicente

Born in 1974.
Lives and works in Auckland, Aotearoa New Zealand.

Selected solo exhibitions:
2006 – *Two Cities*, Quay Gallery, School of Fine Arts, Whanganui.
2005 – *Wet Social Sculpture*, St Paul Street Gallery, AUT, Auckland; *Live Stock*, Starkwhite, Auckland.
2004 – *Tomorrow Never Knows*, Starkwhite, and The Physics Room, Christchurch.
2003 – *End User*; rm103, Auckland and The Calder-Lawson Gallery, Waikato University; *Theme for Great Cities*, Ramp, WINTEC, Hamilton.
2002 – *Another Green World*, Artspace, Sydney.
2001 – *Dell*, Lightbox, Auckland.
2000 – *The Fountain City*, The Physics Room; *Fedex*, The Blue Oyster Gallery, Dunedin.

Selected group exhibitions:
2006 – *Walters Prize 2006*, Auckland Art Gallery Toi o Tamaki; *Zones of Contact: 15th Biennale of Sydney*, MCA, Sydney; *Video from New Zealand*, Loop Video Art Festival, Barcelona; *Islanded*, Adam Art Gallery, Victoria University of Wellington, and Institute of Contemporary Arts, Singapore.
2005 – *Breaking Ice*, Adam Art Gallery, and Southland Museum, Invercargill; *Dimensions Variable*, Canberra Contemporary Art Space; *Snake Oil: recent acquisitions*, Chartwell Collection, Auckland Art Gallery Toi o Tamaki.
2004 – *Everyday Minimal*, Auckland Art Gallery Toi o Tamaki; *Vacancy*, Te Tuhi, Auckland.
2001 – *Fuse*, Dunedin Public Art Gallery.
2000 – *Sister Spaces*, Southern Exposure, San Francisco; *In Glorious Dreams*, Govett-Brewster Art Gallery, New Plymouth.

Bibliography:
Stella Brennan (ed.), *Dirty Pixels*, Artspace, Auckland, 2003.
Stella Brennan, *Nostalgia for the Future*, Artspace, Auckland, 1999.
Andrew Clifford, 'Dive Into A Suburban Fantasia' in *New Zealand Herald*, 21 September 2004.
Sean Cubitt, 'Cities at the Edge of Time' in Stella Brennan (ed.), *0 – 10*, Ondine Publishing, Auckland, 2005.
Tessa Laird, 'Orchestrated Litanies' in Ewen McDonald and Luke Parker (eds.), *Zones of Contact: 2006 Biennale of Sydney*, Sydney, 2006.
Robert Leonard, 'History Curator' in Stella Brennan (ed.), *0 – 10*, Ondine Publishing, Auckland, 2005.

Yuk King Tan

Yuk King Tan works across a multiplicity of media, genres and activities, shifting lightly from photography, video, installation, sculpture and performance—from pyrotechnics to sky diving, shopping to social documentary.

Delivered with highly refined execution, her work is tougher than it first appears, with interests spanning what she has described as the 'history of cities, frontiers, borders and boundaries, the social costs of exploding growth, values and how they are effected by the clash of cultures'. The nature and make-up of power – whether that is cultural, economic or social – is a key element within her practice.

Often her work attempts to construct systems from chaos, such as the recent project *Overflow* (2005), where a twelve-sided dodecahedron snowflake structure was assembled from laid out piles of cheap mass-produced items, simulating the controlled ebb and flow of the late capitalist marketplace. In graphic form, images culled from diverse media outlets formed the same geometric structure, chronologically charting a terse political trajectory from 9/11 to the 2005 London bombings.

At other times she dismantles, or even explodes, existing order, most notably in her series of drawings created through the process of lighting fireworks. In these works either the tempting unlit firecracker or the smoky residue of the burn marks remain like sores on the gallery wall, acting like clues to the frenzied activity that has occurred. Described by Tan as 'a language of creation and uncontrolled decay, collapse and regeneration', the pyrotechnic works act as individually small but collectively compulsive interjections.

Emma Bugden

Born in 1971.
Lives and works in Auckland and Hong Kong.

Selected solo exhibitions:
2006 – *Shelter*, Gallery Quyn, Ho Chi Minh; *Yuk King Tan* Sue Crockford Gallery, Auckland; *Loudspeaker*, Te Tuhi, Auckland.
2005 – *Overflow*, City Gallery, Wellington.
2004 – *Flowers of the Revolution*, Jonathan Smart Gallery, Christchurch.
2003 – *Probable Worlds*, Sue Crockford Gallery.
2001– *Luft-Raum*, Kunstlerhaus Schloss Wiepersdorf, Germany; *Aeroscape*, Hamish McKay Gallery, Wellington.
2000 – *The Territorial*, Camden Arts Centre, London; *passerby*, Artspace, Auckland; *W.A.D.A.M.*, Artspace, Sydney.
1999 – *instant!*, Ludwig Forum Museum für Internationale Kunst, Aachen.

Selected group exhibitions:
2007 – *Turbulence: 3rd Auckland Triennial*, Auckland Art Gallery Toi o Tamaki; *This Place is My Place – Begehrte Orte* Kunstverein, Hamburg.
2006 – *Local Transit*, Artists Space, New York; *China Works*, Art in General, New York; *Pearl River Delta*, Kunstverein Wiesbaden.
2005 – Guangzhou Triennial, Videotage selection, China.
2004 – *Think Local Act Global*, City Gallery, Wellington; *Remember New Zealand*, 26th Bienal de São Paulo; *Nui Work*, Inanui Gallery, Rarotonga.
2003 – *Points of Entry*, Artspace, Sydney (toured Australia, New Zealand, Canada); *Cuckoo at the Critical Studies Test Site*, Rooseum, Malmö.
2002 – *Centre of Attraction: 8th Baltic Triennial*, Lithuania.
2001 – *MultiStylus Programme*, Auckland Art Gallery Toi o Tamaki; *Prospect 2001*, City Gallery, Wellington; *Sightlines*, Te Papa Tongarewa Museum of New Zealand, Wellington.
2000 – *Flight Patterns*, Museum of Contemporary Art, Los Angeles; *Art from New Zealand*, Chinati Foundation, Texas.

Selected bibliography:
Emma Bugden, 'Yuk King Tan' in SCAPE 2004 *Urban Arts Biennial*, Christchurch, 2004.
Sarah Farrar, *Overflow: Yuk King Tan*, City Gallery, Wellington, 2005.
Tessa Laird, 'Yuk King Tan' in *Toi Toi Toi: three generations of artists from New Zealand*, Museum Friedericanum, Kassel, and Auckland Art Gallery Toi o Tamaki, 1999.
Robert Leonard (ed.), *Yuk King Tan*, Artspace, Auckland, 2002.
Peter Shand, *Yuk King Tan: The Picturesque*, Govett-Brewster Art Gallery, New Plymouth, 1999.

Yvonne Todd

How you respond to 'having your photograph taken'
may tell you a lot about your response to Yvonne
Todd. For those few people who are always 'present'
in photographs – unruffled, ready, open-faced – I
think her photographs must seem puzzling, off, or
just plain mean. But for anyone who has felt even
mildly tyrannized by photography, by its claim on
faces and events, by the feeling that the camera does
indeed steal souls – for these people, Todd is an oddly
consoling artist. She loves photography all right, but
in the same way that a vampire loves people with
long necks. It's easy to imagine her as the director of a
shadow photo studio peopled by waifs, consumptives,
and shotgun brides, a nocturnal equivalent of the
wedding photography agency where Todd learned
her craft. In her fiercest (and funniest) photos, the
subjects look at us with a hint of reproof – as if our
attention is exactly what traps them there in their
dead wigs and yellowing lace. Her great talent is for
coaxing a queasy chill from objects and textures: wet
socks, bandage-coloured turtlenecks that immobilise
their wearers, and surfaces so spotless you just know
a phobic is nearby. All of this ought to amount to
a despairing account of the world, but the spirited
bitterness of the photos is the best revenge an artist
could take on whatever images and realities inspired
them. Take *Frenzy*, Todd's portrait of a donkey-toothed
reclining woman whose vastly billowing dress seems
to hide another body. In photos like this, Todd pursues
social discomfort – ours included – as tenaciously as
Ansel Adams pursued light on the flanks of Yosemite.
Frenzy suggests Ingres' grand odalisque by way of *Mad*
magazine. To paraphrase the editors of that venerable
publication, it's portraiture in a jugular vein.

Justin Paton

Yvonne Todd

Born 1973.
Lives and works in Auckland, Aotearoa New Zealand.

Selected solo exhibitions:
2007 – *The Lamb's Book of Life*, Peter McLeavey Gallery,
Wellington; *Blood, in its Various Forms (Incorporating Meat &
Liquor)*, Institute of Modern Art, Brisbane.
2006 – *Blood, in its Various Forms*, Ivan Anthony Gallery, Auckland;
Meat & Liquor, Peter McLeavey Gallery.
2005 – *Vagrants' Reception Centre*, Ivan Anthony Gallery.
2004 – *The Bone of Jupiter*, Peter McLeavey Gallery.
2003 – *The Book of Martha*, Peter McLeavey Gallery.
2002 – *Bellevue*, Ivan Anthony Gallery, Auckland; *Sea of
Tranquility*, Peter McLeavey Gallery.
2001 – *Asthma & Eczema*, Ivan Anthony Gallery.
2000 – *Lace 2*, Ivan Anthony Gallery.
1999 – *The Crisis*, Fiat Lux, Auckland.
1998 – *Fleshtone*, rm3, Auckland.
1997 – *Cabin Fever*, Teststrip, Auckland.

Selected group exhibitions:
2006 – Busan Biennale 2006, Busan, South Korea; *High Tide: new
currents in art from New Zealand and Australia*, Zacheta National
Gallery of Art, Warsaw, Poland, and Contemporary Art Centre,
Vilnius, Lithuania.
2005 – *Mixed-up Childhood*, Auckland Art Gallery Toi o Tamaki.
2004 – *Telecom Prospect 2004: new art New Zealand*, City Gallery,
Wellington.
2002 – *The Sky's the Limit*, Kunstverein Langenhagen, Germany;
Slow Release: recent photography from New Zealand, Adam Art
Gallery, Victoria University of Wellington, and Heide Museum
of Modern Art, Melbourne; *Break*, Govett-Brewster Art Gallery,
New Plymouth; *The Walters Prize 2002*, Auckland Art Gallery Toi
o Tamaki.
2001 – *After Killeen: social observation in art*, Artspace, Auckland;
The Way We Were: the Fiat Lux retrospective, Manawatu Art Gallery,
Palmerston North.

Selected bibliography:
Janita Craw and Robert Leonard, *Mixed-up Childhood*, Auckland
Art Gallery Toi o Tamaki, 2005.
Megan Dunn, 'Auckland Photographer Yvonne Todd's Pictures
Could be Called Sexy...' in *Pavement*, February-March, 2002.
Ron Hanson, 'Death, Rejection and the Fountain of Youth:
melancholy and subversion in the work of Yvonne Todd' in
White Fungus, issue 7, 2006.
Anna Sanderson, 'Humbled, Sharp, Superior, Simpering' in *New
Zealand Journal of Photography* 55, 2004.
Yvonne Todd, *Dead Starlets Assoc.*, Institute of Modern Art,
Brisbane, 2007.

Venice Project Patrons

Jenny Gibbs
Glenn Schaeffer
Dayle Mace
Chartwell Trust
The James Wallace Charitable Arts Trust
Kevin and Rowena Roberts
David and Libby Richwhite
Jim Frazer
Michael Lett
Ann Lewis
Connells Bay Sculpture Trust
Jenny and Andrew Smith

Sponsors

ARTSPACE[NZ]

WORKSHOP®

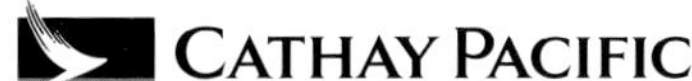

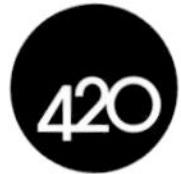

Speculation

Published by Venice Project, Aotearoa New Zealand
and JRP|Ringier on the occasion of the 52nd Biennale di Venezia

Venice Project
c/- Artspace
PO Box 68418
Newton, Auckland 1145
New Zealand
T +64 (0)9 303 1965
artspace@artspace.org.nz
www.artspace.org.nz

JRP|Ringier
Letzigraben 134
8047 Zürich
Switzerland
T +41 (0)43 311 27 50
info@jrp-ringier.com
www.jrp-ringier.com

ISBN: 978-3-905770-75-9

Distributed by JRP|Ringier in all countries except Australia and
New Zealand where it is distributed by Clouds

JRP|Ringier books are available internationally at selected
bookstores and the following distribution partners:

Switzerland
Buch 2000, AVA Verlagsauslieferung AG,
Centralweg 16, CH-8910 Affoltern a.A.,
Buch2000@ava.ch

France
Les Presses du réel, 16 rue Quentin,
F-21000 Dijon, info@lespressesdureel.com,
www.lespressesdureel.com

UK
Cornerhouse Publications, 70 Oxford Street,
UK-Manchester M1 5NH, publications@cornerhouse.org,
www.cornerhouse.org/books

USA
D.A.P./Distributed Art Publishers,
155 Sixth Av., 2nd Floor, New York, NY 10013,
dap@dapinc.com, www.artbook.com

Other countries
IDEA Books, Nieuwe Herengracht 11,
1011 RK Rotterdam, idea@ideabooks.nl,
www.ideabooks.nl

Australia & New Zealand
Clouds, P.O. Box 68-187, Newton,
Auckland 1145, Aotearoa New Zealand
hello@clouds.co.nz
See www.clouds.co.nz for a list of selected outlets

Editor: Brian Butler
Project management: Rob Garrett
Design: Warren Olds, Studio Ahoy, Auckland
Sub-editor: Gwynneth Porter
Editorial assistant: Laura Preston
Proofreaders: Tessa Laird and Deborah Orum

This publication makes use of *Churchward Marianna* for titling. The
typeface was designed in 1969 by Samoan New Zealander Joseph
Churchward. He named it after his young daughter who, at the
time, was also fat

Printed and bound by Musumeci S.p.A., Quart (Aosta) in an edition
of 7000 copies

Many people have given their valuable time and thought to this
publication. We would like to thank the following: et al., Laura
Preston, Nicolaus Schafhausen, Howard Grieves, Gwynneth
Porter, Warren Olds, Nicola Farquhar, Jenny Gibbs, James Wallace,
Jim Barr, Mary Barr, Dayle Mace, Glen Schaeffer, Tessa Laird,
Dan Arps, Murray Crane, Kate Butler, Ariane Craig-Smith, Ida
Moberg, Victoria Henderson, John McCormack, Dominic Feuchs,
Ivan Anthony, Hamish McKay, Gary Langsford, John Gow, Sue
Crockford, Isha Welsh, Michael Lett, Jane Sutherland, Ryan Moore,
Peter McLeavey, Anna Miles, Melanie Rogers, Josie McNaught, Rob
Garrett, William Sommerville, the Artspace Board, Greg Fahey,
Trish Clark, Chris Cherry

Thanks to our patrons and sponsors. Thank you to the curators/
writers for their speculation and thought. And, finally, thank
you to the artists for their commitment and generosity. This
publication is dedicated to you

Cover images: icebergs sighted off the Otago coast of the South
Island of New Zealand in November 2006, two from a flotilla of
around a hundred that broke free from Antarctic pack-ice. They
were remarkable not only for their size, but for how far north
and close they came to the coast. Photographs: Stephen Jaquiery,
Otago Images/Otago Daily Times. © Allied Press Limited 2006

Inside cover image: house where Ernest Rutherford was born, and
surrounding countryside, Spring Grove, near Nelson, New Zealand,
c.1910. Courtesy Alexander Turnbull Library, Wellington